SMILING IN
SLOW MOTION

Derek Jarman's creativity spanned decades and genres –
painter, theatre designer, director, film maker, writer and
gardener.

From his first one-man show at the Lisson Gallery in
1969; set designs and costumes for the theatre and ballet
(*Jazz Calendar* with Frederick Ashton at Covent Garden,
Don Giovanni with John Gielgud at the London Coli-
seum, *The Rake's Progress* with Ken Russell at Teatro
Communale, Florence); production design for Ken
Russell's films *The Devils* and *Savage Messiah*; through
his own films in super-8 before working on features:
Sebastiane (1976), *Jubilee* (1978), *The Tempest* (1979),
The Angelic Conversation (1985), *Caravaggio* (1986),
The Last of England (1987), *War Requiem* (1989), *The
Garden* (1990), *Edward II*(1991), *Wittgenstein* (1993),
and *Blue* (1993); to directing pop-videos and live
performances for Pet Shop Boys and Suede.

His paintings – for which he was a Turner Prize nominee
in 1986 – have been exhibited world-wide.

His garden surrounding the fisherman's cottage in
Dungeness where he spent the last years of his life
remains a site of awe and pilgrimage to fans and new-
comers to Jarman's singular vision.

His publications include: *Dancing Ledge* (1984), *Kicking
the Pricks* (1987), *Modern Nature* (1991), *At Your Own
Risk* (1992) *Chroma* (1994), *Derek Jarman's Garden*
(1995).

ALSO BY DEREK JARMAN

Derek Jarman

SMILING IN
SLOW MOTION

EDITED BY
Keith Collins

VINTAGE

Published by Vintage 2001

2 4 6 8 10 9 7 5 3 1

First published in Great Britain in 2000 by
Century

Vintage
Random House, 20 Vauxhall Bridge Road,
London SW1V 2SA

Random House Australia (Pty) Limited
20 Alfred Street, Milsons Point, Sydney
New South Wales 2061, Australia

Random House New Zealand Limited
18 Poland Road, Glenfield, Auckland 10, New Zealand

Random House (Pty) Limited
Endulini, 5A Jubilee Road, Parktown 2193, South Africa

The Random House Group Limited Reg. No. 954009
www.randomhouse.co.uk

A CIP catalogue record for this book
is available from the British Library

ISBN 0 09 928418 9

Papers used by Random House are natural, recyclable products made from wood grown in sustainable forests. The manufacturing processes conform to the environmental regulations of the country of origin

Printed and bound in Great Britain by
Cox & Wyman Ltd, Reading, Berks

Editor's Preface

Derek kept his handwritten journals in thirty-three black-bound handmade watercolour books, just small enough to slip into his jacket pocket. All bore the legend 'Reward if found', although two volumes were lost and have yet to surface.

He seemed ambivalent about publication, once instructing me that on his death he would like them to be burnt, yet he continued to write and each volume bears a tentative title: *Heart's Ease, A Fit of Amnesia, A Great War of Poppies, Saint's Days, Shot Down in Flames, A Chill in Utopia, And the Day Grows Old* – Derek had always laboured over titles. In a lyrical description of one of Derek's former lovers, who had subsequently appeared in his first feature film, I discovered the title in the only underlined phrase: *There's a moment in* Sebastiane *when he surfaces from the water <u>smiling in slow motion</u>*.

Derek worked on the first volumes of the diaries himself, characteristically revising and re-revising. I was fortunate to assist in the editing of two of Derek's earlier autobiographical volumes, *Kicking the Pricks* and *Modern Nature*, and stuck to the same methodology here. I have coalesced some fragmentary biographical sketches, removed some repetition and for legal reasons have excised some sections. The rest remains in Derek's vernacular, its coherence – like his once beautiful handwriting – degenerating with the progression of his illness.

Derek would keep his journal on most days, only twice resorting to dictation when too ill to lift his fountain pen. In the final diary he wrote without vision, his semi-legible scrawl only possible from his memory of the scratch of nib on paper.

As I transcribed this last volume the writing stopped mid-sentence at a page's end. Perhaps Derek had been distracted by a phone call or a visit from a well-wisher, maybe exhaustion had set in. I took this to be the end of the diaries until months later, showing this page to a friend, the same thing happened to me that had happened to Derek – some blank pages had stuck together. I turned past them to discover that in a pain-filled parody of his calligraphy there were three final, heart-rending pages.

Writing in better health at an earlier time, Derek ended an earlier journal on a more eloquent note:

> *Please read the cares of the world that I have locked in these pages; and after, put this book aside and love. May you of a better future, love without a care and remember we loved too. As the shadows closed in, the stars came out.*

> Derek Jarman, *At Your Own Risk*

May 12-91.

For days now I have tried to start this diary. but the clatter of my existence has warned me off. The first mark on the page eludes me it is easy to put off. The cold weather with its biting easterleys has pinched me to the old stove that roars through the evening white hot. a cruel. sore throat. coughs and a deep depression have left me darting hither and thither mop and duster in hand. Paint brush dipped in venetian red. even my new overalls the colour of faded brick and my suntan hardly cheer me. H.B. drove here yesterday with malcolm it grew so cold we muffled up to visit the swans nest at the Long Pits with its seven small cygnets. The fox decomposing in the shallows a swaying mass of green is surrounded by an army of black tadpoles many thousands of them. H. B.

1991

MAY

Saturday 11

For days now I have tried to start this diary, but the clatter of my existence has interrupted; the first mark on the page eludes me, it is easy to put off.

HB drove to Dungeness, it grew so cold we muffled up to visit the swans' nest, at the Long Pits, with its seven small cygnets. A dead fox decomposing in the shallows, a swaying mass of green algae surrounded by flotillas of voracious black tadpoles, devouring it to the bone. HB throws a stone in the water, sending ripples through this predatory army. 'Father Nature,' he says, 'the destroyer.' The cold weather with its biting easterly has pinched me to the old stove that roars, white-hot, through the evening. A cruel sore throat, coughs and a deep depression have left me darting hither and thither, mop and duster in hand, indecisive paintbrush dipped in Venetian red, even my new overalls, the colour of faded brick, and my suntan hardly cheer me.

I watched TV out of the corner of an eye and sank deep in the ruined sofa with Pepys's *Diaries* – which I crept through with little enthusiasm, at the pace of a snail.

Sunday 12

Today dawned blissful, not a breath of wind, warm and the sun out, a great silence. The nuclear power station – which normally hums and splutters – has not been brought on-line. Heat shimmers off the shingle, weeks of soaking rain have left the Ness a hopeful green.

Alan Beck rang, we discussed a riotous book: *Fags, 'Fatcher, and Fucking*, a scurrilous desktop-published venture; then silence again.

~

These wild flowers are in bloom in the garden: shining cranesbill, spring vetch, whitlow grass, sea campion and broom.

~

Peter Fillingham here with his friend Stephen – who works the bronze foundry in Canterbury; we foraged and beachcombed for wood and metal for the forthcoming show at the Design Museum.

3

Early to bed, restless night, tossed about with waking dreams of hungry boys.

Monday 13

Students from the Royal College of Art film department emerged from the mist at eight this morning, they are filming next door. Any strangers arriving upset me, more cars parked at the side of the road in my view, destroying my illusion of isolation. People wandering across the landscape are unaware of the poppy and sea kale seedlings. Could it be possible for people to arrive and improve the view?

~

All these projects are gathering to completion: my book *Modern Nature*, *Edward II* and the garden exhibition at the Design Museum. At eight last night the telephone rang and I was asked if I would like to take Concord to Washington at one today for the première of *The Garden*. Even *I* can't run that fast, so I'm sitting here watching the garden grow, as the mist blows in, tumbling in chalk-white veils, blotting out the power station across the Ness.

~

Alan Beck visited. We drove to Hastings for fish and chips, calling at Rye Harbour and crossing to Pett Level, which he called the Costa Canasta. We stopped and walked across fields, along a path to the sea, through banks of fern-like hemlock. It took some persuading to stop Alan's friend Billy from tasting it – Alan and I had a friend who made a hemlock salad one fatal summer and succumbed like Ophelia in a stream. Alan said he had read somewhere that it didn't take you too gently.

Tuesday 14

Liam [Daniel] and Philip [McDonald] are here taking photos. The sun is out, the seagulls are fighting over a string of mouldy sausages I threw out. Philip complained that for weeks after the opening of *The Garden* people came up to him and said boldly: 'You're one of the naked rent boys in *that* film.'

~

My American friend Lynn Hanke arrived at twelve with a picnic lunch of asparagus from the farm shop on the Marsh. We made a raid on the Madrona nursery for lavender to restore the circle in front of the house.

After we had planted it we drove via Lympne along Stone Street to Canterbury to see the cathedral – I haven't liked Canterbury since Nik Pevsner and his wife quarrelled violently about the dates of its architectural details. We bumped the car very carefully into a parking space and walked down the ugly heritised main street to the Cathedral Close; on one side a Laura Ashley dress shop, on the other Ratner's jewellery store which was headlined in the *Sun* a week or two ago THIS IS WHAT CRAP BUYS YOU, with a picture of Mr Rat and his wife sitting in a very ugly room.

~

I half expected to see the aisles of the cathedral full of hand-clapping charismatics belting out Bible hits to old Beatles tunes – but the place had the silence of the tomb, muffled feet of plague-black vergers scurrying around the columns of the two Williams. Carey, the new archbishop, was inaugurated at gunpoint, sharpshooters in the west towers. This is where crap takes you.

~

Another sad film on television last night with a gay boy trying to break the hearts of his stolid Christian parents, to a soundtrack of the Pet Shop Boys' 'It's a Sin'.

The cathedral undercroft, ruined by selling stalls, is closed today but the stained glass glows in the sunlight. Our footsteps keep time to the mournful bell.

King's College boys in crumpled potato sack suits, buttons done up, play croquet. My atheistic thoughts harden. Canterbury is an ugly town, erased out of history by improvers.

Back at the car the rubbish that was left neatly in its black plastic sack is trashed all over the seats and a note on the window says: '*You've damaged our car we have two witnesses, you'll hear from us.*'

Driving to London lamenting the sixties, how ugly they were, buildings, clothes, hairstyles – everything was ugly except for Jackie O. The memory of Jackie O. made us laugh all the way back to London, with the blinding sunlight in our eyes.

~

In the evening Richard Salmon invited us all to a dinner for his friend, the multimillionaire painter, Sebastian de Ganay. A restaurant on the Portobello Road with a designer-trashed interior and too many candles. Sat between Lindy Dufferin and Mary Jane. Lindy said Sebastian had the sort of looks you wished to spoil. Richard had a bright tie patterned with pistachio nuts; HB had sewn me into his Katharine Hamnett pants as all the buttons had fallen off – he says she makes them that way deliberately so you remember her. Back to Phoenix at one.

Wednesday 15

Spent much of the day waiting in the green room to videotape Sue Ardille's television programme on same-sex marriage. An interesting time listening to many good arguments from the lawyers: we were happily free of marriage that shackled the straights and came with a long history of repression of women as property; however, marriage provided a framework of benefits, property, inheritance and children's rights.

Women understandably more cautious than men, one already had endured an unsuccessful marriage, though another had her lesbian relationship blessed by the Metropolitan Church. I don't know what use I was in the discussion, I was much older than the others. Supper together with HB invited, it was difficult talking about ourselves in his absence. I concluded the programme by stating I had never been happier.

Thursday 16

A screening of *My Favourite Film* at the NFT.

As we arrive my 'number one fan' is lying in wait for me. 'Did you get my postcard?'

'Yes, I did, thank you.'

'I telephoned Working Title and they said you were so very busy I was not to bother you, but I've been waiting in the café outside your flat, hoping to see you. Would you autograph my ticket stubs?'

As I sign she continues: 'The new Pet Shop Boys show isn't a patch on your one.'

'Oh, really, where did you see that?'

She tenses and glares. 'Paris! Where I sent you my postcard from!'

HB slips between us and manoeuvres me into the auditorium.

~

Griffi's *Il Mare* is an extraordinary film that has been lost for years – it was found for me in the National Film Archive. Much as I remembered it from screenings at the Academy in the sixties: boredom, the possibility of a relationship between two young men – an actor and a runaway – in out-of-season Capri. The landscape takes over the characters, becomes an extension of their thoughts. Finally the actor deserts the boy for a fashionable young woman.

The first faltering attempt to depict a gay relationship before cinema could be more explicit. It is sexy, its camera-work elegant and mannered, the music haunting. It was made in 1961, some years before the tortured, unsexy *Victim*. I wondered if the scenes of the boy washing in a thunderstorm had remained in my mind when I made *Sebastiane* – they are erotic.

Saturday 18

Prospect Cottage.

Came down to Dungeness with HB last night. He had bought new pillows to sleep on.

~

The garden has leapt ahead in two short days. I took out the can and watered, then Peter came in his Brezhnev era Lada and we drove to Hastings to meet Laetitia Yhap, her son Ajax and husband Michael – who was mending his fishing nets on the beach. Hastings beach has been cleaned up – little flotsam there for our show in London. Laetitia is painting the fishermen and their bonfires on the beach. HB did not like the smell of dogfish being gutted, but amused Ajax, swinging him round like a fairground ride.

Sunday 19

Derek Ball, the bon viveur of the Ness, came out of the night in a panic – his cat Spyder had vanished; it came back for breakfast.

~

Beachcombing. In the garden the first purple iris, sea kale, thrift, wallflowers, star of Bethlehem and bugle.

Monday 20

The mournful foghorn sounded all through the night. The moon faded, dawn came up under a milk-white sky, calm and very warm. I took the watering can and watered the front garden. The cold wet spring has left the garden very green. After last year's failure with valerian I have succeeded in nurturing one strong plant. The elder trees cut back by the sharp easterly winds are shooting up. All the wild flowers are thriving.

Tuesday 21

A flummox of friends arrived here all of a sudden at eleven. Lunch in the Light Railway Café, then off to Hastings. HB left at six for London. The RCA boys stopped filming next door, then played football on the beach as the sun set.

Wednesday 22

The weather turned somersaults through the day, blew hot and cold, sun and cloud.

Buttercup and bacon-and-eggs growing at the roadside. Bacon and egg in the Light Railway Café.

Thursday 23

Vaughan Williams' songs, hey and ho and a rumbellow. Jolly ramblers collecting country airs, cyclists and joggers pass, the milkman stops with seven pints – HB drinks one each morning with seven Weetabix piled like breeze blocks in a bowl. In the cereal packet are glow-in-the-dark monsters that he has stuck all over the bedroom wall to protect me from the curious who drop by each day to see the garden.

Here come the letters. I escape into the garden with the watering can and a feather duster to attack the ants that have invaded the beehive.

~

My face itches through the night, the drug cocktail has me tossing and turning. I try to ignore it but it creeps up on me and once I start scratching I cannot win, the irritation is elusive until I'm drowned in the quicksands of sleep.

Friday 24

There is not a breath of wind this morning, a bright redstart hops over my stones. Wallflowers and sea thrift, yellow and pink, patches of fluttering white sea campion, wild mignonette flowering at the roadside.

Washed clothes and the kitchen floor, and watered my fennel seedlings.

Saturday 25

Mist closed in at dawn – the foghorn's incessant boom woke me. The sun made a brave attempt to break the gloom, slight blush in the clouds. A jetliner ruled two bright white lines across the sky, before the mist closed over everything. Raked the fire. It's an English summer – still very cold. My bees arrived at 9.30, to greet them the weather cheered up.

~

The bees are safely housed in the WBC hive, humming sweetly. They completely ignored me as I moved them about with Mr Hart who made a gift of them, within minutes they were fanning themselves happily.

~

Fay Godwin, who sent me her book *Our Forbidden Land*, came and took photos. We had lunch at the Light Railway Café. A young Japanese fan appeared, I made her tea and gave her a lucky Dungeness stone necklace – almost in tears when she left. How strange to travel halfway across the globe to find the garden. As the sun went down a lone sentinel bee buzzed me for getting too close.

Sunday 26
Overcast. The iris bloom white, pale-blue and deep-purple.

~

If you want HB to jump about, all you have to do is say the word 'careful' – this drives him mad. Careful, careful, careful!

~

Walked to the Long Pits. The first yellow flags are in bloom, red-and-black cinnabar moths flutter unsteadily and swallows fly fast and low. There are many caterpillars on the brambles, the air is full of floating gossamer from the willows.

Monday 27
The first Californian poppy opens amongst the white stones at the front of the house. The bees arrive home with bright-orange pollen sacks.

Tuesday 28
My neighbour Brian Yale said that the tragedy of our time was the lack of concentration. He had driven me to Folkestone to see his paintings in the public library. There was a tiny museum – the history of the world crammed into one small room.

By afternoon the rain has set in with a strong wind. Peter came and took sticks and stones in a van to the Design Museum in London.

~

The day grew colder. I retired inside and painted two small canvases. The final proofs of *Modern Nature* delivered to Random Century by HB.

Wednesday 29
May is the driest on record, it is even colder today. I'm well wrapped up in front of the fire.

~

Filled the bees' feeder with white sugar syrup; I was a bit nervous as they poured out and buzzed rather angrily, even though I was quiet and gentle. A bumble bee, scenting honey, dived into the hive and was repulsed by angry workers.

~

A huge scroll pours from the fax machine – twenty-seven points from the publisher's lawyer concerning *Modern Nature* – my dreams are particularly libellous. 'I appreciate that the author's dreams are being described here . . . Mr Jeffrey Archer is extremely litigious and this reference is arguably defamatory . . .' Nearly all the clauses concern the inclusion of 'possible homosexuals' and straights in a queer context.

~

In the afternoon the bees swarmed round the kitchen drain looking for water. It grew colder. Peter and I drove to London, dinner at Poon's Chinese café.

Thursday 30
Breakfast at Bertaux's. Café Brazil closed, shops going down like ninepins in the recession. Boards up everywhere.

~

Michael Cashman plodded through a worthy and very dull programme on the BBC, Stonewall/McKellen connections heavily underscored. No mention whatsoever of Clause 25 – now renumbered 29. Why does he want to fit into a pattern of life that is so obviously outmoded? He called the Pride marchers 'ratepayers' – a horrible call to middle-of-the-road values. Who cares for the *EastBenders* episode as gay myth, the soap was unwatchable. Where is mind and honour in gay politics? Very little in the press, less at Pride, none in Stonewall. A vision of gay aspiration, he seemed bitter and hurt, drained of life at a dull dinner party.

I am intent on putting as many miles between us as I can, can you imagine waking up in the morning with one of them? – what a mistake. If this is what gay has to offer I'm glad I'm queer.

Friday 31
Installed the garden at the Design Museum, strange to be back at Butler's Wharf. The old iron gates that I unpadlocked each evening are there and the graffiti that says '*John Dale Stalag*' is still on the door of the furniture warehouse, everything else is scrubbed, all the fun vanished. The forecourt where we made all the Super-8s – stark-naked boys having it off all along the river wall – is now a car park. I stepped over a barrier and was sworn at by a caretaker.

~

Derek Ball told us the sleaziest story: he was on Hampstead Heath and went down on his knees to give a boy a blow-job. As he put his hands on the boy's bare buttocks he found a flaccid condom dangling, like a tail, out of the boy's arse.

~

Late afternoon drive back to Prospect.

~

Peter [Fillingham] came with sea kale seedlings and HB planted an avenue of them leading to the front door. On the television the Titanic film *A Night to Remember* – shed a tear for the end of elegance.

JUNE

Sunday 2

Warm. The wind died away. HB slept away the morning. I painted the garden, all the flowers start to bloom. After lunch he built a bath for the bees swarming around the kitchen drain so they can drink elsewhere.

~

At teatime John Vere Brown arrived with friends. He seemed well, in spite of his recent heart attack. While he took photos we went up to El Ray and talked to Pat in the garden she's growing. It's years since her railway carriage home was accidentally blown up by a film company – she still hasn't received any compensation, so she lives in the ruined remains of the place with dogs, cats, and her husband Albert. HB threw sticks for the dogs. We admired the night-scented stock and mignonette.

~

Home later to read Frances Spalding's biography of John Minton – fairly conventional writing: 'Congenital homosexual' and the sailors – aren't there one too many of them by the end? The Colony Club must have looked like a scene from *South Pacific*.

Sad drunk generation: Minton, Keith Vaughan, Francis Bacon, my dear friend Robert Medley, all tanked up, squirming and screaming in the glass museum case.

~

Turned in at eleven. The rain that was meant to blow in blew away. Poor dry garden.

Monday 3

Frost has set in, the wind blows incessantly, whining round the eaves, even the refuse collectors have given up. HB cleans the kitchen looking like a French Revolutionary in his Jacobin hat, which he calls 'a National Health woolly knitted diaphragm'.

I water the roses, the wind blows colder, the empty bus passes. Very quiet, no telephone calls. We are forgotten.

~

Anna Pavord came to write up the garden for the *Independent* and left me sea lavender and sweet rocket. 'Simply the finest iris in all England' flowered to keep HB happy – he thinks I'm moonstruck. Californian poppies blazing away.

~

Turned the bee bath into a lichen garden, shut the house up and drove back to London. Supper at Poon's restaurant and then off to see the screaming lambs film that has received so much praise. Anthony Hopkins put the frighteners on the audience, but the rest not up to it, the plot falls to pieces and the murderer is a tedious Gothic transvestite.

Coffee at the Presto, which kept open for us. HB attacked my spots with Clearasil. Dreamt the night away.

Tuesday 4
Naples Yellow has disappeared off the shelves at Rowney's.

~

Sound dub in the gloom of De Lane Lea studios as the sun shines down outside; here the voices run back and forth: *snoozad snoozsat* or rather *kcab dna htrof*. Ken Butler sits beside me out of breath – he escaped from a mob in the south of India into the edit suite. Steven Waddington – my Edward – has got a part with Danny Day Lewis in *The Last of the Mohicans*. He had never flown before and arrived in LA with a videotape of *Edward II*. The BBC wants the beginning with the boys fucking recut.

~

Reptilian highs: Ken says in Bombay the 'in' crowd get bitten by a snake for a four-day high with a thirty per cent chance of death. There's nothing like this in Dungeness – must be pretty dull down there.

~

Simon Turner is going to build a castle in front of the playback screen with scavenged bits and pieces, everyone will contribute something to it. He will complete it with a moat of vodka.

~

Royal College of Arts opening this evening, students as attractive as the work was dull, sculpture more interesting than painting, but all a pale imitation of the past.

Rushed to the cinema with Mike O'Pray, Richard Hamilton, Paul Huxley, to see a student's graduation film, all of us looking rather old, cheerful smiles.

Ken studied at the RCA; he said the tutors treated you as if they were giving you their own money, rather than a grant – it's the same for me with the film-funding bodies.

~

Supper at D'Aquise, Polish beer and sausages. HB's friend Camilla, in Bloomsbury batik dress, described her holiday in Leningrad – waving packets of Marlboro on street corners to stop cars and get lifts all over the city. HB says we should sell up, defect and live like tsars. It would be so cold we would have to spend everything on decent furs – how many packets of Marlboro for an Arctic fox?

Wednesday 5
HB has a horrible thought: as dust is made of human skin, if you hoovered Quentin Crisp's room you'd have enough to make another Quentin. HB is happy – he has a pair of white training trousers given to him by his taekwon-do instructor.

~

In the sound edit again with Simon and Ken. Ken has an upset stomach that he calls Delhi Belly.

By five we are on the way to a complete soundtrack.

Thursday 6
Peter's installation shone like a star in the wasteland of DIY at the Design Museum. Jon Savage arrived with a compilation tape – ninety minutes of London songs. The Thames flows. Bliss was it to be alive.

This evening, HB in the kitchen, he said he was very happy, I am too.

Friday 7
To the OutRage! meeting at the Lesbian and Gay Centre, where it was decided to zap the Isle of Man – as it's still illegal to be queer there – and a homophobic pastor in Tufnell Park.

Saturday 8
Mr Drako's car drove under an articulated lorry; he is in intensive care and has still not found his memory; Manfred Salzgeber telephoned from Berlin. He is ill, and suggested we make a comedy about AIDS. At Compton's bar, amongst the Siamese clones joined at the moustache, twenty-year-old Pete

came up to me and confided he was also HIV positive – tragic smile drowned in disco music.

Sunday 9
A brilliant sunny day. Julian Cole drove me and his friend Eric to Dungeness. The first time I've seen Phoebus Apollo this year. The wind blew warm in the trees so every leaf and blade of grass danced, reflecting drops of light. All afternoon the garden shimmered. Purple and green poppies, petals blown like confetti.

The bees kept indoors as the wind had them crash-landing by the hive door. Julian and Eric are in the kitchen making tea. Julian tells me Paul is newly diagnosed HIV+, he had a wild affair and fucked without a condom; after a week his lover told him that he had the virus. Eric talks about cruising: at least the English attempt to smile at each other, however hard it is, the French just scowl. He said nothing excited him so much as a large half-tumescent cock, promise was better than fulfilment.

~

Later at the London Apprentice a strange encounter: someone came up to me and said how pleased he was to see me out, he spent a night with me in the seventies. I asked where I had met him. 'We met on the Heath and you took me home.'

I met an American architect. We talked about modern architecture, my visit to Philip Johnson's glass house in the sixties, Louis Kahn, Ernö Goldfinger, we were for the moderns. The night went so fast that I left bleared-eyed at five a.m. in bright sunlight.

Monday 10
We start the final sound mix on *Edward*, Simon's medieval title music fills the studio. We are all very happy.

Late last Friday we played the last reel through, the music for the dance sequence sexy and exciting 'Sweet Prince I come', Andrew Tiernan snaky. Early morning sexiness – the snake-charmer boy with his ice-pale green eyes.

~

Simon is crawling around in front of his castle in a Dalmatian spotted kimono, it's 10.30 and we've completed the first reel.

Simon says: 'Do you sweat?' He did, he stripped off.

~

To draw the pliant King which way I will.

~

Peter said he liked the King's protective character, but hated sex in films. We all agreed.

Twelve – we are on reel two.

~

Ken says Gaveston is like some street vixen.

~

2.30 – Gaveston is laughing, I'm heavy with lunch from the Melati. While we ate we watched an elderly man through the smoked glass, buying a leather mask in the shop over the road – others' fantasies.

~

Ken is smoking, we are on reel four; my number one fan is in the reception with God alone knows what to sign.

Tuesday 11

Up very early as I had a restless night tossing and turning in the sheets. I watered the garden at Phoenix House and planted valerian in the sunniest corner.

~

I'm off to the sound-edit, wearing my John Pearse jacket – a King's revenue on my back.

~

Ken arrives, takes the packet of cigarettes from his pocket and curls up next to me on the sofa like a cat. The two pussycats in the sound department are called Stereo and Mono.

Ken lights up, hacking cough, heavy breathing 'and body with continual smoking wasted'.

~

Simon is explaining his castle: what's missing from Simon's castle? The vodka moat, he's drunk it!

~

Spaghetti at the Presto with Peter and his friend Karl. A visit to the Slade show, which had a welcome art school feeling after the Royal College's corporate art. The lawn provided a pleasant and much more relaxed environment for a chat; students served Newcastle Brown Ale, mostly smiles, a few boys with avant-garde scowls. I talked to a friend of Peter's with an open smile, blacksmith's hands, quite a star. Two charming Glaswegians, a girl who had seen my exhibition at the Third Eye; the warmth that people give me like a good coal fire on a winter's day.

Met Ian on his way to Kinky Gerlinky. He said he'd take me out on the town.

~

HB back from Newcastle with many gifts: home-made yoghurt, lady's mantle, blueberries, blue overalls.

Wednesday 12
Little sleep, fury about *that* knighthood and those who said it helped us as they helped themselves. As if a millionaire declared his riches to help the poor. I thought of putting some final words on the credits for *Edward*, calling for equality before law.

~

Bought a purple velvet shirt, which shone in the dark – far too expensive.

~

The *Evening Standard* rang me for a comment on the OutRage! wedding and civil liberties. I wonder if other men and women bubble with the overwhelming anger that creeps up on me in the early hours of the morning? The careerists who came out of the closet when they had feathered their nests and criticised our behaviour, where were they in the sixties and seventies, and even the early eighties?

Wurlitzer Babylon – apparently a descendant of Lord Nelson – objects to the wedding! I asked the *Standard*: 'Which mistress was he born to?' Fuck this country, where we are forced to listen to fools with mouldy names.

~

Back in the sound-edit. Up on the screen Tilda [Swinton] wonderful: 'He shall be murdered when the deed is done.'

~

Simon is still building his castle, Marie Bett says she'll order a skip to remove it on Saturday. The new vodka moat has not arrived. Nothing happened to Simon last night – he didn't fall off his bike, as predicted.

~

A queer wedding, six o'clock, Trafalgar Square. Rain clouds threatening, I walked there with HB, Peter and Karl, sporting my 'Queer as Fuck' T-shirt. Several hundred OutRage! supporters, rice and confetti, a dozen or so couples and Peter Tatchell wearing a pink carnation standing on the column base. A boy in a dress walked up and down the plinth with 'idiot boards': 'Aaaah!', 'Ooooh!', 'Boo!', 'Hiss!'. Outraged charismatics frothing with hate, pelted with confetti and shouts of 'Out Tory'.

The couples were funny and touching: two girls exchanged vows for a second time after six years; Richard and Anthony arrived on a motorbike; two boys in drag vowed to share each other's make-up; two men in toppers brought their dogs as bridesmaids.

In the middle of it all the rain set in and a group called 'Inrage' made a small demonstration against the word 'queer'. The pigeons chased after the rice and Richard, high on the column straddling his motorbike, lobbed a bouquet, which sailed high over the crowd – to my total surprise I jumped and caught it cleanly. HB looked alarmed.

To Christine Smith's gallery in Covent Garden. We shelter in a doorway from a downpour; a waitress at the café under Inigo Jones's arches offers us a seat out of the rain.

At the gallery John Minton's picture of a boy sitting, charming, but thin. My T-shirt upset some; HB rude to John Pearse for selling me a shirt for £160 and two other people having identical ones at the opening: 'At that profit margin they should be one-offs.'

HB has made himself a one-off T-shirt – it says: 'Queerbashers' above a photograph of him brandishing a machine-gun; below it the legend: 'Come and Get It'.

Thursday 13

I slept so badly again last night, HB very uncomfortable, he usually takes a sleeping pill to survive these nights.

~

George is to recut the boys fucking from the first sequence of *Edward* for the BBC's screening next week. We are hoping they will have a change of heart but we are trapped. The commissioning editors are allies, but above them are Mrs Thatcher's accountants.

Friday 14

At six the screening of *Edward* for the investors – a great success. Colin McCabe said Kit Marlowe would have smiled, it was a great improvement on the original.

~

The evening at OutRage! with Patricia Tatchell and a couple of handsome lads talking about our first sexual encounters – Peter said his brought the sun out in his life, others hadn't been so lucky.

~

An extraordinary meeting on the Heath with a young criminal lawyer from New Zealand who led me a dance up and down *his* dale, laughing as he went – he said I was a charismatic hero of his childhood and produced a good bottle of red wine concealed under a tree. The rain set in and we talked for hours in the soaking wet. He wore a knitted woollen cap and a leather jacket, and in the dark resembled my Edward II. I asked him if he worked out. No, he said, he played rugby – flirtation and much good conversation in the shadows. Completely lost, he almost carried me back to the path and with luck I caught a taxi within seconds.

~

Back home late, HB tucked up in bed reading *Zen and the Martial Arts*. Fell asleep with Anger's *Fireworks* and Genet's *Un Chant d'Amour* turning over in my head and dreamt soundly.

Saturday 15
Drove to Prospect with HB, James and David. We made a picnic lunch and beachcombed. HB fought taekwon-do last night and has bruises all over. He has fallen asleep. James and David have left for London and a concert by the Charlatans.

~

The day overcast, I walked along the beach under a slate-blue sky streaked with orange rust that reflected itself in the wet sand. Prospect peaceful. HB hated the Copland that I had bought and replaced it with 'HB music' – Rain Tree Crow. Before the day was over Alan Beck came by to track down David – one of Alan's students is a suspect for a murder of a gay man in Hythe and David had spent time with him over the weekend the murder occurred. [Editor's note: neither of the parties mentioned here were involved.]

Sunday 16
Long article in the *Independent* on Outing. I'm for Outing, after first reservations. Every lawyer's query about *Modern Nature* was over sexuality – the straight world built this prison for us, now we are at the gates. What harm can the knowledge of someone's sexuality do? We need to make

those in high places speak up. There are more prominent people than the gaggle of thespians who claim to represent us – the first to be targeted should be the politicians, then the professions, particularly lawyers, judges and police, and then the churchmen who have havoced young lives.

~

Peter here with his friend Stephen. We drove to Joanna's wild-flower nursery at Dymchurch and bought valerian, which we planted alongside the house.

HB making a nuisance lighting the bee smoker. I was already jittery opening the hive. In the end the honey supers and a large tub of sugary water, queen excluder, and top board were all put in place without a mishap. It is nearly midsummer and the sun barely peeked through the clouds; late in the afternoon it rained. A bright-yellow sign has sprouted next to the house proclaiming: 'deep sea fishing'.

The lads, HB calls them 'the Dungenettes', left for Canterbury and the cinema, and I retired to bed early.

Monday 17

Cloudy, still and warm morning. I woke late, at nine, alone.

Made breakfast and planted the last of the santolina cuttings at the back of the house. Rewrite my will.

The sun climbs out of the clouds as I hang out the washing. There are black tortoiseshell caterpillars on the nettles and the gulls squabble over the discarded food scraps. There's another visitor walking through the garden and a letter from a student in Oxford that demands a reply: 'Dear Derek, I love you madly, I wish you were my father.'

The guns at the range in Lydd echo the thunder, the garden is shot with scarlet poppies, fumitory, smoke of the earth, deep-blue sage, ink-blue columbine, the white sea kale petals blown away in the wind, mauve jack-go-to-bed-at-noon and the blue-green yellow horned poppy, sea pinks and the sentinel red-hot pokers – known as 'Eddies' to HB. There are drifts of yellow broom, foxgloves and valerian – rather a wild bunch, the pink Mrs Sinkins, herb Robert, catnip, bugle and the last of the July flowers all a jumble.

Tuesday 18

The sun shone brightly this morning, then disappeared behind the clouds, poppies that come with the dawn punctuate the garden with scarlet, sending the bees dizzy as they blow in the breeze. Yellow sedum, deep-yellow eggs-and-bacon and purple vetch, all flowering. Small mullein plants where I scattered seeds last autumn.

Planted woad and chicory, the last santolina cuttings and prepared a bed for the iris.

and the white pink mrs sinkins .
herb Robert. kinown of herb kevin here,
Catnip bugle and the last of the winter
July flowers. all a jumble . by two
the poppies had shed their petals . I spent
the afternoon giving an interview for the observer-

tuesday

The sun shone brightly at eight this
morning then disappeared behind the
clouds - such a humming of bumble
bees in the blue sage flowers. Poppies
that come with the dawn. punctuate
the garden with scarlet sending the
bees dizzy as they blow in the breeze .
yellow seedum deep yellow . eggs &
bacon , and purple vetch . all flowering
small mullein plants where I scattered
seed last autumn - planted woad & chicory

Janáček's violin concert too loud and clear.

I dislike my landscape paintings today, they look ill-formed, hurried – the colours have turned to mud.

~

The wind's got up and the pale-ochre grass shimmers in the sunlight, in the late afternoon I watered the garden, back and forth with the heavy galvanised can. I have felt strangely light-headed all day, my stomach has taken a turn for the worse, it is quite impossible to concentrate – it's over four weeks since HB changed the telephone numbers and I still cannot memorise them. People think I'm lying when I say I do not know my own phone number.

In the evening the rain set in. Numbed head, tired eyes, vague disquiet.

Wednesday 19

It rained through the night, the cold that has gripped June is not dispelled by the forecasters' promises. The poppies are blue with cold – iron-grey clouds stacked over a steely sea, the white cliffs pulse at the edge of my headache. I cut back my newly planted valerian as the wind strips it of its leaves.

~

A letter from Peter Burton at *Gay Times* saying they would not feature *Modern Nature* as it conflicted with other material they are publishing, I'm not very lucky in that magazine – I'm either the butt of their scorn, or second-hand. Gave up the gay press, or rather it gave up on me. Curled up on the sofa with Nicholas de Jongh's book on homosexuality and the theatre.

~

In the afternoon the wind got up and the sun came out, the bees took off uncertainly, the flowers danced.

Thursday 20

With HB to see the sixties print exhibition at the Tate, most of the place closed for a Constable exhibition, the galleries like the M20, works and diversions everywhere.

Meeting at the BFI – the price of publishing *Queer Edward* has escalated to £10,000.

~

OutRage! meeting at the Lesbian and Gay Centre – a discussion about whether women want men demonstrating outside women-only bookshops which refuse to stock the 'SM' magazine *Quim*; the Isle of Man action to campaign to legalise us there; the exorcism of Lambeth Palace; 'Hollyphobia' – homophobia in the cinema; Outing.

Home at eleven, very tired.

Friday 21
Still cold and wet. Face red with irritation, felt like fading away.

Saturday 22
Caught the train to Ashford at eleven and met Peter. We traipsed round Sainsbury's with HB in search of 'HB fare' – little packages of nuts and oven-ready stuff that I cannot believe is edible, huge packets of cereals, mountains of yoghurts, processed peas, cow pies – he sits apart, eating his parallel meals.

Sunday 23
Along the railway embankment dog roses are flowering. At Dungeness the first pure white flowers have opened in the garden, bright against the grey rainy skies.

Walked to the Light Railway Café for lunch; along the roadside restharrow, bright bugloss and poppies, starry white Nottingham catchfly and drifts of purple thistles.

HB on the phone to his Geordie friends reports that I brought the Newcastle branch of the Committee for Homely Evenings (Campaign for Homosexual Equality) to its knees over the McKellen affair, he was, according to someone called Tim Bolton-Maggs, 'saintly'; I, the devil incarnate. Saintly is to be understood as 'raised a lot of cash'.

At the same meeting I had mentioned Outing a local Labour MP. HB said not to, as this sort of news might lose the Labour Party the election – well, if Michael Cashman stands as an MP that's done already.

~

It's raining again, the seagulls come in with the catch. Scarlet headaches and buzzing bluebottles.

~

Neil Tennant and his friend Jay arrive for tea.

Neil said a Japanese fan of Margi Clarke had killed herself as they could never swap skins, Margi had attended her funeral where she was the honoured guest.

I tell him about my number one fan; he knows her! She has all of my books and all of his CDs, all signed but never read or played – wrapped in cling-film and on display.

'We ditched our number one fan,' he said with a look of triumph, 'in Whitley Bay.'

I tell him I am to appear at the Christopher Street Parade in Berlin, on a stage with Jimmy Somerville. 'Oh, will you give him a message from me?'

'Of course.' I get my pen and pad.

'Piss off Mary, I'm head fairy.'

Monday 24

HB ironed all my clothes, then danced about annoying me with typhoo chops, he always gets excited when we are leaving – for Berlin today. He packs for every conceivable occasion, from ambassadorial reception to anarchic apocalypse.

Walked to Shipley's in the rain and bought a book on Whistler to read on the plane. HB accompanied me in his little blue tea cosy hat with his yellow bag slung on his shoulder, red socks and T-shirt, green tartan pants and red and black checked jacket for the journey – quite a dandy.

The plane swove and dove in the thunder clouds to Tegel Airport. HB convinced the woman who sat next to us was a spy.

At the cinema we saw *The Dream Machine*, Connie's film *Jean Genet Is Dead* and Paul Bettell's *Illegal Tender*. Then on into the night. I got back to the hotel at sunrise. HB soundly asleep, the waking pigeons cooing as I fell asleep beside him.

Tuesday 25

Tom's House much as we left it, hot water gurgling in the plastic immersion heaters, rooms decorated with huge prints of Tom of Finland's bootboys – our room has a slave market and a leather boy with laced-up flares. The oil painting of a blowsy lady with a rose presides over the dining room. Kurt, the proprietor, full of opera and ballet enthusiasms: 'Now,' he said, as he served breakfast leaning heavily on his walking stick, 'we have two of everything.'

~

Filmed documentaries all day until seven: on the old S-Bahn; in the loos of the old Hotel Esplanade and walking through its ruined interiors. HB retired to bed (via Burger King – the only place for him to eat in Berlin). I had supper at a Thai restaurant with Manfred Salzgeber, who has done more than anyone to support queer cinema.

At one in the morning the bar on the corner spilt out on to the streets, warm night, loud music, the police stopped to make them turn it down. Manfred in his leathers with his new boyfriend from the East in a smart uniform who saluted me goodnight. Berlin – late, lazy and laid back, I wonder if this will change now it has become the capital city again. The rents have risen overnight and accommodation cannot be had for love or money.

Wednesday 26
Manfred took us for lunch at a Greek restaurant. Back to the hotel to sleep, then out to Kreutzberg for a vegetarian meal at a restaurant called The Last Supper and cognac at the Bar Anal. HB protests: 'I can't sit in the window seat of a bar called *Anal*.' HB meets one of his friends, a young English artist called Tony – he makes large signs that read 'Homosexual'. He's been here for two weeks and works in an hotel cleaning the carpets – anything to get out of Great Britain, where, he says, you can't even hold hands.

Thursday 27
HB, hai-ing and jumping about in his tartan pants, says he's going to be invincible – will split any fluff I look at down the middle when he's finished his taekwon-do.

We spent the morning driving in East Berlin. Visited the morbid, over-grown Jewish cemetery, its granite monuments crushed by the frost and toppled by invading trees. East Berlin truly ugly, austere and very unwelcoming, the architecture looks like a cracked bathroom, old buildings have shed their stucco without the patina of decay, even the trees look mangy, not a pretty boy in sight to brighten the gloom. Do the people grow to look like the surroundings? A cup of coffee in a café where the lady smiled – there are few smiles in East Berlin.

HB says that East Berlin reminds him so much of the North-East that he feels at home there. Berlin is not a capital yet, HB says it's like Sunderland on half-day closing.

Kurt went to hear the Berlin Philharmonic last week and the East Berliner audience shouted 'louder, louder' in the quiet moments of a Mahler symphony. The boys still sport tatty jeans, knobbly knees showing – this fashion has long disappeared in London. Bob Geldof's wife Paula Yates was the most startling example of it – her whole arse on display in Faversham. HB, of course, thought she looked fantastic.

~

Back at the hotel James has sent a huge shopping list for John Maybury's film *Man to Man* – everything from light switches to sanitary towels. We've been blessedly free from film nonsense these past days and here's an ugly fax from Basilisk to spoil it.

~

HB has got Franz Liszt's hairstyle, he says he hates it and is going to smother it in gel. He makes a newspaper hat to conceal it and we head to a midnight party in a cinema, which never quite takes off. Late at night we get a lift to the hotel, squashed in the back of a Porsche, arriving just in time for a last drink with Rosa von Praunheim who looks completely unaltered in fifteen years, wearing the same leather jacket and blue shirt.

~

HB calls me a 'bed fascist' – which means I grab all the sheets, covers and pillows, while he freezes on the bare mattress.

Friday 28
Still grey and overcast.

'Twink twink tiddly twink,' HB sings at the wash basin. All our money is going down the drain on James's demands for props. Dagmar Benke, who commissioned the films for ZDF, arrived and we bought £55 of rubbish at the supermarket. Then we caught the S-Bahn to the East and walked for hours and hours through ruined streets to ruined churches and along a pristine theme park street restored to the width of a façade.

At three we stopped off at a squat called the house of queens, HB threw stones at the windows, rousing several surprised boys with badger haircuts – they blinked at us in bleary-eyed disbelief. We watched a curious film made for Channel Four with a horror movie voice-over about their lives and a battle with some neo-Nazi boys and the police.

Home in the rain.

Saturday 29
Another AIDS interview and another screening: this time about that horrible quilt – what bits of cast-off clothing would be sewn on mine? Old taxi receipts to Hampstead and a membership to the Subway.

~

Christopher Street Parade, lots of make-up, dyed hair and drag, dancing to old Steve Strange records – a bit tired, but fun.

The political speeches icy avalanches blurred through the tannoy. The march fizzled out as everyone took their own directions, there seemed little reason to brave the rain and cold to a sports hall in the East. The parade over, drooping feathers and blotched mascara, like a mid-seventies rave in Railton Road.

Berlin strangely enervated, everyone wants to rebuild the wall, the exposure to a new reality too hard to accommodate. East Germany is indescribably ugly and sad, like a cripple in the family – everyone walks slower. 'They don't like us and we don't like them' is the prevailing attitude.

Everyone on the march complained that the party tonight is 'Over *There*'. We don't make it – the address is not on the ticket.

Sunday 30

Eleven o'clock, champagne for breakfast. HB retreated behind a pile of yoghurt pots, taut, middle-aged faces round the table. Berlin is built on sand. Please Mr Sandman, send me a dream.

HB prowls about, packing. The birds in the square are not singing, only the distant sound of radios and washing up.

Lunch at Café Einstein, just warm enough to sit outside. HB throws breadcrumbs to sparrows singing 'Feed the Birds, Tuppence a Bag', a waiter tells him off. HB asks him for a bread roll and proceeds to scatter more crumbs. The waiter returns and says if HB does not stop he will be asked to leave. HB indignantly protests his innocence. There is a solitary 'cheep' behind us and we turn to see a flock of expectant sparrows. The waiter glowers and marches off. HB tosses the birds the entire roll.

Spent the afternoon in the car with Dagmar. The city gutted of culture, the destruction of the Jews like smashing the only mirror in which you can see yourself. Berlin staggers blind into the future, unable to see itself in the dark and gaping hole left in its heart. It's the same in Warsaw.

JULY

Monday 1

Once more into his breeches, dear friend.

Actors can never make good politicians, as they will betray you for the applause. The Labour MPs should be Outed first because they are the ones who should be helping us. I'd turn the key on the Tories and leave them in the closet. As for myself, I always believed in High Art, made my films in *that* Establishment – my critics were too stupid to understand this; and my audience just wanted to dance to Gloria Gaynor, not yawn through *The Garden*; if I hadn't had to fight for my sexuality and respect I'd have been very middle of the road.

~

It's the day of the library: the morning started with the BFI taking on *Queer Edward*; I received the first copy of *Modern Nature*; saw Takashi Asai, who commissioned another book; Century Hutchinson rang for another.

~

After Berlin, London seems frantic with its beggars, workout rent boys and expensive Soho bars.

~

At Dungeness by sunset. Walked along the beach and found an old tin box for planting. On the way home a car stopped along the road with four young men, one of whom asked for my autograph. I invited them back to Prospect for tea. We talked by candlelight, I gave them a book – they came from Nottingham, unspoilt by London, very shy. One of them had my photo on his wall.

Tuesday 2

The rain pours down, great puddles form on the drive, cars pass by in trails of mist, syncopated roar on the roof, the garden drips with rain that has turned my view to green.

The post is full of Christian exhortation and more lost boys from Liverpool signing their letters with hearts.

Lynn Barber came to make an interview. Lunch in the Light Railway Café, where a model boy strips off for a jeans advert.

The poppies hang their heads lower and lower, they sink into the afternoon, washed up on a July day. The rain still falls and the dark closes in.

Wednesday 3

Under the dark rain clouds that have shut out blue skies and clamped the horizon, the field of scarlet poppies sway in the breeze, the sleepy heads of the thunder flowers bowed around the little black house have charmed all my visitors. It was once thought that staring at them for too long would blind you – but they open my eyes. I should count them for you but the hundreds of last year whose seed I scattered have returned as thousands, a great war of poppies flout the transient day.

I wish you were here with me this morning, the sun we had quite given up for lost is playing fast and loose; weeks late, summer is coming in.

The draft of a new will arrives through the door; I sign it.

Delius's *Sea Drift* returns like the tide, washes the morning bright. I worked in the garden, split a clump of thrift and the purple iris, planted out mullein, sweethearts and soldier's tears.

A red admiral circled as I took gorse cuttings. Silvery hare's foot clover shimmers on the bank.

~

Returned to London reading *Peers, Queers and Commons* on the train. Late pizza at the British Museum Pizza House.

Thursday 4

Spent the morning at St Mary's. My doctor had returned from an AIDS conference in Florence; Africa is facing huge problems – a health budget of twenty-seven pence per person per annum. Here things are very different, St Mary's one of the finest hospitals, patients live longer. We dwell on a little futurology, three to six years are the best forecast, the worst next week. On the way home I decided to try to make the millennium.

Peers, Queers and Commons, finished in the waiting room, comes out rather too strongly for the Campaign for Homosexual Equality and Stonewall, and against the abseiling lesbians. The author has no involvement with the arts – Hockney, Somerville, myself completely absent. Surely we helped as much as Cashman and McKellen? The reason we were not at their Downing Street bash was quite simple: because we were not asked – except for paintings to auction later, and when I offered one of mine for their fundraising auction this spring it was not accepted.

There's an art battle going on – who holds the keys of history and why were we not asked? They connived with the straight media which had already turned me, quite falsely, into a dangerous producer of video nasties: *Jubilee*, *Sebastiane* – the Churchill Bill mentioned in *Peers, Queers and Commons*, but the films absent.

~

A long and frank interview with Hugo Davenport of the *Telegraph*, at times very funny. We both laughed at the country ladies of their readership embracing each other at a gymkhana.

~

Too tired for OutRage! fell early into bed on a steamy night.

Friday 5
Thought for today: God is our amnesia.

This morning we watched the first screening of a completed *Edward*, the lighter print showed up more of the dungeon and the fine performances. Marlowe's lines of insight: *the closet of my heart*. Noticed the spitting priests, Gaveston, Edward, Spencer, Mortimer, and the red-hot poker. Marlowe the mirror in which Shakespeare finds himself.

~

It's very hot. Interviews with *Tribune* and *The Scotsman*. HB has gone to Newcastle, sudden quiet, I miss him greatly – somehow all the cleaning, laundry, ironing, shopping and bed-making happens miraculously in my absence. He said: 'the self-cleansing flat is taking a break.'

Walked through the cool of Westminster Cathedral to Random Century to discuss a new book, and then back across Westminster with Tony Peake.

~

Unable to sleep, I spent most of the night on the Heath, talking to a charming silver-haired man about the past and the razoring that the city has performed here, all the undergrowth burned. The Heath used to belong to the GLC and was unkempt and romantic; now, under the force of finance, it has received a banker's barbering. One young man said: 'I want you to know, Mr Jarman, that I love you, but I'm not going to have sex with you.'

The heat brought the tourists, everything most decorous, although two lads were rolling around in the mud left by the June rain. The leather boys clustered round a rather handsome lad who'd stripped off: pale and finely built, he was showered with kisses. Lightning played through the night, a voice in the half-light said: 'It's electric here.'

Saturday 6

The heatwave continues. I sleep in the train to Ashford past the pale-blue linseed fields.

The garden has never looked so fine, ecstatic in the midday sun.

Ken rang to say he had read through *Modern Nature* last night and he found my depressed self quite different from the self on the set of *Edward* that he knew. 'Liverish,' I said, 'those TB bugs jaundice the view, like cracked and yellowing varnish.' I've had the first bug and sent it packing.

I am much more certain where my feet are planted today – and the garden blooms as never before, all the flowers of the wilderness.

~

Alan Beck calls by on his way to the E. F. Benson day in Rye – we talk of the possibility of a gay archive as we walk along the beach.

~

Much later in the silent evening Edward, the red-haired boy next door, shoots at the flaming sun with his air rifle. The dying light turns the poppies deep scarlet, the bugloss spires a burning iridescous purple, my sky-blue T-shirt cool against the glowing timbers of Prospect. A gentle breeze rocks the grasses silhouetted against the angry clouds. Edward fires one last shot as the sun sinks slowly behind Lydd church and disappears into the 'Bungalow for Sale'.

The coming dark smells of the sea.

Sunday 7

At seven a young man with jet-black hair and blue eyes knocked on the door, asking for angling bait.

A heavy dew had condensed in the night, sparkling on leaf and petal. I made myself toast and coffee and, heavy-eyed, settled into the morning. The wind got up and the clouds rolled in from the sea.

After lunch at the Light Railway Café, my neighbours Brian and Sheila drove me to the strawberry field in New Romney to pick large punnets. Later I walked along the beach and brought back an old lobster pot.

The nuclear power station vented steam for over an hour – so noisily I could not hear. A red admiral circled the garden and at teatime a hummingbird hawk moth flew into the kitchen.

The mauve nostalgia of the opium poppies, white sails floating across the aquamarine, at the day's end the lighthouse illuminates the deep-sea wrecks in the phosphorescent depths.

Monday 8

Clouds bring a light drizzle, the wind's got up and is blowing billows across the grasses, wave follows wave. Sweet smell of the warm wet shingle.

After weeks of waiting on my indecision I have plunged in to paint the first ecstatic landscapes. John Adams's *Shaker Loops* dances across Dungeness horizons, the swelling in my heart throws itself into the reds and gold, floats in cerulean, drowns in the cobalt and hides in the deep sage-green of sadness.

Tuesday 9

HB hanging out in Sunderland. I met Donald 'Smudger' Smith on the street outside Russell and Chapple and we spent the morning on a gallery crawl starting at the Royal Academy.

Met Norman Rosenthal, full of the Turner Prize: 'If Anish Kapoor wins, I've lost.'

Up in the lift where Norman ticked off the lift attendant – 'It's too full' – and then the ticket collector for half closing the doors: 'The RA,' he told him, 'is about looking.'

He bustled us through the spectacular new galleries by Norman Foster. Braque and Vlaminck my favourite fauves with violet and mauve skies. Back to the drawing table at Prospect.

We walked down the elegant staircase made of opaque glass so you can see the shoes of those above you.

The Michelangelo lurks behind greenish bullet-proof glass. 'That,' says Norman, 'will have to be replaced.'

On to Totah's, Keith Milow's show at Greenwood's and Richard Hamilton's at D'Offay – with all the eerie strangeness of hotel lobbies, more frightening than Bacon. Damien Hirst's butterfly piece in Woodstock Street quite the best, with tropical butterflies all over the gallery, on the floor and eating syrup on a large table.

~

At five a showing of the final print of *Edward*.

~

Caught a cab at 9.30 to the Heath. Very hot, met Julian. HB had sabotaged my armoury – KY replaced with a tube of Deep Heat and my bottle of poppers filled with perfume.

Wednesday 10

Washed out, but very happy this morning as HB, the long-lost HB, returns from Newcastle.

Chris Woods here, conversation about the Crusaid gala. I find the idea distasteful: one rule for the rich, another for the poor. Until schools and hospitals are integrated into a state system with no private bolt-holes, they will always be in crisis. The rich don't experience them, do nothing to help them, while Madonna sings for them at God knows how many £££'s a ticket.

~

Meeting with Les Blair to talk over the designs for *Waiting for Godot*.

~

HB arrived home with a new seahorse tattoo and an offer to go camping in Scotland with his friend Garry. HB calls me a saboteur as the washing machine has self-destructed and his white hydrangea has withered away.

Thursday 11

Geraint, a photographer from the *Independent*, collected me at eleven and we drove through a scorching morning to Dungeness.

I took the queen excluder from the hive so the bees have a brood and a half, then we took off to the Light Railway Café, where I was photographed with a party of elderly ladies from Folkestone. I had put on my brick-red overalls to look bright in the pale-blue room. By four we were finished.

~

The rose at the kitchen window is in full bloom and the scabious is flowering in the front bed.

Friday 12

I woke at ten o'clock – very late for me – from a vivid nightmare in which my father had transformed his house at Merryfield into the most curious space, a combination of Mertzbarn and Watts Tower. A host of dropouts, extras from a left-bank art show, were being entertained there. The spaces, some distant ancestor of the new gallery at the Royal Academy, were very exciting. I was full of admiration, it had every richness that the original lacked.

~

My old friend Jeffrey Rodgers, who 'sailed' for America fifteen years ago, telephoned. I met him at the William in Hampstead, the first grown-up artist in my life. He said we never realised we were living through golden times.

A door slammed in the breeze, and my stomach collapsed in a dose of the shits. I was unwell yesterday, very sore, it gives me a feeling of unease. I can never quite forget my illness, it gives a finality to every gesture – is this the last flower I will plant? Will this be my last flying trip into my past – the Heath. I go to spite the present.

I am as content as I would be in other circumstances, though I am ready to give up. Fuck this long summer dying. How can I focus with this sore arse?

~

The garden glows fire-bright in the wind, all scarlets and blues, like my paintings for Richard. Peter phones full of woes: I had given him an advance copy of *Modern Nature* on the condition that he didn't show it to James. While Liam, the photographer on the *Man to Man* set, was leafing through it James snatched it – never let a diary out of your hands. The spilt water seemed like a flood on the phone but I'm certain it was little more than a drop. All the aggravating days that led to making *The Garden* were a deluge, there's but a drop on the pages.

~

The wind is blowing so hard the bees, heavy with orange pollen, fail to land. The paint falls off the canvas, my old trousers are splashed with orange and there's a hole beneath the knees.

HB's leek sausages sizzle for lunch at three.

~

Today my only companion is a bluebottle, which makes a furious attempt to knock itself silly on the window.

~

Can you feel I'm quite quite content between these lines?

Saturday 13

Shall I stay here or return to London? The rain has set in, my pictures painted, the garden weeded. All my disgust with Basilisk washes over. I've already had one of their little notes that says such-and-such and this-and-this will happen, and then the schedule passes and no one phones to explain why. I must learn not to care

~

All my flowers are bowed in the rain, what do they care if it blows hot or cold?

I washed the floors. Peter arrived out of the gloom and we left for London.

Sunday 14
Breakfast at Bertaux's, a mound of letters. Review of a book on Boothby in the *Independent* brought back half-forgotten memories – visiting Dorothy Macmillan for Sunday lunch in the sixties.

~

Lunch with James. He describes Colin McCabe rushing around the *Man to Man* set like a balloon squealing with delight as the air rushes out.

Spent the rest of the afternoon dozing on the bed as HB watched *Soylent Green*.

Monday 15
We are off to screen *The Garden* at Moscow film festival. HB has packed two huge suitcases: one with clothing; the other with tinned food, chocolate, cigarettes, chewing gum and toiletries. He calls it 'soft currency'.

The plane, a huge Tupolev built before the oil crisis, gleaming and enormous with fifties Cadillac fins. The wide aisles soon fill up with televisions, video recorders and microwave ovens, the ephemera of capitalism that affluent escapees are taking home. The flight is bumpy and a gale roars through the bright cabin. 'Great!' says HB. 'This really is like flying.'

~

We are met at the airport by our translator Helena. HB slips her something and whispers conspiratorially. She whisks us through the VIP arrivals, bypassing customs to raised eyebrows from the uniformed staff. 'Don't want my bribes confiscated,' HB explains.

Tuesday 16
We are driven on a coach, hot as a glasshouse, to the monastery at Zagorsk. The four coaches drive in convoy preceded by a police car. Helena is quite religious, she frequently recites the Lord's Prayer out loud. She ties a headscarf as she kneels at the tomb of St Sergei in the dark, icon-encrusted little cathedral at the centre of the huge monastic complex. Once, 1,500 monks lived here, now there are 150.

Today the state hands back religious property. No one knows how they will afford to look after this vast palace. Old ladies are everywhere, they are mostly dressed in black and do not look up from their work. Some are polishing the floors and gilded candlesticks, others are singing as they kiss the tomb of the saint. 'Are you a believer?' they asked. 'Are you a believer?'

'No,' I said. 'No.'

Our guide, a young novice, says he's seen the light restored to two blind pilgrims with his own eyes – so strong is the saint in 'This Temple'. The atmosphere is tense with the past, the smell of beeswax candles and the antiphonal sadness of the chant, which rises and falls in the dark.

'This room,' says our guide, 'was given to the monastery by Peter the Great and was used during the revolution as a gymnasium. The Bolsheviks destroyed the icon stands for rifle practice, the current ones came from a church in Moscow.'

We are shown a painted box given to the Patriarch by Stalin for support lent during the great patriotic war – with more than a little irony, as above it are photos of the cathedral he demolished in Moscow to build a swimming pool.

While we stare at icons by Andrey Rublev, HB slips off to buy a set of devotional manuals for his mum, they cost 130 roubles – 4.US dollars. He gives the same amount to the guide behind the desk. Our tour guide has tracked him down and reprimands him, as they are forbidden to accept tips, 'However . . . my wife embroiders altar cloths for the monastery and the gilded cotton is *so* expensive . . .' We both slip him £10 on a deserted staircase. It is six months' wages for him.

Wednesday 17

HB returns from a shopping expedition with his treasures. 'Look at this. The Americans spent millions of Apollo dollars devising pens that would write in zero gravity and pocket calculators. The Russians spent a few roubles on a propelling pencil combined with a slide rule, an infinitely superior culture.' He heads out again in search of more space race treasures and to bribe himself to the front of the mile-long McDonald's queue.

~

Helena drives us to her little flat out beyond the university. She has two cream mongrels that bark and dance at her return with a 'doggy bag', into which we have slipped all the food that was left on our table at the Rossia. Her flat is a clutter of wooden dolls, blue porcelain and old mahogany furniture, with many primitive paintings on the walls. She brews tea and recounts the work of a faith healer, visions of her parents in dreams. She says she has nothing to fear, but shakes with anxiety before our press shows. Helena's great-grandfather was the physician on the tsar's yacht and was spared by the crew who drowned the other officers by throwing them overboard with weights attached to their legs.

She is divorced from a drunken actor and lives for her dogs and God. She has frizzy hair, frightened kohl-blackened eyes, rouged cheeks and a very fast walk. She is slightly stooped and has a charming smile. She says this is the first festival where the interpreters have not had to file reports for the KGB on their charges.

Helena receives 160 roubles a month; a chicken – if you can find it – costs eighty, a dollar thirty. The search for hard currency in Moscow is relentless: caviar is slipped to you at the hotel for fifteen dollars; in the Arbat gangs of smiling boys approach you to sell military issue watches with red stars and portraits of Gagarin on the strap for ten dollars. A ride on the underground is fifteen kopeks, three times what it used to be – some decimal point of a penny. Here we are billionaires, overwhelmed by the sadness.

Helena tells us of two diplomats' wives visiting London for the first time: one is taken to Boots the Chemist and faints in disbelief at the range of products; the other visits Sainsbury's, where she runs up and down the aisles screaming in ecstasy. Both are sedated and sent home, to receive psychiatric care.

Thursday 18

HB returns from his morning swim in a fluster. As he pays his way into the hotel's swimming pool a handsome young man asks him if he will pay him in as well. 'Of course,' says HB – it is less than two pence for towel, locker and pool.

While HB is resting between his innumerable lengths the boy swims up to him. 'You give me three dollars.'

'What for?'

The boy makes kissing noises.

HB swims away, scandalised.

Later the boy swims up to him again. 'You give me two dollars.'

'What for?'

More kissing noises.

HB leaves the pool.

The changing rooms are policed by stern matrons; one asks him in perfect English 'Are you a sailor?' pointing to his bestiary of tattoos.

The boy hears HB speaking and seeks him out. 'You give me one dollar . . .'

HB gives him his swimming trunks, goggles and the contents of his pockets – chewing gum, a packet of cigarettes and a five-dollar bill. God knows what the boy thought he wanted to do to him for that much, so he explained: 'I don't want to fuck you, I just want you to fuck off!'

~

In the evening we are taken to the Palace of Youth, one of those cheerless marble monoliths as ugly as the underground that the Russians are so good at, vacuous pomp.

We stand in the centre of the stage blinded by spotlights. 'This is my friend HB who I have lived with for five years, he's very shy.' The audience of young people, 2000 strong, gasped, then applauded. We had a long and very friendly question-and-answer session, something that would have been impossible on my visit seven years ago. The audience congratulated Helena on her translating. I was presented with a citation from the Moscow Film Club for their favourite film of the festival. It's still illegal to be gay in the Soviet Union – for most of the audience this was the first time they had seen a film that had touched the subject. There were to be no prizes at the main festival. My hosts said if I had been born here I would probably have spent most of my life in lunatic asylums like Parajanov until, like him, I died young.

Friday 19

We visit the department store Gum, which faces Lenin's mausoleum. Helena tells us Gum had just been saved from collapse as an accumulation of thousands of tons of dust had been recently vacuumed from its roof. Gum resembles a nineteenth-century rail terminus, more than half of it is closed during its opening hours, with a tide of humanity with nothing to do but admire the architecture, or gawp at a window stocked with clothes from Benetton – quite beyond their grasp.

~

At the edge of Red Square a row of old ladies sit on the pavement with fading framed photos of young men. A vigil for lost sons in Ngarno Karabash? Or grandsons in a purge? The Great War? Afghanistan? Or the Revolution itself? They are so old. Do these battered bundles of old clothes hide princesses?

Meanwhile the new young businessmen of Moscow are sporting smart Western haircuts, flat-tops, rockerbillies. Stripped to the waist in the sunlight, they hustle the tourists with egg-shaped dolls of the hated Gorbachev with a begging bowl, inside him Brezhnev, Stalin, Peter the Great.

~

Drunks are crashed out on the black leather chairs in the entrance to the enormous Hotel Rossia. At the film festival's closing reception people stand facing the long tables, eating. They are so busy tucking into the cherries and pears they only pause briefly to make conversation; you can tell the foreigners as they are not engaged in eating.

A young man – 'My name is Andrew, I am nineteen and I must see you' – is standing by the hotel entrance holding a rolled-up newspaper. Andrew is a student of music from Izhevsk. He saw the film last night in the Palace of Youth. 'We have never seen anything like *The Garden*,' he says. 'I will remember it in my heart for ever. There is no love here. I can afford to come to Moscow once a year and the situation at home is more desperate.' He has pale-blue eyes, wears an old T-shirt, khaki shorts and sandals that have nearly ceased to exist. I give him all the roubles in my pocket – two more journeys to Moscow – and the phone numbers of friends. He is trembling with fear and repression. I try to calm him, make him smile, tell him it was the same in England when I was nineteen.

I have happily missed Sophia Loren presiding over the prize-giving, sitting on a wall talking to him.

~

It's ten p.m. and the changing of the guard is performed to the chimes of the Kremlin clock, a goose-stepping ballet at the doors of Lenin's red granite tomb. A group of one hundred or so curious onlookers watch rather indifferently in the great empty square, when suddenly an elegant and rather portly man shouts (in Russian): 'I spit on the tomb of the murderous bastard.' The words ring out in the silence, the crowd is hushed, there are no pigeons here, utter silence in the dusk. Within seconds he is pulled and shouted at by a pinched little man in ill-fitting jeans and a leather jacket, and before you can click your fingers a car appears from nowhere and he is bundled into it by the KGB. The car speeds away in the dreadful silence. We had been told that the great terror would never be lifted until the body of its perpetrator had been buried.

A man started a conversation: 'Are you speaking English?'

'Yes.'

'I'm thrilled to meet you. I teach English and you are the first Englishmen I've met.' His English was formal, old-fashioned. He said he was on holiday, had sailed here for ten days in a boat from Astrakhan. He had a kind smile and looked like Picasso. 'I read a lot, Jack London in particular, and Byron, what a great poet he is.' I felt as I spoke to him that I could confirm or destroy a lifetime's work by my deportment.

~

Meanwhile Helena and HB walked back from the scene of the crime. Helena said the KGB would put the man in an asylum, beat him black and blue, and release him after a few days.

My friend from Astrakhan said: 'He was quite mad and probably drunk as well,' though he had seemed quite sane and sober to me. We all drifted apart in the gloom. The weaselley KGB man had returned to his 'job' as a street photographer, *Colour Photos – by Post*, names and addresses taken and the photographs posted to you.

'You see how clever the KGB are,' said Helena. 'They even follow you on holiday.'

Helena spots KGB agents by their clothes: too neat, too expensive, too clean. She walks around arm in arm with HB. They speak in codes, behaving like a pair of spies themselves. When she sees a suspected KGB agent amongst the crowd she says to HB: 'Colour photos . . .' he looks at the 'agent' and, if he agrees, replies: 'By Post.' They do it so often the entire populace must be on the KGB's payroll.

~

At midnight we are taken to an inner party members' haunt on the top floor of a skyscraper. Two huge armed security guards man the entrance, one pulls the door ajar to reveal a half-empty restaurant, the tallest blocks our way. 'Have you got a reservation?'

'No.'

'I'm sorry, the restaurant is fully booked this evening.' He closes the door in our faces while his comrade pages the lift.

HB pushes forward. 'Will *this* do for a reservation?' he says, waving a twenty-dollar bill in the guard's face with a flourish.

'Certainly, sir.' The doors are opened and we are shown to a window seat with a view over Moscow and served caviar. In a few short days HB has fully grasped the nuances of state socialism.

~

Back at the Rossia Hotel, a VIP on the eleventh floor of this vast barracks, I shooed the cockroaches into the dark and lay in the sweltering heat thinking of the past five days in which we had shown *The Garden* in competition at the film festival to an audience who had said in disbelief: 'However was this film chosen?' It surprised me as well and it might easily have never happened; there were many at home who were worried about the reaction to the first gay film shown here.

Saturday 20

Early-morning Moscow dusty and cheerless, the golden onion domes of the churches hardly dispel the gloom, everywhere cracked windows, peeling stucco and pot-holed roads, stale and airless. In spite of the past and the present, people shine out of this gloom with a simple kindness it would be hard to find back in England.

~

Helena whisks us through Aeroflot VIP departures and kisses us both in a tearful goodbye, saying she'll pray for us. She presents us with a beautiful red silk banner proclaiming in gilded letters 'Under the flag of Marxism-Leninism true Socialism shall Triumph'. HB hands her a huge wodge of paper money: two hundred dollars' worth of roubles and two hundred US dollars, five years of her schoolteacher's salary. She looks him in the eye and says: 'You might have done it sooner.' A security guard is eyeing them suspiciously. She narrows her eyes: 'Colour photos . . .'

HB nods. 'By post.'

Sunday 21

HB performed a mammoth wash on all the clothes which he said stank of communism. Read the *Independent* and contemplated the young beggars tucked up in their soiled sleeping bags begging with plastic mugs. The ones outside Phoenix House today are from Scotland. Welcome home.

~

Alasdair came in the evening. he's still quarrelling with young Barry. We both took off for Hampstead Heath at nine. A long censorious conversation: 'What are you doing here? A public figure! It seems at variance with your public statements!'

'What do you expect me to do? Describe Hampstead Heath on television with Jonathan Ross? There's a time and a place.' He left, very grouchy.

It was made up for by a young Greek lad who said: 'Can I get you a Coke?' He went up to the stall at the ponds to buy it.

Back late. Love and sex are not the same – who heard of anyone falling in sex?

Monday 22

Bought a fine silver pen in the market, I shall use it to continue writing this diary. Otherwise the day spent with Maddy [Morris], Rick [Mayall], Nigel [Planer], Ade [Edmonson], discussing *Godot*. Maddy and I decided on a huge yellow moon, blasted willow and the stage flooded – how much of this will we be able to afford?

Late in the afternoon I had my hair cut. HB also chopped off his locks with a Stanley knife, then got his barber to repair the damage. Says I tried to sabotage him by complimenting him on his long hair. He has the haircut of Gary Stretch, the boxer he so loves: he's been 'Stretched'. Now the boys will all be after him and his friend Garry will be happy.

~

My hair is silvered with the stress of the last two years; the grey crept up my sideburns and has now reached the crown. This is a good time to add a few years, when someone enquires about your age – 'I'm sixty.'

'My, how young you look!'

If a gay man of my generation didn't strike out for the horizon then he performed a small betrayal. It was a duty for those of us marked as 'different' to lead adventurous lives. Conforming had no place, particularly no place in the politics of a generation. The eighties attempted to reverse this. You cannot turn time back except on the little Soviet watch HB bought me.

Tuesday 23
Dungeness. In the afternoon Toby and his friend Mark made a videotape in the bedroom. They took a long time getting it quite right. I wrote many letters as they worked away and played an extraordinary CD by B. Tchaikovsky, which I bought for many too many roubles in the foyer of the Rossia.

~

After Toby left a thunderstorm set in as darkness fell, wild lightning played across the nuclear plant, then it crossed over the sea, razor bright. The lights in Prospect flickered on and off. The sun set blood-red and cast a strange violet shadow.

Very silent between the thunderclaps.

Wednesday 24
Gossip travels fast. A couple of nights ago Sir Ian McKellen was called urgently to the Palace as Prince Edward was coming out to Prince Philip. True or false?

The onus is on heterosexuals to explain themselves, their behaviour and the evil they have brought us. They need to come out, not us, and face the prosecution. It's they who have warped sexuality, who have murdered and driven innocents to suicide, they who should ask for forgiveness.

The rain has poured down all morning, the garden is bowed under the weight of thundery drops, the scarlet poppies yield to the deep yellow of the cotton lavender and vivid blue of the cornflowers, the last petals of the dog rose fall like snowflakes. The yucca is in bloom, a great creamy spire of bells, purple lavender and mounds of yellow and scarlet nasturtiums. I wander across the landscape, broadcasting the seeds of foxglove and poppy.

Thursday 25
A warm, overcast day. I worked in the garden planting a wide circle of gorse round the wood henge, cuttings which may set – there are thirteen points on this compass. The rain has produced a cornucopia of flowers, many of which have self-seeded in these favourable conditions. Mallow, wild wallflower, columbine, thrift, at the sea's edge a clump of deep purple alfalfa. An elderly lady arrived with a camera and asked me if she could take photographs: 'I find it so peaceful here.'

~

Ken telephones. He says that all men are homosexual, he can see it in their eyes. This accounts for the paranoia.

Back to London.

Friday 26
'Show print' of *Edward* at Mr Young's at nine o'clock.

~

A young woman interviewed me for the World Service on Outing. Stonewall are strongly against it. I must say that made me strongly for it. As for privacy, what is private behaviour? The rich protect themselves with comprehensive libel laws. The royal family flaunt their couplings and Hollywood, which sets the pulpy agenda, keeps us firmly locked out of the studios. What are a couple of careers in the movies or politics compared to the terrible isolation of young men and women?

I'm a much better role model than the Stonewall gang who do not represent me in any of their aspirations, whether acquiring knighthoods or being served white wine at sad little dinner parties.

As the Establishment always writes the history, I wonder how I'll come out. A bitter man who resented life? Took it out on those nearest? Put the clock back for homosexual reform? If you read *Peers, Queers and Commons* there is a vital element missing: its thesis is that the steps forward will occur through parliamentary legislation. This is a mistake, steps forward came by the example of our lives, one David Hockney in 1960 was worth more than the 1967 act and did more to change our lives. The aim is to open up discourse and with it broaden our horizons; that can't be legislated for.

Sunday 28
Dungeness. A cotton wool mist blowing in veils from the sea, the horizon disappears making a very secret garden. It's midday, the foghorn booms three times every minute.

I open the hive and put the third super in place. Maybe we shall have honey in September.

The *Sunday Times* has Outing as the lead article, Tatchell in the limelight, Stonewall lagging. It's very selfish for Matthew Parris to argue that it would have damaged his career. If careers exist they shouldn't be pursued at others' expense. He talks about inching forward, we're talking about jumping. It's suggested that only one hundred careers are at risk. Who gives a fuck for these fat cats who have built their careers, how far are they going to fall from the House of Commons? Into a boardroom. So carry on Outing.

Tuesday 30

You're better off in the cinema for cocks – they look too small to be effective on stage. Alan Beck, HB and myself went to see the Chippendales at the Strand – we were the only men in the audience. Several hundred screaming middle-aged ladies with frizzy hairstyles and bottles of vodka hidden in their handbags re-lived their youth at a Beatles concert.

I wasn't particularly turned on. The Chips never flashed their dicks, but rolled around with pillows and towels. They were so big and muscly their dicks would have looked incredibly small. On the whole, they made rather ineffective sailors and bike boys. The ladies queuing at the ladies' asked if we were their minders. HB much sexier than all the Chippendales put together.

AUGUST

Thursday 1
The Outing campaign by FROCS called off – they said it was a media hoax, I can't believe anyone will be happy about that. They should have left the heat on over the weekend and seen the line of MPs who would have voluntarily Outed themselves.

Friday 2
To Dungeness with Howard Sooley. We visited Joanna at the wild-flower nursery. Tucked the bees up after opening the hive – they have exploded in numbers.

Staked the gorse and weeded the front bed. HB rang to say the *Queer Edward* book looks fine.

A magical sunlit day that stretched out into the evening.

The nuclear power station roared through the starlit night, sending a great spume of spectral steam high into a pewter sky.

Sunday 4
Cast and crew screening of *Edward II*; the BFI set up a stall and sold over two hundred *Queer Edward* books. The audience liked the film, my old friend Robert Medley – who arrived from the Charterhouse – loved it. We ate pizzas at the British Museum Pizza House, Robert told us of Benjamin Britten's first boyfriend who was killed in a plane accident.

Dozed off – all the excitement during the afternoon – and at nine took off for Hampstead Heath. A dull voyeuristic sort of night, two short-haired lads with fine physiques put on a public display, snapped on condoms like surgeons with rubber gloves.

Wednesday 7
There's a review of *Modern Nature* in the *Guardian*, the first article that I've had for a book in a national paper.

~

OutRage! 'riot' at Lambeth Palace – casting out homophobia from the Church of England. Fuck it, we've the book launch – I'll miss the fun!

Thursday 8

Lunch at Richard's to launch *Modern Nature*, many old friends: Yolanda Sonnabend, Ossie Clark, Andrew Logan and most especially Brenda Lukey and Roger Ford, who she hadn't seen in twenty years. I rushed round the room back and forth so fast I can't for the life of me remember what happened – not even a shred of gossip. HB taekwon-doed Phoenix House, it's all being dismantled for the great move; we're going to live on the floor with no bed or chairs, even the mantelpiece is going.

Friday 9

A book-signing at Shipley's. Spent the evening on Hampstead Heath.

Saturday 10

Caught the train to Dungeness.

Sunday 11

Dull, overcast day, rain spitting. I dug the front garden. HB arrived with Peter and Karl. All the furniture from Phoenix House is installed.

HB weeded the stone circle in the afternoon.

Monday 12

Brilliant, sunny morning, shimmering silvery flowers of the hare's foot trefoil bobbing up and down. The front garden looks very formal – rather tidy, all the summer flowers are at an end, the dried sepia of autumn overtakes them, only the burdock is left to flower and it's putting on its mauve.

~

The *Sunday Times* notes that I give equal importance to everything, the mark of the naïf, I see everything through the past but claim a modernity for myself. Most English artists have put on the specs of Albion and see the present through an imaginary past.

~

The sink has overflowed, flooding the kitchen, I'm paddling about, barefooted, with a mop.

~

I open the hive – the bees are near to swarming, their numbers have exploded, they are building comb everywhere.

~

When we got back to London, HB reluctantly showed me an unpleasant review in the *Telegraph*, the nastiest I have ever received.

Tuesday 13
Christopher Hobbs walked with me to the new National Gallery extension and then on to Royal Academy. Met with Norman Rosenthal and Sophie Hicks – who is designing the Pop Art show. Back to meet Norman's wife Mañuela and their new baby, who was fast asleep on the bed wearing a little royal-blue suit.

Wednesday 14
HB worked in the flat cementing the floor. Then we went on an abortive shopping trip for some trousers Sophie had recommended from the Gap. HB got cross as I thought the pair we singled out too ordinary but wasn't prepared to pay for something out of the ordinary. He muttered 'too ordinary' all the way home. I really want to steal all his Katharine Hamnett trousers which he hardly ever wears – they suit me so well.

Thursday 15
Trip to St Mary's and then on to the Edinburgh shuttle.

We checked in at the film house and met my American friend Lynn Hanke. Then we all went for a long walk, ending up in the second-hand clothes shops where I bought a suit for £40, tailored long ago in Shanghai and never worn.

Lynn walked into a junk shop and spied a sawn-off tree trunk: 'Wow! That would make a fantastic table in my Fifth Avenue apartment. I don't care how much it costs, I simply *must* have it!'

The owner's face was a mixture of delight and disbelief – as they organised shipping he put up the 'closed' sign.

Early to bed.

Friday 16
Another long walk in the morning, I had my shoes repaired, then HB and I walked to the National Gallery whose gloomy maroon torchlight swallowed up the pictures. I think the idea was that it should look like a Victorian country house – but these were never the places to see paintings, just to acquire them.

~

Three hours of lectures and interviews, a quick bath, then the *Edward* opening at the Cameo cinema. Extreme nerves – how would Tilda like the work? The cinema full, no one left the screening, not even for a pee, I've sat here for all my films, this is the first time this has happened.

Saturday 17
The Icepick. I'm a captive audience, HIV infection invades a relationship, the play needs a couple of tender moments, otherwise it's the best I've seen, without sentimentality. Saw the play with Nicky de Jongh. I think he was quite taken by it.

We had supper with the actors, then all left for the Oyster Bar.

HB left for Newcastle, I crept home at 4.15 as the sun came up.

Sunday 18
Flew back to London.

Monday 19
The moth holes in the suit I bought for £40 will cost £100 to invisibly mend, shut my eyes and told them to do it.

Tuesday 20
Chris Woods and Malcolm Sutherland down here. Much conversation about Stonewall – the closed shop not the riot. Why should we leave this little cabal to control gay politics? Decided that the name does not belong to them, many histories came and went.

Peter arrived and rebuilt the main stone circle, then he went swimming in the sea, besieged by large mosquitoes under a moonlit sky.

Wednesday 21
Cherish a few friends and insult the rest.

Thursday 22
Back to London. My doctor, Mark, has prescribed an ointment containing lithium, which after a year and a half of torment has finally cleared the irritating rash from my face.

Saturday 24
Drove down to Prospect with David.

Peter shingled the garden and built a bench for passers-by. Alasdair appeared out of the blue on his bike.

~

Later we walked over to Derek Ball's, who threw an acid-house party for a group of tipsy boys from Brighton. It was a marvellously warm night. As we walked back at midnight we could hear Derek reciting the *Book of*

Homosexual Verse at the top of his voice almost to Prospect Cottage – a mile away.

Sunday 25
A glorious, sunny day. Received a letter from the young man of Izhevsk in the Soviet Union.

~

As the full moon came up, bats flew around the house.

~

Alasdair found an acid party in the bushes near the power station, arrived home late.

Monday 26
The honey we stole from the hive last night is light and very fine; we are going in again this evening. Delius's 'Song of Summer' playing very loud. HB still far away in the North with his friend Garry.

Alasdair invaded the hive. It has gone completely out of control, the bees working in the gaps between the supers. Angry bees followed him out to the sea's edge. We gave up, and I caught a taxi to Ashford and a train home.

~

Late night on the Heath. HB gone leaves me quite adrift.

Tuesday 27
Woke very late (midday), hot and flustered. Two meetings with James and Daniel Miller from Mute.

Wednesday 28
Slept through the day with the blinds closed, the room is strangely cut off – a perpetual twilight. No usual postcard from HB, he is definitely on holiday.

Saturday 31
Dungeness. A crew from a Japanese magazine arrived and took thirty-five colour plates and a hundred 35mm shots of the garden. We all had lunch at the Light Railway Café.

~

Alasdair arrived and slept on the beach.

SEPTEMBER

Sunday 1
Alan Beck arrived and explained at length why *Prospero's Books* was truly dreadful – middle-class tits and arse makes a nonsense. *A 'P' and Two Noughts*.

Monday 2
All go, phones buzzing, the sun still shining. I'm feeling fine, my face no longer burns, the lithium has done the job.

~

Sleeping at Phoenix House like the old days – a futon on the floor – a good sense of well-being.

~

Meeting with Howard Sooley and Stephen Pickles to find a photo for the cover of the republishing of *Dancing Ledge*.

~

Mike O'Pray came to interview me. I potted up some honey.

~

Hottest of wild nights.

Tuesday 3
I'm wearing HB's blue shirt. I met Aiden Shaw this morning as I went into Bar Italia. He said he'd got a very big dick, slightly hooked for his 'punters'.

Much talk of the Conservative Family Association. They have been writing articles and making broadcasts suggesting that we should be locked up for our own protection. From whom? Ourselves? The concern of the supremely unconcerned.

~

HB returned, growled about the honey, which has got into every nook and

50

cranny of the flat – there had been a honey explosion. He refused all cuddles till it had been cleaned up.

Donald 'Smudger' Smith's very good show at Chelsea, where I bought a silver painting.

Wednesday 4
A day of meetings, these short diary entries reflect the whirlpool that swirls about.

Saturday 7
Venice, for a hectic few days at the film festival. Carol Myers put us in the grand Hotel des Bains on the Lido. The whole gang here: HB, my sister and niece Kate, Christopher Hobbs, Tilda and her friend Joanna. The hotel was as extravagant as the spotless white-and-gold uniform of the head porter.

Sunday 8
Our first day here is relatively free, only three hours of interviews in the morning; in the afternoon we caught a boat to Torcello and walked round the deserted cathedral, which has been beautifully restored, its golden frescos glittering and awe-inspiring.

Lunch at Cipriani's cost an arm and a leg.

Monday 9
I started interviews at 9.30 and worked continuously, with only a glass of water for sustenance, until seven in the evening. Yesterday's interviews printed in all the Italian newspapers.

At 8.30 we drove to the Excelsior and walked to the cinema, Tilda wearing a black velvet lampshade by Dior, HB arriving on a weaving motorbike with Joyce Pierpollin. The film was well liked.

Tuesday 10
Another day of interviews and an earring hunt for Kate, I find her some beautiful ones in a tiny shop, hot with the glass-blower's torch.

We crossed the Grand Canal on a swaying gondola, the first time I have done this.

Wednesday 11
Returned to London.

Tuesday 17
My first free days this year. Sat in Dungeness with butterflies as my only company in very still and sunny weather.

Sunday 22

It's no small thing to be made a saint, especially when you're alive and kicking, and have to give your consent. In spite of the Sisters of Perpetual Indulgence's warnings not to let it go to my head, I had to take it seriously. I am, after all, the first Kentish saint since Queer Thomas of Canterbury who was murdered by his boyfriend, Henry, in 1170.

Eileen in the Light Railway Café asked: 'Why are you being made a saint?' 'Fate?' I answered.

The sun came out and the wind got up, blowing the sisters' habits this way and that. A congregation of a hundred people arrived from here and there to rehearse the order of service in high palare by Sister Celebrant, Mother Fecundity of the Mass Uprising.

~

I dithered about my costume like any old queen off to a ball. Should I be plain ordinary Joe Saint, or something a little more *glittering*? I gave in to temptation and chose the sparkling golden coronation robe that Steven had worn as Edward II.

Friday 27

Great waves of unease swamping my best efforts to smile, hate mail saying I was 'a disgrace' – I had appeared in the *Independent* with the sisters. Meanwhile Ian McKellen has tea with the Prime Minister.

Must keep my head up and at the risk of more hate, put the case against the airless Stonewall. We cleared a few briars and they set up camp and announced that they spoke for us. Why kowtow to the enemy? Why not demand what is right rather than beg? They are the enemy who attempt to put our clock back – whatever *you* think, *I* know – they are my generation.

~

The grandfather clock strikes the hours and left to its own devices would strike thirteen. I'd be better off in London this weekend – I'm so neglectful I cannot cook for myself, a sort of anorexia is overtaking me.

~

Dear Alan Beck drives me to Ashford. Thunderclouds dark as whetstone here, the last summer sun swallowed in a hazy dusk and there are storms forecast throughout the weekend.

Have I lived too long? Passed my sell-by date? *Edward* on the horizon, the possibility of a film of *The Picture of Dorian Gray*, set in the closet of Wilde's heart, a prison movie.

Endless journey back to London, squashed into a corner by some noisy girls who called themselves lager louts.

The hate mail plagued me all day.

I switched on the washing machine and opened a pile of letters, all asking for something: an interview, photograph, autograph, or that I should read an enclosed script. Help! I cannot even write my own any longer.

Alasdair seems out of sorts as well, perhaps it's the autumn.

HB finally arrived home after a seven-hour journey from Newcastle.

Saturday 28
Wet drizzle. Lunch at Poon's, a visit to the Brief Encounter to pick up a *Pink Paper* and *Capital Gay*.

Mike and his boyfriend Ian call round. We go to see a rehearsal of *Waiting for Godot*. I leave at the end of Act One. Beckett's fifties Parisian nihilism translates heavily, the theatre he was up against vanished years ago, Pozzo tedious, Lucky's speech the only bright moment, however hard Rick and Ade try, the laughs are mostly for 'business'.

Returned to shuttered Phoenix House and turned in with the Wilde biographies.

Sunday 29
The grim, dark autumnal isobars have brought with them a deep depression. Norman took me to the Ivy and pushed the gloom back for an hour.

Everything in the art world is insured, the moths of debt are munching on the canvas. Suicides: Norman's friend ate a lobster then threw himself off a cliff last week; Adrian's pompous funeral concealed that the gold was merely Dutch metal, as the funeral processed in debt – the ashes buried in Assisi near St Francis. All the stories are like this, the dizzy boom has bust and the antiques returned to bric-a-brac.

~

Timothy Taylor came for tea: blond, wispy hair and as sweet as ever. Left alone, I spiralled into an autumn low. Went to the Heath in the pouring rain and spent the night talking to an old friend about the past. Walked back at three in the morning. The cold has set in.

Monday 30
Bought paint for the front room at Dungeness – a bright-yellow to replace the rather dull Naples-yellow that has faded in my eye. The sun was out, blue skies.

~

The first Coxes are in the market, flushed with red, tart flavour of autumn. I'm much happier today. Met Paul and his friend Mario. Noticed Mario's beautiful amethyst ring in the sunlight, Paul had bought it in Spain.

Bought *De Profundis* and marvelled at the classics I had not read. Almost bought *David Copperfield* but the type was so small in one edition I could not read it and in the edition I could read the book was so heavy I could not hold it.

~

John Maybury here; his film of *Man to Man* is on the rocks. He was very gloomy. Bunked off *Godot* – it makes me so very depressed. Late in the evening I feel I should not have survived last year and Beckett brings that on.

Bumped into the Pet Shop Boys; they had just been to a screening of *Edward* – I think they liked it.

OCTOBER

Wednesday 2
Sky bright as Giotto blue all day, all the stones in the garden a-glitter. A host of letters, including one from a seventy-nine-year-old gran, with nine grandchildren, who went to *Sebastiane* – 'quite something' she said.

All the plants that Howard and I brought back from Madrona nursery are planted by the time the fishing boats return across the bright deep, rocking back and forth in the waves with a thousand itinerant gulls.

I finished painting the front room a cheerful primrose.

Thursday 3
Andy Bell from the group Erasure came here. Shy fish and chips at the Pilot Inn. He wants to get involved in a film.

Friday 4
Gardening under the bluest of skies – very warm in the afternoon, I walked in the woods. The bees are taking the dark-yellow pollen of the ragwort. The hawthorn and dog roses are scarlet with berries and hips – I must plant hawthorn and circles of wood sage, which are a deep rust and would look good as edging.

Saturday 5
It poured down all day. Alan Beck drove me to Brighton; we visited the HIV drop-in centre, sploshed through the town and ended the day with John Roman Baker of the AIDS Positive Theatre.

~

Met a lad who had demonstrated at the Labour Party Conference, absolutely no discussion of law reform there. How could there be? Labour has been driven far off course, they would do anything to win the ghoulish public vote.

Sunday 6
The grandfather clock, which refused to work for weeks, now ticks through day and night but has invented its own numerology – it strikes thirteen quite

regularly and then it's anyone's guess, five, eight, ten and thirteen again.
don't ever remember telling the time from a grandfather clock; they usuall
ticked away in the shadows of a Victorian hall, the heartbeat of the house
sometimes a smiling sun or moon circled.

Raked the front and back gardens, and then, with the sun still shining,
left for London.

Monday 7

The morning spent being interviewed for *Edward II*.

HB finished scraping paint off the cupboard doors, which I had starte
five years ago, perfecting his dojo.

Tuesday 8

Richard's daybook *Today and Tomorrow* finally arrived, it was schedule
to be finished December last.

Met young Tom on the street and took him to Shipley's. Armed him wit
books for his first days at King's.

In the evening went to see *Jacob's Ladder* with HB – a film he muc
admires.

Wednesday 9

European script fund meeting for *Dorian* – too much to-ing and fro-ing t
get these projects afloat.

Friday 11

To Dungeness with Michael. Temperature soared to 102°. Returned t
London. HB rang the hospital.

Saturday 12

Temperature back to normal, a bit wobbly but off to the North.

Sunday 13

A day in Durham visiting the cathedral which, with Ely, is quite m
favourite. We paid our respects to Cuthbert and Bede in the autumn gloom
with the bells roaring overhead. Then drove in the rain to St Peter's a
Monkwearmouth, devastated by sixties improvements, the famous towe
eroded and tottering on its foundations, its tombstones shoved aside for
sorry municipal green – a vandalism as devastating as the destruction of th
medieval shrines. Those tombs left were inscribed with no fewer than thre
Isabellas and two Hannahs, another was in German – the grave of a se
captain from Stett in Pomerania dating from the 1840s.

The young Welsh vicar who showed us round ran up as we were leavin and asked what had brought us to the church. Were we a group of archaeologists? I felt like saying 'No we're a group of fags', but thought that might be taken unkindly – he had interrupted writing his sermon to show us the last trace of a Saxon carving, an X that marked the spot, the door through which Benedict, Biscop, Cuthbert and Bede had passed.

~

Both of us rather relieved that the *Edward* opening was over, HB's whole family in the audience. *Edward* was received with a great deal of sympathetic laughter in Leeds – a young student audience – and rather seriously in Newcastle with an older audience who squirmed audibly at Tilda's assault on Jerome.

The squatters at Stonewall took up the rest of the time and indeed, much of the weekend, as the gathering after the screening was almost a political meeting in which Stonewall seemed at best tolerated with suspicion. Generally it was felt they were useful for the Tories in their election campaign and not much else.

I said that if John Major was that interested in taking tea with old queens he didn't really have to look much further than his cabinet.

Later, talking with Right-On Richard and Martin John Bless the Bed that He Lies On – all the boys here have long nicknames – they said they knew that one of their local MPs was gay. You see, the closet really works.

Monday 14

HB woke me up by bouncing on the bed with a thump and saying: 'What does it feel like to have a big Geordie lad on top of you?'

An autumn mist had closed over the weekend, and by this morning the leaves were cascading down as we walked across the park and past immaculate allotments, to meet HB's friends for breakfast.

We left Newcastle on the express train at ten.

Received a postcard of a boy lying on a metal bed, staring at the ceiling with a hard-on. Thought of HB landing on me this morning.

Tuesday 15

Gym boy Tim walked into Bar Italia and recounted stories of a holiday spent in the sand dunes at Studland – the rougher the boys were the more he liked them. He said he could never hold on to them as they were always married. He was off to the Marshall Street baths, where he said the police cadets swam early in the morning.

Spoke with my agent Lorraine to stop all interviews; the further you go the further they push you and mine have reached the shores of anger. I need a space for myself, so I'm not spread all over the breakfast table with the toast and marmalade each morning.

~

HB is very lively these days. He bounces around, flexing his muscles, and says: 'Look what I'm making for you, Fur Beast.' He also leaves warning messages on the answerphone to deter annoying callers.

Lunch at the Presto where Maria tirelessly piles spaghetti and makes compliments – others' good fortune she sees as her own.

~

Edward opens – a benefit for research at St Mary's. An immense amount of work done by Michael Christie to get it organised: he sets about all the little panics and comes away smiling.

Pet Shop Boys' light show spectacular. HB changed mid-performance from purple velvet to Fred Perry. Sandy dressed in gold thigh boots and basque stole the show. Happy to see how young the audience were.

Wednesday 16

I have married Ryan and John from Middlesbrough – I instructed them to kiss and count up to one hundred and, being practical, suggested they count down in the same way if they wished to divorce.

Thursday 17

The doorbell rang three times at 4.30. This has often happened over the years – drunken friends leaving nightclubs without the wherewithal to get home. Sometimes I've opened the door, but unless you are prepared to spend the rest of the night coping, it's the end of sleep.

This time HB and I lay in the silence, then HB got up and stood on the balcony. He came back and said he had no sleep left in him and lay on the bed, complaining of my fidgety self.

A terrible nightmare in which my bedroom was invaded by a TV crew as I woke, arguments, they left. I fled, driving a bike up a country road in the hills – a flower-strewn tapestry.

~

A surprising blue-rinse review from Alexander Walker in the *Standard*. I suppose I could have set myself up as the loudmouth he suggests I am by insisting on mixing life and celluloid, but there is more than a little homophobia here.

~

Walked down to the NFT at six. Clear, cold, sparkling evening, earth hath not anything to show more fair than the view from Waterloo Bridge, which must be one of the world's finest.

The NFT besieged. Ossie Clark, looking so elegant with a paintbrush thrust through his chignon. A good question-and-answer session – Gen P. Orridge said later that it improved as I got more political. Over one hundred books signed.

Dinner of oysters at Groucho's with Colin McCabe and Ossie – a string of near-hysterical jokes that rocked not only our table but the whole restaurant with Colin's wild laughter.

Ossie brings back my so dimly remembered youth; he said Tilda's make-up was immaculate.

~

Back home the dour Simon Callow on television – pronouncing on the film 'as a gay man' – I didn't make it for 'gay men', I made it for queers.

Auden said British theatre ceased to be of any interest after the actors became gentlemen back in 1660. Certainly Callow's appeal to some dim and tarnished value looked odd. He said he was dismayed by the film – bumbling old vulgarian.

Friday 18
A long lunchtime conversation with Malcolm, who said that Simon Callow's remarks were so redolent of a theatre stuck in the fifties, an ivory tower of aesthetics untouched by everyday life. With Callow we are dealing with one of the brighter thespians, which makes his inarticulate intervention so sad.

At twelve, Stephen Pickles arrived with the reprint of *Dancing Ledge* – it looks very handsome, less arty than the original, and is now rededicated to HB.

Sunday 20
Ian flew a kite round the moon.

Monday 21
We have moved into a little office above Anne Summers's sex shop with a view down Old Compton Street, enough room to swivel a chair, 'AYOR' written on the doorbell. Across the alley a bar, 'The Village', full of pretty shop boys sipping Earl Grey in their break. Michael is very happy, as these eighteen-year-old 'Essex boys' are his type. By four, keys were cut and the desks laid out. The office is a great addition, though money still races through my fingers.

I left at six and was in bed very early.

Tuesday 22
I picked up my silver pen fizzing with fury and took the first stab at *AYOR*. The new office is a fine place to write.

Wednesday 23
HB returned from Newcastle with a flat-top haircut exactly like the one he sported when I first met him five years ago: 'The Barber said "Usual, Sir?", and continued where he had left off.'

The cold weather has set in. It must be very cold – HB is wearing his pyjamas.

Thursday 24
I sat and worked in the cold on *AYOR*.

HB's friend Steven came by. He is known as Peaches Minnelli – Peaches because his adolescent bum was once described thus and Minnelli after Liza. Peaches brought his 'boyfriend *du jour*' – a young American lawyer. He had been described as six foot seven but he was no taller than HB.

Another early night. Cold cloudy weather has set in. HB offered to type up *At Your Own Risk*.

Friday 25
Fellini's *Amarcord* playing in Bar Italia this morning, set the day off on a good foot.

At twelve we are off to Dungeness.

Walked to the Long Pits, deathly still and very silent; picked rose hips and sowed them across the landscape.

HB sat himself in front of the TV to watch *Thunderbirds*.

Sunday 27
Derek Ball here at breakfast; much talk about Alasdair's highs and lows.

Sun out and very warm. I planted the parterre alongside the house, then gathered stones on the beach.

Disturbed a large owl sitting on the broom near the beehive.

Polished the floors.

Monday 28
One of my vivid recurring architectural dreams. I think I was with Lynn Hanke. we were definitely in Corfe, trying to get a taxi to Worth Matravers. It was raining and the driver moaned but changed his mind and took us. The road to Laughton changed and we suddenly found ourselves driving through a vast quarry the size of a cathedral, shored up with wooden pit props. Far ahead were tombs, rather Victorian-looking, being finished by a stonemason.

OCTOBER

The landscape changed, the sun came out and we found ourselves in the courtyard of a ruined sandstone house with crumbling classical details, very pronounced and massive. The walls looked naïve but the effect was charming.

An old man was climbing a long stone staircase, which cascaded down to a lake; the view over the walls was of a landscape that was almost provincial: fields, stone walls all glittering in the sunlight. Beside the lake a huge pavilion wing of the house with the same heavy overblown classical details. An old woman received us in the courtyard, said: 'It's yours if you restore it.'

DECEMBER

Tuesday 24
I've been here for nearly two weeks with the days spent rather fitfully. I've planted to no great ends, been rather more successful hauling manure; read Richardson's book on Picasso and *The Beggar's Opera* and, of course, tended the fires and scrubbed the house.

Thursday 26
Christmas! It's over, thank Bethlehem, no good time to be Queer. So alienating celebrating the super-celestial family, the family's family with crumbs of cake and the chemical turkey.

Tuesday 31
The new year came in with fireworks and a bonfire on the beach at Maddy's grandparents' house in Littlestone. Derek Ball, roaring drunk, after all the straight boys, flung himself about with David Gingerbits. The party was well under way when we arrived at eleven so no one heard the chimes of Big Ben on the little radio crackling in the static under the stars; everyone forgot to make a wish. Alan Beck said: 'This is the first straight party I've been to for years.'

The handful of us were rather quiet in this rowdy crowd of art school boys and ended up sitting round the kitchen table sipping Lapsang from Alan's thermos – which he would carry to the very ends of the earth. Turan [Ali] talked over a zap on the *Evening Standard* – that truly provincial metropolitan paper. At 2.30 Alan brought me back to Prospect Cottage, where I fell asleep. Curious that I had survived another year.

HB was far away, headed to a Northumbrian village where the men dress as women and carry blazing butts of tar on their heads.

1992

JANUARY

New Year's Day

I woke early this morning washed out and rather dazed. The old year broken like the waves that are running high along the Ness.

I'm wondering where Derek could have ended up, perhaps corkscrewed on a sofa with some of the art school boys. He certainly hit Littlestone like a bomb from another decade and rocked the old house – he primed himself before going on a curious mixture of Nina Simone (rather maudlin) and a scratchy rendition of Beethoven's Ninth recorded in 1942 by Furtwängler.

~

I know I'll not keep this diary up, it will flag like the cocky boy with the enormous dick in my Christmas present from Peaches – a video called *A Matter of Size* – who rams, or rather donkeys, his schoolteacher. A good video for the students at Canterbury, where another chapter of the Sisters of Perpetual Indulgence are plotting to saint Marlowe, or Radclyffe Hall, or both.

Canterbury, the daughter church of Dungeness, forty-five minutes by car along Straight Street, needs some saints to rescue it from the creeping suburbanity that has settled like a chancre on the old town.

~

The wind is up today after days so still and dark you could hear the mice nesting under the kitchen sink. I've been hoovering my mind all through the holiday for a project for this year but found nothing except an enormous lethargy. Two days ago Nicholas de Jongh gave me the fright of my life: some new recipe for disaster cooked up at St Thomas's – a drug that the researcher described as capable of further slowing the virus, so we poor guinea-pigs can limp on for another year or so.

I have an idea that once you are dead time speeds up, about a minute after you have died all your friends join you, five minutes later it's the final trump.

~

Andrew – Derek Brown's taciturn and charming friend – came to tea, crippled with arthritis which has laid him low for several months. He buried his boyfriend some years before he met Derek who had also done the same. What an extraordinarily sad time.

~

I have good news to start the year, the plan for an extension at the back of Prospect to build a bathroom and a small studio is to be passed by the planning department. I've been reading their decision either way as I'm not certain if it will be worth the expense and trouble, and might complicate this simple house. A bathroom would make *such* an improvement and I would finally have a spare room.

I missed the first phone call of the day, rushed through the house to pick it up, but the phone went dead in my hands. HB runs away from the phone, I run to pick it up. I phoned him. He's off trekking along Hadrian's Wall.

~

At 3.30 Derek Ball rang, he had a terrible hangover. He had walked home – five miles along the seashore in the freezing cold without his clothes at five this morning.

I went to Maddy's house to retrieve Derek's jacket – they said he'd left in the small hours wearing it back to front.

~

A spectacular carmine sunset over the power station. A few forlorn and freezing protesters have ringed it with cycles as it's been given a reprieve and is to stay open. Their pamphlet says: '*Get Dungeness before it gets us*'. As the sun disappears right between reactors A and B it grunts into life, strung with lights like a Christmas window to the future.

Thursday 2

Derek Ball rings me at 9.30. He says he feels a little fragile. I'm sleep-bound, have been sleeping in. It's cold, grey and rather windy.

I throw myself into the day accompanied by a rowdy Shostakovich symphony. In London the offices are back to life, down here nothing marks time, no rush hour, or weekend, just a few fishermen as the tide comes in.

Derek comes up the drive at 11.30. His first words are: 'I've just about recovered.' I think these words are true for all of us. Thank God it's January again – the sun comes out.

~

The exhibition at the Design Museum has led to another spate of beachcombing with Peter. All of the installation was returned so there are new sculptures, new stone circles. The side beds are planted and although the winter has been cold it has not been inclement. We have had no scorching winds to blacken the broom, the bulbs are peeping through, the poppies are up. I have carted manure these last weeks and tucked it around the roses and elder. The planting has gone native. I have mallow and fennel, daisies and mullein. The dog rose I planted next to the kitchen window is up to eye level. I've picked the hips and planted them.

Friday 3

I leave for London with Richard in the racing-green 'They used to make aeroplanes' Bristol. Richard promises to drive slowly. Via New Romney, stop and buy pies at the bakers HB has renamed Fairy Cakes and look in the antique shop, which has a great Edwardian chair. We drove slowly back to London, discussing the two exhibitions and the recession – which is hitting art dealers hard.

~

Back in London a pile of letters, the most surprising that *Edward* has won a large cash prize in Belgium.

~

Bumped into Johnny Volcano, Spud's sparkly friend, in his studded leathers – chatted in the bar.

~

I sat in the empty flat for half an hour, half hoping that HB would return, then went to the Heath in the New Year drizzle. I'd not been there long when a young man came up, a broad, open smile with friendly eyes, he started a conversation. He'd lived in London for eight years doing odd jobs as, at sixteen, his parents had thrown him out when he told them he was gay. He'd only returned once for his grandmother's funeral. He lived alone, preferred it that way, rarely went out, and if he did, went to the Heath – it was the most honest way to cruise, the meetings uncomplicated, he did not want a relationship. He was emphatic that he was not there because he was repressed. On the contrary, he felt those trapped into the commercial scene were victims of their desires. We walked up to the hamburger stall by the pond, bought a cup of tea and returned briefly to the blazing deserted fire.

He said he'd been here many times but had yet to have an orgasm, he was quite happy to just talk. He had first slept with a man at ten and had not stopped. He shouted in the firelight that he found heterosexual men and their competitive masculinity claustrophobic – coming from a working-class background he should know. We talked of repressions, self-oppression,

Outing – he didn't think that would help. He'd once seen an MP here but he couldn't remember which. He had one particularly exciting story: he had advertised himself as a 'builder' in a gay magazine and had been contacted by 'X'. He took along his younger brother, also gay, pretending he was his lover, and soundly spanked the ex-MP – he described him as a gentleman.

Saturday 4

A bishop had called us 'unrepentant sodomites' on the radio; it almost makes our mundane sexuality sound exciting. I think we should burn his cathedral down.

A book sent anonymously on the Marian movement, sects and movements acting like watch committees. I am deluged with letters of the type: 'Christ died for your sins.' I write back a saintly rebuff: 'How stupid of him. Why didn't he stay alive and die decently of old age?' These letters are accompanied by books, which usually have rays of light with an eye in them on the cover, written by luminaries who have doubtful initials like 'SJ' after their names.

~

Robert Medley's eighty-sixth birthday party. Talked with Maggi Hambling about the lesbian and gay archive. She said: 'I hate that word "lesbian".' Looking at Philip Prowse she added, 'We're all queer on this side of the table.' It's no problem for fifty-year-olds, more so for those forty-year-olds, the Gay Liberation Front generation. I never liked the word 'gay' – it seemed to mark us with a false optimism.

Sunday 5

We work on the book. I'm hung-over as I went to the LA last night – full of friends and acquaintances: Julian Cole, Sean O'Connor the theatre director and his actor friend Gareth. The place was packed, noisy and energetic, friendly faces and a couple of cruisy glances. Home before dawn.

Monday 6

Worked all day on the book. HB returned with tales of adventures from the North.

Tuesday 7

Isaac Julien is across the corridor, editing a series on black cinema for the BFI. He pops his head round the door. Finish *AYOR* and send it to Random Century.

Jimmy Somerville came to tea, he's planning a new album called *Juice*.

Wednesday 8

My face is irritatingly sore, shaving a horrible experience, the razor grinding across the inflammation, it itches on the pillow at night, I still toss and turn, I was up twice last night. Poor HB.

~

Sit in the office and write cheques and letters, the first day for months I haven't felt under pressure.

~

Queer people should demand equality in all aspects of life: legally binding unions, the right to bring up children, adoption rights, rights of access and property, equal opportunity in employment, an end to proscription in the military, an equal age of consent, inclusion in all sex education, a bill to outlaw homophobia in the media, an end to Church pronouncements on homosexuality, deletion of anti-queer statements in the Bible, establishment of teaching facilities in universities, a national archive.

Monday 13

Out with Nicky to the Gardens – the old roof gardens of Derry and Toms. Cold damp night. The restaurant gay, suburban, all the boys in baggy suits with overproduced girls and understated drag queens. David Inches came to our table, overexcited by a young man called Deadly Weapon – a stripper from the North, good-looking, broad-shouldered, baggy suit. He was sitting next to his manager – a moustachioed clone. David flashed a naked photo of Deadly Weapon, the staff were so carried away they almost toppled over, spilling the soup. Nicky said: 'If you want attention here you've *got* to strip.' We walked round the garden and saw the two pink flamingos.

Home by 12.30. HB returned from seeing Ron Peck's *Boxers* film.

Tuesday 14

Howard picked me up at 8.30 to drive to Prospect Cottage. The road through the City was clear so we decided to turn off to Bromley and search for the sempervivum nursery. We arrived at a suburban house with conifers and clipped lawns. The entry in *The Plant Finder* said: 'strictly by appointment' – Howard paved the way. Mr and Mrs Smith almost destroyed their front door trying to open it, but suspiciously invited us to see the plants. Mr Smith has exhibited for the longest. Even though there's a man in the States who has two million sempers and Jovibaras, he poured cold water on all opposition. He names the cultivars – two hundred new ones each year, one in a thousand worth it.

We chose ten plants. There was a long wait as they all had to be meticulously spruced up with a pair of tweezers and labelled with his uncertain name tags.

Howard and I fascinated that anyone could sustain a forty-year obsession with the plants, climbing mountains to track down rare species.

The colours were all wrong in January, Pink Flush was emerald green, the 'spiders' webs' that sempers sport dissolved in the fog.

At Prospect we potted up in old tin cans from the beach. A handsome young fisherman with a sparkling smile came and talked to us.

We stayed just long enough to open the mail and walk round the garden before leaving for Hastings, fish and chips and the second-hand bookshop.

Back in London by eight.

Wednesday 15

Lunchtime walk with HB to the National Gallery. A large building site has opened up on the Charing Cross Road, more clip-on classicism. Through Leicester Square to buy ice creams – we ate them in the freezing cold – past a queue round the Prince Charles cinema which has brought its ticket prices down to £1.00.

I bought a pullover from M&S – very warm. Ian Shipley and Clem both dressed in M&S. HB reluctant to shop there after he found they prosecute shoplifters for burglary so they have a criminal record; says they make enough profits without ruining lives as well.

~

7.30 – journey to the ICA for the Damien Hirst opening. A nice young gallery man talked briefly of not much and in the handshake the artist seemed a bit of a crosspatch, as gran would say.

Over to Cork Street and down to earth with Spud and Johnny with their smashing hairstyles and leathers, then on to Stockwell to see James Barrett's show of HIV-related work, which I liked.

Thursday 16

Slept in very late.

Dan Farson in Bertaux's, struggling with a piece on Mantegna. I suggested he was an art historian artist, this pleased Dan. Bertaux's in its usual fluster, the till rang up a coffee and croissant for £48.

Back to the little office at midday to write a statement for Glasgow. My face has cleared up – feeling very rested and rather happy.

Friday 17

Peter Tatchell called by, we had tea in The Village. He is having a terrible time – the flat above his has been squatted by a group of right-wing rowdies who hammer the floor and shout 'fucking poof' throughout the night. He says they spent two days shouting, swearing, throwing bottles and the furniture at each other. The council evicted them, then they moved into the flat beneath him.

~

I walked over to Cowcross Street for the OutRage! meeting. Very cold night, shops shuttered and out of business in High Holborn.

The lesbian and gay centre was packed. A small demonstration against the use of 'queer'. The *Standard* zap organised – Aamir and Sarah are to go, a Spanish journalist said he had a personal siren that could stop the show, everyone in the room is going to demonstrate outside the Savoy.

Turan had written an excellent paper on Tony Richardson: 'The Secret Shame of Freddie Mercury (Why Dying from AIDS is Not Heroic)' and my own treatment in Alexander Walker's obituary review.

The main time was given to a discussion on fascism and if we should affiliate with the Anti-Nazi League.

On the way home an old man collapsed in front of a bookshop, his hands clasped in prayer.

Saturday 18

Dom Sylvestre Houedard's obituary in the *Independent*, two nights ago Nicholas Logsdail rang to say Sylvestre had collapsed and died, running to meet a London train.

In the late sixties Sylvestre made the Lisson Gallery a second home, you could be sure to find him in the little room upstairs, his hands dancing across the typewriter.

At my first one-man show in 1969 he sent little messages to me during the private view: '*Mrs God invites you to her opening. Sylvestre.*'

Bald, with pointed ears, in his black monk's habit and his NHS inquisitor's glasses, Sylvestre was one of the liveliest minds to attend the meetings of GLF, his kindly earnest manner and immense learning would suddenly dazzle. I remember him creeping into a screening of *Rosemary's Baby* without the audience noticing his monk's habit – when the lights came up at the end of the movie a girl sitting next to us jumped with fright at the devilish smiling face in the stalls.

I made a sculpture: *H as H is H* for his show at the V&A. Sometimes he stayed in my Bankside studio on his return trips from Guernsey – where he was born in the early twenties. Once he brought an enormous bottle of duty-free perfume and poured it all into the bath. When I made *Sebastiane* he sent me pages of closely typed information – a scandal sheet for the Emperor Diocletian's court. Sadly, many of his laminates disappeared, but others I framed, *Greece* and the *Gloster Odes*, they hang on the wall, quiet and thoughtful.

Sunday 19

HB says I'm like a storm-tossed ship at night; we have to lie in bed for two extra hours to make up for lost sleep.

~

Spent the evening chatting with Jonathan Hope about the *demi-monde* of the sixties. He met Robert Mapplethorpe at the same time as myself, and Sam Wagstaff with his Sam Shepherd looks. I thought Sam was sixty when he died – although he didn't look a day over forty – Jonathan said he was seventy, had fought in the Second World War. When Sam met Robert he said: 'I'm looking for someone to spoil' and gave him a diamond brooch in the shape of a monkey, which Robert pinned to the lapel of his leather jacket and forever after balked as people pulled its tail. Jonathan had met the misanthropic Paul Morrissey who told him that Jim Morrison of The Doors was queer without a doubt.

~

Later with Nicky de Jongh for a *Boyz* party in Bayswater. Pretty professionals chatting. We'd both expected something a little raunchier as I had met the handsome host in the LA – maybe they were on their best behaviour.

~

Arrived home at one to find HB awake. He jumped up and down and fought for his side of the bed, and then at 1.30 put on the television to watch an awful horror film called *The Wicker Man* that ground its way in lewd singing through the night.

In the middle of this Alasdair and his friend Barry arrived, blind-drunk, and forced an entry, making so much noise that for our neighbours' sake HB let them in. Undeservedly sleepless night.

Monday 20

Visit to St Mary's. Dr Mark said the AZT had given me an excellent 'suntan', everything else seems to be in order. We attacked the spots on my face with liquid nitrogen. I put the idea to him of painting with my blood. He was enthusiastic and he said he'd find out if it could be sterilised. He suggested I took the AZT out of its packets as it is illegal to enter the States with HIV infection. This makes immigration a true panic, but I refuse to have my passport stamped 'HIV+'. So all I can do is cross my fingers and hope to get through.

I'm going to be as calm as possible.

FEBRUARY

Sunday 2

A cold, foggy day. Jet-lagged, slept fitfully. HB and I returned this morning from two weeks in the States where we made new friends and lost old ones.

Five days at Sundance Film Festival in Deer Park – a little town near Salt Lake City.

We were met by Pat, who wore a fur jacket and a miniskirt in the sub-zero temperatures. She said she had visited London to see a Lloyd Webber musical. Pat carried a crocodile skin briefcase and her fur turned out to be the first of many. Deer Park ladies look like groups of furry lemmings in a great slaughter. Our condominium was four times the size of Prospect Cottage, with a jacuzzi that would have swallowed a football team; it turned out to be so chlorinated that it was unusable for me – burnt the skin off my back. HB sat in it for hours.

HB walked up and down the mall of Albertsons supermarket buying trinkets for me – a huge sausage called 'Jimmy Dean'. Main Street had an unusual antique shop with Wild West artefacts and sold foot-long twigs of barbed wire like cast-iron brambles. In the shops piles of dead bear (polar and brown), lynx, wolverine, antlers formed into chandeliers, jackrabbits sprouting horns.

The festival turned out to be friendly: Isaac Julien – whom Pat described as 'A big fat eight ball' – and Hanif Kureishi from London; Colin McCabe, who is making a new film with Terence Davies – *Vile Bodies*, set in a New York SM bar.

All the young queer film-makers were there for a panel, which was obsessed with violating the political correctness of seventies gay lib. Todd Haines, Tom Kalin, Isaac Julien, myself, Saidie Benning, chaired by Ruby Rich. Ruby introduced me as a 'cultural icon'. The film-makers were articulate and enjoying themselves.

On the way to New York in the plane, sitting beside Jim Jarmusch, lots of complaints that the Sundance Festival had grown too big – I was quite happy, but was pleased when the plane flew above the fog that filled the plains around Salt Lake City and turned eastwards across the snowy mountains.

~

Five days at Mark's. The sun never gets to his apartment at East 62nd so the lights burn continuously even at midday. This arrangement is not improved by heavy curtains and Venetian blinds. In midwinter you notice how sunless NYC can be; I found myself crossing roads to walk in the little patches of brightness.

America is falling into the soup. George Bush stumbles through a State of the Union Address, Mark says their future is hopeless. No wonder Boris Yeltsin is smiling at the UN. The fall of the wall was like pulling the plug from a bath. With interest rates at four per cent, no one will borrow a cent, the old heavy industries sink like lead. Everything is half price here, electrical goods, CDs, clothes, food – a McDonald's for fifty-nine cents, a fraction of what they cost back home.

~

My fiftieth birthday spent with Malcolm Leigh in his very beautiful flat in the Chelsea Hotel. Malcolm and I now add up to a century. Everyone we knew is either dead or mad. Patrik Steede has joined the dead. Poor straight-gay Patrik – I'd lost contact since the mid-seventies, going it alone on *Sebastiane* brought the rift and though he said he had 'forgiven me' we never got close again. He shacked up with a New York model girl and that was the last I heard.

Amadeo picked up a stranger, was knocked out, doused with petrol in the bath and torched. He joins the long list of people who are dead or murdered.

Malcolm is particularly amused by ██████ ████████; he says he designs his foot fetish shoes as torture chambers for the rich: 'He practically crippled ██████ ███████ in the seventies.' I once remarked on a pair of Tilda's shoes, '██████ ████████ – they make my toes bleed.'

~

HB and I walk round and round, and end up at the gay bookshop where George at the till smiles at me. We keep meeting Faye Dunaway – shouting 'Hello Boys' on a pushbike this morning near the Strand bookstore.

~

Neither of us knows what to make of the States, we are glad we came and glad to leave. Distance preserves friendships, Malcolm Leigh and Keith Milow visited. I wonder if I'd know them if they lived in England. Keith has had cable TV installed specially to watch the TV trial of the mass murderer Jeffrey Dahmer. He has TV obsessions: last time I saw him it was the Olympics and Greg Louganis – the pretty high-diver who looked like a kouros, all thighs and pecs.

~

I return to England fifty, with a pair of spectacles, five CDs, a couple of books and much kitchen equipment – Mark's parting gift. In the customs hall at Heathrow a huge bottle of my favourite liquid soap explodes all over the luggage. HB discreetly dumps it in the gents'.

Monday 3

Drove to Prospect with Howard who took two photos of a rather unwilling HB up by the Long Pits – HB had hoped to find toads, but not yet. The garden seemed hardly changed in three weeks, there was a purple box containing a euphorbia from the Beth Chatto nurseries and a letter from Beth amongst a pile of sixty letters and cards – well-wishers for my birthday.

Tuesday 4

Spent the day replying to the mail – calculated at this rate I spend two weeks a year writing notes. There is a new pillar box as if to welcome my efforts.

Wednesday 5

Up very early for telephone conversation about queer politics with Michael Howard, the local Tory MP, he at sixes and sevens, me a little too angry – though it wasn't too hard to get the blood pressure up over his ridiculous suggestions: the army was a special case as officers had great power over the men – get killed on my orders but don't let me seduce you. I realised quickly into this debate that we have the high ground, all arguments were stumbling, emotional and incoherent.

If big tough squaddies are so scared of queer boys we should have a special mincing faggot infantry unit, only unleashed to set the most fearsome enemies retreating.

~

It's warm again today with the sun making a brave effort to show through. I worked in the garden for a couple of hours – all my strength permits. Planted ivy-leaved toadflax in the front garden, the irises have sprung up – four inches of new growth that pierce the February gloom.

~

Took my pills; I'm very shy of them and stare at them for minutes on end before I force myself to swallow them. Invariably they lodge in my throat and have me choking. My itching wakes me once a night for an hour and then calms down. Last night I slept quite successfully.

~

At three a young Japanese musician arrived, quite unannounced, and wept in the kitchen. He brought me his music, we walked in the garden and he took photos, after that the phone kept ringing.

Thursday 6

Two demos, one reported, one present.

Woke early for a radio interview, then caught the slow nine o'clock train to Charing Cross. As the train slipped through the Kent countryside I thought I saw a field of American bison.

Changed into my sober banker's coat and walked with HB to Bow Street, where there were more photographers than demonstrators and even more police. Speeches were made: Alan, who is nineteen, on the age of consent of twenty-one; a moving speech from a lesbian mother; I stood up and said a few words, encouraged by Jimmy Somerville smiling in the crowd. I said goodbye to HB who we decided should not be arrested this time as there is a deadline to finish *AYOR*.

The very orderly, non-violent and good-humoured march wound down the side streets to Charing Cross Road where we would be in contravention of the law which forbids demonstrations within a mile of the Commons – Sarah Graham, Jimmy and I carried a banner saying 'Gay Rights Now' and linked hands. At the entry to Charing Cross Road the police loud hailer van announced we would contravene Sessional Orders of Parliament.

Peter Tatchell, who is an extraordinary organiser and without whom I cannot see this type of intervention succeeding, told all those who did not wish to be arrested to move on to the pavement and not to block it. The Mrs Thatcher drag queen cut a pink ribbon, telling us she washed her hands of it all and we were now Mr Major's problem.

The police van trumpeted that a group of five could proceed to Parliament to hand in the petition for our rights but they could not carry any banners.

We walked on to Charing Cross Road and lay down – probably forty to fifty of us. We were warned again while the cameramen shouted and scrimmaged through the police. We tucked the banner around us as if we were in a huge queer bed; staring up at the sky, Sarah noticed a nest in the plane tree above us with a rather annoyed pigeon, and then one by one we were arrested. All of this happened in dream-time and was over before a twinkling. I found myself in a police van staring across the road at a smiling but worried HB, being frisked by a pretty policeman.

I think I had rehearsed this moment in my mind ever since I came to London as a student. The law reform of 1967 went through in my twenty-fifth year. I was a criminal for my first twenty-five years and a second-class citizen for the next twenty-five. I was finally arrested for being myself in this disgraceful society, illiterate in human complexity – the pen splutterers.

We were driven to the police station near the Oval and queued for our details to be recorded, we were photographed by the arresting PCs – many of whom were friendly and quite a few rather good-looking, but more at ease with the women than the men.

Pockets searched – all my bits and pieces signed for and sealed in a plastic bag.

We were locked up in cells with our names chalked on a blackboard on the door. I shared mine with Alan, who had given the speech, and a young man from Newcastle. We amused ourselves with stories and chatting through the spyhole in the door to the women across the way. Sarah gave us good advice about cautions and whether we should accept them.

Suddenly it was all over, property returned and on the street again.

Friday 7
Finished *AYOR* once and for all. Celebratory scrambled egg on toast at the café with HB. A sombre photo in the *Guardian* peering out of the police van. The intervention made all the major news bulletins and most of the papers. The *Independent* gave us the most thoughtful coverage. Drove down to Dungeness at nine with Alan Beck and Gingerbits. Alan is to become a sister on Sunday, Gingerbits got himself handcuffed at twenty-one – legally.

Saturday 8
A gloriously sunny day and warm. I worked in the garden mulching the roses as there is a continuing hosepipe ban.

Brian Clarke, the builder, drove past to say that most of the objections to my proposed extension have been dropped and we should be able to start work in March.

~

Brief report from Sandy Powell. Sandy's protest at the *Evening Standard* Awards fantastic! She wiggled on to the stage in her skin-tight all-rubber gala dress – 'Annie LaPaz had been Mr Sheening me all day' – to amusement. Soon the audience were gasping, her intervention so impressive she was joined by Shirley MacLaine, who left the ridiculous Bubbles Rothermere's party in support when she found out Sandy's ticket was torn up in her face.

Sandy has been fêted in the bars all week; she said she had terrible nerves but at the last minute they disappeared.

Aamir and Sarah told me there was next to no security and they had walked on to the stage quite casually. The demonstration was carried gleefully in the press the next day and also televised without any cuts.

Sunday 9
The Canterbury chapter of the Sisters is formed with Alan as Sister Latex.

Housework, cleaning the black dust away that flies up as I stoke up the fires with anthracite. Driving down here last Friday night with Alan we almost had to stop because of the fog; when I was a kid it would have been a thick pea-souper from all the coal fires.

Monday 10

The day dawned bright with sunlight.

David Thomas is concrete-mixing next door; I'm hard at work scrubbing the floors.

Mark Jordan here making a video interview. I explained to him my colour-coded theory of revolution: red and videotape don't mix, hence Mrs T's success and the end of the Soviet flag. I'm wearing blue this evening.

Tuesday 11

Drove north with Howard and Piers, the fog cleared and the drive over the Lake District was in sunlight, the hills in the palest ochres and sage-greens, rust bracken and dark-green gorse speckled yellow. The roadside cafés grew emptier. In the last one the bread was varnished and untouched. We bought Kendal Mint Cake instead.

In the Manchester City Art Gallery the gallery director, looking like Clark Kent, nervously asked me the name of the show, a cesspit at the heart of Manchester, decided on *Shipwrecked*.

In Glasgow we were stuck in interminable traffic lights. Dinner at Café Rogano's – Howard had haddock and Piers a toothy bream.

Wednesday 12

In the evening a full house at the Glasgow Film Theatre for *Edward II*. A strange beetle lady insisted on taking photographs and the DJ bar endorsement.

Thursday 13

The show opened, lectured at the art school – everyone kind and happy to see us. Mrs T came to Glasgow and no one came to see her, so she was given a guided museum tour in which she related everything to her mantelpiece – 'This would look good over the fireplace' and muddled *Sunflowers* – 'Who are they by?' – with chrysanthemums: 'Such expensive chrysanths.' She was totally out of touch – in a world of her own. Now she is beavering away founding a Thatcher Institute. It all sounds infinitely depressing.

A young man at the opening with a broad smile. Flirting, he sat on the chair in the middle of the gallery with his leg pressed against mine, called me 'Uncle Derek'.

Friday 14

We drive south and leave the road at Penrith as it starts to rain. Through the Lake District in low cloud and mist, then back on to the M6 where we stopped at a Rank Eater.

Read the obituaries in the *Independent* over mushroom soup and breakfast tea.

Tuesday 18

Tegel Airport, Berlin.

Sat out the last few days in a truly ugly hotel, the Savoy, whose brassy gilt interiors are the physical embodiment of mental illness.

These film festivals are now a trial – I'm going to have to call a halt. I've been on the road now for over a week. The interviews began though I did stop them up – used my appalling cold that has got me by the throat to divert some.

It's snowing and the jet is waiting to board.

Berlin is full of contradiction and no argument. I felt as if the audiences had been told to like *Edward* and had complied for 'kulchur'. The screenings were cosily West and I had an audience who had grown old with me.

The sun's out, the snow has cleared and we are boarding with noisy children. I really do hate children on aeroplanes, they should be banned to some corner with the cigarettes.

I made the audience laugh. What can one do but laugh at the cinema? All small minds and inflated public egos.

I'm seated on the plane. The sub-Bach that BA plays to lull the senses comes and goes as people slam the luggage lockers. One and a half hours to go. The seats next door are empty. If I cough and splutter perhaps they will remain that way.

A lunch with a few bright lads and an interviewer who, thank God, did not like the film. I complimented him and said: 'I'm not going to defend the film, you're probably right about it.' I think this confused him. I hate most films as well.

I ask the interviewers: 'How long do you have to survive to have survived?' I've survived two years. Manfred says that AZT dislikes him. I tell him I live on a tightrope, shipwrecked.

There is a whistle on the life jacket for attracting attention. 'Please study the safety card carefully.'

Tom Kalin and Christine Vachon, his producer, kept me smiling. Yesterday we caught a taxi to Sans Souci and walked in the empty gardens as snow drifted through the trees and around the gaudy Chinese Pavilion, an ancestor of the Savoy Hotel.

Somewhere in time Prince Frederick's Pavilion of Sicilian boys, all curving buttocks and biceps.

Modern Berlin boys in Tom's Bar sit as silent and motionless as museum exhibits in front of a large porno video screen – they are wink-proof, frozen like ice.

They are spraying the wings with de-icer.

An interviewer tells me his boyfriend has died, somewhere deep in his mind he hated being queer. I say I find it exciting.

I can't believe this, they've put a baby in the seat next to me! I cough and splutter, and say loudly to HB: 'My AIDS is playing up today.' In alarm, the entire family relocate.

The kids are crying behind me and shouting: 'The plane's taking off!' We turn on to the runway and roar into the midday sky. Berlin cold and grey below, with a powdering of snow.

Through breaks in the cloud, grey and white fields of the old East Germany, sad drab streets of frozen little towns. West Berlin hugs its affluence to itself, the brightest thing in the East is the restored dome on the synagogue.

In the gay bookshop I bought James Purdy's *Narrow Rooms* and looked at the Hervé Guibert but decided my French was not good enough. Was he a drama queen? Or did I ignore the problems? He seems to have been led a dance by his doctors in Paris, or was it *all* fiction?

We are above the clouds in the sunlight, the plane is incredibly noisy. I hate flying so much, the claustrophobia, the terrible dead-looking meals, the struggle to get out at the end.

I met a young actor. We agreed that the British theatre is riddled with death-watch; he's moved to Berlin. I've never fucked a British actor – they are not attractive, not even worth the trouble of fuck 'em and forget 'em. They took radical parts and led conforming lives, as much energy as the leather dummies in Tom's bar.

We're a little further on and the plane has gone quiet. I've refused the lunch.

Good to be heading home with HB.

Wednesday 19
Spent the day at Richard's planning paintings.

Thursday 20
Woken by Derek Ball telephoning from Grimsby where Graham Cracker fades away. Graham has been mortally ill now for two weeks. He declared his HIV status and waited an age at the outpatients department at Westminster – they sent him away with indigestion pills.

Derek in a panic to contact Alasdair. Alasdair so poor he begs about the

81

office for money for his train fare. I feel fragile as a packing case of glass, one slip . . .

~

It's cold and pinched, and my hands shake. Michael Christie and I walked around Bond Street; some shops closed between Asprey and Versace. 'Must be the only shop that sells cement in Bond Street' – Michael, looking into a recession-hit gutted interior.

Michael is gloomy, talking about becoming a rent boy now his job at TV AM is no more. He said it might make his dream of living in Soho a reality.

Friday 21

Howard at Phoenix House at nine. We drove through the cold sunny morning to Dungeness.

Lit the fires, made tea and took off to Great Dixter where we bought helichrysum at the nursery and then on to the Cyclamen Society. Home as the sun set apple-red alongside Dungeness B.

I wrote twenty or more letters and then the phone rang: a journalist calling from the *Independent* – the videos that Psychik TV made ten years or more ago were the subject of a television programme, *Despatches*. My presence in them has made me an associate, the non-story has been picked up by the tabloids. I hung up, only to be rung by the *Mirror*.

Jon Savage phoned. He thought I should leave Dungeness, perhaps the garden would be written up as 'satanic'. This is more than I wished for. I need peace and quiet, and now a journalist is pursuing me on another's fuck. I looked up *Dancing Ledge* and reread what I wrote in the early eighties *Filming the Psychik Rally*. Alan came and rescued me from the tabloid attention. I spent the night in Canterbury.

Saturday 22

Alan drove me to Gillingham, a town where they gobble their syllables. I stood on the filthy platform for a train to Blackfriars.

Walked up the stairs in Phoenix House, cold and tired. HB waiting for his friend Peaches. We all walked to the Day of the Dead show at the Museum of Mankind, then back to Presto for tea.

Graham Cracker died at eleven. I have a fine portrait of him in the photograph albums.

The last time we saw Graham was in New York. He had been asked to *trompe l'oeil* a Manhattan dining room to look like a sun-baked prairie. Graham painted a beautiful desert with cactus plants and Joshua trees; as he put the finishing touches on the sky he included a tiny twister, almost invisible on the far horizon; it looked so good he made it larger and then larger. After a week of frenzied repainting the dining room was transformed: storm clouds and lightning flashes circled the eye of a thunder-dark tornado. The best work he had ever done.

The millionaire owner returned from his vacation as Graham was making the final brush strokes. He hated it and threw Graham out on to the street, screaming: 'I'll see you never work again.'

Sunday 23
HB and I caught the bus to Camden Lock market. It seemed deadly uninteresting, music from *Blade Runner* playing ominously on one antique stall, horrible cheap frying smells and scratchy old records, vile art deco and rotting second-hand clothes – damp and depressing. We walked to the garden centre, which was being dismantled, plants dying with neglect in the winter drought.

Monday 24
Warm, very still, overcast, the sun hovering in the mist. Julian drove us down to Prospect and we walked out to the Long Pits. The water is excessively declined from previous years. The gorse is in flower and the pussy willow is bursting open. There are crocus and snowdrops in the front garden, which I watered until I had emptied the rain butt. I bought cider vinegar and covered my itching skin with it – Danny's recommendation, I stink like an insalata.

Dungeness quite deserted, Janáček playing. HB prowling through the library.

Tuesday 25
No sign of the promised sun today, grey as a school blanket. HB naked eating his cornflakes; he likes being cold, says he's from Sparta, his tattoos look quite arctic.

Walked to the beach, tide far out, nothing to see as the mist is blowing in an easterly.

HB removed almost half the compost heap and shingled the compost heap at the back of the house. Planted the santolina I bought at Great Dixter and the fern that was left outside the front door in a purple box from Liberty. Cornflower and poppy have sprung up, and the iris are nearly a hand's breadth high. The still and relatively warm winter has left most of the plants thriving, there is a yellow wallflower coming into bloom.

The bees are flying in the cold to the gorse bushes, the golden flowers burst in tiny showers of pollen.

Lorries belt up and down the road taking shingle beach to prop up the nuclear power station. HB says the population of the world has doubled in his lifetime; by the time the power station is burnt out there won't be any room left.

Wednesday 26
The elder is breaking into leaf. I am reading a book called *Machiavelli in Hell*.

Graham died of shingles according to Alasdair. All this death is depressing, horizons pinched in, drifting with no direction. My skin itches and drives me to distraction. It is early in this history of sorrow, intense fragility of purpose.

I pick at my lunch. HB says there are mice in the kitchen dancing in the crumbs, trapezing amongst the wire storage unit – athlete rodents. A seagull cries in the mists that swallow the power station, ghost-writing this diary.

~

There is constant pressure from well-meaning people who want to visit me – three or four letters a day announce the imminent arrival of strangers, the possibility of filming, photographing, or taping an interview. I've started to throw the letters away unanswered as replies generate more mail. Whole days pass writing replies – sometimes as many as thirty, books of stamps, envelopes and paper are always near to running out.

~

I potter in the garden, rescue the foxglove from an infestation of caterpillars, weed the stone circles and wait for the rain – which never comes.

My teatime cat, a mahogany tortoiseshell, arrives across the shingle. The blue hyacinths droop lower, sending waves of scent through the house.

~

The sun was up and HB said it was like five a.m. in the summer, but it soon went and he did too – lolloping down the road with his yellow duffle bag on his way to Newcastle and a haircut to make him attractive again. As he disappeared into the distance I felt so sad and foolish to be ill and in love.

Thursday 27
A bright dawn, very warm, the slightest breeze. Showered myself with cider vinegar to stop the itching, which tears me apart in the small hours of the morning. I don't think it is changing things, but here's to hope. Cleared the side of the house and fetched shingle for the stone circle.

Watered in ivy-leaved toadflax, watched a crocus open in the sunlight, watered the sempervivums. The bees are out in force, collecting pollen from the gorse and from the snowdrops in the flower bed.

Walked over to the fishing boats and back to lunch. Janet Thomas stopped her car and drove me to the shops in Lydd. She is going to start a nursery at the other end of the Ness.

The sun shines all day, shirt-sleeve weather. I put the blue hyacinths out and HB catches the Newcastle bus at one.

As the dark sets in a blue tit is catching caterpillars in the sage bush.

Friday 28

A hawk swoops across the broom, circling a sparrow, which he catches. This morning I caught a mouse in HB's chocolate-baited trap.

Pulled myself together with a bucket and mop, emptied the cupboards, polished the furniture and dusted the cobwebs. The sun sank into a mist and I made a good resolution: that I should fight this gloomy lethargy that puts me to sleep on the sofa each afternoon.

The coal is delivered, but it's so warm today that I've left the doors open to air the place. The fire dies in the grate.

As I write I feel I'm pressing against some unseen barrier – if I could only break through.

~

Setting sun haloed in chalk-white dusk. Pale-pink shingle swallowed in the mist.

A knock on the door: friends of Boris: 'Can we look at the garden?'

Sun sets, telephone call from LA – an interview. It's nearly six and the sun has gone.

Two young women appear out of the dark holding a tape recorder, I tell them to come back tomorrow.

Saturday 29

It's 8.30, the sun is shining. Derek Ball rang to see if I would be down here this weekend, but I'm waiting for Alan and Gingerbits who are coming to take me back to London – as I wait for them the bees are fighting over the crocus flowers and the first daffodil is opening. I hope for lazy days with no direction except the spring.

London by one. Spent the afternoon exploring the West End with Gingerbits.

MARCH

Sunday 1

Long telephone conversation with Nicky, he's certain my phone is tapped –
'What's that noise?'

'Only the washing machine.'

'That doesn't sound like a washing machine to me.'

He felt that Sir Ian, whom he described as 'impossibly grand', should
retire to the Isle of Man. Norman Tebbit was on the radio advocating gay
law reform, no doubt he's had one of *those* visits from Sir Ian. Tories and
their fag friends conspiring to win the election. I said I'd sell up at Dungeness
and move to the Isle of Man – that would be news.

~

I'm lying on the floor of this wasteland. HB has well and truly transformed
Phoenix House, he's the Giles Gilbert Scott of domesticity.

~

Nicky arrives for lunch, it's a cold grey day. Workmen, digging a ditch to
put down a bright-yellow plastic gas main, wear fluorescent orange
overalls – the only colour on the street, everyone else as monochrome as
the day.

We eat at the little Poon's, then walk round the bookshops. A very long
conversation about Wilde, an infuriating icon for queers – the complicity
with snobbery, the foolish in him and the writing less interesting than the
life. I found a first edition of *The Ballad of Reading Gaol*, which seemed to
be an omen.

~

I'm finding it so hard to concentrate, focus, wonder how I will get by
without work, a time has come to a close, how are others in my state? More
cheerful? Gloomy? Relieved? Fate dealt this blow, with Graham gone only
Alasdair remains, but Alasdair will somehow always remain, pickled in
indecision. The end of the book brings its own ending, is not indexed, too
many people are knocking at this door.

I pick up *The Raft of the Medusa* – death raft – and drop it. I think I should make a film of a garden, Monet's garden, flowers, and sail away right out of life.

Monday 2

Sparrows singing on the balcony. Toured the shops for books on Oscar Wilde.

~

At midday caught a cab to Richard's studio in Edwardes Square, where Piers had already started putting together a large canvas, which we sized and covered with multiple copies of the *People*: *Sex Boys for Sale at Queen's Grocer*, it looked quite impressive. Another cab to go shopping: John Bell and Croydon Medical Suppliers, in Wigmore Street, where years ago we bought plaster bandages for making masks. The place had become a large chemist's, we didn't find anything for our collage. Nearly every second shop in Wigmore Street was empty and boarded up.

The sex shop in Berwick Street produced no surprises and at that moment I realised I had lost my spectacles, which destabilised the rest of the afternoon.

On to Bird and Davis, the colour-men, which is now much reduced in size in a shop behind Drury Lane. It was here I bought tins of Brunswick-green in the early fifties to paint my landscapes in the Northwood attic. Piers remarked that I knew all the back alleys. Russell and Chapple, the canvas suppliers, was plunged into gloom by a power cut, lit by a few candles – when I got back to Phoenix House the same had happened there.

Rushed back to Richard's, where Digby had found my glasses, and then back to the cold, dark flat. Perhaps this is the first tremor of the collapse of the West.

Maria in the Presto gave me candles, I lit them, rang the London Electricity Board and took off into the night.

~

The Heath, damp and cold. Met an Australian dancer/stripper with thick, straight black hair. He was carrying one of those workout shoulder bags. He had given up a degree in psychiatry, said the people he worked with now were much more fun. He had a Chippendale smile and heavy workout thighs, said he hated bars and pubs, and came here as he 'got what he wanted' quickly. We talked of HIV – he said he never put himself at risk, was tested negative last week.

Thursday 5

Painting with Piers and Peter at South Edwardes Square, working here we are carried away. I missed the OutRage! demo, but finished eight paintings: *E II R Sex Boys for Sale at Queen's Grocers* – large, black and scarlet; *Blood* – a scarlet painting, over a *Sun* headline: AIDS BLOOD IN M&S PIES PLOT; *18*; *Vice Boy's Revenge*; *Spread the Plague*; and *Vile Book in School*, with a letter written on its bright-yellow surface.

~

I wrote a statement for the show in Manchester:

> *I painted these pictures fast and loose through the popular press. The landscape of my 1980s, dark and obsessive. I had not had a studio in years, I had forgotten to paint large and public, I dreamt of the paintings of my youth, I hadn't enjoyed much since that time, shipwrecked and lost in this work. The paintings burnt back the years. The heady smell of turpentine that filled my childhood with youthful optimism. My spirit guide is Goya, I saw this, this is the present in which my friends were lost, they died in these headlines behind the cups of sugary tea. Which blood? Which books? What revenge? What vice? What virtue?*
>
> *I painted these pictures with no hope and wild laughter, you are the jokers, the laughter is on you. Tears fall behind the headlines. 'Discover yourself' they said at school, I found a terrible subject. Was my sex ever safe? There were no queers in* Coronation Street *which had nothing to do with my life, I lived in other and better Englands, this is no soap.*
>
> *I painted these pictures with half-closed eyes as quickly as possible with the arrogance of second childhood. I discovered I had never forgotten my canvas and the paint went on with ease, it wasn't difficult.*
>
> *Shed no tears over this work.*

Peter and Piers are gluing *Gay Santa* [with large breasts] *Gets Sack*.

Outside the camellias are flowering and there is a carmine japonica ablaze in the railings. We ate a pizza for lunch in a marble-white restaurant decorated with Picasso fakes.

Peter says Parisians are literate in images. Piers is harassed by Richard, who keeps interrupting from New York, and has the most annoying telephone ever: a horrible buzz that could drive you to madness.

HB came back with two proggy mats from Chester Le Street and a buzz cut.

~

Julian Cole came for supper at Ragam, we stopped off in Marchmont Street at his young Los Angeleno friend's flat – a blond surfer with body piercings, he had a silver barbell through his tongue.

Left HB fuming on the street, the 'Thursday Caller' pressed the doorbell at Phoenix House and delivered a death threat, this happens each week. HB says: 'When I catch him, *he'll* die.'

Friday 6
Breakfast at Bertaux's, trip to Covent Garden art shop where the 'minimal' paint, paper, and glue for a poster was £23, the price of the first batch of paintings is over £1000 – I spent £250 on a few cans of paint.

Midday, caught the bus to Richard's – it took for ever. London packed in the warm spring sunlight. At Marble Arch we passed a beggar boy wrapped in a duvet asking for 'spare change' – he looked not a day older than fifteen.

At Richard's a charcoal drawing was delivered and an Auerbach head that had cost £23,000 – Digby said it would have cost twice as much at Marlborough a year before.

The gardens in the square looked ravishing, the japonica and the camellias have been joined by the most delicate prunus blossom, as white as snowflakes.

The painting *Sold Out* finished by four, *Cocks and Arses for the Tory Classes*, *Forward With Britain at Fortnum's*. Maybe the little beggar boy should have walked to Fortnum's where the *People* could have snapped him as a 'sex boy for sale'.

Saturday 7
Drove with Howard and HB to Dungeness. Peter joined us from Deal. It was colder and raining, the garden looking greener, all the daffs out. We drove to Rye, knocked on Neil Tennant's door – he was out – then on to Dixter to buy plants. HB and Peter talking Geordie in the back of the car all the way.

Took the first steps towards a film of *Dorian* – a black painting with a gold figure who steps out of the canvas, Dorian a queer-boy gigolo for women, set in the present day, Basil played by Julian Sands (his studied queen in *Naked Lunch* the best thing in that film).

A poor mouse whacked by HB's trap in the middle of the night.

Sunday 8
The tortoiseshell cat that HB gave a can of food to is back. It's scratched up the front flower bed, but made little damage. It's here, chattering away, sitting at the kitchen door hopeful for more sardines.

~

The garden is putting on the colours of spring, the inky purple *Crambe maritima* uncurl like medieval capitals, sap-green elder, pale-blue rosemary flowers, garlic racing with the iris, crocus punctuate purple and yellow, the snowdrops are over. I scattered white campion and corncockle seeds amongst the poppies and cornflower seedlings, and planted the santolina we bought at Dixter. The miniature train has started to run again, hooting as it passes the house.

~

In the afternoon I watered the sempervivums, the secret of their culture is to pretend you are the melting winter snow. The sempervivum or houseleek is also called *Jovis barba* – Jupiter's beard. Four hundred years before Christ, Theophrastus mentions Aizoon the ever-living.

~

I searched the beach and brought back wire and floats to make a serpent sculpture. As the afternoon ended the sun came out and caught the tiny buds on the dog rose bursting into life. The tortoiseshell cat returned and danced in the long grass.

Monday 9

Richard phoned to say he was thrilled by the new paintings, especially *True Blue*.

Ruby Rich phoned to complete the article on 'New Queer Cinema', some complaints over the mostly male Sundance Festival and *Edward II* – people find Isabella misogynist. I said if that's the case then there are no wicked queens in history. It's my 399-year-old collaborator, Kit the unreconstructed.

Today the sun is out, the crocuses have flattened themselves in the warmth, borage shooting up by the front door. The larks were singing, invisible in the blue sky as I walked along the beach looking for flints.

The taxi lady arrived at ten to put me back on the train for London. I have felt a dizziness behind the eyes for a week as if I was stoned. It's this that gives me a lack of concentration for writing or reading and wondering if I will ever get another film made – though this doesn't worry me much, as painting is exhilarating and the garden more so.

~

At Richard's, horror of horrors, we had stretched the canvases too taut and they had all buckled. Howard, HB and Piers undid the damage. The paintings came apart with a sharp crack like a rifle shot. Late in the afternoon painted *Dear Santa, Please Send Me Time*.

Tuesday 10

The taxi that brought me to St Mary's smelled strongly of my grandmother's perfume.

I have a slight headache as I sit in the waiting room at the Wharfside, which is as silent as a tomb. No one reads, they are all staring into the air, shifting uncomfortably in their seats. Opposite me a Marky Mark lookalike boy, big brown shoes, jeans, silvery jacket and a back-to-front hat, sits next to an elderly man with gold glasses. The silence continues, just a cough. The Marky boy stares at me as if wishing to break the silence, one piece of hair has come adrift and sticks up through the hat like a unicorn. He has his finger in his mouth, looks so glum, his gold earring catches the light as he tilts his head.

'What's the next plan?' asks someone. The boy slouches deeper in his chair. Over the years the posters have proliferated: *Positive Youth*, *Positive Discounts*, *Newly Diagnosed*, *Social Work*, *Support*, *Confidentially Yours*, above all the *Concorde Study* continues. The boy stares at the ceiling, hand on the back of his cap, half angry at my interest. He has beautiful eyebrows, he's laughing, a nurse has sat down with him to work out his problems with housing and payment. 'There was a gap,' she says. 'Did you get the Giro? . . . caught in the machinery . . . hang on to it . . . council rent . . . housing . . . the weekly claim . . . ill . . . hospital . . . backdate . . . monthly tenancy . . . Glasgow . . . see what happens . . .' She laughs. 'We're wasting our time ringing.'

'They put me on a drug to stop me having fits,' he says.

'They'll sort you out quicker than I can sort you out,' says the nurse. The boy is smiling now.

The clock ticks past midday. The Marky boy sighs and picks the stones out of his shoes. He has a diamond ring on his middle finger.

The silence is broken by the receptionist tapping the keys on the computer.

Positive Discounts, *Travelling by Train*, *Single and Homeless*, *Do You Need Rest and Respite?* The phone is ringing, no one picks it up.

The room is even more silent, someone says 'Hello' in a whisper. A social worker has arrived to ask the Marky boy for an interview, he's going to be here on the 31st. I would love to break into his silence, not to mention his pants.

Dr Mark said to avoid the Mississippi Valley – strange fungal infections. He burnt the spots on my face and then I had my blood taken. Several men were having transfusions.

With a deep breath I walk back into the sunlight.

~

Nearly three hours taken out to see *Angels in America* at the National. The seats at the Cottesloe very uncomfortable, unwelcoming. The play seemed curiously dated (1985), some mad camp Armageddon. The audience laughed without stopping, but there seemed little to laugh at. The best of it was the tacky – the angel more a Christmas tree fairy – I couldn't see the point of the bed collaged with Hollywood divas. The fuck scene was uncomfortable. It all seemed a bit dramatic after St Mary's.

Wednesday 11
On the top deck of the number 10 bus to Richard's, stuck in Oxford Street, more bomb scares, the tube closed down.

A boy in a red jacket, short-haired, tall and melancholic, is the only other passenger. I can feel his eyes boring into the back of my head. The papers are unreadable, full of the small print of Mr Lamont's budget, squabbling about with the spare change.

~

I'm going to paint *Whore*, *Spunk* and complete *18* at Richard's. Noisy painting. London rolls by, seems like a place where I no longer live, part brochure, part film set, the people bizarre – designer mishmash, extras. As the years have passed I have grown out of it, it seems ever more tawdry, less satisfying. I guessed that the boy in red was an art student, he got off at the RCA.

John Dewe Matthews, Sarah, Alison, all came to the studio.

Johnny very funny about Maggi Hambling – she calls all her students by their surnames. Johnny said when they came to his show, he only knew the elderly ladies as Sinclair and Wilson.

Sarah said she wished there was a cruising park for women like Hampstead Heath – which is deserted since a Tory MP was caught up there with his pants round his ankles.

~

I'm rushed off my feet, there seems to be so little time, I'm falling over the hours and minutes. My 'poppers cough' – that's HB's name for it – stops me short.

I gave a lad a condom on the Heath, he threw it over his shoulder. 'Like salt,' he said, 'for good luck.' I found the condom later, kept it as a souvenir of these times. I'm still coughing, though.

~

HB was up late too, working at Sandy's *Orlando* sweatshop – he just popped in for a cup of tea and a snog, and ended up whaleboning Quentin Crisp's corset into the small hours.

MARCH

Thursday 12

I'm standing waiting for the number 10 on Oxford Street outside the electronics shop, which is blasting unreasonable music for my headache, cold rain blown in my face, attacked by a persistent Hare Krishna boy selling enlightened books – perhaps he should get one to the mendacious Archbishop who has banned a queer prayer book.

~

A bag lady with a little circus dog passes in front of the bus; she hauls her huge load over the kerb.

~

People stare when I roll up my trousers and scratch my itchy legs. The bus's movement pushes the diary along.

~

Piers says: 'This floor is a losing battle.' I've just scooped the last of the paint on to *Love Sex Death*, and attacked *Spread the Plague*, which looks like a background to an Otto Dix. The enjoyment of paint is hard to describe, wild as any film, even though I've got the turpentine headache – what surprises me is the return of colour in these blues.

~

We all went to lunch, Ken looking like a large young David Hockney. Richard tells us an Oscar Wilde story: Oscar at dinner with Gide in Paris, telling the old prune that his previous night's lover had murdered his wife earlier in the week. Once dead she had all the beauty of a spent rose bush in the rain.

Dicky thought he could be happy in the San Reno building in New York; we weren't so sure, though Keith does seem happy there. He said if he moved there we could all stay – so we all agreed he would be happy. We talked of the people who died of AIDS this week, and Patrik.

~

Patrik the disappeared – uncomfortable memory.

I first met Patrik in King's Cross, at The Place – the dance centre set up in an old drill hall by Robin Howard. Robin was very tall and had lost his legs, so he walked leaning heavily on a stick. Patrik had helped open The Place and was planning to work with the young choreographers and artists who flocked there – Pat always had plans but never fulfilled any of them. He was enthralled by film, particularly bad and trashy film, *Beyond the Valley of the Dolls* was his favourite; he took the students from The Place to see the film and set it as an essay topic.

Pat lived in a tabula rasa, a blankness that allowed him a certain mystery. He was tall, had long brown hair, wore tight blue jeans, a denim shirt and cowboy boots – he was never fashionable. He had a mind as sharp as a razor and would tell you the worst about himself – as he had nowhere to live, no job or money, he was chained to those who had. He laughed quickly and often, and was able to move in. He moved into Bankside – my studio at the top of a ruined warehouse on the riverside.

Pat loved to shock and between us we had a riot of a time, no more so than the fortnight of drag – the result of trips to the second-hand shops for couturier dresses to wear at Andrew Logan's first Alternative Miss World. Classic Balenciaga or Dior cost a fiver and Pat, with his angular body, slipped into them hand in glove. Pat wasn't a drag queen, not a trace of camp about him, he was just a young man in a dress, we talked about Radical Drag but it was just Dressing Up.

Our first adventure was a performance of Peter Maxwell Davies's *Songs for a Mad King* in the Queen Elizabeth Hall; we severely disrupted the audience in evening dress. I don't think Max was too pleased but said nothing as the season was launched at a reception in my studio.

Pat won the Alternative Miss World, without a touch of make-up, by getting into the dresses the other contestants had taken off – a spur-of-the-moment decision, but much funnier than anything anyone else had dreamt up for the occasion. A year later he conceded his crown to Eric, looking like an eighteenth-century squire after an orgy in *Tom Jones* – blue denim, cowboy boots, with an immense boa constrictor wrapped around him like those haute couture dresses.

Pat's favourite evenings were those we spent in Bianchi's with a bottle of wine and a plate of carbonara. Bianchi's was quite beyond our, or I should say *my*, pocket but it was quite the best of the Soho restaurants, packed with theatre people, simple, unpretentious, and run by Elena who left to run L'Escargot when Bianchi's finally closed. Pat and I had such laughing times; there was a corner where we laughed at everyone and ourselves until we were in speechless stitches and then walked back home, giggling all the way.

Pat had a soft spot for bent aristocracy – in those days they gave weekend parties. The best was an orgy which was thrown, on the spur of the moment, for a very confused group of Soviet dancers from the Bolshoi, most of whom, unlike here, were straight. The orgy was memorable because the aristos assumed that all Russians did it – at least that was the impression that Rudolf Nureyev gave – and Pat told the confused gang from Leningrad that all the British aristocracy, and most of the others, take it up the arse; sodomy is an old British custom, bugger thy neighbour – and out of politeness some of them joined in.

94

Pat was a gigolo, rich ladies, rich men. He brought the perception of an acid drop into their bland and repetitive lives. He was the perfect company at dinner and was always paid for.

One night in NYC Edward Montagu – who was always leant on by good-looking young men for a dinner – took Pat and a gang of freeloaders to the very expensive Four Seasons. They had caviar and champagne, and more of it, running up a bill of thousands. Montagu secretly put a couple of hundred dollars into Pat's hand and, when the bill came, divided it up, put his cash down, and passed the plate to Pat in front of the astonished and worried gang. Everyone waited with bated breath, Pat produced the money and he and Edward departed, leaving the rest scrubbing around in their pockets.

Pat had a mind as sharp as a razor and a complicated background in Wiltshire. His hunting-and-shooting mother had chained him to a meat hook in her medieval cottage and whipped him with a riding crop for some indiscretion. This had established a lasting bond, or maybe bondage, in their relationship – there was not one moment when the thrill of being whipped by his mother was not uppermost in Pat's mind – hence his love of Sebastian tortured by the arrows of desire.

Patrik liked to be spoilt, I don't know if he grew out of this in NYC but I was always treating him, whether it was spaghetti carbonara or a holiday in Italy.

With the help of my mechanical father we bought a battered old Austin 40 – one of those half-wooded Tudorbethan ones – with the idea of driving via Amsterdam, where the boys were easy, down through Germany and Austria to Venice and even further. We got to the ferry and the car broke down before our adventure even started. We should have heeded the warning; the kicking, pushing and shoving that eventually got it going were to become a way of life during the next month.

In Amsterdam we booked into a hotel near the Rembrandtplein. I had stumbled across it in 1970 with my friend Ken, who was as beautiful as a movie star with his chestnut hair and grey eyes. We got the same room, the one in which he was 'fucked rotten' – as he put it – by a bloodstained butcher's boy called Vim. Pat and I unpacked our bags and collapsed into the sheets, to be woken in the early dawn by the landlady hammering on our door. A cat burglar had been in our room, repacked all our clothes and taken the suitcases. He had left our dirty socks and underpants. Money, passports and the car keys had gone, along with my beautiful jacket, silk-screened to look like a leopard, the cast-off of some fifties group.

We spent the next forty-eight hours repairing the damage in banks and embassies, and when we weren't in official queues we were in the flea market where we bought worker's overalls, T-shirts and second-hand shoes.

The customers of the Doc and Coc, the oldest gay bar, gave us a wide berth – we had no money for drinks. The sauna was better – stark naked without the overalls we had a chance, though sex in the sauna was so easy it lost some of its excitement. The Dutch sauna, unlike the American ones – which sported camouflage decor like an army barracks – was white-tiled and antiseptic, almost like the waiting room for the clap clinic. As we left we saw Duncan Grant, aged ninety, sketching boys in the restaurant.

Kitted out like two unemployed window cleaners, Pat and I took off down the motorway to Venice. Within an hour the car seized up and boiled over. This time we were rescued and towed into a small town, where we remained for a day while the local mechanic found spare parts. Pat developed the clap – an infection on holiday is always a nightmare, you end up with doctors who'll put out their hands for the cash before they'll treat you and then ask embarrassing questions. Sometimes it's painful – they insist on poking bits of wire down your stinging cock to take smears for slides and their cures seem to be as diverse as their methods. I found you could buy tetracycline across the counter, I think it was illegal but no one refused me. *Ambramicina*, I still remember the name, went into my tooth bag and toured with me.

Next day we were on our way. Pat's clap cleared up overnight but 'Hilton', our Austin 40, did only ten miles, slowed on the slightest gradient and then stopped in a cloud of steam – the garage had forgotten to put water in the radiator.

The more disastrous our journey in Hilton became the more Pat laughed at our predicament. We got to Venice, stood in front of the mosaics at Ravenna and then drove down the spine of Italy to Salerno, where Hilton, right in the middle of a three-lane highway intersection, packed up.

Hilton was finally pushed on to the car ferry and abandoned in Dover for ever.

I never had sex with Pat, though a lot of my friends thought we were having an affair. Unlike mine, Pat's sex life was very discreet. He disappeared like a cat, liked to be thought of as straight or at worst bisexual, ended up living with Chrissy, a famous New York model.

Patrik was always planning to do this and that, but to have completed any of these dreams would have grounded him like a paragraph in this diary. Though I had not seen much of him for years I expect he was still dreaming. Behind Patrik's charm lay an impenetrable sadness, he had a certain snakelike indestructibility, it seems improbable he could be dead. Maybe the afterlife is reserved for him alone.

~

Horrible night of scratching, migraine confusions. It got worse when I thought I had more bodies than one. HB kept awake by my tossing and turning.

Friday 13

Sitting in the ten o'clock train with HB. HB near nude for such a cold, wet day, just a cherry-red Fred Perry, blue jeans and a pair of black trainers, buzz cut peeping over the *Independent*, his little yellow duffle bag on the seat next to him.

~

The turpentine has given me such a headache. HB has given up the *Independent* and fallen asleep.

~

At Dungeness it was blowing a gale, but the sun was out and when the wind dropped it was warm. The sea kale had grown an inch – the measure of spring. I worked in the garden while HB rearranged the books into alphabetical order and complained about the Stravinsky music: 'some horrible din'. In the end we settled for silence and good humour. 'Typical,' he said. 'You put on a horrible din and go outside to avoid it.'

Saturday 14

The flesh-coloured hyacinth droops in an excess of perfume in the kitchen. HB is showering, he has caught my cough. *The Rite of Spring* advances us into the cold March morning. The tortoiseshell cat arrives and stalks through the house, I'm christening it Tiger Lily. Gingerbits is driving from Canterbury and bringing it some treats. It's curled up now on the wine velvet cushion on top of the broken chair, quite asleep.

HB leaves for the Long Pits, I see him walking in the distance.

In the bookshelf I find my old telephone books – where are all these half-remembered faces? Some I know have died, others, I wonder, morbid curiosity. Where are Olaf, Daniel and Johnny M? Who fucked too many for their health? Johnny made it like a porn star: 'Fuck that tight arse.'

My porn star friend Aiden thinks he's the Stryker of the nineties. Jeff in Manchester said when Aiden was a student he was excessively shy and clean-living. Since then he's had a most successful career selling his body and has just returned from the set of a porn film in the US.

~

Driven by Paul and Gingerbits to Canterbury for the Queer Art Festival.

Sexy photos on display and *Sebastiane* flickering on a television. I bought one of Della Grace's photographs of lesbian boys with cocks – the one that Sarah had said caused a stir.

Della great fun, left the audience in a good mood. Della said: 'Let's have a show of hands. Everyone in the audience put up their hands if they have never had a same-sex relationship . . .' (There was a large show of hands.) Then she finished her sentence: '. . . and would like to.' Six hands were left up. Couldn't imagine this happening thirty years ago.

Paul, a maths student, drove us back to London. We met up with Michael and all went to Poon's for supper, Paul very surprised that strangers had to share tables.

I've never seen London busier, it was a fight to get down Charing Cross Road, rubbish blew down it in a tidal wave.

Monday 16

Aurelia pulled me an espresso in Bar Italia and a dewy-eyed Italian youth in a long white apron who was sweeping up the floor flashed a smile and brought my coffee over to me.

~

On the train to Heathrow. HB tired, he stayed up to the early hours washing and ironing and packing my suitcase for me.

~

Trees along the railway line green with spring.

~

Articles in the newspapers on Tina Chow's death from toxoplasmosis. It was noticeable that her high living – unlike Freddie Mercury's – was, quite rightly, not called into question. She had known four sexual partners.

~

Meanwhile the unpleasant ex-MP caught and cautioned by the police on Hampstead Heath is in his own words 'not gay'. Thank God – he voted for Section 28. I'm glad it is no longer considered gay to be unbuttoning another guy's flies at midnight in a gay cruising ground.

The *Independent*'s article on the Heath is very even-handed. The *Times* goes for shock horror and quotes *Modern Nature*.

~

We have just passed Cork at 35,000 feet. HB has built a barrier of cushions and blankets against my AIDS-related fidgeting.

~

For the first time for years we are not staying with Mark in East 62nd Street – his mental state has put him away. There are rumours he thought he was the Holy Ghost, though he never expressed that when I was in hearing distance.

~

HB and I are booked into the Mayflower Hotel on Central Park. The lift is as large as the flat and has perpetual canned muzak – we dance a two-step, cheek to cheek, surprising guests waiting on intervening floors. We get the lift to ourselves.

Tuesday 17
Still dancing in the lift with HB, who has got the hotel to bring up an iron and ironing board for his meticulously packed clothes.

Friday 20
Los Angeles. The rain is pouring down. We've been trapped at the Chateau Marmont for an eternity, no one rings, no one seems to know we are here, except Donny who met Howard Bruckner on a mountainside and his present boyfriend on a street.

The TV has sacrificed all channels to profit, you flick about and nothing comes up. Even the layout of the *LA Times* is squeezed and chopped by advertising, and it rains and rains.

This is the second time I've been here – that time we were trapped in a condo with no furniture.

The Chateau has an Olde Worlde charm; once stars stayed here, then they died here, some keep trunks of clothes in the basement. It's full of German starlets who will gain nothing from being here – there was only one Marlene.

~

One happy HB moment: we met Gary Stretch – the boxer – at a hamburger stall. HB was photographed with him – not at all homophobic, but not at all homosexual. When he left he stood up and stretched, and thrust his bulge right into HB's face. HB so fazed he couldn't finish his chips.

~

Edward II opened the Lesbian and Gay Film Festival – thoroughly middle-aged, middle income and respectable. Donny and his hustler friends the only 'youth'; one lad with an iron ring through his nose, another in a dress – who complained that my characters are too straight. The strangest meeting was with a man who came to Upper Ground with Tennessee Williams for my party in 1969, he remembered it clearly. That past seems so long ago that if he had said it hadn't happened I would probably have believed him. There was sex enough, drugs enough, and quite enough rock and roll, but not enough of any of them to give you a hangover.

Rain poured down through the screening, washed out the party – so we came back to the Chateau with the girlfriend of HB's marine biologist friend Dr Ruth and ate yet another plate of smoked salmon – this seems to be the mainstay of Marmont's cuisine. We were in bed before midnight. Most days we've been in bed at eight. HB, who keeps London time 'to avoid jet lag', gets up at four a.m. and takes long, long baths.

Saturday 21

Hollywood is bracing itself for an assault by gay activists for the Oscars ceremony.

Melody, who is small and kitted out in a black pyjama outfit, shuffles the interviews, all charming, all gay. I get the impression that I'm to be kept in the ghetto for always here, that straight people wouldn't be seen dead at a gay movie, even an Elizabethan one.

Steven Waddington did not turn up – his filming schedule interferes. No Julian Sands, no Lee Drysdale, not even David Hockney – should I ring? No, it will only complicate Melody's schedule.

I do hate photographers, staring into my face at the patchy irritated spots that the HIV has thrown up. Actually my spots are getting better as Dr Mark's liquid nitrogen attack wears them away.

~

It's ten. One hour on the phone with Gus Van Sant. Gus seems worried about how much of an activist he should be – it's much more difficult here than at home.

~

The rain has stopped. We have three hours sitting here before Donny arrives with his beer and his W. Burroughs T-shirt. Donny is big, gangly and sexy, his hair out like a haystack, yet he seems curiously insecure, perhaps that's the LA lifestyle – Donny is a Midwestern farm boy. Donny takes photos for two hours and the sun is out. Both the film premières – NYC a benefit for the film festival, and here – have been well organised and Fine Line seems to be quite happy to be open in its publicity. One of the reviews (which have all been favourable) says: '*The film has a fine sense of jewellery.*'

~

Donny took us to a gay rodeo. Was it fun? I don't know – the people there seemed to enjoy themselves. The rodeo looked like a scene from a B movie – somewhat over the hill. The stalls were totally apolitical, no books, pamphlets, no one collecting for AIDS, just shoeshine boys and clothes salesmen, and these gaunt, middle-aged men with cowboy boots and Stetsons. Roly-poly dykes line-dancing in a tent where the same old drag queens routinely camped it up in moustaches and high heels.

Donny had his boots shined and met a 'fluffer' from Colt Studios – a rather nice young man who was employed to give blow-jobs to porn stars to warm them up before they were filmed or photographed.

We drove to Ronnie Cottrell's house – he served us tea with his hair encased in a henna pack.

Ronnie had a folio of nineteen-year-old nudes most of whom were crystal casualties, or had been locked away for stealing food. How strange this place is, people relate to each other like fast food, any sexy boys have left to be in Bruce Webber photographs.

There were rumours of a 'gay industry' party: presumably executives and out-of-work fluffers who haven't made it in porno yet. The homophobia in the power structure sits strangely as even straight men, like Gary, flaunt their arses and cocks – it looks quite exciting, but honestly it's too much trouble. The young boys here seem to be after drugs not sex. Everyone talks of the recession, I'm not quite certain what this means here, everything is half the price it is back home and everyone has more of it. Prospect Cottage would look like a pauper's shack in these tropical gardens.

Drove back to the Chateau with very loud in-car music blasting us into silence.

Sunday 22

Poor HB arrived back late – the hands on his London body clock pointing this way and that, he's sitting on the bed saying he feels 'all strange'. He had gone out with Donny who got more and more drunk and out of order as the night developed. HB had expected to go to the 'gay industry' party but ended up in the heaviest SM leather bar 'wearing cashmere' – he said it was a great relief to meet Spring, who had driven his motorbike down here from San Francisco.

~

A long wait at the Chateau Marmont (we are prisoners here) for the car to take us to the BAFTA awards. I've no idea what to say except 'thanks'. Perhaps it is a bad idea to tell a joke – I never tell them. They sent me a tape of last year: Dan Day Lewis charming – kept it short; Kenneth Branagh, via satellite from Tokyo, went on about his Britishness and they cut him off.

~

HB has gone for a walk in the rain, I told him no one walks in LA. I've swallowed my pills. Donny said he had to come off the AZT and ddI as they didn't agree with him, but that may be due to the alcoholic punishment he is inflicting on himself. The worst of the spots on my face have gone.

~

It's so silent here, the hum of the fridge, birdsong and a distant dog barking.

~

One of those ubiquitous long dark limos came for us and took us to BAFTA. We found ourselves sitting alongside Jodie Foster, whom we all love – I was whisked off for the presentation, so little could be talked about. Vanessa Redgrave introduced a very strange selection from the old movies, not award stuff but I survived it – how strange to be shown your obituary before you have died. I hope my acceptance speech didn't sound ungracious. The award must have been the first for a queer film-maker, thankfully the dreaded 'g' word was not used in Vanessa's citation, I didn't use it either – I think it's pretty evident.

Collared by a *Sun* reporter who said: 'We are just the people who you dislike.' I smiled, took it all in my stride. The *Times* was pushing me to say I thought all the closeted stars should be Outed. 'Perhaps they should, perhaps not.'

~

After six years HB and I are happier than LA itself; we are both glad when the car comes to pick us up for the airport.

The award weighs a ton, I've been lugging it through the airport. I'm sitting next to HB who is writing postcards. When he's posted them we'll go through passport control.

We're both braced for the journey; it will be great to get back home and leave the fluffers behind to struggle into the movies.

Tuesday 24

Very tired, back to reality, the stretch limo recedes into a dream, a pile of washing waits on the floor.

HB was on the TV talking to Jodie Foster in the early hours of the morning, there are thirty messages from his lesbian friends.

HB returns from signing on – he calls it 'The Arts Council of Great Britain'. At the dole office he bumped into Sandy's boyfriend, Alfie, who shouted right across the crowded office: 'How did you do that? I just saw you live on TV from LA with Jodie Foster.' The whole dole office turns to look. 'Must have been someone else,' says HB – then tells Alfie all about it when they get outside.

Wednesday 25

All the dykes at the gym pestering HB for Jodie Foster's phone number.

Julian came at eleven with his Californian friend with the silver piercings. HB grumpy in the car – I think this was because they were smoking dope. In Ashford Sainsbury's buying food for the day HB asked if we could stop at the Little Chef for lunch. I said yes, so he only bought a cream split for his pudding. When we got to Little Chef corner I made Julian go straight to Prospect, HB so furious he squished the bun in my face. After a while he recovered and laughed his way through the rest of the day.

~

Dungeness cold and grey. We drove to Rye and walked around the antique shops, then back to Prospect, Julian stoned – weaving all over the coast road from Camber, so much so I worried all night of HB's safety on the road back to London.

Played myself to sleep with Shostakovich and slept well in the wind-buffeted cottage.

Thursday 26

All day long the sun tried to break through the clouds, twice it started to rain and then thought better of it. I could feel the cold on my back as I worked in the garden planting cistus, teuchrium and two new iris. Busy as a lark, industrious as a bumble bee – I saw a large one in my daffodils. HB hates daffs, says they look vulgar. Here they stand surreal in the shingle, quite out of place; Mrs Jekyll would laugh at them but they bring in the spring and once, when they were rare in the shops, were such a treat.

The grape hyacinth loves the shingle and each year increases itself by bounds. They are sturdy, defy the salt winds and last for months, some have been out for weeks, others are bursting into bloom.

The sea kale have grown inches in the last week, the deep inky purple has a touch of green in it, the same colour as the wallflower buds. The sea, which was roaring rough yesterday, is a calm, milky turquoise. The seagulls are squabbling with the crows, fishermen are repairing the boat that was stove in in the storm. The bees, bright-yellow with gorse pollen, are blown off course and crawl around the hive waiting for a lull in the gusts.

~

HB starting to scan *Narrow Rooms* into his computer. We met James Purdy in New York on the night that *Edward II* opened and took him to the film in a stretched limo. He told us that Edith Sitwell took him under her wing and had a furious row with Gollancz when they tried to take the word

103

'motherfucker' out of one of his novels. He seemed very happy for us to take on *Narrow Rooms*.

Friday 27
A fat rain fell from the north all night, washing colour into the stones, which sparkled in the dawn, curled up on the sofa with Mrs Jekyll, vision of her swatting wasps around her berberis with a ping-pong bat.

Cold damp condensation fuzzing the view. All the spring flowers have shot up in the last week, the soft green of the irises and ornamental garlic are a foil to the silver green of helichrysum. The pinks have puffed themselves into fine cushions, the first flowers have opened on the wallflowers, the rosemary comes into bloom, pale-blue, and the gorse cuttings are putting out pale-green buds, the older plants are ablaze with yellow flowers – my bee gold.

It is too cold to work in the garden today but I picked up stones on the beach as the tide went out. In spite of the cold and wind the bees were out on the gorse, nothing deters them now the spring is round the corner.

~

Marjorie Althorpe writes from Glasgow to say she is disgusted by some of the *vox populi* graffiti in the Glasgow show. As I open the letter a cold hail falls.

Brian the builder drops by. The new studio is going to set me back the best part of £15,000. I decide to do it, I still have money from Father in the bank, enough to cover it.

~

At midday I walked to the sallow woods by the Long Pits, they rattle in the wind, bright grass-green moss on the trunks and a silvery hint of pussy willow coming into bloom. There is one primrose plant – the rabbits have dug the other ones up, violets are out, as are starbright periwinkle. As I walk home I pass my bees flying in the opposite direction. Everyone on the Ness seems to have watched the BAFTA awards, they stop and smile.

The rain set in and I curled up with my herbals. When I lived in Upper Ground the alley alongside the studio was called Paris Gardens – it's long since disappeared under 'redevelopment'. I have always remembered the name, a mystery solved when I stumbled across herb Paris, which must have been grown there. Gerard says:

> *The berries of herbe Paris given by the space of twentie days are excellent good against poison. It hath been used against the alchemist and witches to doe wonders. In truth they are all but drowsie dreams and illusions.*

Saturday 28

Very cold and wet, with a high wind, the sea boiling white, all my garden bent to the ground. It's ten and I'm waiting for the taxi lady to take me to the station.

Finished off the work on the New Contemporaries with Marina Warner and Guy Brett. We've chosen nearly all women artists, only four men. Guy brought a new catalogue of Helio Optica – whose show he curated back in 1969 at the Whitechapel.

~

In the evening Alasdair called by and we went to an indifferent Indian restaurant for a small curry and Bombay Duck that cost an arm and a leg.

Alasdair quite resigned to Graham's death. He shaved Graham after he died, felt Graham had gone with no regret.

Sunday 29

Derek Ball collected me at 9.30 and we drove down here by way of Canterbury and then across the hills to Hythe, a pleasant change from the usual way through Ashford.

We drove to Appledore where I bought a broad rake and some new knives to replace the rusty Victorian ones, which make HB throw up his hands in disgust.

Back to the Light Railway Café for lunch and plans to throw a midsummer party.

~

There were two people waiting to see me. I was a bit short, too many unannounced visitors and here I was an easy prey weighed down with carrier bags. The house was freezing cold and the fire started sluggish.

Opened the letters – more demands for signed photos. Worked in the garden. As I was weeding a fine Jaguar pulled over and Johnny Phillips clambered out, it was a pleasant surprise. Johnny is very attractive: I can only describe him as a fresh-faced Sandhurst sub lieutenant. He spent the day here and then we were cooked a great supper at Derek's who produced pasta and huge bottles of wine. Johnny left at 9.30, by which time we had demolished several generations of London boys. Derek very against David Hockney, said he found gruff Yorkshiremen a pain in the arse, he had always found Yorkshiremen opinionated and closed. This was his view as an outsider – a South African who has lived here a quarter of a century. 'David Hockney,' he said, 'would always steal a conversation. If someone told a joke you could be certain that he would butt in before they had finished with an alternative punchline.'

Johnny thought Philip Prowse the most interesting of the bunch, with the vanity of talent. I said I'd always admired Philip's move to Glasgow, more surprising than David's to LA. The generations whizzed by, Johnny thought Michael Clarke blindly ambitious, even his 'wild' lifestyle coolly calculated, a big dancer with a small talent.

Leigh Bowery – much loved, and it just goes to show, if you wear silly clothes round Soho for long enough you'll get to be famous. Steven Linard – Bond Street Grand. Others dead, others dying. The misspent nights slipped by, the fashion of a generation out of fashion, not much to say for it all.

Monday 30
My skin itched like Nessus all night. The clocks changed, the rain poured down. I don't know what time I went to bed, chased from the TV by the election, the tedium of getting rid of the Tories after all these years, misspent years. Why, if we 'never had it so good' and made more money than ever, did they leave it in such a state of decline? Major is really minor.

This morning it was still raining, cold and windy, though I did see stars peeping through the small hours. I picked up a mop and bucket, and started a spring clean. Halfway through, the paperback edition of *Modern Nature* arrived with Howard's grand, sad cover photo.

I find it mysterious that all the years that have passed should lead to

Prospect Cottage – perhaps it is the tin roof which reminds me of the Nissen huts of an RAF childhood in the forties, so thrifty and far distant; maybe it is the flower bed which runs in front of the house – it has the same lumps of concrete from some long-demolished fortification as those in Abingdon and Kidlington; or the stoves which roar in the wind; or maybe the name Prospect.

Today there is solitude, a half-hour has elapsed without a car passing and the phone is silent, and though it's cold I'm well wrapped up in my grey sweater and an old corduroy jacket – as worn as a moss-grown wall. I feel higgledy-piggledy. No appetite today.

A view of boats fuzzed by the dismal rain that patters on the metal roof. The smallest money spider is building a web on the desk light, so fine that my breath swings it back and forth. It's possible to be alone here.

The mice have got in under the bed and destroyed the antique silk saris stored there, nibbled little holes through all of them. I'll take them up to London and give them to Sandy to make HB lavish shirts, gossamer as the fabrics that the Baron von Gloeden draped over his Sicilian lads.

My spring cleaning creeps towards the kitchen. I polish the knives and forks with Duraglit. Duraglit purposely made to shine the silver and leave you with black fingers and little black wads of the stuff everywhere. All those 'marching on the spot' days of childhood, Duraglit and Blanco, belt buckles and buttons on the CCF uniform, the tarnished smell of it. A forced march along the clifftops on the isle of Purbeck in weather so evil the ice formed on you to windward and you went deaf with the cold.

~

The thirtieth, my parents' wedding anniversary, comes again. Three years ago it was warm and sunny, the ivy-leaved toadflax out by the lifeboat station bright with flowers. Today there is no hint of them. Mother of millions, fleas and lice, wandering sailor, monkey jaws, braving the cold. Each day brings different colours to the crambe leaves, some are pure magenta, others overtaken by a cobalt-green.

Living at the brimmes of the sea where there is no earth to be seene, but sande and rolling pebble stones.

Chou Marin d'Angleterre was described by the French as 'barely edible' but used to be brought to Dover market in cartloads.

Tuesday 31
The sea this morning has a silver lining brighter than any cloud, a great dark ship steams westwards along the tinselled horizon under clouds, duvet

heavy, sailing in the opposite direction. Curiously silent after a week of wind and rain.

All the phone calls that come in are the ones I would dearly miss, the demands on me are aggravating, particularly the demands for photographic sessions that will take over a day and leave a record of wrinkles.

Alasdair said he felt Graham had not gone. This idea of life after death frightens me – can you imagine anything worse? Will I find myself sitting here for eternity as the house crumbles to dust around me? The mice chew the purple curtains and the spiders build webs to hold the tattered velvet together, finally birds fly through the roof and one last pane of glass floats in eternity.

I wash the antique saris and they flutter along the line, yellow, pink and emerald.

The sun comes out, the bees with it. An elderly lady came all the way from Canterbury to see the garden with a copy of *Modern Nature* to sign, it was her birthday.

Worked in the garden tidying the front bed. Silent Edward passed by and then ran across the shingle to the sea. March is gone, mad-haring it.

APRIL

Wednesday 1

A clear, cold day. The bees have settled, I cleared the hive – last night I dropped a honey super and they got so angry they chased me up to the house. I extricated myself from the beekeeper's suit with only one sting.

~

HB and Howard arrived at eleven. They brought the papers, the court case of Jason Donovan – Straight as Hell, while the rest of us are Queer as Fuck. If Jason makes any money out of this it can only prove that for years we have laboured against the odds.

The Oscars are on TV and Queer Nation demonstrates. Jodie Foster – also the subject of an outing campaign – receives her Oscar; meanwhile two young fans of Jason who've been to see him in the *Technicolor Dreamcoat* forty-five times say: 'We don't care if he's gay, we love him.'

~

Down the lanes to Great Dixter, HB tickling my head from the back seat. The woods spangled with star-white anemones turning their faces to the sun and primroses, batter bright. We spotted two yellow brimstones, which flew alongside the car on a lane to Bodiam. HB got out and chased them.

At Dixter we bought lavender and rosemary, and later at a supermarket of a nursery *Santolina vivens* – the green kind. Peacock and tortoiseshell butterflies amongst the heathers. Lunch in the fish and chip restaurant at Hastings before one last nursery, Madrona, and home. HB and Howard walked to the Long Pits while I packed for London. It was a beautiful day.

Thursday 2

London.

Our drive along the Sussex lanes seems an age ago. The rain has set in and I walk to the bank in my – HB's – duffle coat with hood well up against the cold. Dr Mark's new pills seem to have got the better of my itching – I slept quite soundly last night, rested for the first time in months.

In the record shop I'm asked about my health – I said it was like describing a will-o'-the-wisp. The tickling drives me to distraction – it covers my whole

109

body from the top of my head to the tips of my toes, it stops all my concentration, makes it impossible to sit and read, to watch a film, I find myself with my trousers rolled up like a grandad paddling on one of those comic seaside cards. I found a great card in Hastings of a boy holding a large stick of pink rock, wearing only the briefest pants, with the title: *What a Sweetie*. Bought their entire stock. Late in the afternoon HB walked with me to Heal's looking for coffee cups. We passed a large shouting lady who looked like Divine.

~

Richard had cleared both his studios for his party to celebrate the five years of his gallery. I found a corner with Tom Kalin, Christine Vachon and HB, smart in his pinstriped suit. Tom had brought rubber trousers, Christine her Geordie girlfriend.

Norman and Nicky like Gog and Magog. Simon Watney with his hair brushed forward over his glasses like a Roman emperor. What did we all talk about? The election? No. Art? No. AIDS? Thank God, no. Mostly old scandal.

Richard banished *EIIR Sex Boys for Sale at Queen's Grocers* as Lady Helen 'Melons' Windsor was expected. Tom regretted there was no sleaze in the salon and certainly no boys as good-looking as the surroundings.

We all left for the Ragam where we had a very happy dinner, with Christine snogging her girlfriend to the surprise of the clientele. A great evening.

Friday 3

Some days start in panic, today was one. The phone rang with a friend asking for a huge sum of money. HB, I think quite rightly, got cross.

An interview at ten with the *Guardian* with a pit in the stomach. I could feel there were going to be no smiles or jokes. The interviewer was so obviously disturbed by *AYOR*.

HB banished by the interviewer – 'I can't conduct an interview when there is someone else in the room' – to the kitchen. He got angrier, packing for Newcastle. She finally insisted that we were left alone, so he is evicted into the rain.

At the beginning of *AYOR* I wrote: '*Those who have not lived this might think the world I'm describing distant.*' My interviewer had all the facts but seemed unable to understand – on a day when a second-string actor was about to be given more damages for a small magazine article than I have received in fees for all my films nearly twice over!

She defended the foolish *Guardian* article that said a gay man was the end of the line, she seemed unable to understand we had children and families.

Had not the slightest interest in the fact that my whole life has been spent under assault.

Only those who have lived with HIV can understand the terrible emotional stress. How can you do the 'right thing'? It gave such ammunition to those who would deny us the right to love, to be celibate was to connive their censure. I sensed that behind all this questioning she wanted me to say 'Yes I do have unsafe sex' so they could put a tombstone over me and, like the confused, trapped in police custody, I almost falsely confessed so that it could all be over and done with. I pointed out that safer sex was only half a decade old. In 1986 there was no talk of condoms in a list of dos and don'ts in the gay press.

By the end of the interview I saw not a chink of understanding and felt either I was mad, or so old I could no longer communicate with those who had grown to adulthood in the 1980s.

~

At five Paul Burston rang: 'I have something to warn you about. The new arts editor of the *Guardian* has decided to commission a hostile article.' That's why I had endured such a negative and upsetting morning, the *Guardian* does have an agenda, the Ides of March come two weeks late. I wonder if he's right.

Saturday 4
Aching, near to exhaustion, I drag the wheelbarrow across the shingle. I've a permanent stitch in my side. Still angry and upset. My paranoia is shared by many of my friends. Paul's telephone call seemed to echo what I had felt so strongly but didn't express. My weakness is my inability to grasp that literate and intelligent people could do anything but agree that this time is all awry.

~

I attack the small canvases with knife and bradawl until the paint bleeds. Little murders. When the author of these scowling canvases has gone the heat will be turned off and all that will be left is the ash. My mind, unable to concentrate, grey as cinders. HB says: 'Finish your sentence, go on, I dare you.'

~

I've swallowed my pills, lurking behind the glass of cold water, I consider a wild and deadly revolt. Dr Mark says most of his patients give up on them and lie about it. Balanced on the moral tightrope, swaying in the hurricane of prejudice, I push on.

~

A large bumble bee sails round the garden in the cold easterly. The sun is still shining.

The old fisherman who, face to the ground, cycles past each and every day, as weatherbeaten as the nineteenth century, has forgotten something and turns back.

~

Nicky rings and says the new arts editor of the *Guardian* has been gunning for me for a very long time, but since he was a sub, no one took him seriously. Journalists at the paper are upset by his attitude – after all, surely there must be other targets for this tabloid treatment. That the *Guardian*, which I read all through my childhood with such relief, should, when presented with serious issues, decide to trash them has made me more confused than usual. I hope this continual sniping doesn't undermine what is left of my 'health'.

Sunday 5

Silent, sunny day, cool to the touch, and I have to leave for London. I would give my heart now to stay at the edge of the sparkling sea. London seems so dark, wearisome, sad – all my troubles are there.

Alan comes at eleven with Gingerbits; they drive me up to London. I put the washing in the machine and walked down to Poon's for lunch.

In Whitechapel a huge poster of John Major had a Hitler moustache drawn on it. Maybe the long dark dictatorial night of the Right is about to end and the country that sold its heart for shoddy goods will wake.

Monday 6

I went up to the Heath and sat in the cold, chatting to old friends. I had no sex – dear *Guardian* readers – as it was freezing. I sat on a tree stump and looked up at the sickle moon and thought how horrible these journalists are, people who make another devalued pound out of our misfortune.

Tuesday 7

Painting the Manchester show at Dicky's. The gardens of Edwarde's Square ablaze with camellias, japonica and spring bulbs – the blackest hyacinth I have seen, only a touch of purple. We eat each afternoon in the local Lebanese restaurant – salads and a delicious cold semolina pudding with nutmeg and pistachio.

Piers has brought a thick quince jam mixing agent to build up the canvases, they have become thicker and simpler, with single words on them.

Wednesday 8

We all go to the ICA to see Connie's films. *North of Vortex* was particularly stylish.

Home via the Rembrandt show – full of low-angled paintings of troubled psyches. Rembrandt included lots of fancy dress as if he were trying to escape the dull reality of the black-and-white puritan fashions.

Thursday 9

Down to Dungeness on the train clutching the *Guardian* article. A horrible picture of me grafted on to the body of Michelangelo's *David*. The *Guardian* should shrink itself to a tabloid instead of disguising itself as a broadsheet of repute. Struggling with HIV in the open is far more difficult than coming to terms with my sexuality in the 1950s. A wasted opportunity for that paper to do something decent. Why are people so negative? The phobias leapt out of the journalist's averted eyes – the interview was so seedy.

Not that I really want to be liked by them – it is something of a relief to escape their conformity.

The garden was ablaze with flowers: white narcissus, wallflowers, hyacinth, grape hyacinth, cilla and bright yellow Siberian wallflowers, my gorse cuttings are sprouting and the elder is bright green with new leaves.

Whitebait at the Pilot in the sunshine to the sound of distant gunfire.

Friday 10

Donny rang to say I was on the cover of the *LA Times* with the headline KING OF QUEER. Over there I'm a gay guru.

AYOR arrived with a rather tacky cover – I threw my hands in the air and decided to enjoy the contents.

~

The bright spring sunshine and warm days did much to dispel the election gloom. The one moment of excitement Lavender Patten's shrew-like face as her podgy little husband was booed, smarmily congratulating his opponent.

Brian came over and said the country had voted for the totally unimaginative.

Saturday 11

HB and Sarah arrived, he put his Rachmaninov piano concertos on and they promptly left, beachcombing.

The sun shone on and on, Gingerbits's hair and the gorse bushes shining as red and gold as can be. We took photos; everyone complained about the *Guardian*.

HB cooked a leek and bacon pie. I turned in and they all took off to the beach for a midnight bonfire.

Sunday 12

Grey clouds rushed in to cover the dawn. I worked in the garden briefly, planting nasturtiums and some red hollyhocks.

By ten it was greyer and cold. I put on my coat to walk to the sea.

Derek left the Sunday papers on the doorstep, pictures of City streets strewn with skyscraper glass.

The maroons went up and the lifeboat launched in the sunlit mist. I wrote my letters, while HB cleaned the kitchen, moved the dungheap and rebuilt the stone circle. Then we took off for lunch at the Pilot and sat outside in the sunlight.

~

I'm cold and very achy, with a headache hovering.

~

Sarah, Gingerbits and HB discussing if they would sleep with someone to Out them. HB says he would sleep with Jason Donovan, Cliff Richard or even Norman Tebbit if it would bring down the Tories, but would need psychotherapy for the remainder of his life.

~

Skate and chips at the Pilot, then HB gives me a piggy-back home.

The rain set in. At four Derek came by and all of us and his cats left for London.

Monday 13

HB says I slept peacefully.

On the number 10 sailing round Hyde Park Corner, the sun comes out.

There is one and a half billion pounds of IRA damage in the City. All is normal.

Tuesday 14

Painting at Richard's all day, much more successful than yesterday – interrupted by too many visitors.

Made an all-white painting called *Jason Death Threat Kiss*. The turpentine in the paint makes me dizzy, causes a bad headache most days. At moments I wish my physical self would evaporate, cease, no more aches and pains. HB tells me to hold on.

Put Rock Hudson newspapers on to a new canvas, then Howard drove me home.

Malcolm Sutherland telephones – asks me if I would like to direct at the Citizens Theatre in the autumn. Tilda as Hamlet?

Wednesday 15
A begging form letter from Stonewall, Michael Cashman Chair, claims to have changed our lives – fiction. I want everything to change, even my life; I sit here waiting, a sitting duck. HB waited with me in the freezing rain for half an hour at the Number 10 stop – he has a terrible cold.

We turn round Hyde Park Corner, wet and cold, only the plants are enjoying this. Monet paints his garden, I paint the wilderness of illness, my sad subject, no *Jazz*.

Thursday 16
Howard and HB drove me down to Prospect. We stopped at a nursery in Faversham, bought cistus, stole sempervivums and then came down here.

Imagine my surprise, the building work had started! The concrete foundation was laid, a huge new pile of stones to locate from the excavation. Brian had worked carefully so that nothing was out of place – the foundations came right up to the wild rose hidden in the grass, I hope it will survive the upheaval. We left for Rye bookshops and more nurseries near Udimore.

I bought a smashing new watering can – perfect for Mrs Jekyll – more plants and back home. HB picked gorse to dye his Easter eggs. The gorse as bright as gold is as warm as the weather is cold.

Friday 17
A very cold easterly, grey flannel sky, the plants none too happy and some scorched by the winds of the last week, particularly the leaves of the garlic and the last white daffs, which barely opened.

April brings these winds each year, the garden is blown about but soon recovers. Many plants have seeded, lavender, lovage, fennel and the Californian poppy, sea kale, mullein, foxglove, dog rose, grape hyacinth, wallflowers, aquilegia, valerian, sea pea, borage. I took the protective wigwams off the sea kale as they were beginning to restrict its growth, planted up the cistus and ornamental artichoke, then, forced back inside by the cold wind, curled up with Jekyll's *Gardener's Testament* and a loud Tchaikovsky trio.

Saturday 18
The blackthorn is out with its white flowers like a whisper of snow. On the path to the beach there are blue-white star of Bethlehem – peep-o'-the-day,

just two plants that struggle into life by the boats at the sea's edge.

Worked building a bank from the shingle excavated to build the new rooms. It was strangely quiet for a holiday – except for a few fishermen working on a boat there was no one on the sands, a vast and quiet emptiness. The only sound the song of a lark lost in the grey mists and my feet clattering on the pebbles as I turned home.

At ten the sun came out and brought back the spring. I took out the dead cuttings from the gorse circle and replaced them. The circle is now complete. A fiery orange marigold has opened, the first of the year. The fennel has seeded itself in the broom – it is spotted with ladybirds like drops of blood. A large white butterfly drinks nectar from a chrome-yellow Siberian wallflower, it fights for its space with a large bumble bee.

Lunch: bread, cheese and an apple. At one the cabbage white was followed by a peacock. Walked with Brian and Sheila to the woods, stumbled across a sea of violets on the way back.

Easter Sunday

Overcast, but very warm. Drove round the coast with Derek looking for a boot fair, we didn't have much luck till on the way back we noticed one behind the Jolly Fisherman. Joanna had a stall with her wild flowers, she gave me lavender and valerian.

We drove back in Derek's old Citroën with the Sunday papers, cruising the boys along the seafront. Derek singing 'Sultry Weather'.

The lifeboat went out at one and the clouds closed in and brought rain. Gingerbits arrived from Canterbury and worked in the garden, moving the enormous mound of stones thrown up by the excavation.

Derek invited us to dinner and cooked a brill.

Monday 20

Cold and grey. Packed Gingerbits off to Canterbury. Derek came by. One chalk-white iris unfurled by the front door as we left Dungeness and drove without a stop back to London, which was warm and sunny.

Lunch at Poon's, a walk through Covent Garden – much too crowded – and tea at Bertaux's. Bought Gertrude Jekyll's *Colour in the Garden*.

Tuesday 21

Number 10 to Richard's. This is my last week painting in the studio as all the work goes up to Manchester next week. I need ten pictures for the show, I've painted seventeen, so there is a choice.

HB in Newcastle. Derek suggests we drive to France.

~

Awful AIDS awareness concert for Freddie Mercury – hairy old rock dinosaurs lumbering across a too-big stage, their bodies oozing out of twenty-year-old fashions, Liz Taylor the only one to put it straight to the audience, some of whom shouted 'get off'.

~

I left for the Heath, even older crowd, mostly OAPs. Delightful shirt-sleeve weather, cool.

Take a deep breath and get ready for the *AYOR* onslaught, there is going to be no good press – I can feel it, I've had more than my fifteen minutes.

Wednesday 22
The *Independent* joined those who condemned Freddie Mercury without looking too closely at the history of the epidemic.

~

In the evening I took Sarah up to Hampstead to interview the cruising boys for a radio programme she is making. They were all quite charming to her except for one middle-aged and shrivelled man in a leather hat. We were home by twelve.

Thursday 23
I've finished the show for Manchester. Howard came and photographed, and we walked in the garden in South Edwarde's Square where we discovered a geranium with the most delicate black-and-purple flowers.

Richard remarked that Howard's sense of colour – a maroon cardigan under a pale green cardigan – was like the colours in the square.

HB playing about. I told him he was the sort of person who if he discovered the secret of the universe would keep it to himself. He tells me he has and he is.

At five Piers ran up the stairs and said that David Hockney was walking up the road outside the studio. I leaned out of the window and shouted down to him. He was very surprised, came up, thinking I lived there.

He'd been to Safeway with his young friend Ian, both of them were here to work on a new opera at Covent Garden. David looked thin and very fragile, time seemed to have shrunk him and his deafness gave him a stoop as if he was taking a curtain call. He talked of little except his deafness – said he had got used to the idea of living in silence, would only miss the music.

He said: 'I've hardly been in London these last ten years, it seems very remote, I never go out, just live in the garden with the two dogs.' He seemed resigned to his unhappiness. When he left I felt alive and rather well.

~

In the evening Nicky de Jongh telephoned and we had supper at the Presto. Much discussion about royalty, sparked by Richard's sinister obsession with blood lines and employment of Helen Windsor.

Nicky could see no English play worth restaging, nothing from America, thought I should acquaint myself with Max Frisch. Perhaps I should write my own play. Nicky is one of my friends who cares for me quietly.

Friday 24
The week has left me feeling very fragile, concentration becomes very difficult. I told HB that I might not be able to work again, he offered to look after me.

Saturday 25
Dungeness. The door in the extension is up. It's very cold and windy here. I'm not feeling at all well.

Sunday 26
HB and Derek left for London at nine, I stayed here. The wind whined around the house all night and very little rain fell.

I wrote letters and painted my landscapes, and became increasingly worried at my inability to concentrate.

Outside, the garden blows back and forth in the gale, looking more battered by the minute. The white comfrey is flowering at the front door, so are the forget-me-nots and borage, the cillas are no longer at their best and are swallowed in a riot of spring foliage.

Monday 27
The wind whined through the night, though the sun came up pale at dawn. Sat eating breakfast watching a wren bob up and down in the sea kale. My back aches intolerably, I can feel the muscles in spasm. Walked round Prospect three times and decided it was better to be alive with all the discomfort. It is just possible to forget all this illness for a moment, then it attacks again.

It's nine and the sun is out full in an overcast sky, the sea a sheet of silver so bright the fishermen's huts are silhouetted black.

Came up to London on the 12.04 and fell asleep. HB bounced around in my dreams. 'Look what I've made you,' he said, flexing his muscles.

Tuesday 28

Slightly fuzzy in the head, I sit at St Mary's – it poured with rain on the way, soaking HB's duffle coat. Discussion with Dr Mark about scent and smell. The clinic is about to move to Bart's – so if my health holds I will not be back here.

An offer from the States to publish *Dancing Ledge*.

~

At Edwarde's Square the rain rattles on the windows. Richard has sold the painting of Madonna to Andy Bell for his birthday. This is good news as I have £500 left in the bank and no particular work, the VAT man and tax man loom, and my head aches and aches. The pictures look very good this morning.

At twelve a television researcher rang to say that Francis Bacon had died, could I say a few words?

Francis said that he was 'optimistic of nothing'. He also said he couldn't understand abstract painters having such dull palettes – surely if you are to paint abstracts your only advantage was colour, look at that horrible maroon in Rothko. Richard said Bacon once pulled a mirror from his pocket and stared at himself muttering: 'So unhappy, so unhappy.'

~

At five I left for home, met HB at the National Gallery to see the new Holbein, there were just two old ladies in the room fascinated by the details in the clothes of the lady with the squirrel; she looked very serious and a little uncomfortable at having her likeness taken.

Stopped off at Shipley's and signed *AYOR* – it was delivered this morning, he has sold five.

Wednesday 29

Most restless night, though I woke quite clear-headed. Piers and I painted *Francis Going to Work*, an homage.

Tilda came for lunch, straight off a camel in Uzbekistan, most of lunch spent discussing the madness of the hyper-rich in America: Mark taking leave of himself; Lynn's charming husband Rob who was scheduled for Apollo and the moon.

~

My interview for the *Observer* was cancelled – they are writing a piece on Bacon instead. Nicky rang to say the ████████ ██████████ █████████ ████ ███ █████████ ████ ████████ ███ ██████ ██ '██████████' – ██ ██ ███ ██ – ███████ ████.

In the evening we went to a rather ominous show at Karsten Schubert's – brightly-coloured trolleys of junk with 'Final Reduction' notices – we all hope the gallery will survive the demise of art.

HB cooked a very stylish toad in the hole and I was in bed by nine.

Thursday 30

Rather restless night dreaming I had lost HB in a Moscow underground station full of refugees. He also had his recurring nightmare about the Kraken. HB, 'look what I've made for you', resembles a muscly Jerusalem artichoke this morning and is eating a huge bowl of cornflakes and little tubs of yoghurt.

It's very cold again today, but Edwarde's Square is a drift of lilac and wisteria, which mists the old houses and smells delicious. I stayed just a few minutes at Richard's and left him, rather gloomily dealing with bills, that he has little resource to pay any longer. 'This is such a waste of energy,' he said. Piers lit the fire against the cold, it roared away. In the square I noticed a pink cherry that had left a perfect circle of fallen blossom on the new-mown lawn.

HB went to the science library and I grabbed some duck and rice at Poon's before walking very slowly round the National Gallery. Ribera's *Lamentation* over the dead Christ and the beautiful Degas painting of the girl holding the back of a chair stopped me short.

MAY

Friday 1

HB's in Newcastle, I'm in Dungeness. It is cold but the sun is out. The house extension is up to the roof, you get a very good idea of how it will look, a very bright, sunny room.

Clement Freud arrived this afternoon with a smashing cake. I'm afraid I was a bit of a culinary desert, I've never cooked, never wanted to, *Yea though I walk through the valley of the shadow of burnt toast*, I find myself hard-pressed to rustle up a decent meal, the kitchen never looked so near a wilderness.

Clement described how to poach an egg with little hope in his heart that I would be able to follow his simple instructions. He put me in a very good mood, better than I have been for weeks. I can't think why, he was only here for an hour. I was the most hopeless host, he even made the tea!

Saturday 2

Played the Henze Violin Concerto to the rising sun. Walked round the house, and round again. Weeded the front bed, planted two lavender bushes and the last of the gorse, but it was too cold to continue working outside.

~

At five Alan Beck arrived with Gingerbits and made a great pasta supper. We watched the *Matthew* of Pasolini as Gingerbits hadn't seen it. Alan told me that the Indian director Ray had enquired after my health, saying he liked my films more than those of any other British director, it seemed so extraordinary. It put me in a good mood, thinking you cannot tell where you will find friends.

They left after the sun set.

Sunday 3

The warm weather is back. The sun hot on the back of my neck, not a breath of wind. The garden bright with wallflowers and the bees humming in them. The back garden is a delight, though there seem to be few irises – maybe I should move them. The rest looks fresher than I have ever seen it and many plants are well established. The elder is over waist high, the dog rose higher,

121

the rosemary covered with blue flowers, as is the ivy-leaved toadflax, the sea kale busy with flower buds, the *Crambe cordifolia* by the kitchen door has turned into a very large plant.

I opened up the hive, the bees have started to build the honeycomb – though it is slightly distorted as the foundation has collapsed. The butterflies are back, a peacock has circled the house all afternoon and a small copper was sunning itself on the thorn blossom. The lizards were out basking on the flower pots.

Read Horace's *Odes*.

Monday 4

I'm feeling much better this morning, better in the head! The rash is still there – I ate an inordinate amount of garlic to see if it would attack the itching, how much garlic dare I eat? HB is totally allergic to it, as frightened as a vampire, it makes him shudder.

The wallflowers are deliciously scented, they waft their fragrance into this room on the sunrise. I wash the sheets and hang them out to dry.

~

A young girl arrived on a white bike, she had cycled from Dymchurch. An odd couple stopped and put stones into a plastic bag, the man laughed, he had the most unpleasant laugh I have ever heard – like a buzz saw, it even stopped the larks singing.

The first swallow of summer looped into the sky. The chalk-white flowers of the sea kale open, so does the star of Bethlehem; the valerian are in bud.

Derek drove me to the station, I arrived in London at 6.15.

Tuesday 5

Piers and Richard managed to muddle all my appointments today, I rescheduled them at the studio. While I waited I dealt with a huge mad correspondence: a pretty boy sent a love letter to my mother; another asked for tokens of love for his two sons; someone sent me a long prison letter; another railed on about sodomy; requests for pictures and autographs; someone asking me to decorate an egg cup. Should I push the whole lot in the bin?

Last night a young man in Hampstead clutching my book. He had come up to sit under the trees as his boyfriend had been diagnosed with HIV and was in hospital after a suicide attempt, he was called Dorian and was from Wales.

This morning my young interviewer was in a similar predicament. He said he had reacted by shutting himself away for two years, reading really boring novels published by the Gay Men's Press.

At four I made a television interview with Richard Jobson, we walked round Lincoln's Inn, he lamented that no one wrote about London like Dickens. We had a great hour, looked into the old hall, then came to the Presto who were all in their Sunday best – Maria had put on lipstick!

HB returned from Newcastle, he brought me sea-softened glass pebbles from Roker and said that for a visual artist I was very unaware of my immediate surroundings – I had not noticed his starfish tattoo, now a month old.

Wednesday 6

Michelle has repainted Bertaux's – the first time since VE day – and mended the clock, which was stuck at 9.45 throughout the winter.

HB bustles about tidying up as I have an interview here at 11.30 – as a special treat I am allowed to stroke his neck, though not a lot before he says 'enough'.

He's gone to the gym in his bright-green pants and red socks, complaining that I borrowed his jacket for the TV yesterday and got it all smoky. He sniffed around this morning and declared that my clothes stank and threw them into the washing machine. I am wearing the suit which has hung for years in the cupboard. I cast jealous eyes over HB's clothes but he won't let me steal them – I wear his clothes on telly and then friends ask him: 'Oh, is that Derek's jacket you're wearing?' I think my soul is wedded to the idea of a Mao suit, something practical, never changing, a blue shirt and trousers. I feel very uncomfortable in new clothes, unless they're HB's.

Walked to the post office in Trafalgar Square and waited and waited. On the way back paused in the bookshops and bought a book on the Madonna and Baudelaire's letters.

Rather frosty interview at Bush House, another of those homophobic ladies they wheel out to interview me. She thought that the virus had made my sexuality obsolete.

Walked back through Covent Garden with HB, who stopped off at a noisy diner for a hamburger.

Off to the Barbican with Nicky. Pity, 'Tis Pity She's a Whore, quite sexless and suburban. The comedy was good, but the rest of it gobbled too fast. The play is really rather unpleasant and becomes quite unhinged in its last minutes. I'm glad that I only ate a lettuce leaf with Nicky before we started, £18 for that and a piss-poor bottle of indifferent white wine. Ned Sherrin in the audience with a muscly Australian lad with a smile as broad as his biceps.

A man crossed over the Pit in the interval and said: 'My HIV doctor has told me to keep out of the sun, but you look great.'

I am sunburnt after a day in the garden and have been all winter. People think I am on a permanent holiday. I am, maybe, I can only thrive on this attention.

Thursday 7

Is this illness imaginary or real? Has it become real after being imaginary?

Ended the day at Waterstone's reading from *AYOR* to an audience of two hundred.

Friday 8

With Howard and HB to Dungeness. HB obsessed with poison, all the way down the M20 describing methods and poisonous pets including a lizard with a poisonous bite and poison dart frogs.

We stopped off in a herb nursery and bought a peppermint geranium, and in a junk shop found a painting of a saint with her eyes turned to heaven.

When we got to Dungeness the extension was being roofed in a very high wind. HB and Howard went to see Janet and her purple orchid while I planted a purple-veined dock, a bright blue comfrey and a cranesbill.

We drove back slowly, I fell asleep in the back of the car.

Saturday 9

Start the Week with Ned Sherrin – Brian Forbes very kind and also amusing about the past; Laurie Pyke got me to sign a piece of paper for her friend, Hibiscus.

Up to Islington to be interviewed about Kenneth Russell – I hope I was coherent. HB said I was amusing on the radio. Ned's shows are quite difficult, as you feel you have to shine at ten on a wet Saturday morning. Emma Freud leant over and said: 'What are we to do with Terence Davies? He hasn't had sex in years. Don't *you* fancy him?'

'Everyone fancies Terence but he likes to think they don't.'

'Well . . .' she continued, 'after I interviewed him we got many requests for his phone number.'

~

Lunch in Poon's – we met Derek's friends Tod and Tim. Tod has bought an Elizabethan bed in strange circumstances: the girl who lives in the flat below him showed him pictures of her father laid out on his deathbed. Tod didn't notice the corpse but fell in love with the bed and she has sold it to him. He said it has a brand-new orthopaedic mattress – that her dad had pegged it on, ugh!

~

Driving to Manchester with Michael and Piers. We stop in Oxford to see my sister and her collection of paintings from my schooldays – she made us a picnic lunch and her charming husband David poured the wine.

Michael had booked us into the ██████████████ hotel – once an insurance building by Waterhouse finished in fine Victorian sepia tiles. The interior had been done over, zhuzhed in decorator's chic, huge draped curtains à la Neil Tennant, the entrance as big as a barn and the bathrooms complete with gold-plated taps.

Michael complained to the manager: a miniature of brandy cost £8 and the telephone five times the going rate – as compensation they left him chocolates on the pillow.

HB arrived and said the bathroom carpet smelt of rot, he got the manager to call a plumber.

Sunday 10

Above and around the hotel the rest of the building was empty. HB mounted an expedition through a window and across a precarious ledge. He climbed the clock tower, found the handle which wound up the clock and immediately put the whole of Manchester at sixes and sevens, leaving each of the faces reading a different time.

Howard found a huge mirror and some Victorian tiles, he was secretly smuggling them back to his room in the lift when the doors opened, revealing a surprised porter carrying a tray of glasses. HB barged past, Howard pressed the button, the porter stepped forward to get in and the doors shut with a crash, sending the tray of glasses flying.

Monday 11

I did two readings from *At Your Own Risk*: a lunchtime sandwich affair at the Exchange to one hundred and eighty people – the organisers turned the same number away – and in the evening to three hundred at Waterstone's. I signed books till my hand fell off.

Tuesday 12

We hung the exhibition and Mark Jordan started to make a video of the work and people's comments. Margi Clarke arrived with her new baby tucked under her arm like a bag of shopping.

In the afternoon we walked through a huge derelict warehouse that used to manufacture rubber gloves and is now a cruising area, knee-deep in used condoms. I recce sexual nooks for later, HB looks for salvage furniture for Prospect.

In the evening a screening of *Edward II* at the Cornerhouse, followed by a question-and-answer session. No one in Manchester was happy about the Cornerhouse, it seemed to draw universal criticism.

Wednesday 13

Back to the warehouse with Howard – he took a whole series of nude shots in one of the burnt-out rooms.

On the way home HB insisted we visit the gents' toilet under the railway arch where his hero Alan Turing, the computer genius, was arrested.

Thursday 14

'Do you like the Pet Shop Boys?' – one Parisian boy to another to discover his sexual orientation.

The Pet Shop Boys were in Manchester to play the Hacienda as part of its tenth birthday celebrations. Neil came to see the show and we ended up chatting in the gallery with Piers – who has seduced a different girl each night, straight boys make out easily, no such luck for the queer boys.

The Pets' protégé Cicero, a hunky little Italian Scot, supports them. Chris said Cicero always got a hard-on when he performed, I looked but saw nothing. The Hacienda was hellish hot, the light show cancelled out the film backdrops and, as usual, it was quite impossible to get through the security – as Michael had given us all different passes.

Neil was dressed in a grey Madam Mao outfit and Chris had a floppy grandad hat. The crowd fainted and applauded, the volume was overwhelming. Everyone had a great time except Michael – who parked his car outside the emergency exit and promptly lost the keys. The AA were called and he managed to bribe them with autographed albums.

Friday 15

Michael had a great time after all – he met a Blackpool boy who had his twenty-first the previous day. He'd obviously been getting in a lot of practice as he couldn't get enough of it. His name was Jason and, as he was writing a paper on my films, I let him interview me; he was stocky and had a ravishing smile, which, said Michael, had reduced Chris Lowe to unusual silence.

~

The Victorian palazzo which is the City Art Gallery bore a huge banner which proclaimed: *Queer – Derek Jarman*. This is surely a world first for civic gay pride. The gallery looked splendid – all the large pictures we have painted during the last months are up, as well as the little landscapes and black paintings that were in Glasgow. Catalogue and postcards finely printed and designed by Jeff, who was wearing a splendid Vivienne Westwood shirt razored with Elizabethan duellists' slashings.

The show opened at six and the gallery goers flooded in – by 6.15 the place was already full.

~

Lynn, Richard, Nicky and Ken all arrived from London. Ken said he loved the show. Nicky wore a bright waistcoat and had his head wrapped in a scarf – he looked like a Pirate from Penzance. He was upset by Matthew Parris's remark in his review of *AYOR*, that I contracted HIV through being homosexual. The review was otherwise complimentary, although he did end by saying that I was completely mad – the sort of thing you might say about any friend. We all took off for a Thai meal. I sat with the former Lady Mayoress, her councillors and the leader of the council. I suggested that the Alan Turing toilet should have a blue plaque, one of them said they were closing down all the old loos for economic reasons, but that one was forcibly reopened each time.

They all came dancing at the sweetest queer nightspot. Manchester has a great red light district with bars like NY NY – the sign in pink neon with a limp-wristed Statue of Liberty, run by tranny barmen with a boy looking as if he had stepped off a tennis court at the door.

Everywhere I go people come up and say 'Hello Derek' – it really is friendlier here. By the end of the evening I was exhausted but very happy.

Saturday 16
We drove across England slowly, through the Cotswolds and across the chalk downs. We diverted off to a nursery – not very good – and on the way back to the main road were engulfed by a terrible stench. HB said: 'I can smell death' and he was right – just in front of us a lorry with a skipful of dead sheep, legs pointing skywards. We overtook, miraculously, as a few minutes later we were stuck in a traffic jam in sweltering heat for thirty minutes, just six cars upwind of the lorry, while a police helicopter circled a crash.

Stopped at Hidcote House – ruined by the National Trust, expensive, uninteresting plants and a pot-pourri shop which my dad would have said smelt like a 'tart's boudoir'. The National Trust tarts up its properties until they are rather like over-cleaned paintings and Hidcote, no exception, has been truly overdone. Fortunately, with HB as our leader, we walked backwards through the exit and saved the £20 admission.

Stopped at the Piltdown pub, with its sinister skull and crossbones sign, for supper. Arrived here in the dark, the meandering drive had taken twelve hours. Beds were made in all the rooms. Howard collapsed, exhausted.

Sunday 17

Drove with Lynn to Rye, picked up Neil and his friend Tom and took them to Great Dixter. The garden was idyllic, summer meadows with buttercups and wild orchids, swallows swooping around the old timber house, building nests in the barns.

On the way back to Rye we passed a house with three hundred or more doves and pigeons perched on its steep roof, none of us had seen anything like it. We planted acanthus and cardamom in Neil's garden. Lynn and I found a rag rug, which we sneaked into the front room to surprise HB – he was thrilled by it.

I bought a jasmine for the new extension – its windows are nearly glazed and the interior will soon be plastered.

The week away has been drenched with sunlight and has brought everything out in the garden: honey-scented sea kale, iris, wallflowers a blaze of mahogany, pink-cushioned thrift, star of Bethlehem, bright-orange Californian poppies; my own cardamom is enormous, as is the lovage. Tall decorative purple and white garlic sway in the sea breeze.

Gingerbits made two planters out of driftwood with detailing in old cork floats and turned as pink as a prawn in the sunshine.

A strange young man from Potsdam appeared – in spite of endless telephone calls saying I didn't want him here, he actually asked to stay the night! This invasive manner seems extraordinary. My mother would have said he had been badly brought up, perhaps privacy in Germany was abandoned, was squatted there first by Herr Hitler and then by Erich Honecker, for all he knew I could have been ill.

I made him tea and put him back in a taxi to Rye.

We've had a great day.

Monday 18

God is an atheist.

Tuesday 19

The sun beats down. The extension is being painted black. Brian came with some finials for the roof, a detail I had thought of asking him about.

A letter from the grandson of the Richardsons – who built the cottage in the nineteen hundreds. Did the house still stink of piss and boiled cabbage? He says Grandad Richardson was a bit of an old sod, he always appeared angry. His other grandfather, Jerry Bates, built most of the cottages. He sent me a photograph of the first garden being built in 1905.

At four in the afternoon I keeled over and went to bed, shivering from too much sun. Restless night.

Wednesday 20

I stayed in, very drained with a nasty cough. A good script on Wittgenstein by Terry Eagleton was sent to me by Tariq Ali.

My bees nearly swarmed, but then decided against it and went back into the hive.

In bed by nine.

Thursday 21

I'm up at 6.30 brewing a cup of tea. I'm right off my food, find it difficult to eat cornflakes, toast; cough, sore mouth.

The bees swarmed, it was spectacular: they landed on the broom a couple of yards from the hive – all afternoon bees were flying about in a tiswas, five came into the bedroom. Gary, who is glazing the windows, has five hives and lost a couple during the winter, he came by in his truck and put the swarm in a cardboard box, packed the lot of them up and they were gone.

Friday 22

I've noticed the length of my diary entries reflects the state of my health.

~

Opened the hive and replaced one comb that had warped, in spite of the swarm of thousands of bees the hive still seemed crowded.

Clement Freud rang and faxed me his article, his recipe for me was a French Onion Soup from the old Paris Market.

Clement Freud's dish for Derek.

A special onion soup.

This is called soup à l'ivrogne – drunkard's soup – and used to be available to home-going revellers in the cafés of Les Halles – the vegetable market – before the developers came. For two people.

Thinly slice a good-sized onion and fry the pieces in 2oz butter until they are soft and begin to colour. Pour into the pan half a bottle of best sparkling wine or worst champagne – such as you get in quarter bottles when flying Club Class to Brussels. Heat and decant into a French Marmite pot, cover the top with a thin slice of Camembert cheese strewn with toasted white breadcrumbs, place in a mark four oven and when the top is crisp remove it and cut it in half, decant the liquid into soup bowls and anoint with the baked cheese covering.

Clement's article brought one letter that remembered Mrs Monger's toenails – the apple slush in the huge cauldron with the pips and grated cores that I've written about in every volume of autobiography since the year dot. My letter writer was under the illusion that they were Mrs Monger's husband's toenails – the odd-job man and stoker of boilers at Hordle. He asked: 'Do you remember the 4 o'clock buns?' 'Bun o'clock' would be called.

~

Walked with Gingerbits and Alan to the Light Railway Café – cod and chips – and, spotting Derek's white Citroën, came back via 'Bohemia'. His garden is looking splendid, especially the blue poppy.

Derek wanted to know what we had been up to – conducting a video relationship, Gingerbits and I have become experts in the patter: 'Shove that big cock up me' or 'So you want that big cock up your tight arse?' 'Tighten that arse.' This is the vernacular of Jeff Stryker, the most famous and exquisitely boring sexual mechanic.

On Derek's television was one of those forties war films where everyone speaks so fast but clips their words so the film editor can get his scissors in. I wonder if other European languages in film have changed as much as ours.

Back at Prospect Gingerbits kept us laughing as Alan made us supper. Aren't we all secret nellies with tough-as-fuck exteriors? I asked what happened when HB's gang stole the mirror from the derelict building in Manchester, who was the first to zhuzh their hair? They all went into a derelict washroom and saw HB adjusting his hair, then he got his claws round the mirror and ripped it clean off the wall.

There was also a dyke room-cleaner with a gravelly voice; she barged into Gingerbits' bathroom, he dived under the bubbles so only his muff was showing, no longer ginger but scarlet. He said: 'Us girls should stick together' and she retreated.

Saturday 23

My temperature shot up to 102° last night, this morning I lay on the bed listening to all the little noises as HB goes about his work. It is so quiet and peaceful, all the bright flowers are dancing on the breeze. Californian poppies of every shade of yellow and scarlet. The first blue cornflowers are out and also the burnet rose. Big bumble bees cruise around the purple and white alliums which sway about on their long stalks, like grannies' woollen balls. There are a hundred coppers or more on the honey-scented sea kale, red admirals, peacocks and the biggest, furriest tiger moth caterpillar asleep in the *Crambe cordifolia*.

HB and his gentle friend Garry have gone off on the miniature railway to Hythe, to do the shopping. HB returns, calls me 'tickle fascist' – I can never get enough of my head being tickled – throws everything out of the kitchen and starts to prepare the walls for painting by scrubbing everywhere with sugar soap.

In bed early.

Sunday 24
The thunderstorms we were promised never materialised though I was kept awake most of the night by my cough and temperature sweats.

Half an hour before the sun rose, in the first white light of dawn, the shingles are a ghostly bleached bone, grisaille silhouetting the grey of the shrubs and black of the broom, a silent light unshattered by colour.

I rang up the six queens in 'Bohemia', got Derek who promised to get me Listerine for my raging mouth, temperature 100° again. I asked HB to bring me a choc ice, but it was painful to eat.

We had the briefest quarrel about ringing a journalist. 'You promised,' he said. HB very firm on promises. They'll be queuing to get their fucking recorders going on my deathbed.

~

My first pink dog rose came out at lunchtime and hours later was covered in flowers.

~

Alasdair came over for tea. He's been dead broke but Graham's family gave him all of Graham's clothes – Alasdair now sports the most stylish underpants by Calvin Klein and socks to match. We ate a little before he left for 'Bohemia'. He's going to start despatch riding on Tuesday.

~

I'm piling into the Wittgenstein biography. Bed early.

Monday 25
The sun is so bright it hurts my eyes, the butterflies love it and so do the bumbles and sand lizards. HB and Garry go for a walk. They have a secret

language like that chirping sound cats make. The Bohemians came by, beachcombing, it is scorchingly hot. Richard worries on the phone – says that he has had good feedback from the Manchester show, maybe sold a painting.

Brian comes over and worries about the monument to Bomber Harris, why didn't the RAF sort out something more abstract? A bomber crew for instance. There is no doubt that Dresden was a disaster, but the bomber crews who bore the brunt of it deserve some public recording. Dad was always rather short when Fighter Command came up and not one for Battle of Britain films, too polite to say anything. The popular heroes remain the boys from Biggin Hill. I have a 'graduation' photo of dad with Harris. I feel there should be some public record of their part in the war.

Tuesday 26
Brian the builder happy to wipe out the Artex roof finish in the extension – I call it impetigo. My mouth so sore I had no breakfast.

Long taxi and train ride to St Bart's. Nice spruce rooms, Dr Mark's has sunlight. Everyone finding themselves around. We arrived at two and left at five, as the pharmacy is very slow. Mark says to stop work – that's how I interpreted it. The mouth is a vicious HIV-induced attack of gingivitis. The X-ray – it took three goes to get it right – showed up my chest infection. An extraordinary selection of people in the X-ray department – bent stooped 'clerk' as bald as a vulture, in a worn suit jacket; large, beaten-about bearded wino; a selection of very old couples dressed for winter, very quiet and lost in the hubbub of ringing phones; a cross old lady called Florence wearing a bonnet who bobbed up and down at the desk; the Ediths and Bills fascinated me, their struggle to maintain a threadbare gentility under the assault of the last years of their lives, values and pockets made me sad. I imagined them as young men joining up in 1939 and their vibrant young girlfriends and wives struggling to make do with hope in their hearts – you could see that hope betrayed.

HB wonderful all day. He held hands, said I was his duty.

Wednesday 27
Ill all day today.

Thursday 28
Kept poor HB awake coughing all night. In the end he got up at four a.m. and walked to the all-night chemist for cough mixture.

This morning he was growly, everything I did annoyed him. He growls if he doesn't sleep properly, 'let sleeping dogs lie'.

My temperature is still 99° plus, though the sore mouth is on the turn.

Friday 29

Saw Dr Mark who said I was stoic, this cheered me up. My lungs are a bit shot up, I'm going in again tomorrow to see if there is PCP or TB lurking. My mouth is less sore and I'm sweating myself back to normal.

I feel a shadow crossed my path this week.

Saturday 30

Ken said he met my old friend Dom Dom, 'Quite huge.'

'Like Keith Milow?' I asked.

'No, much bigger.' He's about to take his bar exams. Ken said Dominic's dad Robyn Denny was horrified when he found he was seeing me when he was eighteen.

Dad danced, so Dom Dom took him to the Subway – the wildest gay bar London ever had – to show him what a good time he was having. Dad didn't get his point of view.

Dom Dom is living in Cheyne Walk so everything is not a disaster.

~

Long conversation about Wittgenstein, how do you make images resonate? They can't be illustrative, there's not much point in making a film 'about' something, much better to pay for a TV ad for the *Tractatus* and leave it at that. Personally I don't have the mind to approach the book, but its incomprehensible density attracts me, particularly that which cannot be spoken.

Wittgenstein said there was no such thing as a good British film and never would be, and here we are, making a beginning. What about putting him in as the hero of a Western? Of course, I love the idea that Ludwig hated the Bloomsbury set and their threadbare veneer of culture.

~

Ken went to lunch with all the Stonewall luvvies in Narrow Street. One of the spokespersons for the luvvies' club said that it 'would be disrupted by openness'. It's a pity that when closed shops were made illegal closed minds weren't outlawed as well.

The luvvies got drunk and stoned, and clucked on their various perches. In the roof garden sunset the luvvies fall over themselves to get down a skylight, as a helicopter – they thought from the *Sun* – circled above for the Outing photo of the late twentieth century. Drag them screaming from their closets and finish them. Maybe the *Sun* would have done us a favour. 'They were tripping over each other,' said Ken. 'You would have died laughing.'

~

I am back at the hospital and Dr Mark says I am much perkier. We talk of the Wittgenstein film.

Lunch at the Presto where Carla talks of Madam Bruna: she who worked there for years, cursing the customers, clattering around in her orthopaedic shoes, looking like an Easter Island statue bent double with age. She'd tap her fingers and look at the floor over her gold bifocals, waiting for an order with such obvious impatience, her iron-grey beehive as old as the cardigan hanging from her shoulders. Madam Bruna got her P2 and the next day, after all those years, disappeared. She didn't say goodbye, or even send a postcard.

~

I've got the *Tractatus*, everyone looks impressed, like a vicar with his hymn book.

~

HB is tapping away at *Narrow Rooms*. We are thinking of making it here in a studio, give it the beauty of lighting.

~

I am much better.

Sunday 31

My cough cleared out in the night. I dreamt all night of writing a book on colour, not scientific or in any way academic, free floating through the spectrum. Maybe the *Tractatus* unlocked it.

~

David Lewis came at 10.30 and we drove to Dungeness, caught up, as he has been making *The Gay Man's Guide to Safer Sex* – which stars Julian's very young American boyfriend, Aiden Shaw, and Phillip Williamson who was in *Angelic Conversation*.

Dungeness was a riot of blossom, the poppies a wild masquerade, valerian and huge bunches of clove-scented pinks. The rain which poured down put several inches on all the plants, most of them into bloom, the inky blue aquilegia, lovage, a new crop of alliums white and dusty pink, the wallflowers are over but the foxgloves are marching, purple in the bright-yellow broom, thousands of them. Splendid.

After lunch with Eileen in the Light Railway Café, we all drove to Great Dixter.

MAY

English Nature have planted the stinking hawksbeard in patches in the back garden. I had my first bath in the new bathroom, the extension is nearly finished, waiting for the glass in the large windows and the electricity tomorrow.

JUNE

Monday 1

Dawn came in a great, grey, dewy mist, it drizzled all night, the grey washes an intense colour into the garden. The poppies bow their heads, the mullein caterpillars are back, bright green-yellow and black, there are metallic blue lackeys on the roses and my friendly tiger moth caterpillar is now very large.

~

The glazier came after lunch and then we drove into Rye and bought a corduroy-covered Colonel's chair. The electricity will be connected on Thursday and Brian says that he'll be out before the weekend.

~

The garden is a riot of flowers, the yellow horned poppy is out and there are hundreds of seedlings along the road that have sprung up from seed scattered last autumn.

Tuesday 2

London. A cheque for £700 from *Angelic Conversation*, that film is making me more money than any of the others. Walking to the paint shop, Emma Freud zapped past on her way to the hairdresser's, her front room is also pale, clear yellow.

Wednesday 3

Dr Mark happier at the hospital.

HB and I combed London for floor coverings, paint and other household necessities; we were completely unsuccessful. The weather was hot and stuffy.

I saw Richard, he is as happy as a hare – made four sales from the Manchester show.

HB worked very hard all day to finish editing *Narrow Rooms*.

Asleep by nine.

Thursday 4

Mint tea with Carolee at Bertaux's. Carolee described the fire that spread

Rainbow's end. Monday 24 November 1992

Silence. October 1986

Landscape. 1991

Landscape. 1991

Blood. March 1992

Dead Sexy. 1993

Do Lalley. 1993

We lit a large candle for HB. Chartres Cathedral. Thursday 27 May 1993

Monet's garden, Giverny, *a mass of iris, peonies and dew-laden roses.*
Thursday 27 May 1993

across the bay in San Francisco: how a little puff of smoke became a raging inferno. She sat on her balcony catching black ashes from the burning houses that floated past her like bats in the twilight – part of a map of Russia, people's accounts, fragments of the classics. How the catastrophe seemed so far away in the stillness of the night with the lights twinkling on the bridges.

She'd had a great time in Hull and Wolverhampton. London's air, she said, was worse than LA's, the traffic snarling around its old-fashioned elegance.

Carolee warm with kindly lines on her face, much smiling, a great glow of friends. I feel much better, all bright gifts of strength and purpose. I wobble down the street, breathless but happy. Carolee suggested I took up Helmholtz for colour, none of the bookshops had heard of him, the art shops the most clueless. I did find Wittgenstein on colour and Newton's *Optics*.

~

Sat in the window seat of the Amalfi on Old Compton Street, sad Neapolitan music, the drizzle falling in barely formed puddles. The elderly waiter seemed more than usually sympathetic, brought little treats, garlic oil, amaretti.

The man opposite made it difficult for me to leave, I had to edge round him. I think he was cross that the waiter had brought his rum baba over to me by mistake.

One ravishingly handsome boy in jeans and black T-shirt, jet-black hair, youthful vigour, standing on the street corner laughing, made me shrink even further into my ill health.

HB thinks Old Compton Street the second worst in London after Carnaby Street. I'm still in love with it. Soho, though it changes, has a resilience and the tourist shops are the first to bankrupt. I bought vino santo and biscotti di prato in Camisa. I'm determined to pull myself back to eating even if it costs a fortune to get my strength back. Why should one be defeated by a pneumonia?

Met Sandy on the way to the market with her friend Alfie with his swashbuckling moustache.

~

HB says: 'Tickly tickly tickly legs' without looking up from his typing.

I ask, 'How do you know?' He says he has the hearing of a god. HB likes to be kissed on the back of the neck, the keys of his little laptop patter in the still of the afternoon.

Nearly at the end of Ray Monk's Wittgenstein book.

~

In the evening went to the Goethe Institute with John Maybury and saw

Cynthia Beats' beautifully observed film with Tilda called *The Party*. Wonderfully eccentric Simon Turner played the piano. Dave Curtis, Peter Wollen, Diana Mavrolean, all there.

We ended up in D'Aquise, telling funny stories about Ken Russell, as Tilda contemplated playing Lady Chatterley.

Friday 5

Drove to Dungeness late with Howard. We kept missing our turnings and ended up crossing Kent along Straight Street from Canterbury. The old chair looked frozen at the back of the house though the garden is thriving in the damp. The house is at sixes and sevens, little piles of objects everywhere and everything powdered with plaster dust. HB is painting the kitchen and we are planning a journey, where?

Paul, the lighthouse keeper from Portland Bill, arrived with photos of the Ness and many tales. Photos of his great-grandmother and great-grandfather at Spionkop. His grandfather, the old rat catcher, who built the houses and ran the post office and gave a fortune away helping the fishermen through hard times.

At lunchtime we took off to Starvecrow Lane. Howard took two and a half hours looking round the nursery and came back with a huge box of plants. I fell asleep in the car and woke up with a cricked neck. We drove on to Hastings for a meal. Hastings had a washed-up charm in the drizzle, the shutters up, even the amusement arcade was empty, only a handful of disconsolate foreign students wandering about. There was nothing in the junk shops and we left at six for home. HB quietly working, putting the new room in order. The first music in the room John Adams, which HB liked and to which he happily painted into the night.

Saturday 6

It rained all night and HB found two very bedraggled swarms from the hive. We rang Gary who came and put them into a super and then opened the hive. It is packed with honey and in spite of the three swarms is also full of bees. I've cleaned out some of the queen cells and as we did so a young princess hatched before our eyes, sleek as an arrow; we left her in the hive. HB took the beeswax and with turpentine and soap brewed up a furniture polish.

Gary suggested we bought a new super to give the bees more space, so we took off down the misty twisty marsh lanes to Mersham, where an amusing bee-man gave us the bits and pieces we needed. We carried on over the hills past Ashden to Hythe, where I bought two grand chairs for the west wing.

Simon Watney arrived. HB made spaghetti and salad aux herbes de Dungeness. Simon said he'd taken a spade through his life like a clump of hostas; he had a new job and was going to let his flat in Camden become a home instead of an annexe of the Terence Higgins Trust. The awful devastation of AIDS has left everyone disillusioned and with little fight – though he, like myself, has found great strength in the young: Chris Woods, Keith Alcorn, and Edward King.

~

Walked up to the Long Pits – the dainty Nottingham catchfly in flower, pink and chalk-white, found an oak eggar caterpillar and brought it back on a mushroom for HB to inspect.

~

By lunchtime the sun was peeping through and then came out in a glorious day. The bees were still troubled – I found two dead princesses with little clusters of itinerant workers, I removed them and put the new super in.

~

At three Diana Mavrolean arrived with friends, they painted and photographed the garden.

The night ended in gossip about the Princess and her unhappy marriage, which has swept like a septic tide through the newspapers. Diana Mavrolean maintains the royals are going, undermined by Mr Delors and Chancellor Kohl, aided and abetted by Rupert Murdoch, who must hate them as much as any Australian. She said she couldn't care less for the royals but felt sorry for both of them as people. The intuitive Charles forced to be a macho king while his brother is allowed to be theatrical. Diana, who seems to have grown up through these difficulties, perched at the top of a loveless social precipice. And here we are carefree.

Sunday 7

The foghorn boomed through the night in a dense mist, which left the garden sparkling with dewy spiders' webs. As the sun came up the mist glowed an iridescent white. For an hour you could see only a few yards, though it quickly cleared, leaving the garden with a myriad diamond drops, the poppies with their hairy leaves were strings of pearls. At seven one of the washed mauve opium poppies opened.

I sat by the front door wafted by the clove-scented pinks, it is an idyll: *et in Arcadia ego*. I am so in love with the place please God I see another year.

~

I prepared the frame for cuttings and marked out the next phase of the garden. My stomach is settling, my cough disappearing, but sunlight is devastating – I wear a hat as much as I can, as within ten minutes the AZT brings on a terrible irritation.

~

The mist swirled in again so I worked on the house cleaning the floors and polishing the furniture with HB's beeswax polish.

~

Billy arrived at ten with some undercoat that looked like Heinz tomato soup. While he worked HB painted the workbench with woodworm killer – I'm a bit worried as it is very toxic, but the bench is shot through with little holes. The bees have settled and bring back three types of pollen, deep-yellow, mid-yellow and almost white, the green pollen has disappeared – it must have been the crambe that produced it.

~

Peter Fillingham and his friend Stephen the foundryman call by. Peter had been to see Dicky who had offered him a show and bought his sculpture of a lorry – he's about to make a giant Lada. I've missed him as he has had a scholarship in Paris from the French Government for most of the year. He's moving to Wales, where he has a caravan and looks after a five-foot water monitor that was found in a field, HB wants to bring it to Dungeness. I'm not too fond of giant lizards with a poisonous bite and teeth as sharp as broken glass.

Besides art talk, Peter has one of the most adventurous minds. He talked about the Englishness of Dicky's taste – he bought a Duncan Grant yesterday, a Steer last December and has several late Sickerts.

Peter's mother is Indian and he has inherited dark and smiling eyes and a Gandhian calm, he is the good samaritan, always brings gifts – often his mother's hot pickle. Peter is the sort of man who if he had money would make bad investments. He was thrilled by the west wing. He and Stephen stayed for an hour, then left for home.

Monday 8

The foghorn heralded the dawn, I was up before the sun and watering. As I opened the back door a cloud of little yellow moths flew up, so many they caused the lost racing pigeon, who sits on the roof, to blink. The sun burnt away the mist very quickly.

~

The royal marriage takes over, is everyone obsessed by them? The Press Complaints Commission went theological and talked of an 'invasion of the soul'. Soul, I thought, was so elusive and hidden that was an impossibility. The Archbishop, Canterbury Charismatic, popped up and complained of the effect it would have on the children. I wondered about *his* effect – moon-faced and podgy, a clerical Bunter, the school bully in a mitre of lurex mattress ticking, a lifeguard in the sea of faith. Faith, I suppose, stops thought.

~

The mist rolled in, the foghorn carried on to midday then fell silent in a blazing sunlight.

~

I weeded the front garden, planted out the iris, took cuttings from the sage. Billy painted the windows at the back a bright yellow. After he left, silence overwhelmed me.

I watched the cabbage whites dance in the magenta valerian. The second opium poppy opened, this a deep reddish mauve or morve; I like morve – a dying nineteenth-century pronunciation. Opium poppies shed their petals as you blink, their dusty colours almost a little sad, dreamy, contrasted with their scarlet cousins and the harlequinade of their Californian relatives. The most delicate is the yellow horned poppy, even more fragile than its narcotic brother.

Violet intuition, opiates, the violet hour, Jean Cocteau born in that mauve decade fascinates, the Compte Ferson's jade opium pipes, the opium view from the Villa Tiberio high on the cliffs at Capri – the little boats sailing so far below. I have smoked opium only half a dozen times, its acrid smell sweet as silence, a danger in the dreaming.

~

The sun is reflected a dazzling pale orange in the sea. It is very quiet.

Tuesday 9

I'm invaded by the lost pigeon – every time I leave a door open it's in the house shitting and then panics and crashes into the window; it's been here three days too many. These pigeons are a hazard in Dungeness, they all are exhausted, and end up eaten by the hawks and foxes. Billy says he sent one back, it cost him £23 and the owners didn't even send a postcard to thank him. I can't imagine anything odder than pigeon fanciers, though I could fancy pretty well anything – even Peter's water monitor. Pigeons are so dumb – I shoo it away, it circles the house and lands at my feet again.

~

I planted out the nasturtiums, took santolina cuttings and dug in another clump of iris before nine. The sun's up, the mist has cleared, all goes well.

~

Long conversation with Tariq Ali about Wittgenstein: abandon Cambridge; abandon narrative – except for Wittgenstein telling his life straight into the camera – abandon Moore and Keynes; keep the ninety-year-old Russell with his radical politics; bring in Dora in the thirties, hopeful, free-loving; make Paterson a boy in love with Wittgenstein and his motorcycle; hold the whole thing together with Wittgenstein in his empty room, talking to himself, philosophies of silence that cannot be understood, only felt; extreme austerity, the visualisation must mirror the work – no competition from objects.

~

Howard, HB and my niece Kate arrive. Kate brought a huge fruit cake, we made tea and explored the verges – the restharrow is in flower, a pinky rose with sticky grey leaves. We all caught the lizards that have taken up residence in the santolina, they are green and brown, some speckled, some with red bellies, they don't seem to mind being handled.

We drove off to Appledore and found many metal containers, old buckets and a rusty iron bell to plant the jasmine in, also a very heavy hoe with a wooden handle that had to be de-wormed. HB bought *Salvia guaranita* – a sage with flowers that hang like bells the colour of a night sky.

The thundery close weather made us all most sleepy.

~

Howard, HB and Kate have gone to the woods, leaving me alone with the Janàcek violin concerto. We've had a wonderful afternoon, the only sadness the thunderstorm that deluged Lydd did not come here so the garden is bone dry.

Wednesday 10

HB is searching through his Fred Perrys. I ask him how many he has. 'Enough.' I've secretly counted them, there are forty-three! Today's is a lovely green, very special, some red socks appear, he's off to Newcastle to swim with Freddy the Dolphin: 'Maybe Freddy will drag me to a watery grave.'

~

A letter arrived which began: 'This may come as something of a shock' – a request for £3300 from our landlords for repairs to the building. I wrote them a very angry letter as many of the tenants here will not be able to pay. I expect to see a flurry of flats on the market and richer, less interesting neighbours. You might have thought they would spread the load over a few years but no, they sacked the caretaker, sold his flat and let the building fall apart. After ten years of neglect we are to foot the bill or be put on the streets.

~

Walked down to Ian Shipley's and bought books on colour for my Harlequin book. London is full of unpleasant surprises, I can hardly cross the road without someone demanding an article. Help. Back to Dungeness tomorrow and away from all of this.

~

The day is fresh and sunny. I'm very happy, on my way to St Bart's.

The waiting room was an agony – I hate people coughing and spluttering all over each other. The nurses were discussing uniforms, perhaps pink? Shocking pink? Pink pyjamas and thirties nighties? I said: 'Why don't you invent your own? A touch of Florence Nightingale with a *Star Trek* tunic. Have a competition for the most originally dressed nurse.' They didn't think Bart's would approve.

Dr Mark is going to make a final assault on the molluscum spots on my face with his liquid nitrogen gun – sprucing me up for the Penguin Books publicity photo. He said: 'I must keep a closer look on you.' He says the hydrocortisone tablet gives me twenty five per cent of my energy. I have to carry a little card: *I am on steroid treatment which must not be stopped*.

We did an extensive burn-up on the molluscum on my face with a new pencil-thin freezer. I came away feeling well stung.

I waited for nearly an hour in the boiling-hot queue for the pharmacy, gave up and went over to the Charterhouse to see Robert Medley. His hip operation has been a success, though he leans heavily on a walking stick. He was interested in the colour book, mentioned the red carpet put down by Clytemnestra for Agamemnon, an act of hubris.

We ate an excellent melon and talked about his new picture, a portrait of the Charterhouse reverend. 'Everything's closing in,' he said, 'My sister is now in a sheltered house and consequently I am no longer able to go to Yorkshire.'

~

Julian called by – he's just returned from visiting his young Canadian friend Jamie, the twenty-year-old with all the ironmongery set in his tender parts. Julian said he had more conversation with Jamie's father – a professor at the university. A visit to San Francisco and trips round the bars left him more than relieved to return home. America's getting more selfish as the decades pass – so fucked-up no one knows anything different, a little common sense could solve most of its problems.

Friday 12

I loaded up very early with fruit and veg from the charming blonde girl in Berwick Street Market.

Tony Peake wonderful company and listened to me 'wittering on' – as HB would say – as we sped down the road to Dungeness in his Citroën.

Billy had finished painting another side of the house.

Mark Booth appeared ten minutes after we arrived, we discussed the new book.

Had fish and chips at the Light Railway Café, and then I was alone here with the wind roaring around the house in the bright sunlight.

~

The sun set behind the tower of Lydd church in a blaze of pink and purple, and the clouds turned to indigo in a full moon which sailed through them into the night.

Put John Adams's *Harmonium* on the hi-fi and read Horace's *Odes* louder and louder till they were also sailing, like the moon, across the iridescent music.

> *To grovel in prayer because the mast is groaning*
> *Under the gale is not my style; I will not*
> *Haggle with heaven: 'God save*
> *My bales from Tyre and Cyprus lest they go*

> *To swell the greedy sea's collection!' I just*
> *Bob through the storms of the Aegean, safely*
> *Tucked in my rowing-boat,*
> *Sped by the weather and the Heavenly Twins.*

Saturday 13

Up at 5.30 this morning. Worked for two hours transplanting the iris and planting the exquisite small climbing rose I bought at the Madrona nursery, its colour (an orange), scent and shape – it looks as if it has been pinched – are all very unusual.

Amnesia stalks me. I forgot my razor – I've never done that before – and now I've opened a CD case of *Fearful Symmetries* and it's empty. I've searched through the house with no luck. I phoned HB in Newcastle to see if he knew where I'd put it. How could he? At his suggestion I found it in the box of the CD that was playing.

Went to Rye with Alan Beck, we searched for Virgil's *Eclogues* in the bookshop but found instead *In Praise of Folly* in one of those Folio Society editions which I used to think quite dreadful. But time passes and it's now possible to look at Liz Frink's inappropriate illustrations for Horace's *Odes*.

When I was seventeen I built an enormous plaster and wood sculpture of a Golem that Robin Noscoe, my art master, christened 'The Frink'. From that moment anything too large or too grand was called a Frink – 'I see you're Frinking again Derek.' The art school – a wooden hut with an old metal coke stove – was shrouded in potter's dusty clay. We had a haphazard collection of books and a very good collection of postcards, which Robin kept up to date.

From thirteen to seventeen I painted every day, sometimes in all my spare time – flowers, self-portraits, other invented pictures, one of a bus queue which my mother loved.

One afternoon I painted some tachiste work – forty canvases for which I was severely punished – Robin said I had used the entire term's paint ration. I tried painting a copy of Rubens's *Silerius*, all fleshy pink, and ended up painting several canvases in tones of pink. In the eye of memory they still seem startling.

The post-impressionists ruled my childhood, particularly Van Gogh and Gauguin, you were going to live the life of an artist: exiled, knocking back cordial glasses of lime-green absinthe. The reality for a Dorset schoolboy was much different: trips to Beauclair chapel, reproductions of Nash's *Inspiration of the Megaliths*, Coventry cathedral and more Frinking. Truth, above all truth to material in anything we made – homely pots glazed with wood ash. I went through a Rouault phase – who remembers him now? – of stained-glass abstraction, a cubist phase scrambled with the late Braque's still lives. I got lost in the writing of Paul Klee, read *The Cloister and the Hearth* at thirteen and Delacroix's *Journals* at sixteen. The smell of turps hung around me like an expensive French perfume – the other boys laughed.

I got prizes for art: books on Van Gogh, impressionism, and a large Phaidon volume on French medieval paintings from my first sale. I fell in love with the Avignon Pietà, I adored the translucent sap-green cerulean blue. We painted on old boards, bits of timber, anything except canvas – which was too expensive – with 'Georgian oils' and sometimes the real artist oil colour, which stretched the purse to breaking point.

All the paraphernalia of the artist: the easel – I was given an old studio easel by my aunt Pegs – drawing board clips, charcoal in spindly sticks, a blowpipe and fixative that smelt of peardrops and blew you dizzy, the palette – I never used one but possessed one like a coat of arms. My father complained that I pressed the toothpaste out by the top of the tube, my paints were always in a similar mess. I was in a hurry, the linseed oil and turps would congeal in the jam jar, the forgotten brushes set solid. Robin pulled me up for my slapdash habits. I was no technician, I experimented and made my own pigments, which set like chalk, and drew on the sides of old cardboard boxes. There were self-portraits and still lives with glasses, very meticulous, silvery.

We hung the summer exhibition in the squash courts. I had a wall with twenty paintings, their sizes dictated by old frames I bought in junk shops in Watford. In the same shop I found an etching of a potato picker by Millet for 3s.6d. We did not study the Old Masters, they were closed off from us, we were Modern then – we learnt the inventions of the century without understanding: collage, surrealism, cubism, rayonism, tachism, isms ruled the fifties school and were neatly stored in the postcard drawer. What ism might I become?

~

The garden is ablaze with poppies and cornflowers, the extension complete. I settle in and read Horace. Alan is a classicist, knows it all, both he and I lament the passing of a classical education in the hands of Mrs Thatcher's Gauleiter of the eighties. I wish my childhood Latin lessons had been these poems rather than Caesar's *Gallic Wars*.

Sunday 14

Opalescent dawn of sunlight, mist and dew, refracting rainbows.

I'm up at five, planting iris and rue. I do just a little each day to conserve myself, though these early mornings are the effect of the cortisones, for once a pleasant side effect.

Splash in the bath, wash the towels and curtains peacefully, brew porridge, squeeze fresh orange juice, delicious hot Assam tea – I've stopped drinking coffee as it was giving me stomach cramps.

~

A bright-green lizard wanders in and crosses the floor in little fits and starts.

~

Derek arrives with the Sunday newspapers and peppercorns. He likes the west wing, says it's cosy – it is – the house can now make visitors welcome when before they had to squash up on the sofa or sit on the floor.

~

Another poppy has opened, magenta as a Spanish dancer; these poppies are so transitory, some that open in the dawn have shed their petals by noon. The tall opium poppies are only here for a week, fluttering in the sea breeze.

~

Nicholas and Ken came to tea with a huge box of biscuits. Nicky lies in the sun by the beehive and enthuses about the garden – I promise him a packet of Prospect seeds.

~

They go to the beach, I ponder a trip to London for the evening. My chest aches a little, maybe I shouldn't – it is very hot, too hot.

All the day's work is brought in, it's six o'clock, solitude and a warm west wind rolling through the ochrous grasses. The hawk is hovering by the kitchen door. My pen seems to skip across this page, nothing much happens, another day.

~

Nicky and Ken return across the shingle. Nicky is wearing a barmy hat. Ken, in white shorts and a T-shirt, resembles a tennis star at this long distance.

Nicky, sweating profusely, takes off his shirt but keeps on his Mr Toad hat. We pull away from Prospect Cottage. Ken chimes like a clock in his conversation 'do you reckon?' – he's lit his second cigarette. As we turn on to the main road at the end of the Ness there is a terrific hooting behind us – the car has a flat. 'Damn,' says Nicholas, 'we'll ring the AA.'

'What? To change a wheel?'

Ken solved the puzzle of the jack. 'Do you reckon it's this way?'

I kicked the bolts out and Nicky worried. Half an hour passed in a great improvisation, the car went up and down, and not up enough, then the new wheel was on. 'Tighten the bolts,' instructs Nicky and we're off. Three queens and a flat. 'Do you reckon?' says Ken.

~

The journey back passed without event and several long traffic jams. Nicky complained of the heat again – I suggested he got the job of the theatre critic on the *Icelandic News*. He stripped off, the horn blaring as we passed other drivers. Nicky says Ken jumps and says 'Oooh!', sits nervously on the edge of the seat.

Ken diverts the conversation, describes a wild night with an Australian, his boyfriend Anthony crossly waiting, brewing the coffee when he returns at breakfast. 'What does he expect? That I should break off in the middle of the night?'

Later I walk up to the Heath, nothing except a full moon and the fragrance of wood smoke which hangs in the trees, the slightest breath of air as the sun comes up. I walk home at four. London, with its empty streets, looks like a metaphysical painting by De Chirico, the enigma of a Monday morning.

Monday 15

Mark's assault on the *Molluscum contagiosum* seems to have worked. I'm peppered with little scars. I'm going for another burn-up on Thursday. The molluscum have annoyed me more than most, I look as if I have acne in the wrong light – 'vanity kills,' says HB, each time I have my photo taken. The deal is the complete set of the Penguin Classics for the hospital in return for the end of these spots – Penguin is giving them to me for appearing in an advert.

~

The day is stiflingly hot. Billy is painting. I have cooked spaghetti.

~

Long conversation with Anthony Root. He's nearly convinced by *Narrow Rooms*, has agreed that HB should play the Renderer.

~

Searched through half-empty cans of house paint to see if I had any pink. The old bathroom was pink, soon to be a library. I feel a pink library would be something of an innovation. I found all sorts of colours, dried out and quite useless. Remember not to keep the dregs of paint cans in future.

~

Fay Godwin arrived, weather-beaten in a bright-red dress. We talked of health – she has had cancer and a friend of hers is dying in a hospice. We sat drinking tea and eating a large slice of Kate's currant cake.

The phone rang: Anya was in a car with John who was made a Knight of the Garter this afternoon in Windsor, they were on their way home. 'Is he driving in that big feather hat and his velvet robes?'

'No, he took those off.'

'It's going to be some competition, you'll have to go to the wildest dressmaker to compete.'

John came on the line, seemed happy – Anya is coming down to see the garden on Monday.

~

I found a small elephant hawk moth in the attic. Walked to the sea, a cool breeze and salt smell, the wind is in the east. I continue watering. The sun sets and a large moon, burning orange in an indigo sky, ushers in the night.

Tuesday 16

A strong easterly wind blows in the sunlight, sending the flowers reeling in its fluttering gusts, red, yellow and blue petals will all fall before July. June is the time of the garden, it is overwhelmed by sunlight and drought. I go back and forth with my watering can in garden clothes that have faded and frayed – washed-out blues and ochres. The wind grew in intensity and blew all the flowers out and the clothes line down.

At the sea's edge waves crashed, sending salty spray in veils across the Ness – not good growing weather this. Mrs Sinkins has browned off, the geranium leaves are bronzed, my lovage leans like Pisa and the wind whistles on, sending me to sleep in a storm-tossed siesta – sleeping in the afternoon is a bad sign.

Wednesday 17

I slept fitfully; today the view is frosted with salt on the window-panes.

All my garden scorched with the salt blown in the gale that roared around Prospect Cottage last night. Bone-dry, the leaves are blackened, the poppies hang dead from wilting stalks, the lovage wilts, the elder lists, all the rest bent to the ground, the vinegar plant has closed its flowers, the bees stay at home – hard pressed to fly into the gale.

~

Tariq Ali arrived at midday and we went to eat lunch in the Lydd pub. He had read *Modern Nature* and was surprised to find I had been to Pakistan. His family had a house in Natia Gulls, he spent an idyllic childhood holiday there. He said the Pathans were gay almost to a man, perhaps they learnt that from Alexander. He remembered his mother warning him about them as they sometimes kidnapped good-looking young men.

Tariq said many of his friends in the former Soviet Union were very troubled; they said: 'At least *you* know where the opposition lies.' There it was grey, no one knew who was who. Tariq did not like Greenaway's films, very eighties, he said, with an audience who went overboard to endorse what they did not understand, if there was anything there to understand. He described meeting Bertie Russell and how Harold Wilson at a reception for Kikan Knumah had stretched out his hand ostentatiously and Bertie had equally ostentatiously put his hand behind his back. 'I wasn't going to shake hands with the man who was endorsing the American intervention in Vietnam.'

Tariq, I'm certain, has a host of stories.

We talked about Wittgenstein and I took him up to the station. He was full of fun, optimistic and prepared to give it a go, even with little money. I like that. He retains an element of barefoot, no shoes at all, and has a luxuriant moustache. Impossible to equate him with the bogeyman the press made him in the sixties.

Thursday 18

Up at 5.30 and on the 7.45 train to London – £21 return, as I'm on my way before nine. The fare is normally £10. With taxis this journey to London is going to cost nearly £60, three times what it cost HB to get to Newcastle and back.

The train was out of order, commuters boiling under their cheap suits – many stood all the way. British Rail mumbled a bit and then gave up after announcing we would be stuck for another twenty-five minutes.

I bumped into HB at Charing Cross – he had came to carry my bags. We walked back to Phoenix House past the bookshops.

I swapped a large number of CDs in the Record Exchange and then went to get a list of pigments from Cornellison. I met Gawain, the young Scottish photographer with wild eyes. He had been marvelling at the jars of colour in the shop, rose-madder and permanent-green.

~

At two I left for Bart's and Dr Mark prescribed another course of antibiotics and burnt my face with liquid nitrogen; my X-rays look 'better'. I'm still not well. HB, very cuddly, says he misses me. At 6.30 he walked me down to Charing Cross, another hour and a half brought me back to Ashford, and I arrived at Prospect as the sun was setting – the wind is still blowing, the garden burnt black, not a drop of rain.

Friday 19

Slow beginning to the day, my face is very sore and I hesitated for minutes before shaving. The cold wind is blowing so I will not go out. Batten down the hatches and work on the colour white.

Saturday 20

Vivienne Westwood accepts an OBE, dipsy bitch. The silly season's with us: our punk friends accept their little medals of betrayal, sit in their vacuous salons and destroy the creative – like the woodworm in my dresser, which I will paint with insecticide tomorrow. I would love to place a man-sized insectocutor, lit with royal-blue, to burn up this clothes moth and her like.

~

HB arrived weighed down with emulsion paint and rather cross as he had walked from Camber to here as the bus unexpectedly terminated there.

HB painted the bathroom. The wind blew on through the night and died away in the dawn.

Sunday 21

Too many visitors today. The garden perked up and I worked in it. I cooked Sunday lunch for HB who painted the kitchen a fine Naples-yellow, then we drove to the pick-your-own strawberries fields.

Monday 22

Anya rang to say she had left Preston. HB scrubbed and polished, and hid away any Tesco products. I worked on the garden.

HB answered the phone and came outside to say the Palace was ringing: Lady Di was coming down with Anya – would there be space for her and two armed bodyguards to spend the night? This was not so far-fetched that I did not believe him. 'Just as well you did the housework, isn't it?'

'Oh, God Del, what do we call her?' he asked as I rushed to the phone. 'Ma'am,' I replied. When I got to the phone it turned out to be the publicist from Penguin Books. HB went wild with squeaks of laughter. For the rest of the day he was going round saying 'So much for your republicanism Derek. MA'AM.'

'I was well brought up,' I said, 'and whatever I might think there's no need to be impolite.'

In the event, Anya arrived loaded with fresh vegetables and plants from her garden – I haven't seen her for years, she looks very like my sister.

~

HB comes in, giggling at his trick. Then he kisses me all over the back of the neck.

~

Anya described John's investiture as a Knight of the Garter at Windsor. The deep-blue carpet, fiddling around with bow ties, some of the old boys couldn't fasten them and the Queen had to help. Harold Wilson, very ill and stooped – Mary Wilson spends all her time looking after him. At lunch she sat between Charles and the Duke of Edinburgh, Diana sitting across the table. They chatted about this and that. Anya said this was remarkable as that morning the book about Diana had been published; not a shadow of what was going on passed across her face. After lunch – Anya said the royals didn't eat *anything* – they all traipsed down to the chapel for the ceremony, the new Knights-to-be leading the way.

~

We made an excellent salad, walked along the beach and planted Anya's gift of a wild strawberry in the tub at the back of the house. The garden had recovered from last week's gales and was a mass of poppies and blue cornflowers.

~

Anya left at 3.30. HB spent the rest of the day laughing with friends over his Princess Diana tomfoolery.

~

Peter Logan telephoned, dear old Vera Russell has died. Vera will long live in the memory. Vera's theatrical training enabled her to play her part, she swept into our lives wearing a Cossack hat and a ring. She was self-willed and alarmingly rude. At a dinner party she noticed that Richard had been placed next to David Hockney, whose life was ruled by Vera like a fortune teller – he could barely pick up a brush without telephoning her. Vera looked at Richard and said: 'There seems to have been a mistake' and swapped the name cards round. Vera, in the absence of any men in her life, bullied the fags. She could hardly be termed a fag hag – that unpleasant epithet from the strangled past – but she could be called a fag baiter, a Russian matador who circled round you and stuck in skewers. This was immense fun for all unless they took slight. 'I think all of you homosexuals are damaged,' she once proclaimed at one of Robert's parties, probably under the illusion that she was the only bisexual present. Vera had a forthright manner which was endearing and sincere; all loved her, we cherished it. She was not intimidated by anyone and was courageous. She would have told Hitler his breath smelt. Born in Russia, she would have made a great arts minister if her family had stayed there.

Vera's entry into a room would cause a visible tremor and you would notice people in corners swapping tales under their breath. Vera was present even in her absence – she was the prop of every artist's dinner conversation, there is no one in the London art world who hasn't a Vera story.

Vera was immensely grand and loved by all, none of us will forget her. God alone knows what she's up to in heaven, but he must have been subjected to a few frank discussions in the last forty-eight hours – she's probably haranguing the saints at this moment.

Tuesday 23

Woke with a headache and a slight temperature after a rather sleepless night. My chest still aches and I'm breathless in spite of the antibiotics and an avalanche of pills as prophylaxis.

I managed to plant the last of the irises and scatter the first cornflower seeds.

HB went for a long walk and found a caterpillar, but the surprise of the day has been a merlin – a small delicate hawk, rather rare – that hovers a few feet above us without a fear and catches lizards and mice. It seems to spend most of the day hunting round the house.

~

I'm chased by the radio and the papers to comment on the unfortunate young man who is supposed to have given the virus to several young women in Birmingham – the *Sun* has one of its 'Killer' headlines. I refused. I know where at this moment most of my sympathy lies. The witch hunts of the tabloids and in this case dotty Labour MPs – Clare Short said his name should be published, what about confidentiality? Hardly words of wisdom or comfort.

Wednesday 24

HB and I boarded the train for Ashford and met Ken Butler in Charing Cross. Ken and I took off for Oxford to meet Terry Eagleton who has written the Wittgenstein script.

Tariq provided a feast – cooked by a Mauritian friend who has a small restaurant – lobster, spiced fish and a plate of exotic fruits.

Terry Eagleton sang a song, Tariq full of life and laughter. The changes to make the script 'work' within our budget discussed, Terry seemed quite happy, worried a little by the humour, but otherwise we decided that Wittgenstein might be too gloomy.

We all returned to London at three. Ken and I had cakes at Bertaux's and visited Cornellison, buying some bright pigments – rose-madder was sold out, but I found a rare permanent-green that dazzled the retina.

I felt in equilibrium – life flooded back all day. I almost forgot the HIV, surely *that* happened to someone else? But the necklace of pills doesn't let you forget, there is a terrible desire to cut them out, to deny them their strange powers. Surely I can survive this without them.

~

I plant the garden and will be here next June.

~

Richard and I went up to King's Cross to watch Michael Clarke's new ballet. The hall was spectacular and the audience young and very attractive. The ballet was touched with genius, the solo that ended it was as fine as anything I've seen, but the whole piece left me curiously distant. The soundtrack, except in the first moments, seemed wilful, and Stravinsky's *Rite* left what followed (the Sex Pistols) a pallid grey. Leigh Bowery's costumes had a touch of humour. There were poses, the birth was the best, but it brought out the fact that these tableaux are rather static. Michael, whose toes and fingertips seem to touch outside the vision field, performs as if he was in bondage – his hands are often together as he progresses across the stage with little corkscrew motions. I wanted him to leap out of this – the narrative nature of the work seemed heavy, like starch.

~

On the way back, Richard and I stopped off at the little Goan takeaway and had a curry. There was a stunningly good-looking Indian man opposite us who never stopped smiling. He had been to the ballet as well.

Thursday 25
Spent the whole day taking photos for Penguin Books' Classics. The sun shone, the garden still looks like a packet of liquorice all sorts. I have a new CD of cello sonatas. Washed and went to bed at sundown.

Friday 26
A large parcel arrives from Shipley's of 'colour books', Kandinsky, Alberti, Ad Reinhardt, Albers.

~

Four o'clock, Alan arrives with Gingerbits, who's grown big all over. I demonstrate my bottomless overall pockets. We lock ourselves out of the house and Gingerbits discovers some muscles and breaks the door down. We take off for the strawberry fields, driven along by Sister Latex of the Immaculate Protection and Sister Jocasta Dementia Prëcox who is to be vested at Pink Pride on Saturday. The Sisters of Perpetual Indulgence has its saints by the balls.

Gingerbits's future in bondage is discussed, he is to get a BA in SM, maybe with honours, at Kent University. Kent University has a thriving SM department – it's the dominant faculty and is well funded by Mr Major.

~

In the raspberry canes Gingerbits told me his gypsy story. Bored with Canterbury's one seedy gay pub he stopped off after work in a bar which everyone avoids as there is a possibility of ending up in a fight.

Gingerbits gets talking to a nineteen-year-old gypsy boy who spins the just-out-of-prison-for-the-usual-GBH yarn. He's very handsome, so they carry on talking and he says: 'I've missed my last bus, can I stop over?' Gingerbits says: 'You can have the couch.' When they get back the gypsy boy goes for a piss and returns. 'What are all those photos of naked men doing in the bathroom? Are you gay?'

Gingerbits takes the risk of a fight and says: 'Yes.'

'I am too,' he says.

Gingerbits, always the gallant, offers him the sofa.

'No,' he says, 'I want to sleep in your bed, with you in it.'

'We did the business,' says Gingerbits.

'That's not a very good description,' I reprimanded. 'You've taken nearly ten minutes to get to it. I'll have to have a word with your tutor.'

Gingerbits gets a little more poetic: 'He had a cock like an aerosol.'

He said: 'I hope I won't spoil your fun mate, as I don't much like getting fucked.' He fucked Gingerbits for five hours, on the sofa, on the stairs, everywhere except in the bed. After it was all over he said: 'You see, I *am* gay. I hate fucking my girlfriend. I always pull out before I come, put my hands over her eyes and spit on her belly, and she thinks we made it and she's happy for a few more days.' Gingerbits said he had jet-black hair.

'Don't all gypsies?'

'No, he really was a gypsy – I found that out later. I met him at a friend's house. He fucked me again while my friend was in the kitchen making tea. It was over before the sugar was in the cups.'

'Did he wear a condom?'

'Yes, it was absolutely safe.'

'Well, that's a good thing,' I said. 'What would have happened if you caught the virus? We don't want Clare Short locking you up.'

~

She was on the late news again, ██████████ ████ ███████ ████ ███ ██ ████████ ██ ████████. ███ ██████ ████ ██

████'█, they are struggling with the funding of eight beds for the dreadfully sick. The description of Birmingham made the queer world I live in seem open and respectable. Pity to be a straight now. Thank you, the tabloid press, for telling them they were not at risk. I think the last laugh is on the *Daily Mail*. ████████████ █████ █████ ██████ ██ ███████ – ███ ████████ ████ ████ ██████ ██ ████ ████ ████ ████ █ ███ █████ ███ █████ ████ ██. ███ ███ ███████ ███ █████████ ██ ████████████ ████████, ███ █ █████ ██ ████ ███ █████ █████ ████████ ███ ██████ ███ ████ ████████ ████ ████ ███ ████-██?

~

After all this excitement I managed to make some excellent gooseberry jam.

Saturday 27

Alan arrived very early with the lads and drove up to London for the Gay Pride march. I'd been up since five pottering about the garden.

As we passed the Tenterden roundabout Alan said: 'Well, last night we went to the Sisters of Perpetual Indulgence nuncheon in the crypt of St Martin-in-the-Fields, an international gathering of sissies, technically a screecks.' Like every organisation they've come of age and had a schism – the row, of course, was over make-up. Two sisters have fallen for the Boots counter and have taken to white pancake, the other sisters are plain and use soap and water. They all still promulgate universal joy in spite of the fact that Sister Moses of the Parting Cheeks has an illicit lipstick hidden in his habit.

~

We parked in the National Theatre and walked to the Embankment. There were more people than I have ever seen on the march, less police. Nicky said they looked less happy, perhaps at the size of the march – over 40,000. There were whistles but few slogans and even less chanting: 'Major Major Major, Out Out Out' – half-hearted. A group of lesbians still singing: 'She'll be coming with a woman when she comes.' Every year the march becomes less 'political', more a celebration. Old lefties squat the march, members of Militant, you can spot them a mile away as they are the only ones with loud hailers. We walked from Hyde Park, then we split, half to go to the stalls and party in South London, the other to lunch – it was stifling hot so I joined the lunch lot with my old straw hat to protect me from the sun. As we left we passed a group of twenty near-naked fluffers in little white underpants performing a synchronised routine – half dance, half gymnastics – sweating it out in Hyde Park and a group of topless lesbians looking *very* proud and happy.

~

At lunch Paul Copson said there was a wild gay life amongst the teenagers of Dungeness in the fishermen's huts. He said: 'More of your neighbours are gay than you would imagine.'

~

Gingerbits and I walked through Covent Garden, where I emptied my pockets buying an antique silk kaftan which is the coat of many colours. I consoled myself that it will make a good cover for the book of colour.

~

Alan turned up at the flat at 9.30 and we drove to Dungeness, getting here at midnight. The boys all curled up and asleep in the back of the car. Alan said the day had been a great success.

Sunday 28

It is even hotter today than yesterday, not a breath of wind. The mallow is a mass of mauve flowers and the poppies have recovered from the gales. I walked round the garden scattering seeds of all the plants that have come to the end of their flowering season.

~

I'm blessed with the kindness of neighbours – Brian and Sheila came and took me to the strawberry fields. The season is almost over before it begins and the berries are much smaller than last week, but much sweeter. The out-of-season strawberries that we are almost used to are woody and bitter, picked unripe; all American fruit is like this – gorgeous to look at, sprayed with paraffin wax and next to inedible.

Brian helped me bring back some soil and Sheila admired my sage, which is covered with dazzling blue flowers.

It was too hot to garden, too hot to go out, so I wrote in the shade of the front room and polished the furniture with HB's home-made beeswax polish, gorgeous scent of turpentine. Quite a few garden visitors but I siestaed through them and put on Messiaen as a deterrent. Later I came to and did a little watering.

Monday 29

5.30 – the sea reflects a salmon sun that is hanging in a 'shepherd's warning' sky with great blue-black clouds all of which have silver linings. The landscape is softened by a mist, the ochre grasses stretch away to the silhouettes of the little fishermen's huts.

~

I worked in the garden till eight and then came in as the sun was too strong. I planted two of the anchusa that Anya brought and moved a couple of clumps of sedum. The garden has came back to life as the curry plants and viper's bugloss have taken over from the poppies and the cornflowers. Walking about I discovered a pure white bugloss, the only one I have ever seen. I've tied a bag around it to collect the seeds and planted a little dog rose at the back – I've grown quite a few from hips dug in last autumn.

~

I was in the middle of faxing a whole series of changes to the Wittgenstein script when Minor Minor (Gerald Incandela) walked in. I haven't seen him for five, or maybe six years. Nothing had changed. We took up the conversation where we left off, no catching up was needed. Julian had driven here too fast and they both looked shaken. They stayed for a couple of hours, we walked through the house, along the beach and bought three large crabs from Bob Tart which Gerald insisted on eating, so we sat outside – as they make such a mess. The bluebottles got the best feast.

I can't remember much that we talked about, we didn't get into the past with its ups and downs.

~

I met Gerald in 1973 when I went to Rome with Ken Russell to design sets for his *Gargantua* in Carlo Grimaldi's steel and ferroconcrete palazzo at the edge of EUR – a really horrible daily journey through the snarling Roman traffic. In the room next door to mine Pasolini was putting the finishing touches to the *Arabian Nights*.

I had taken my friend Patrik Steede along with me as he was to research a script on Saint Sebastian, with whom he was in love – particularly in his manifestation at Omleto cathedral.

At the weekends I cruised the Olympia Cinema, full of provincial Italian soldiers looking for blow-jobs – Euneno from Sardinia and another called Paolo who took me up to the Borghese Gardens where I fucked him. Soldiers like it up the arse, it's an erroneous perception to think otherwise – the tougher they are the more they want it.

I came down with an appalling infection with a high temperature and was confined to bed in the Albergo d'Inghilterra. Bedridden and then imprisoned at Grimaldi's with Ken breathing down my neck, all the living was done by Pat – I had the sex, he had the rock and roll.

Eventually Ken's film collapsed, we were moved out of the Albergo, one of Rome's grander old hotels, into lodgings and I found myself free to go out.

Pat met a man who gave him several ounces of hash, Pat returned in a druggy state of love and took me to a tiny flat near the Vatican to visit his new friend. Gerald was sitting cross-legged on a bed beside a very beautiful young girl with a shock of long black curly hair, both of them wearing white and both stripped to the waist.

In what happened more than once in my relationship with Pat, I took his place, fell for Gerald and invited him back to London. Gerald decided to come and gave up a job on the periphery of Italian cinema for a different life.

I brought him to England, bought him his first camera, introduced him to the American collector Sam Wagstaff – Robert Mapplethorpe's panacean, who took him to New York and set him up.

We split over the gold lettering on the Caravaggio book. Gerald drove Nikos Stangos to distraction and beyond, and then turned on me – he has a poor sense of proportion.

I had stood at the crossroads of Gerald's life on several occasions and sensed a cutting of the umbilical. Perhaps this artistic tiff was a way of saying 'I'm independent of you'.

Pressure of personality parted us, as it did Patrik Steede – my great friends. Patrik probably had grounds for his quarrel, Gerald none, just vanity.

Gerald spent the last hours with Pat and was the only mourner at a crematorium two hours from New York. Gerald waited for three hours with Pat's Brazilian boyfriend, who spoke no English, before a furnace became available. Gerald took a dozen red roses, there was no service, just a shuttle of bodies being incinerated. And now Pat is gone, all that hustle turned to ash in New Jersey, and I hear about it second-hand.

The truth behind this is that Pat fell for Gerald, Gerald fell for me and they got together without me at the end. Was it my wallet or my cock they wished to suck?

JULY

Wednesday 1

It rained very heavily in the night, the garden looks refreshed. I planted and cleared the beds. I worked on Wittgenstein – I've made huge alterations to Terry Eagleton's script, which makes me slightly nervous.

~

Alan and Gingerbits drove over from Canterbury. We took off almost immediately to New Romney and bought raspberries. They are restoring the splendid tower of the church, which was literally crumbling away after 900 years of sea, gales and sun. It was early closing day, which put an end to the second-hand bookshops and the army surplus, so on to Sandgate, which looked very seedy and was completely deserted, not a sign of life on the streets or in the houses.

Stuck in a traffic jam caused by the most handsome young scaffolder, brown as a berry. Gingerbits got very horny and wanted to turn back: 'I bet he's got a big aerosol.' When we did return he had gone.

Thursday 2

A gale blew through the night, damp grey clouds hung low over the Ness. The last of the scarlet poppies bob up and down in the rivulets of wind that scurry through the ochre grasses, the broom is revived to a dark green and the clumps of woodsage, emerald with the palest of grey-green flowers. There are bugloss and cornflowers and yellow horned poppies, the helichrysum hovers like seaweed in a strong current, the first bright-blue flower has opened on the chicory and next to it the last bells of a foxglove sway in the wind. There is a sharp little bird, pink and grey with black wings and a black stripe across his eyes, hopping about and avoiding Thomas, the ancient black cat, who sits meditating in front of a bush of catnip.

~

I was up very early, crept about the house to avoid waking Gingerbits and then burnt the toast and set off the fire alarm.

~

I find our national inability to describe our sex lives pathetic. As I write my diary I'm struggling with Wittgenstein's almost blank biography. The ghetto performs like a daisy chain, I wonder which daisies he plucked, Maynard Keynes? Anthony Blunt? Wish there was a foreign power I could spy for – wrong generation, unfortunately. In any case who would want to know the secrets of Mr Major's dirty linen? My sympathies are totally with the spies – it was the only honest thing to do to that rotten privileged imperial society. It is sad that Stalin should have destroyed hope so that their pure motives, their patriotism, could be called into question.

~

Anthony Blunt was more intelligent and more charming than any of the ghastly people who made hay with his unmasking. It's a sad turn of history that they should still have the voices, theirs are ones that would be better silenced.

Friday 3
The rain pours down. Gingerbits and I have a meal in the Pilot, which is hot, stinks of cigarette smoke and is full of gross people who are overweight.

~

Rung up by a frantic producer who is making a programme on Shakespeare. He couldn't find any actors who would talk about this.
  'Sir Ian?'
  'Oh, he's away and in any case he's too grand.'
  'Oh, I hope you're not going to ask Michael Cashman.'
  'No.'
Thank God. None of the actors have an education, otherwise they would get out and produce original work. We have academics who dispute Shakespeare was gay. Well, he wasn't – that term hadn't been invented and the either/or ghetto with it. He was much more likely to be queer, which includes all of us.
  The academics refute the Sonnets, say they are 'a convention', their terms are all twentieth century. The academics might have their professorships in literature but they haven't got their O levels in life. The Sonnets are a convention like portrait painting, or allegorical painting, but no one would deny that the boy you see in a Bronzino existed. It's the same with the Sonnets: Shakespeare doesn't have to have fucked with him. It seems the sex act is the way we confirm or deny our sexuality. This is not the case – it's quite possible to be a celibate queer.

~

I can't see how you could possibly think of *Edward II* as a gay play where sexuality lurked in the background, I just decided to emphasise it. As for Shakespeare's theatre, there was no need – Romeo and Juliet would have both been played by men and would have been a same-sex play. All these academics should go back to their books – civilisation is queer, particularly the Renaissance, distinguished by the fact that most of its artists didn't marry, unlike those in our own century. From the moment Lorenzo, who slept with boys, commissioned Ficino to translate Plato things changed. Neoplatonism was a manifesto for living, not something dead. The monotheistic dictatorship of Christ was over. You couldn't burn fourteen-year-old boys for sodomy, as they did in the 1430s, after Lorenzo.

Leonardo was tried, Michelangelo wrote tortured sonnets, Botticelli turned into a religious maniac under Savonarola, Rosso, Pontormo, Cellini, Caravaggio, all the main artists, Shakespeare, Marlowe, Bacon, and I suspect all the rest. To deny this is not only to betray all these artists, but civilisation itself.

These actors who cannot face the cameras are traitors. They'll camp around Stratford in slap, and slap the Bard in the face. I suspect if Elizabeth I was dishing out knighthoods, Shakespeare would have been at the front door with a begging bowl, Marlowe would have run a mile.

~

Bed very early, my cough still lurks, maybe it is the rain. It doesn't keep me awake but I lie awake from dawn at 4.30 and have to pee at least twice, stumbling down the corridor. Alan is arriving at nine to take us to Rye.

Saturday 4
It is now eleven and Alan still hasn't arrived. Gingerbits said: 'Put an hour on.' He underestimated.

~

A magazine drops through the door, *Christopher Street*, with an interview with Sir Ian 'call me Serena' McKellen that confirms my view that the theatre is totally out of touch.

> Well I had no example, there was nobody in British life, full stop, who'd come out, wait a minute, wait a minute . . . Derek Jarman . . . maybe! [my exclamation mark]. Derek Jarman, a few people on the fringes of society who'd come out, but no gay politician and no gay actors.

So that was where Hockney and all the rest of us stood, from the perspective of the National Theatre. Almost everyone I knew was out by the end of the sixties. McKellen came out in 1988. We, it seems, are periphery, the thousands of men and women who marched and fought. God help us, apparently politicians and actors are at 'the centre'.

> *You mentioned Derek Jarman before . . .*
> Yeah.
> *I know that when you were knighted by the queen he criticised you and said you shouldn't have accepted such an honour from a homophobic government.*
> He couldn't have been jealous could he? I didn't say that! (laughing)
> Okay.
>
> No of course he wasn't jealous. Derek doesn't approve of the title anyway, and I'm not sure that I do really. But if you're living in the real world, if you want to change the laws of the country, I tell you to be Sir just makes it that bit easier to open the door, you don't have to knock on the door, it opens.
>
> It gives you clout and you get your point of view right where it wants to be heard, it's all very well going out in the streets.

The words 'if you are living in the real world' are the key. I think I am right to have reacted as strongly as I did. Everyone I know obviously does not live in the 'real world'. The British theatre, with its lack of democracy, its fear of the rest of us, is clearly portrayed here. I suppose Ian, like the rest of his kind, who have never accepted living artists but only dead ones, can continue to place a world-famous film director, who has written, designed and filmed for twenty years, on the periphery.

Peripheral is the way the straight world sees us. It's a sorry day when 'England's leading gay man' sees the rest of us this way. Maybe Ian has just a gay façade and has a heart as straight as a die.

~

Alan arrived with friends and we took off for Rye for the E. F. Benson Society day. Alan was wearing a shirt printed with mauve cabbage roses, the rest of us looked more respectable. The society had set itself up in the Red Cross rooms, across the road from Radclyffe Hall's house. Every fluffer for miles around had congregated in the tearoom, so in Rye's Saturday high street an impromptu gay bar had sprung up, full of old queens like myself and little bevvies of hair-cut boys with shaved necks, looking like seals.

The food was excellent, particularly the cakes, which were laid out for the fluffers, along with home-made lemonade. There was even one good-looking black boy, perhaps the first Rye had ever seen.

The boys munched away, playing their mothers at a garden fête. Alan

163

took off to climb the hill to E. F. Benson's tomb, Gingerbits and I walked to the bookshops, where I found a beautiful morocco-bound edition of Ruskin's *Modern Painters*. In the second bookshop the proprietor said: 'E. F. Benson that way' before we had walked through the door, and then carried on while both of us tried to find books on colour.

Eventually I said: 'I don't like E. F. Benson at all.' There was a bit of a hush. I thought I had been rather rude so I said I was there with the founding fathers of the novelist's admirers, a group of screaming fans.

'Bring them in, bring them in.'

Later he accosted us, holding a yellow rose for the tomb: 'Have you brought them in yet? Have you brought them in yet?' He was waiting for us in every tortured cobbled street. We went shopping and failed to find cheese, tea, or a copy of *Moby Dick*. Rye is a heritage town, as well stocked as Disneyland. At four Alan drove us back to Prospect, where Gingerbits and I collapsed. We were in bed by ten.

Sunday 5

I woke rather late, so missed the dawn. It was a grey day, so I was quite thankful.

Washed down the floors and then sat and worked on the white section of the colour book. Alan and his gang arrived for tea on their way home to Canterbury. He said to make sense of Benson you had to be one storey up on the *piano nobile*, not at street level.

~

Rye at night was empty, expensive and in curfew. Spying through the window of Radclyffe Hall's house they saw what must have been a heritage lesbian, looking just like Whistler's mother.

Monday 6

HB arrived with Howard and Sven, who had stayed the night in London and brought his thesis for me. He's finished school and is going to start a foundation course in the autumn. We had a glorious day, driving to: Appledore; Rye, where I bought books; Winchelsea, where we paid respect to Edward II; then to Hastings for fish and chips in the little blue-and-white restaurant. In the corner two old queens, brown as berries and sporting gold earrings, one of them had the brightest blue eyes, they were fishermen from the boats.

HB, in his element, had chips and poached egg and a spotted dick, which he said was too light – no suet, more like a cake with custard.

~

I set off for the second-hand bookshop, where I found a copy of Horace's *Odes* for Howard and the *Trierene Riwle* for Gingerbits – to guide his wavering steps.

Very merry, with a large amount of head tickling, cuddling and noise, we took off to Great Dixter. Howard found a clematis and a verbena. There was a spectacular mullein candelabra, like a branched candlestick, at least seven feet tall.

We got back to Prospect before five for a long three-way conference call with Sarah Radclyffe, who wants to leave Working Title – the company she set up – and Anthony Root, who is off to San Francisco to televise an Armistead Maupin novel. They think that *Narrow Rooms* probably could not be made in America, so I phoned Christine Vachon in NYC to see how we might progress. HB finished the second draft script and will take it to Working Title tomorrow.

HB and Howard took off for the beach where HB swam and Howard took photos. Back here he padded around in the bathroom, which has an engraved glass fingerplate on the door: 'HB Paradise'.

Diana Mavrolean arrived with some tinker lads and we all ended up in the George in Lydd, before they took off for London. The sun shone all day.

Tuesday 7
Gingerbits finished typing white. I worked in the garden, wrote a dozen letters, walked along the beach, windy and sunny the washing dried in minutes. The wind died away in the evening – very silent.

~

Brian Clarke came with a very splendid photograph of the white viper's bugloss.

Wednesday 8
Overcome by a terrible itching in the night, it got so bad I thought insects were crawling all over me.

~

Bright sunlight brought the chicory flowers out by the front door, they are bright blue, look as if a child has cut them out of paper and last only a day.

Squeezed fresh grapefruit for breakfast, ordered up the original scripts from the archive.

Started the red section for the colour book and packed up for London.

~

A long, dreary journey from Ashford, the glittering sky at Dungeness swallowed by the pollution of London where it had been drizzling all day.

~

HB very happy to see me and upset by an incident on the bus in Camden. A drunk had tried to get on board and the driver had refused to let him on, locked himself in his cab and stopped the engine. The drunk had become progressively more abusive, 'fucking cunt' had turned into 'fucking poof'. At that point Have-a-go HB's patience snapped and he got up and shouted: 'I'm one of your fucking poofs and if you don't get off the fucking bus now I'll kick your fucking head in.'

The drunk backed off, the bus took off and HB returned to his seat. The lady who was sitting next to him gave him an unpleasant look and, although the bus was packed, stood up with the rest of the standing passengers. He was left alone with his empty seat, no one would sit next to him, he said it made him feel terrible – so much for the vision of a just society.

The urban British are stupid, dim-witted, none more so than the dullards in Camden. They were quite happy to sit grumbling in the heat and quite unprepared to so much as nod in the direction of someone who helped them get home.

~

I hate having my nipples tweaked, which is a green light to HB who is on the attack. He drives me crazy, says it calms him down and makes all sorts of manoeuvres. He's decided the word 'careful' gives him the right to grab them.

Thursday 9

I woke HB up in the middle of the night. I had a dream in which I met God.

'Did he speak to you?'

'Yes.'

'What did he say?'

'Oh, that he'd given me you, he said: "Hinney Beast is your helpmeet." '

~

Searched through the bookshops for books on colour. Grand lunch at the Presto, as the clip Richard Jobson taped in the restaurant is on the air – literally. It is part of one of those BA transatlantic video magazines and their business has improved.

~

While we were waiting for my pills in the pharmacy we went to see Robert at Charterhouse Square. Robert was very interesting about Ben Britten – he had gone with him to the first performance of his string quartet in Golders Green and afterwards Ben had 'come out' to him about his passion for young boys. Robert said he probably never had sexual relationships with them, but that they were his passion. He said that Pears had sex on the side.

Ben was very difficult, said Robert. Wystan Auden lost him as a friend when he lectured him about coming clean about his sexuality. Ben was very offended by the remark that unless he did so he would never become a mature artist. Auden was distressed at his reaction, they never made up.

HB flexes his new tattoo for Robert who says: 'Silly boy, now the police will always be able to identify you.'

Friday 10

Collided with Danny Maggott at the end of Berwick Street Market, bought fruit and ended up having tea in The Village. Good little piece in *Capital Gay* about living in the real world and the fringe. We should interpret 'fringe' like fringe theatre, i.e. the only serious place to be. I've spent thirty years being relegated to the unreal world by straight critics and the film world; now it's the turn of the gay world to marginalise the queers.

Danny stayed and chatted until seven – we had supper in Poon's. He's made his tattoo film and shown it in Hamburg. There seems to be a tattoo film made by every generation of queer film-makers. Tattoos are recidivist, the neat remains of the woad that Pliny said made the British look Ethiopian.

The very tattooed HB left for Newcastle.

Saturday 11

Up at seven, coffee at Bar Italia, Aurelia makes the best in London.

Happy picture of David Hockney receiving a doctorate at the RCA on the front of all the papers.

I got to Richard's at 11.30 in the number 10, the journey passed quickly as I read Manlio Brusatin's little book *A History of Colors*. Piers and I set up three canvases: one a *Mirror* headline about the Birmingham man alleged to have infected several women, with a marriage photograph – *For Richer for Poorer* – and we weighed into two large landscape pictures. They were painted with rubber kitchen gloves that I was using to protect my hands. The results are amazingly directed – Piers mixed the paints and I slapped them on by the handful.

Lunch at the Italian restaurant, then a taxi to the Tate – admired the Anish Kapoor sculptures and spent an hour in Richard Hamilton's exhibition. Richard Salmon, who was sceptical, came out a convert. He thought the hospital installation remarkable – a hospital bed with a TV on which Mrs T. gives a Party Political Broadcast.

Gingerbits was cruised throughout the time we were there by a handsome gym fluffer in blue jeans who kept his hands in his back pockets and hitched them up his bum ostentatiously. This was a bit of an interruption as we had to walk around Richard's show with eyes in the backs of our heads.

The cruiser disappeared in the sculpture gallery. We walked through the Hockney show which looks very grey, I remember paintings like *A Bigger Splash* being brighter. Richard said the acrylic was deteriorating. The paintings look a little slapdash now, particularly after the surgical precision of the Hamiltons.

George Grosz's *Suede* a good painting, my crimson colour is very territorial, cannot be invaded. The Miro is wonderful. All the more daring experiments of the early century seem to run out, though there is a fine Sickert of Peggy Ashcroft painted in Venice in greens and pink.

Home and went to bed to rest up.

~

A long conversation with a charming young man on the Heath about a review of *At Your Own Risk* in *Gay Times*. He said it was critical and using the silver snuff box quote: 'Derek puts his sexuality into a silver box and snuffs it.' Whether true or not, it brought up a whole chain of thoughts.

The concept of positive images was born out of gay liberation in the 1970s; *Gay Times* is of that time and Brighton-based. I don't know how one should describe Brighton, perhaps Façade Amnesia, the town for gay people. There are no queers there, it is often violent, has a huge sex-for-money scene – as there is no other employment. *Gay Times* has been gunning for me – they are theatrical. There was a disgraceful review of my films by their positive image 'film critic' Steven Bourne. Positive images are an illusion, like commercials – they are not the stuff of art.

All steps forward have been made by those of us trying to grapple with the problems in our daily lives. Life was not *The Sound of Music*; if you climbed a mountain it was a sweaty affair and you might not reach the summit. The great queer artists dealt with the negatives, this is why Pasolini and Genet will last long after *Gay Times* is forgotten in a world of false hope and illusion fed by adverts. A film like Salò is a necessary antidote, you could hardly call Pasolini 'gay'. The word is an illusion, it was a necessary rallying point in 1970; with it came the 'gay community' to give us focus but it soon became a method of marketing nightclubs and clothing. The Pride march this year was a mere amble with a lot of noisy whistles, whistles – easy to blow and no need for slogans, no thought but the good time. I enjoy this sunny afternoon, but we need this *and* the anger.

I didn't discover my sexuality to sell *in* – I want change. 'Gay' itself was a problem for the artists I knew, it did not describe us. If we had come up with 'difficult' that would have been better *Difficult News*, Difficult's The Word, thank God for Queer – *Capital Queer*, *Queer Times*.

As Mrs Thatcher's eighties took us over, even those of us who were not joiners, another element of 'gay life' came out of the woodwork – the cocktail queens who kept their suits on even at the weekend. They were rich, narrow-minded and their arrival was heralded by the Theatre Knight. They had always hated artists, perhaps more so than the positive imagists, and I, in turn, repaid the compliment. To them, we who fought for their space were on the fringes of society, we did not live in the real world of banks, the opera and weekends. The old *Gay Times* was caught up in all this and added another insult, class.

To set up a focal point that robs everyone of focus is a treason that the arts can perform quite easily in their concrete bunkers. It would have been much better for our 'community' if the arts had to involve themselves directly. To call Pasolini, or myself for that matter, 'gay artists' is foolish and limiting, one day maybe we will dispense with boundaries and categories. I was never gay, queer maybe, difficult certainly, with good reason. Betrayed by *Gay Times*, who carved no space in the world outside their ghetto.

Conversation rambled through the night. I wish it were raining, rain concentrates the mind, the blue sky is an illusion, behind lies an infinite black.

Sunday 12

Sodomy is straight. Sarah says forty per cent of women have practised anal sex; statistically there are more straight arsefuckers than queers. Kinky sodomy as subversion, it transgresses all notions of Judeo-Christian family values, pleasure without responsibility.

Monday 13

Bought books on Russell and Wittgenstein, and read the *Independent* at Bertaux's. Albert Pierrepoint, one of the last hangmen, is in the obituary columns. Born into a long line of public executioners, he dispatched more than 500, 'an honest, decent and conscientious man'. Albert admitted that no good had come from his job, no foul deed averted, he was just the instrument of revenge. Albert was born in Clapton, Yorks, in 1905 and died in Southport. There was a charming photograph of him, you can only get them done properly in Yorkshire.

~

Julian takes me to Dungeness at two.

We join a traffic jam, the roads round Ashford get worse, the return fare is now over £20 on rail, the lack of husbandry in public affairs is one of the

Tories' blind spots, the railways are subjected to 'market forces', those in Europe are subsidised five times over. To let the money markets float may or may not have been a good thing, but to apply the same principles to transport? To talk of freedom in relation to the car is utter foolishness – freedom to join a traffic jam. You bump along the roads to get to London, the only city in the world that has no civic administration, no Lord Mayor and, regrettably, no Ken Livingstone. Responsibility shirked, and on the radio in the traffic jam Mr Lamont – who looks like a mangy badger – shuffling intelligence and honesty with statistics: 'it's getting better', 'this has dropped', 'this has risen', 'here's a per cent', 'no we've lost it again', 'it's slid down the index'. Led by a government that has abandoned responsibility, the crime rate soars and the tottering public sector falls about their ears.

Market forces, which make nothing cheaper; food, electrical goods, cars, property, all are more expensive here than anywhere I've been. The only thing subsidised is the trash in the Palace. The Windsors truly reflect our society, privileged, unpleasant, a decade's pay for less than a day's work, all of them stupid, unable even to relate to each other, at least Fergie can give good head and she's out on her arse.

Diana was having an affair with her bodyguard – he was killed by the security forces, they crashed into him, another road accident.

~

I'm dying slowly on my feet.

~

We've got tragic Paul with us – Britain's leading expert in the archaeology of construction workers. He gave a fishmonger a bath last week; Julian interjects: 'washed the scales off him'. We are stuck somewhere as the tyre blows up and Julian weaves into a service station. We are alone, a quiet nervousness overtakes the crippled car as we wait for the man from the RAC. Paul is contemplating him in the bath. We read Julian's Rimbaud script and watched a fifteen-year-old putting diesel into a lorry. 'God, he's cute,' says Julian.

Nothing's happening, 'maybe . . .', 'maybe . . .' maybe he's forgotten us. 'Let's go to the Little Chef, we can sit and drink coffee and smoke cigarettes. At least I can,' says Julian. The Little Chef has its usual spotty fryer, it's good for breakfasts and burgers, the decor is scarlet and the fare carnivorous, Soylent Green. We contemplate eating people. I suggest that butchers should display photos of the people who became prime cuts – it might put you off your dinner, it might bring sexual preference into the family roast. Paul contemplates roasting a Macedonian shepherd. Julian, who's a food snob, will only eat royalty. God, what one does to pass an hour.

~

The RAC man has arrived, it's four.

We drove to Rochester with the breakdown truck and while the tyre was replaced found a second-hand bookshop. Paul found a history of Rome and I found two books on Horace Walpole. We got back to the car where Julian said: 'What is the difference between a coffin and a condom? They both have stiffs in them one coming and one going.'

Paul said Caesar's aquatics swam the river Medway in armour. It's five and we are on our way.

Julian says: 'I can say I've been to Rochester now.' The South rolls past, rows of grim villas, clipped roundabouts and street lamps, some of which are burning. The afternoon is gloomy, overcast, threatening and airless.

~

Long chat on the phone with Simon Watney. He is very upset that *Gay Times* has cut his AIDS column for lack of space, surely the only thing that cannot be cut. He said he could understand if they employed someone else. 'Well,' I said. 'You should see the review for *At Your Own Risk* – the book is written off as a disgrace and I as unregenerately middle-class, *that* apparently is my problem.'

I'm not exactly sure how I become working-class, do a Mother Teresa? I racked my brain to see if I knew a case of the downwardly mobile; the other path from working class to middle class is apparently acceptable and admired.

Julian said: 'They hate your middle-class background as it gives you an unfair advantage to be critical; to rise from the working class you have to conform.'

I might be on the fringes of society but *Gay Times* is on the fringes of intelligence, like Stonewall it would do us a service if it folded.

Tuesday 14

A grim gale blew through the night. My stomach collapsed and I found myself staggering through the corridors with fouled sheets.

I woke up washed out. Watched a thin drizzle mist the windows as I struggled to swallow breakfast. Except for the curry plants, which toss and turn in the gale, most of the flowers of summer have gone – like the hot June weather, the wind, which blows shrouds of salt, has burnt them up, but there are a few campion, bright-blue chicory and pink thrift.

Howard rang to say the Royal Horticultural Society had never heard of white viper's bugloss and were very excited, so *Arvensis Sooleyii* might get quite a lot of attention.

~

HB rang me from Newcastle to tell me how shocked everyone was about the article in *Gay Times*, particularly the suggestion I was building a career out of AIDS. If there was a career in being more open about HIV status more people would have taken the opportunity – one could challenge the magazine by inviting people to write in with their names and addresses. The piece is so distorted by this observation. I can hardly have foreseen what would happen when I opened up this closet. I thought it would be the end, if not of life, then of my work. Who will insure me for the films? I don't suppose *Gay Times* know that all film directors have to have a medical before their films are financed. What do they think it is like to be under the continuous eyes of the curious as I walk down the street? They have no concept of the insecurity – HB walks beside me in case the next encounter is not one of a well-wisher.

~

I've been sick all day. I wish my vomit had been spewed over *Gay Times* rather than wasted down the toilet. So many of those who made a few bob out of us in the seventies were brain-damaged by convention, now they are entombed in it.

Wednesday 15

At four this morning the moon looked as if it had been scratched out on a contact sheet, deadly still, grey dawn with the foghorn booming through the mist. I was up at five. The sun is up, pushing the clouds back.

~

Altercation with a lady who was picking flowers along the verge – so angry the kettle boiled dry; summertime on the edge of violence. I decided to invite her to see the garden. She left almost in tears.

Thursday 16

Terrible upset stomach that's left me so drained and dizzy I can barely write this sentence. Thumbed through my copy of *Blast*, maybe that's the way through to red.

~

Several fan letters, two from painters, cheered me up. If you put a queer painting in a civic space it helps – the letters sent by young men in Northern art schools say the Manchester show has made space. Back in the seventies *Sebastiane* did this – an overtly homoerotic film in provincial cinemas, not

Victim, not *Sunday Bloody Sunday*, but a film, however faltering, in the tradition of *Un Chant d'Amour* – it helped to make a space for younger film-makers, if that was all I achieved it would be enough.

I wobbled down the corridor and painted a small canvas in scarlet and viridian: *Et in Arcadia Ego*.

~

Carol Myers rings me to invite me to Bueños Aires on the sixth. I don't think I'll make it, as if my stomach goes on the plane it would be quite impossible. I can barely get down the corridor and if I had to queue for thirty seconds I would shit myself all over the aisle and fellow passengers. Fuck it all.

~

Three young men arrived from English Nature. I took them round the garden. They said the brown tail moth infestation had cut back the sloes. They were defending Dungeness against nuclear reactors, deep-water harbours, shingle diggers and flower pickers, dune buggy riders were beyond their powers.

~

In a swift few brush strokes I threw all my pent-up frustrations into three more pictures and solved my landscape problems.

Saturday 18

Woke at six with a headache, which stopped me getting to work. The grey English summer has settled in. Alasdair arrived and made enquiries of Derek Ball, he of 'Bohemia', who has not been seen for many a week. After breakfast he suggested we walk up to his shanty and enquire within. Things alter slowly – the new house near the lifeboat station is complete and there is a rash of repainting – several of the houses are going back to their primal black. The rain has tinged the straw-coloured grasses green, the broom is very lush with jet-black seed pods, the woodsage is flowering and the viper's bugloss nearly over – like the blue sky overwhelmed with cloud.

~

Alasdair clipped back the santolina. I dozed all day, weak as water at the knees. Recovered in the evening, sat and listened to Whitman's poems set by George Crumb – I'm getting more of his music, Lynn is coming over on the *QE2* and bringing some with her.

Sunday 19

Drizzle sets in, Alasdair dozes, I doze. I wish I could experience one day of good health.

~

Alan arrives with Gingerbits; then John and Miriam Cartwright call with huge clump of irises for the garden; shortly after that Johnny Phillips, who is searching for a place to live outside London. We all walked along the beach, which was quite deserted.

Monday 20

The foghorn boomed through the night, warm and misty morning. We all ate a long breakfast – sugar puffs, tea and toast – and then set up the computer in the west wing and started in on red. Red is a difficult colour, both Gingerbits and I feel this way.

Tuesday 21

The worst electrical storm I remember raged across southern England last night. It started as the sun set, an ominous purple cloud hung low over the Ness and within minutes the power lines were down. HB rang to say London was rocked by thunder and then the phone went dead. We lit candles. Ever since the hurricane, inclement and extreme weather has made me feel insecure, I worried and hardly slept through the night. There was a second storm in the small hours, the world awash in continuous sheet lightning which lit up the clouds over Dover. At five the lights suddenly came on – I thought Alasdair was getting up to return to London, but both he and Gingerbits were sleeping soundly. It's early, I'm up and they are still asleep. HB will probably visit, he said he would if the electricity was on.

~

Sylvia has a new tame crow that has taken up residence on her washing line, where it performs aerial acts. It follows Ken about and stands on his head.

~

The garden looks damp and very sorry. The rain has flattened the curry plants, the cut-back cotton lavender looks grey, there is a last flowering of poppies and cornflower, but nothing left to flower in the autumn – even the mallow is stripped of its flowers.

At five HB arrived with Howard and Sandy. She's doing a new film, a large budget, but the same amount for each costume as the low-budget films she is used to – all the money is going on stars' fees.

Wednesday 22

Woke with a splitting headache, though HB was more than usually cuddly all night.

The sun beats down. Howard has made a set out of a tarpaulin. HB is putting some stretchers together so I can paint next week. Howard took photographs of me in the garden stark-naked but for a see-through spacesuit and in the middle of the shoot two besuited Jehovah's Witnesses arrived, they looked quite surprised. I asked them to put their magazines through the door. Cherry Smyth rang. I read her book on queer notions, it is very good and the first considerable writing.

Bought lunch in Lydd, took more photos, the sun carried on shining.

~

We drove to London, stopping at a nursery in Hawkhurst where I bought geraniums.

We walked to the new Tesco where we bumped into Kenny, very hot under the collar. He objects to the order of restraint put on Andy – the Thursday caller. I can't understand why he or Andy should object; having the doorbell rung with threats at all hours of the night when I am feeling ill has to stop. If this is the way, so be it.

Thursday 23

I woke late – ten. HB had gone to the gym. Breakfast at Bertaux's. An article in the paper about the Parthenon turning black. Bought Lucretius and Bishop Berkeley at Pordes's and a couple of colour books, then HB walked me to the number 10 bus stop.

~

I spent the rest of the day in Richard's studio giving a series of interviews, first to a Japanese documentary, then two C4 productions on Michelangelo and Shakespeare – who were they?

My observation that civilisation is homosexual is easily defended. Tolerance and an embracing of human sexuality is accompanied by a flowering of the arts.

Plato is a blueprint for same-sex relationships and a handing down of wisdom, from one generation to another, in each other's arms.

Alcuin, who reorganised the schools for Charlemagne and wrote love poetry to a young man, is another pivotal mind. In ancient Rome same-sex marriage was common.

Ficino, translating Plato for Cosimo de Medici, was not involved in a dry academic exercise but in providing a blueprint to open up mono-theistic Aristotelian Christendom to the pagan gods, each one constellating images.

The Ganymedes of the Renaissance recognise the existence of same-sex love. Michelangelo sent a drawing of a Ganymede to his Tommaso;

Leonardo, and much later Newton, founded modern science in same-sex beds.

Michelangelo's art reflects his torment – the slaves are struggling to get out of the rock, like the Neoplatonists from Christendom, they never quite succeed. The great image of Greek love, the creation of Adam, is at the centre of the Sistine, Adam had no heterosexual identity when he was created and the image is of the young man lying languidly as his fingers, touched by the older 'God', are charged with sexuality. The church will still not come to terms with its queer artist. Art historians still make the mistake that his life did not affect his art, only someone who has not created a painting or sculpture could maintain that the sonnets are not written for Tommaso, the beautiful victory crushes the tormented artist. Michelangelo's is the art of bondage – to his patrons' God.

Tommaso, enthralled by the body beautiful – he would have loved to be on a Pride march with all the bevvies of near-naked gym boys. It is not possible to look at works through the eyes of the past, only the present, and no one coming to Michelangelo or Shakespeare should ignore this unveiling. Civilisation is same sex, Shakespeare answers the blind in sonnet 17:

> *Who will believe my verse in time to come*
> *If it were fill'd with your most high deserts?*
> *. . .*
>
> *If I could write the beauty of your eyes*
> *And in fresh numbers number all your graces*
> *The age to come would say, 'This Poet lies . . .'*

Home in a taxi, early to bed.

Friday 24

Left HB in front of St Giles church at twelve. 'What should I write in the diary?'

'HB off to Newcastle, I'm off to the Heath,' he says.

~

London hot and exhausting, it's so close today the petrol fumes sting your eyes.

Is my lurking headache from the heat and fumes, or the dreaded *Toxoplasmosis gondii*? Heat and fumes.

My jittery immune system is in better shape than the economy. We are passing the Palace which is flying a limp royal standard. A group of sweaty-looking guardsmen, all unattractive, are marching round the Victoria memorial; this lot are wearing brown pleated kilts – a skirt and a ginger moustache are not my dream ticket, the idea of pursuing guardsmen seems forlorn.

Snarled up at Hyde Park Corner, everyone at cross purposes, a group of Indian dignitaries with a blotch-faced Lord Carrington sit in landaus with a mounted escort at the Park gates which, like the Albert Memorial, are in restoration. At Palace Gate the traffic slows to a halt. We are passed by a bald man with a large dog and a telephone sticking out of the arse pocket of his jeans, police sirens, derelicts selling copies of the paper *The Big Issue*. The best description of the passers-by is 'weird', weird clothes, weird hairstyles, the land of weird – a visual illiteracy.

Thank God, I've got to Edwarde's Square. Lunch with Richard, pouring curses on the bank – he sent them a quote from Lear: 'You can't make nothing with nothing.' Piers went paint hunting, I produced a landscape.

Saturday 25

An early start, coffee at Bar Italia. The newspaper boy stopped me and asked me how the nuclear power station was doing. Another hot and close day.

I did my shopping and then came back to write up this diary, heavy with sleep as last night I went up to the Heath, where there has been another massacre of holly bushes by the moral guardians. It's sad to see the place raped by the city which now condemns the old trees to the bonfire if people make love under their branches.

~

Sarah arrived at 12.30. I tore the precious sonnet 'Let Me Not to the Marriage of True Minds Admit Impediments' from my book and hung on to it. Sarah had a great Wilde quote, so the past was well represented.

We walked down to Piccadilly Circus, several hundred demonstrators blended with the Saturday crowds. Eros was boarded up behind black hoardings, rather sad when you think that he was the child of the rainbow. The demonstrators blew whistles, banged drums and chanted: 'We're here, we're queer, and you'd better get used to it.' Peter Tatchell organised the proceedings through a megaphone with his usual flair, without him, I'm sure these manifestations would fall apart, as it is they are very good natured.

Isaac Julien remarked that he hadn't enjoyed himself so much for a long time, this was echoed by nearly everyone.

I read my sonnet, which went down quite well – I should say I shouted the sonnet through the megaphone. The crowd was decorated by the Sisters of Perpetual Indulgence and two of the tallest young men in immaculate drag with picture hats – one of them had a black miniskirt with 'safe sex sluts' written round his hemline, very stylish. Gingerbits had his arse stroked by him whenever they collided. Pat Arrowsmith, Jimmy Somerville and a host of friends including Julian Cole and David Hurst. We were at Eros for an hour – speeches demanding an end to discrimination – Pat Arrowsmith, very eloquent and angry, drew a cheer from the queers by saying she was lesbian and hated the word. I think it showed the good humour of all concerned.

We moved off to Downing Street and sat in the road, more speeches were made – there was one angry protester who thought Operation Spanner should have been mentioned, a platform was offered to her but she didn't accept. The angriest protesters were marching at the front with Aamir, who I think is absolutely sexy, very fiery. Sarah presented our petition for equal rights at Number 10.

Then we marched off, led by a drag queen Britannia who squeered the 1967 act on her trident. Halfway down Victoria Street the police aborted the party that was to have taken place at the Victoria memorial. Armed with ice lollies, we left at four, very hot.

I think queer politics have arrived.

~

Andy Bell's concert a delight, we all danced along in our row. Subliminal messages to a largely straight audience – he sang 'Somewhere Over the Rainbow' for me and his parents. The most handsome fan came up in the interval, we held hands for a second before we were swept apart in the crowd. The Odeon was an inferno, but no one cared as the concert was alive with swans, wellies and feather boas. Andy very good at bringing his songs to a snappy finish, he gave one lad a condom and talked of Hampstead Heath. Later, I went there.

Sunday 26
Very funny photo of us in the Observer, all looking grumpy through a distorted lens. Sarah's face creeps into the corner with goggle glasses. I noticed the Observer calls us 'gay demonstrators'. There is no mention, as usual, about our grievances. Coverage in the Independent is better – as Peter has written a clear article. As usual, we are shoved aside by the straight press – its tacky interest in David Mellor's love life gives us the elbow. He's not my idea of a sex symbol, give me the fluffers on the OutRage! demo any day – FILM DIRECTOR IN ACTIVIST LOVE NEST.

~

Piers collected me with Digby at one, to Dungeness with a freezer Peaches had given me and bags of food. As we left, two large white butterflies were dancing round the plants on the balcony – butterflies on the Charing Cross Road, right in the concrete centre of London.

We stopped off at the Little Chef on the Marsh and an overgrown wasteland of thistles alongside the building was alive with a mass of whites, literally hundreds of them feeding on the purple flowers, also peacocks, admirals and browns. The hot weather and rain has kept the weeds thriving and has brought more butterflies than I can remember.

The fields are already harvested. I'm certain they are four weeks in advance of my childhood in Curry Malet; perhaps they'll be harvesting two crops a year. Digby said they'd never get the irrigation together if they couldn't even get the garden hosepipes flowing, the reservoirs would run dry.

I planted my geraniums by the front door and went to sleep as the sun set.

Monday 27

Feeling very under the weather, I started to work on grey.

Outside the road is up as the water supply is restored. We have peat-brown water as the pipes are so old and rusted. We are assured it's safe, but it's very disconcerting. Whites wash sepia, a bath looks uninviting and the water you boil for tea is indistinguishable from a strong cup of Darjeeling. There was a time when we drank tap water, but now no one who can afford bottled does. Vichy and Badoit have been drunk off the shelves, instead we have St Yorre. I think if you're buying water it should taste. In the supermarkets there are fountains of spring water from distant highlands. I said to Piers the water was safe, he retorted: 'That's what they said to those Devonians whose hair turned green last year.' A glass of Devon water wounds the brain. Here the Folkestone and District Water Company is doing its best to keep us informed, their worst fears are to run out of the product – a huge percentage seeps through faulty pipes and for that we have had a hosepipe ban for the last two years.

~

The sun came out and the sea turned the brightest deep-blue I remember, I almost see round the corner to the white cliffs of Dover.

My neighbour Samantha, the youngest householder on the Ness, brought round iron for a magnificent new sculpture, which we put up at the back of the house.

Tuesday 28

Bright, fine dawn, deliciously cool. I worked in the garden until the sun became too strong at nine. There are even more white butterflies in the garden, I counted a dozen on one bugloss plant and they are fighting for space on the thistle. Outside, the men are working on the drainpipes, the water is off.

At four Christopher Lloyd arrived with some young helpers and took notes, everything looking sun-drenched – all rusts, browns and pale grey-greens; the sea remains a bright, deep blue.

Wednesday 29

With the water off life seizes up. I had just enough for one cup of tea this morning before the workmen rolled in. The damage to the plants along the verge is considerable, though the white viper's bugloss seems to have escaped. That can't be said for my bank of yellow horned poppies, which have been mashed into the shingle. The men who are working on the pipes are friendly and, when they are not playing the radio, quiet.

~

Posted a dozen letters as far away as Brazil and New Zealand after enquiries about the garden. What will happen after the film shows?

I walked to the beach and brought back a float – large, hexagonal, rusty, diamond-like – planted it, then took cuttings before settling down to grey.

A foolish schoolteacher drove her car into the garden this lunchtime, missing the white bugloss by feet. She arrived with four other cars with children who were crawling all over the place.

The odd thing about Dungeness is that people behave as if the normal courtesies don't exist: because we have no fences they decide to walk across our gardens. They are often so forgetful they will drive on the wrong side of the road. They pick the wild flowers – which my neighbour Janet says are disappearing.

The old people are the worst, they would do well to learn from their children or grandchildren. They think nothing of stripping the landscape and when there are no flowers left they dig up the plants, and if they find no plants they steal the shingle, and return to dump their rubbish. If this is what happens in a SSSI in England then there is no hope for the rest of the planet at all and these kids will be burnt, or starved to death, by Mother Nature.

Give a silver-haired teacher a car and she behaves like a barbarian. If I had my way I'd ban the car from the Ness, on yer bike Miss Smith. As they pulled out I thought of shouting: 'Kill yourself with the exhaust fumes and save the planet.' I thought better of it. I could see she was a nice person, like one of mum's friends, and I was turning into a policeman. Maybe that's a solution – the constabulary could give up arresting queers for consensual sex, which cost £25,000 last year alone, and arrest and imprison the same number of mindless people who throw cigarette packets and soft drink cans on to the verges.

At the bottom of the road a film crew is filming one of the old houses. They've parked at least fifty cars and lorries on the shingle verges . . . poor wayside flowers.

~

Now they've all gone – teachers, workmen, film crew, tourists – and I'm all alone with a thousand white butterflies.

Thursday 30
Tried to get to the shops but the taxi service seems to be on holiday, so I gave up, cleaned the fridge and swallowed a pint of UHT milk for breakfast.

~

My new role, as Ness watchdog, drew approval from my neighbour Sylvia. She wants to turn the road into a toll road, or at least build those bumps to stop the vehicles rushing by.

~

Just finished Anthony Grey's book *Quest for Justice*, a catalogue of justified woes. Mrs Whitehouse comes over not as muddle-headed or in the slightest well-meaning, but as pig-headed and prepared to ignore anything that might undermine her phobias. The picture in the end is of a country awry, where reason and common decency have long been ousted by prejudice. I can't understand why Anthony Grey wants us to join it, it seems appalling that in order to change this we have to conform. This is the weakness of the assimilationists' view.

~

Nicky rang in a flap to say he had fifteen minutes to write a piece for the *Standard* on 'coming out at the fringes of society'. Meanwhile the white butterflies are dancing in the unreal world I live in and I walk the verges scattering yellow horned poppy seed to undo the damage of the last days.

Friday 31
Went shopping in Lydd. I had almost run out of food as I've been down here for nearly a week. Primed canvas and watered the garden, which is holding its own. Thunderstorms are expected. At Spionkop they are restoring the old semaphore tower.

At four Sylvia's crow suddenly landed on one of the poles in the garden. I found it a little cheese and fed it – it's quite shy, does a sideways glance, grabs the cheese and flies off a few feet to eat it.

Later Mr Crow returned, but much bolder, he started to hide the pegs from the washing line and carried off a silver foil sweet wrapper.

I rang HB to tell him the news, he's off with Peaches and Nicky to see *The Sound of Music* at Sadler's Wells – Nicky billed it as 'So bad, it's a must.'

AUGUST

Saturday 1

Up at seven, a stifling-hot day, too hot by nine to be in the garden, breathless, though last night a sea mist sprinkled dew across the garden. Now even the white butterflies flutter lazily through the bugloss.

Mr Crow is hopping around looking expectant, much more fun than a cat or a dog and also rather more pretty.

Isaac and Topher arrived with Julian and we talked queer matters. Isaac very complimentary about Peter Tatchell and the OutRage! demo, well organised, like a film shoot.

Isaac is working on a script about Roger Casement, but we all seemed pretty gloomy about the chances of making a film. Working Title sums up the disaster: if you have a success, overheads increase and the accountants move in to pay the bills. Films cost £20 million now; no one, except Sir Richard Attenborough, knows how to do that here. British films are in competition with American films, it's not in the interest of Hollywood to help, one box office flop and your company is bankrupt.

I told Isaac I don't care any longer, making films here is for fools and the deluded, no one in their right mind would bother.

Sunday 2

Wrote grey in seven pages – my headache came back so I was glad to finish.

A lot of silly, ill-informed letters in the *Independent* about the word 'queer' and Peter Tatchell's very well thought-out article. I read them and then fell asleep on the sofa.

Marked out a second circle in the shingle, which I will plant with gorse.

Warm close weather, which even the cold breeze failed to freshen, sweltered as the sky grew increasingly grey.

Monday 3

The promised rain passed us by and by nine the sun was blazing down. The landscape is the colour of bleached bone, a desert of dried plants rattling in the wind. I watered the four flower beds until overcome by my headache. I think I should leave for London and let the doctors check it. It hurts particularly in this bright light.

HB and Howard arrived. Howard's photo in the space suit with everything showing caused huge laughter. He doesn't think Century will put it on a cover – Howard says they are very conservative in the art department.

We planted a Russian periwinkle, the bluest of flowers, watered the garden and inspected the new gorse circle, took more photos and, as I still had a headache, HB rang Dr Mark – who gave me an appointment for two tomorrow.

Tuesday 4

Took breakfast in the Bar Italia – the burning sun already up. A strange, troll-like person on the pavement swaying around and slapping his lips. Old Compton Street becomes more weird by the day. HB says it is full of rent boys with pagers and mobile phones, it all seems quite quiet at eight.

At ten I walk to the bookshops and buy an original Chevreul on colour – Graham in the bookshop looks worried, he's going to visit Dungeness on Thursday. We wondered if a book titled *Victorian Nosegays* was about some hidden nineteenth-century perversion. Bought Steiner at Watkins where I have to negotiate my way round the till, my eyes seem fuzzy, which worries me.

My dream of visiting the Alhambra fades. I don't think I will be able to cope with the heat and the sunlight. This sudden return to London has caused chaos – David Hirst, whose telephone number I haven't been able to find, is visiting me in Dungeness this afternoon.

Long telephone conversation with Lorraine about acquiring the rights for *Narrow Rooms* – they are £1000 for the first year, I ask her to take them up as then we can talk about making the film and here I am, feeling a closing in at the edge of my field of vision.

~

Dr Mark put belladonna in my eyes so I left the hospital in a blinding white dazzle. HB, who came with me, had to ferry me over the road. I'm to have a brain scan on Monday. In the meantime Dr Mark tapped my reflexes, looked into my eyes for cytomegalovirus – none present; looked at a mark on my leg – not Kaposi. We laughed at that, one down and two to go; he held his arms out and waggled his fingers at the edge of my vision, he seemed fairly satisfied. Then we did a liquid nitrogen burn-up on my face to get rid of the molluscum.

~

Back at Phoenix House, David Hirst said Prospect looked like a chapel in a sauna. We all went to a Mark Nash film at the Bijou – Jimmy Somerville, his friend Sparkle Eyes, Isaac Julien, Cherry Smyth, Paul Burston, quite a gang.

The film accurate, psychoanalytic and, as Mark said, depressing. David said it was only too accurate. HB thought it very strange.

Wednesday 5

Wrote a letter to the *Independent* supporting Peter Tatchell and then spoke to the *Pink Paper* to do the same. OutRage! getting too much undeserved criticism, though anyone who gets into the minefield becomes a target.

I pointed out to a young correspondent from Edinburgh that his fortune to come out at sixteen was the gift of rowdy GLF meetings and his platform in the *Independent* the gift of those who turn out on the OutRage! demonstrations.

~

Nicky came by, we had lunch together; no new news, but much gossip.

HB very sweet all day.

Thursday 6

Graham, Jonathan and a young airline steward came to take me to Dungeness. I asked the young man if he had joined the 'mile high club'. He said that a first-class passenger, alone in his section, had once taken out a huge hard-on and asked: 'Do you want to blow it?' He put his jacket on to conceal his excitement and set to work. When the stewardess came through his section she said: 'Why are you in that jacket, isn't it hot?' He told her he was cold, so she turned the heating up. Eventually he blew the guy. 'Well,' he said, 'I knew something was up. As I performed the various safety regulations for him he rubbed his cock all the way through, as if I was a go-go dancer in a gay bar.'

~

Dungeness dry as a bone. I planted out my cuttings as we are expecting thunder tomorrow and the end of three weeks without rain.

~

Derek came down here late – his first visit here in six weeks. He was exhausted, had spent a week sleeping on the floor of a hospital looking after a friend with meningitis. Most of the time his friend was in a coma, the doctors had thought there was no hope, but he pulled round.

Friday 7

I was up at seven and I put on Lynn's gift of the Messiaen symphony, cleared my letters. Watered the garden in anticipation of the storms.

~

AUGUST

Howard and I drove to Hastings. The August gardens were uniform and violently coloured, the lawns had turned brown, the straggling flower beds were full of snaggle-toothed burnt-up roses in livid colours, hydrangeas, dahlias and lurid bedding plants. My garden is quite over by July, these are in gaudy glory.

Hastings mirrored the gardens – trippers in fluorescent greens and pinks, a little old lady in baboon make-up was pushing a pram full of dolls down the main shopping street.

In the bookshop Howard bought a tome on plant diseases but found no reference to rosemary dieback. A second plant, one of my oldest, has succumbed by the back door.

I bought Zola's *Paris* and then we sat and had tea and cottage pie. Outside a huge funeral, packed with lads with haircuts and bulky suits, all of them to a man had a large gold fisherman's earring in their right ear. As the hearse went by a group of them stood on the pavement sobbing.

We walked up to Laetitia's and found her and Michael just returned from an exhibition, her wild terrace garden covered with spectacular brambles with huge very sweet blackberries. Ajax, her son, caught newts and showed us a dead slow-worm the cat had caught. We left Laetitia and drove up to Bexhill – a total contrast to the eccentric trippy Hastings: Laetitia was sporting a bottle-green mohican, here ladies of her age had bleached their hair a premature grey and had it styled in the cabbage rose fashion of the seaside elderly. No fluffers on these streets.

Howard searched for an Opal Fruit ice cream, which was quite impossible to find. As we left Bexhill we got lost in a suburban estate and drove in a circle until we found a country lane to Battle, from this moment we seemed to drive in circles through increasingly beautiful woodlands. Battle played out, we turned in a driveway whose owner glowered at us from his garage. Off again via Pett Level to Camber, where we clambered out of the car along the beach; everywhere we went we saw ginger boys.

Back at Prospect we watched Fay Godwin's programme with Mavis Nicholson – who is suitably serious. Fay, who has had cancer, seemed indestructible and frail at the same moment. Her photographs are marvellous and her commitment to the landscape pulls them out of any feeling of 'heritage'; when anything is heritised it stinks of camphor.

The expected thunderstorm never came, so we walked up to 'Bohemia' for a very merry meal with Derek, who cracked open a bottle of champagne, and my rather modest bottle of Burgundy.

Derek said he had seen a masked flasher in Hyde Park being jerked off in full view by a rather grand-looking lady in a grey pleated skirt – they were so involved that they didn't notice an incoming lady returning from Harrods. She was horrified and started to scream. The man scuttled off and the lady who had been 'comforting' him started to scream as well – the two women ended up consoling each other.

The rain came down.

Saturday 8

Howard and I planted up the second circle. Derek arrives, hyper, after seeing off a schoolteacher with her roaming terrier dog which had killed his gorgeous cat Baby. We climbed into the Citroën. I said: 'New Romney.'

Derek asked: 'Why do you want to go there? It's so dull.'

It's very hot and misty. Derek, ruminating on his garden, says hydrangeas grow as large as houses in Cape Town. Howard says they need water and if they don't get it they're in big trouble.

~

It's eleven in the morning and Derek is already hooked on the idea of a trip to Bottoms, Folkestone's alternate monthly gay disco. The last time Derek went, drunk again, it was a straight night and he mistakenly cruised all the straight boys – who were so surprised none of them put up much resistance.

In Hythe we waited and waited for the breaded plaice in the chipper whose customers had a combined age of 100,000. The cod was fossilised and Derek was missing a Bette Davis movie and his afternoon nap.

We walked round the market as the rain came down in large, warm, wetting drops, Derek waiting to curl up with a romantic novel.

Back home, Howard and I clipped the helichrysum, which was blown flat by the wind and rain. A passing photographer asked to photograph us at our work, then a young gardener from Sissinghurst asked if he and his friend could look round.

~

The sun is setting and the first ravers from the acid party at Lydd airport are walking round the Ness. The light is going in a golden mist, a slight wind rustles the yellow flowers of the ragwort. Above them the sun sets a soft pink disc in the grey, the merlin has flown from the telegraph wires, dragonflies and fast flying admirals, black as the floaters in my eyes, fly like arrows across the shingle. Howard pruned and watered until it was time for him to leave for London. I sat here worrying about my right eye, the field of vision seems to have narrowed at the edge.

I wondered quietly how I would cope with blindness.

Sunday 9

Stiff sea breeze, overcast. Cut back the valerian, transplanted a borage to the back bed, swept and washed the floors and read my colour books for green.

Two students from Leicester came to see the garden, one confessed he had sent me a love letter when he was eighteen after seeing a programme on television. A very charming lad with a big smile, he was having problems with his born-again parents.

Strange feeling, disembodied eyesight; there is a distinct falling off of vision on my left, a grey area that comes and goes, the whole visual field is a will-o'-the-wisp.

Monday 10

Trouble at Bertaux's – Michelle nearly burnt down by a blown fuse that set the fridge on fire. She was dressed in spectacular red and black this morning, which was blurred by my eyesight. She said her Yugoslav boys, all Albanians, call her Madame Drama. The best workers were the army boys, their passports all stamped quite easily at Heathrow, about 400 are arriving each week.

~

10.10 – I'm sitting waiting for a CT scan in a crowded corridor in Bart's. The *Independent* read, I sit with the diary. Many old and crotchety men drinking some yellow liquid that smells of aniseed, some doubled up on wheelchairs. Hospital staff bright and efficient as usual. I worry a little about losing my eyesight, I'll have to go into journalism. Perhaps I should do a Lynn Barber and interview all those people I would wish to meet. I wait in the ultrasound waiting area, a couple of younger people have arrived and the place is becoming empty.

I'm wearing HB's green polo shirt and the staff are similarly dressed, perhaps they think I'm a nurse as no one has spoken to me for a long time.

My more macabre thoughts dance a deadly tango. Ah well, it's two years since the foundations tremored. Evil eyes. I can't imagine going blind. Maybe that was the terrible premonition read in my hand all those years ago by Umberto Tirelli in Rome. I wonder if I could paint blind, why not? Piers could photocopy the tabloid headlines, I could write the remarks, not too difficult.

My life is so far removed from this slow queue.

One of the nurses has his hair tied back in a rubber band. Horrible light from fluorescent tubes behind frosted glass, grey ceiling tiles pressed out to look like Travertine marble, grey-flecked lino, no windows, white walls and a fake wood reception, scratched. Notices are dotted all over: 'Resuscitation – dial 222', 'Break Glass', 'Please Do Not Eat or Drink', 'Do Not Enter When the Light Is On'. There is a spider plant, an ivy, a fan, it's airless, though mercifully it rained last night and everything is much cooler. At 10.30 I run out of ink.

SMILING IN SLOW MOTION

~

The brain scan: laid out and strapped in under the white plastic arch, the scanner hums, do re me, melodic and meditative, like drones by George Crumb. I'm given a radioactive iodine injection – cold as ice up my arm – and shuttled through a second time.

On the way home Stephen Pickles bumps into me, he said: 'The closets are rattling all over England and you've driven Simon Callow straight.' In Oxford Street people disappear as they pass me.

~

I'm sitting at Phoenix House, the blinds drawn against the sunlight. HB is back from Newcastle – as the washing machine is roaring away and the fridge is defrosting – but he's gone out.

~

Sarah came by with a letter from the *Pink Paper* defending OutRage! Howard came with the paperback cover for *At Your Own Risk*. Dr Mark phoned to say the brain scan looked OK.

~

Decided to paint a canvas blind to see how I got on, it should be possible with Piers to help.

~

An invitation to Dinard festival. I've turned down Bueños Aires, Jerusalem and others this year. One of the problems with HIV is the feeling of being out on a limb. I was never much of an adventurer, now I'm a stay at home, at least the work gets done and, though they are all at pains to deny this, one festival is much like another as cinemas are much the same everywhere with the audience and critics all facing the same way.

~

One of my correspondents wrote that he found the lack of film information in *Modern Nature* curious. I can't see that writing about a visual medium can be much of an enlightenment: who wants to read an analysis of a Van Gogh? I've never read film theory and never bought a cinema book unless I was interested in a life. I've two bookshelf feet of Pasolini, Murnau, Cocteau, Eisenstein and Buñuel – who wrote an elegant autobiography. Tarkovsky, with all his religiosity, seems dull and bombastic, and yet his films like *Stalker* are among my favourites; Herzog sounds a bore in spite of *Heart of Glass*; Fassbinder was a bully – a friend of mine locked him in an empty house while he was location hunting, threw away the key and left him. A reputation in the cinema is as hollow as the books that are written. Unless there is purpose, who cares for a well-made film or genre? Not I. I wouldn't know what a genre was, am I one? Life was always more important than celluloid, a reputation will last as long as aniline dye, we will all be forgotten like the masks and pageants of the Renaissance and, for the most part, good riddance.

Perhaps the archaeological fragments will lead others to believe there was more than meets the eye.

Tuesday 11

The day started out back to front when Tania at Bertaux's had pointed out that my clothes were back to front and inside out. Since hardly anyone was in the place I took them off and put them right then and there. The next shock was a cyclist who drove right across me. I didn't see him until he almost parted my hair.

Dr Mark thought he could detect lesions in the back of my retina and put the stinging eye drops in. While that was taking effect the nurse got the liquid nitrogen and burnt the growths on my face. It stings and looks quite dramatic – like a witches' cauldron – smoke comes up from the swabs as they scorch white holes.

Eyes again, a terrible blinding light. I was put on a succession of machines. 'Look left, look up, look down, look right.' The torch was blinding, but worse was to come, as the CMV, now diagnosed, was photographed. A blinding flash into the eye while you concentrated on a small flashing red and green light, a green moon after-image and then the world turned magenta. The photos of my eyes looked like one of those colour photos of a distant planet. 'Like a pizza,' said the doctor. 'We often use culinary terms in the hospital.'

Back in the consulting rooms Dr Mark gave me the option of being a patient in the ward or coming in twice a day for two hours – I decided to stay at home.

A young South African doctor came to inspect the damage. I won't get the vision back this time, though when the bleeding in the eye is stopped it might improve slightly. Blindness is on the cards. I'm relieved that I know what is happening, the worst is the uncertainty. I think I have played this scenario back and forth nearly every day for the last six years.

I walked home thinking of Jack, the Great Orlando, how he had coped with blindness and become such a great clown. I'm so surrounded by goodwill.

HB I can see is sad for me, it's much worse for him in many ways. I made him promise not to give up his course as a gym instructor, whatever happens.

It is strange sitting at a table of four and finding the person at your right completely disappeared. This is what happened this evening.

Peter here from Wales, he's learning Welsh, and Howard.

Wednesday 12

My sight deteriorated a little more in the night. I'm sitting at Bart's with HB, waiting to be connected to the drip of DHPG (Gancyclovir).

HB offers his blood. He says it will kill everything and it would be romantic.

The drip trills and gets going, I watch the blood drain back into my arm.

I monitor myself with my outstretched hands, I've lost half to a third of the vision in my right eye. It's a strange sensation, like being accompanied by a shadow. HB, walking beside me, appears and disappears. I can still see his face and hand, but everything between is a blank. I have lost my sight in a central band. The sister says it should stabilise and it could be good for some time: 'I have known people on the drug for a year, or years.'

I make a decision to go for *Wittgenstein* in time and colour. The child could tell his story into the camera. Black drapes. Could the students be Romans? Could we build a room and paint it in different colours?

I had never thought of the outcome of all this in any other way, but thinking blind is quite different from becoming blind, though maybe something else will carry me off. HB more than usually loving, if I couldn't see him I think I could still be happy. My only panic is my morning shave. I couldn't bear anyone else to touch my face as my skin is so irritated, even when I do it myself I hold my breath.

~

We catch the number 24 to Parliament Square, then walk through Westminster School down the empty streets to Queen Anne's Footstool and on to the Tate, where we met Howard and Sarah. I left them to walk round the Hamilton show and went to see Philip Guston's paintings, which I have long admired. The bright white walls of the gallery and the crowds coming and going made me somewhat dizzy.

I've always been able to see the next picture in a line, now there is a blank – the blank isn't black, but white, so very difficult to 'see'. People suddenly appear very close and I think I'll bump into them. I rehearse a confrontation in which I say: 'I went blind today.'

At the Kapoor sculptures I nearly had my first accident as they had surrounded the two large Klein blue rocks with a low rope fence. I nearly went over it – HB grabbed me just in time. Both sculptures are a treat. I don't agree with Norman, who doesn't like them, I would be happy to live with them.

~

We all walked to Random Century, where Howard had a meeting with the art department, and then to the Horticultural Hall in Vincent Square. I bought a dozen snowdrops – they are best planted as early as possible, as the bulbs dry out easily and die.

Home. HB sees Steven Waddington walking up the street and shouts down to him to come and visit. Looking very well, he amused us with gentle stories. He is not working at the moment, though Nigel Terry has signed a contract for five years on an American medieval soap.

~

Back at Bart's, very quiet music in the background. Nurse Gary fights to hit a vein in my right arm, at the third go we strike blood. Steven had said he would faint if a needle was put in his arm. You get used to it, though I still close my eyes. On my way here I was haunted by memories from *The Ruin* and other Anglo-Saxon poems, fate is the strongest, fate, fated. I resign myself to my fate, even blind fate.

The drip stings, a big lump swells up, out comes the needle, it feels like an electric shock is running down my arm.

~

I left the hospital in a downpour. Standing at the entrance an elderly woman trapped in the storm. I hailed a cab and asked if I could give her a lift. 'Can you take me to Holborn tube?' On the way she broke down in tears, she had came from Edinburgh. Her son is in the ward – he has meningitis and has lost the use of his legs. I'm helpless as the tears flow. I couldn't really see her sitting next to me, just hear the sound of her sobbing.

~

Back home HB, my true love, had bought me a khaki-green silk shirt. Whatever happens to me I'll look good, he has an impeccable sense of style.

~

On the television *Out* very good, Simon Watney discussing priorities in healthcare and Peter Tatchell invading Sunday mass in Westminster Cathedral, a clip that reminded me of *Ivan the Terrible*. He shouted at the Christian murderers from his megaphone, the organ started up to drown him out, he was attacked by devilish priests and a moon-faced boy who crossed himself repeatedly after shoving him about. The rest of the congregation kept their eyes firmly fixed on the altar in tunnel vision, or spat at him.

HB said I went wild. I've always thought that the priests should be put on trial rather than the politicians. There is nothing of value in religion any longer, just narrow-minded hate. The blank faces of the born-again confirm this.

Thursday 13

In the ward at nine. I'm sitting in the waiting room, television blaring, with a young woman switching between the demented channels.

~

A discussion has been going on about the needles, the girl next to me had a line in her neck. Nurse David came and attached me to the drip and saw I was writing. 'You're not doing another book? I haven't even read the first.'

Three-quarters of AIDS and HIV organisations are not providing safer sex information for gay men: 169 organisations gave no warnings, fourteen districts believed they had no homosexual community there. 'You might try district X, *they* have a theatre.'

My eyes, I hope, have stabilised. Dr Mark said I had caught the infection very early.

~

HB and Howard arrived as the drip ended and we drove to Dungeness. Bishop Berkeley: 'If you can't see the chair it doesn't exist.'

~

It rained, I answered the mail including a fan letter from a lad in Western Australia who had sent a handsome photo of himself.

~

Howard and I faced the blustery weather and planted wallflowers, HB caught earwigs and sacrificed them to the pitcher plant, and then fell asleep in the west wing. I packed up all my books on colour and we drove back.

I think I have come to terms with my blind fate, there is so much to do, if Beethoven could write the ninth without hearing, I'm certain I could make a film without seeing. There are concerts, books and painting – none of which need sight. I wonder how long it takes to learn Braille.

~

I used to work at the RNIB in my Christmas holidays on their appeal with dear Miss Punch, who arrived on her Harley Davidson each morning to keep us on our toes. Her job as a gardener left her with time to spare in January. Sixty-five, a leather girl, she was the first out dyke I ever met. Closeted and frightened by my sexuality, she gave me immense confidence as an eighteen-year-old confused virgin. If Miss Punch had said 'Climb on, I'll take you for a ride' I would not have been happier.

I opened the thousands of letters with donations, sometimes a tatty parcel would be full of old white fivers, or a child had sent a silver thrupenny bit from the Christmas pudding.

Miss Punch would speed the flagging: 'Chop chop! Derek.' She had more energy than all of us and the power of her beloved motorbike. She looked like Edith Piaf and wore a cock-eyed knitted beret at a saucy angle. She bossed all the other 'girls' who came back year after year for the company.

In the dark midwinter the RNIB was fascinating. The library was typed up by retired people who had learnt Braille; they each took a chapter of a book so it could be transcribed within a week.

Friday 14
Headache during the night. HB crept out of bed while I was still sleeping.

My eyesight has closed in even further, I watch the shadows drawing in. Felt very sorry for myself as I walked to Bar Italia for a coffee, then pulled myself together.

I noticed a blind man at the bus stop.

~

Nurse Gary is on the phone to the doctor, he is to look into my eyes.

I think the indecision is what hurts and a quite normal instinct to feel that I might have escaped all this. The hospital is very quiet, almost hushed, how can I write this? I have a sinking feeling in the stomach and feel very defeated. My mind as bright as a button and my body literally falling to pieces, a naked light bulb in a darkened ruined room.

~

Red Pentel test: held at arm's length and moved in – when does the red appear out of the dark? Peter, the young Irish doctor, says the CMV hasn't progressed much. We talk of Wittgenstein; he says Wittgenstein's cottage in Ireland was literally at the end of the world on a lonely fjord.

~

The nursing staff in Andrewe's Ward full of laughter. I was made toast and did further tests in a dark room. I can describe my sight this morning as 'drunk'.

~

To the BBC where Turan recorded a programme for Monday morning. He was as impressed as I by Peter Tatchell's invasion of the cathedral, also by Simon Watney and his statements on female-to-female transmission of HIV.

The carpet at the entrance to Broadcasting House is royal-blue, there are bright-blue and yellow pamphlets on the table. I pay attention in the way a painter does to describe simple things that the rest ignore: the pipe on Vincent's chair, Monet's glass of pink roses.

~

I walked to my bank in Oxford Street and then returned to St Bart's for my drip.

Saturday 15

The pit of my stomach has gone. I'm very nervous crossing roads as if shock waves had rebounded on me across my sight. Everything seems to have stabilised. I have a bad headache from swivelling around. I can see friends are very shocked.

Tania very sympathetic at breakfast, I tried to make light of the situation.

I'm phoning people up as I know there will be a terrible rumour that I'm blind. HB asked who I wanted to be at my funeral – I had broached the subject. 'Everyone, and the Sisters of Perpetual Indulgence.' One day, many many years from now, I hope he will be buried with me, no dates with destiny. HB made me promise to give him a sign if I go first. What if I'm not there? I might insist on my democratic rights to throw any afterlife away.

HB has been IV trained and is about to hook me up to the drip. It will take at least an hour.

Sunday 16

HB sitting next to me reading the papers. Heidi explains the possibility of having an implant so I can treat myself. It's very quiet – there are only three patients here – the drip purrs away. I worked on green and brown, and then walked with HB to the National Gallery. We stayed only a few minutes as it was so crowded and the gallery-goers stepped backwards looming into my vision field and leaving me feeling insecure and seasick.

I noticed how all the green had faded from the sixteenth- and seventeenth-century paintings, the verdigris turned copper-brown, the paintings seemed very dull. The Impressionists a little brighter. As we left I said: 'Colour is a twentieth-century invention.' Only the lapis-blue, deserted by the fugitive colours, remained to remind us of past glory.

In Holland brown ruled Rembrandt's palette and everything was drowned in dirty varnish.

Sarah brought a book on sexual dissidence and left for an evening of *Alien* films with HB, who was cross because I called him 'duster top' in bed this morning. He put his hand into a tub of gel and now has rock-hard hedgehog hair that would break a comb.

~

At seven I dragged my irritated self back to the hospital; my eyesight has deteriorated since Monday but has stabilised.

Monday 17

Side effects of Gancyclovir are: malaise (very Victorian), sore throat and nose bleeds, headache, dizziness, abdominal pain, constipation, diarrhoea, muscular twitching, cough, pruritis urticaria (itchiness), incontinence and abnormal blood levels in a few patients.

The drip is playing up, a slight move of my hand stops it.

I was stopped in Waterstone's by a young man who took endless notes about where I shopped for books. I bought Francis Bacon's essays and the Leyden Papyrus which I will use at the beginning of the colour book.

HB came to the hospital and we were entertained in the TV lounge by Lewis and his friend. Lewis in a wheelchair, his hair awry, munched through a packet of dry biscuits, as slow and deliberate as a praying mantis. He spoke enthusiastically but almost incoherently, because of the brain damage that has trapped him.

He complained of the noise and the cutting down of the trees for the building of the new wards. Of the London Lighthouse he said: 'You can't be too careful who you mix with there, there's no way of telling the visitors, patients or staff apart. The staff have nothing to identify them except they're all into leather, the place is like Sadie Masies' – the SM club at the Lesbian and Gay Centre.

~

A good explanation for my tiredness is that I'm working overtime to correct the loss of sight. Blink and squint.

~

Mayday.

Tuesday 18

HB in the kitchen with greaser's hair, protects the space against my intrusion. He's taken to calling it his 'office' and guards the washing up like I guard my papers. He's worried about going to Newcastle at the weekend, but I insist that I can always admit myself to the hospital. I should be able to cope physically.

~

HB comes back from the eye department where all the notes are muddled, says: 'It's like Romania in there'. Two sixty-watt light bulbs, murky, grey and most depressing.

The dolls in a doll box in the eye clinic are so grimy. Dr Mark shrugs, says the kids don't see them.

HB is struggling with the hospital phone, which has been designed with a cord so short you have to kneel on the floor to use it.

~

Tommy Nutter in the obituary column, HB spots it. Tommy was always a delight and very handsome. When HB first came to London, on our first date, Tommy came into the restaurant and said hello. Tommy, immaculate in his Savile Row suits, took a shine to HB. HB saved up and bought an expensive shirt from him and dreamed of a suit. On the day he collected his shirt Elton John had just been in and spent £30,000 – Tommy closed up shop and took HB for a cup of tea. As they walked down Savile Row, Tommy pointed out Gieves and Hawkes, and said: 'Arafat has his suits made there.'

~

A long talk with Dr Mark as he lanced my boils. 'Ugh!' said HB.

'I quite enjoy it,' said Mark. He thinks I should take the long-term view, years rather than months. He suggested joining a test for oral Gancyclovir that is being run by Mr Migdal, the eye specialist. The drug is consumed by the liver and up to now they've been unable to administer it orally. They've tweaked the molecule to fool the system. At the moment they have no indication of the results but he feels that to join the trial is not much of a risk as I will be monitored very closely. I think it's best to be adventurous, to treat this as the dodgems, music, bright lights and the bumps.

Dr Joseph felt the infection had been halted. The bright light left afterimages of the blood vessels in my eye.

I suppose this is every visual artist's worst nightmare, but it is only a bad dream. What does it really matter? I will remember the colour of a blue sky and eat the cheese of vivid dreams.

~

Christine Vachon and Tom Kalin were at home after I returned from Bart's at eight. A long discussion of queer marriages of convenience, the bed-snoopers from immigration who appear out of the blue at three in the morning, interview you in separate rooms asking, 'What colour toothbrush does your loved one have?' If your marriage is of mixed race then the heat is up, rifling through your photo albums and dirty linen. The rights of marriage are sacred only in the church. Here as everywhere, different values are applied.

Walked to est. with them and stopped at Bar Italia on the way home to chat with Chris Woods. He was spotted on television by an irate mother – she recognised him as her teenage son's lover and wrote to the Channel, the police and her MP. Chris says his TV days are over. I wonder if Woody Allen's film career is in the same state after the revelation that he is fucking his stepdaughter.

Wednesday 19
Oh drip drip drip.

~

Gancyclovir.

~

I wait for James and David. We are driving to Dungeness to water the plants – though thunderstorms are forecast. We will talk of the blue void of Yves Klein. James thinks there is no chance of making films here, the future of the BBC hangs on a soap made in Torremolinos, *El-Dora-Do*.

At Prospect Cottage there is a pile of post in the hall. I entertain two gardening enthusiasts who arrive as we do. They were very knowledgeable, said the garden was a breath of fresh air. Gardening, like everything else, is backward-looking – the idea of a garden is the restoration of some gigantic nineteenth-century folly. Prospect looks to the future.

They had been to a research establishment in Arizona and said my garden was what they were dreaming of. We discussed the lack of imagination that leads to a cracked drive, brown lawn and the scorched flower bed.

At Prospect, flowers are just a bonus and are not really necessary. Some, like the sage, flourish; others, like the iris, are often blown away in a salt easterly and are just there for the foliage as much as the flowers.

~

James searched the Ness for mushrooms while I sorted out books to bring home. At four we piled into the car and had a cream tea in Rye before returning to London, exhausted.

~

I asked the nurse if I could sit in an empty room as the TV lounge is full of patients and visitors smoking, and the awful blurred television blasting away.

~

I decided to make *Blue* without images – they hinder the imagination and beg a narrative and suffocate with arbitrary charm, the admirable austerity of the void.

As I left James in front of the hospital he asked: 'You won't change your mind, will you?' I promised not to.

~

Drip drip. Countdown from 100 to 36, one hour nearly gone. I'm exhausted this evening, can't get back to my wild HB whom I love and who loves me.

~

A young man, frail as Belsen, walks barefoot down the corridor in his pale-green hospital pyjamas, very quiet, coughing.

The roar from the central-heating ducts outside the window.

My face burns from the chemicals, my anus stings from the boils and my jugsy eye hides the people who walk past.

Thursday 20

This morning Antonio made me two cappuccini with hearts inscribed on them and enquired of my health. I'm light-headed and headachy today, but my early morning visit to Bar Italia wakes me up.

Bar Italia is always a bustle, Pavarotti – music's Incredible Hulk – is belting out some air from the Risorgimento to the accompaniment of the hiss of steam in the cappuccino machine. Tarta della donna – granny's cake – is the best, as are the cappuccini, presided over by a huge boxing poster of Rocky Marciano.

After the Verdi there's the news, today it's the story of Fergie's toe; sock it and suck it, the Duchess of York's sex life at Balmoral on the civil list. Fergie's relatives are such a dull lot, the rumours about the rest of them make the odd blow-job on the taxpayer seem saintly. At least someone is having a good time.

~

By nine I'm at Bart's. I sit watching life ebb away in the Andrewes Ward. It is the lack of hope that is so distressing, as the HIV always wins, knocks you for six just as you are beginning to forget it. A bullet in the back of the head would be easier, just a moment of terror, over before you register it. With this illness you can take longer than the Second World War to get to the grave, ending your days looking like the tympanum of the damned at Autun.

~

I have laid out the books for my book of colour – Aristotle to Wittgenstein, the Leyden Papyrus to *The Doors of Perception*. The problems with books of colour is that they turn out like shopping lists, the unscientific Goethe reads better than Chevreul and Wittgenstein's terse statements cannot be read, only analysed.

~

Christine Vachon and Steve Clarke-Hall here, very enthusiastic about *Narrow Rooms*. Christine thinks we should set it in the fifties so we can have Senator McCarthy and cold warriors on the radio to give it dimension. Casting, which you know you can never afford, but it's worth a dream: Dirk Bogarde as Dr Ulric, Matt Dillon, Faye Dunaway and HB.

Della Grace had sent me photographs of lesbian boys which Christine admired. They are great and they confuse. Any queer is bound to look at the enormous dick before he realises it is a strap-on dildo worn by a boyish girl.

~

Ken returns from a trip to Seville and the Alhambra, which he said was the most beautiful building he had ever seen. Poor Richard was on the telephone and fax all day, and only appeared at lunch and dinner before returning to battle the recession. Richard is St George and the art market his large bankrupt dragon.

Ken and I worked on the Loony Ludwig script. We put in his life, now we need the philosophy and love, and then we should be there.

HB goes to the opening of *Alien 3*. He made his escape as the pills have turned me into a wind-tunnel, my farts could solve the energy problem.

Friday 21
HB left for Newcastle this morning. I was in high spirits as I know he wouldn't have left me if he had thought I couldn't cope. It was a vote of confidence that I could live my independent life. Let's hope it stays this way until the end, which may be in the room I'm sitting in at the moment with my drip. I think I am resigned now to my approaching death. I hope I can embrace it cheerfully. Up until this battle with CMV a part of me felt I might slip through, cheat fate with a new drug. Now I realise that is improbable.

HB and I are in love and will remain so until the end of both our days.

~

Ken and I settled down to *Wittgenstein* and decided to rewrite in order to include more information. Could John Messenger be put into tracksuits the colour of angels? Could Jody play the young Wittgenstein and tell the story? Let's take leave of ourselves.

HB thinks the Palace spilt the beans so they could take possession of the children – Fergie has appeared for the second day running like an oven-ready turkey from Tesco. A spokesperson in scarlet, half newscaster, half lady-in-waiting with a county hairstyle said: 'We can't have those children brought up by foreigners, they're *royal*!' An extraordinary observation to make of the happy family who are all mongrels.

Royal scandal shows the extraordinary lengths a society will go to to avoid reality, the royal family is like any family, the myth is 'family life'.

~

My neutrophil count has gone down, the white cells under attack from the Gancyclovir.

I cooked myself supper and retired early to bed.

Saturday 22
Worked all day on green.

Dr Mark took me off AZT as my cell count had plummeted – he says it opens me to infection. Derek's friend died in the week. He is alone, and sounded depressed.

Sunday 23
Breakfast acted by Michelle and Tania who lose their Yugoslav waiter – he is leaving for Istanbul and Austria. Michelle says that when Sarah Armstrong-Jones came to tea he said 'You look like a princess' before she and Tania coughed and changed the subject. He's a Don Giovanni and has three gold bars hidden under his bed.

Mathilde comes in with a carrier bag with her name on it and we talk of dyeing. She tells me the dyers made the rainbow for the miracle play of the flood. She squints through her glasses and adjusts her cardigan of many colours. Harris tweed is still dyed with blackberries and lichen – naturally. She uses chemical colours for her work in the theatre.

The corporation is cleaning the streets with a lorry that shoots water in every direction. Michelle runs out and kisses the operator and promises him coffee and croissants every time he passes.

Tania's friend drives me to St Bartholomew's, every road is shut, we go round and round – a ten minute journey takes half an hour.

I'm writing with my right hand and my left hand is being bandaged by Jane and the drip started; it never stops.

~

'HB? Where did I put my?. . . trousers, socks, books, glasses, toothbrush?'
 Long silence. 'I know where it is.'
 'Oh, where?'

AUGUST

'At your arse-end where you left it.'

I haven't lost anything but him this weekend. I miss the constant rustle of an HB, the clatter of typing, the whirling jug-jug of the geriatric washing machine that tumbles its soapy water on to the kitchen floor, the clatter of the desk chair as he searches through his forty-three colours of Fred Perrys in the cupboard. There's no fun in stealing his clothes if he's not there to protest 'You're stealing my look!' HB is very superstitious about his 'look'.

HB rustles about, he irons my shirts – which never saw an iron until he arrived; he opens the window and the sound of Charing Cross Road roars in; he vacuums – I'd never possessed a vacuum. I sit in the chair with my legs in my arms as he roars past; there is cooking and washing; and the exact brand of lemon lavatory cleaner flushed down the loo.

HB is up before six and off to the gym to see his taekwon-do instructor. HB's favourite pastime is the gym: 'Look what I'm making for you, Fur Beast.' When I wake up he has run my bath, he soaps and tickles my foot as he eats the great wall of cereal. 'Tickle my foot, tickle my foot. Twizzle my hair.' I am so itchy from drugs and general dilapidation, it's almost the only thing to take me out of myself.

HB growls and does the accounts for the VAT man. I'm always surprised that these authorities are so relentlessly unforgiving, since I can't even add up and develop an amnesia for numbers. HB, on the other hand, shines with numerals, reads *Nature* from cover to cover – he disappears to the library to keep abreast with developments in the sciences. Last week someone developed a solid that is lighter than air, wonders will never cease. HB retired from the acme of computing to come and live with me at twenty-two. For six years now I have been wildly in love with HB. HB is fanatically loyal, studies taekwon-do to protect me, and his constant and amusing attention has kept me alive.

HB is growing his hair and says no one looks at him any longer, this, of course, is crocodile tears. Tania thinks he is incredibly handsome and has a face you never forget. I think the same. HB, of course, will never believe this. He's modest, thrifty and conducts his life with the rectitude of a Methodist – his father is a lay preacher, his mother is the chapel organist, from her he inherited his eyes. HB has incredible eyes, they are green with lashes like spiders.

HB has tattoos, an ancient British tradition, he says. I never notice them, there are flowers and bees, a lizard, a seahorse, a fish and actually he's right, I forget the rest though I like tattooed boys.

I met HB in the most romantic of circumstances, in the front row of the Tyneside Cinema, and rang him later to wish him Happy New Year – he came down to London with a bag on his shoulder, like Dick Whittington, and eventually came back to stay.

I knew the moment I saw him that I would live with him for the rest of my life. When I am gone I would like to think he will be buried with me. Perhaps we should have three spaces, as I hope he will fall in love again. He is my first true love at fifty and I am his at twenty-seven. Some of us are slow, it was worth the wait.

~

The drip is nearly finished, it has counted down from 100 to 25.

Monday 24

Howard called by with the post from Dungeness and we talked brown and green flowers as we walked through the bookshops on the way to Bart's. I met a man in a mustard coat, he said he bought it in a Japanese store where it was described as green.

~

The chocolate trolley arrives, no chocolates for me today. We've been to Foyle's and bought books on the eye instead of colour – I am turning a blind eye to my faulty blood count this morning.

~

Heidi demonstrated the mixing of the drug. 'I've never been much of a cook,' I say and then she sets up the infusion pump. 'How does it work?'
  'Like your gut.'

~

I'm working so hard on the book that I sleep – when do I ever *sleep* now? – with a pen and paper by the bedside. I can write quite legibly in the dark and the best thoughts seem to flood at four, though in the morning they never seem quite as sharp as they did in the darkness, where they flash into the mind with no competition, isolated like a single flower in a specimen vase.

~

Last night passed in a hurricane, like Hurricane Andrew, which threatens to wreck Florida today with winds of 150 mph.

~

A blind hospital worker with a white cane walks past, she is smiling.

~

I worked through the afternoon with Ken on *Wittgenstein*. He brought in the script, which is witty and informative, then we went to the café for Ken's favourite – liver and sage, and apple crumble.

Back at Phoenix I settled down to a book on Pliny that cost me £40 at Foyle's – it will save me having to read the whole of the *Natural History* – then worked on the colour brown.

~

Back to Bart's at seven in the pouring rain, dripped, returned to watch *The Garden*. C4 has sensitively put the adverts into close batches, as a film of image and music is disrupted badly by these little narratives – any one of which cost more than my film. *The Garden* wanders about and then settles down to tell the Passion. The *Independent* said it was muddled, but it is the muddle of necessity, its paths are signposted: 'There are many paths and many destinations.' The suicide of Judas, Pilot and the Pentecostal scene, the crowning with Thomas and the final drawing apart, all as clear as a bell made in Christendom. Film critics have no visual training, they are writers who make their pronouncements through the fog of Eng. Lit. There are no words in the camera, the cinema started in silence, acquired piano, organ and then a soundtrack. I don't think it regressive to abandon the wordy narrative. The film has poems, a poetic narrative. I kept wondering what this will look like fifty years from now. I hope I can watch it from a corner of the afterlife over the shoulder of an old friend.

Tuesday 25
Had a long conversation at Bertaux's with a young man who was reading Ray Monk's book on Wittgenstein, then over to Bart's for a meeting with Dr Mark who seemed happy with my 'progress'. He said the white flashes I experience in the eye are common when the retina is damaged. The retina might peel away – which could be a problem – as the eyeball shrinks back to its original size.

Talked to two young men, one of whom had just been diagnosed with cancer – he told me this in a whisper – the other may have a touch of TB. A man is wheeled past in a tall chair that looks like a child's high seat.

~

Ken said a young architect friend stayed at the London Lighthouse. He hung on as a party was thrown for him at the end of the week. Sixty friends gathered and he was wheeled in. He took one look at them and said 'I'm too tired', went upstairs and died.

The Lighthouse was a topic of conversation in the TV lounge here last night. Someone had a friend who was dying and he asked for a cigarette. The staff said: 'This is a no smoking area, but you can have a bottle of champagne if you like.' However much the place is needed, private charity is an affront to all of us *and* the NHS, there is no morality in charity when it lets others duck their responsibilities.

~

Started my chapter on colour in antiquity, 'Shadow is the Queen of Colour', and worked steadily through the day until I had tidied up all my notes. I met a young Australian who sorted out some books for me at Zwemmer's.

~

Read Pliny on extravagance in Rome. I like the story of Rotundus, Claudius's slave, who was so rich he had a solid silver chaser that weighed two hundred pounds, and twelve side dishes of one hundred and fifty pounds each. Pliny wonders what kind of banquet could be served and how many slaves would be needed to carry it.

~

I caught myself looking at shoes in a shop window. I thought of going in and buying a pair, but stopped myself. The shoes I am wearing at the moment should be sufficient to walk me out of life.

Wednesday 26

This morning Tania and Michelle were all in a fluster, they go to Edinburgh tomorrow with *The Maids*. Tania's friend David drove me back to Bart's.

My post becomes stranger. I had a request for an autograph from a boy in Nashville, Tennessee, who wrote, 'I bet you've never had a letter from Tennessee before.' At HB's suggestion I wrote back that of course I had received mail from Tennessee before, Elvis used to correspond regularly. Requests for autographs from Czechoslovakia and Poland are quite common, I had one each last week. It seems a strange pursuit to me.

There are two charming men who always seem to know when I'm going to the BBC; they produce the same old photo of me as a child in Italy and I have to sign for them.

I've left all my post in a pile and have not answered anything, either I am a correspondent or I write my book and make films. I'm alone here and I cannot possibly ask HB to deal with my mail when he comes back this evening. I have never had a secretary, though HB has typed up all my scripts and books in the past.

~

At three Dr Mark rang and said I had drawn lucky to go on a course of pills. This was an enormous relief as tomorrow I was to go in to have an operation to put in a permanent drip turning me for the rest of my life into a 'bionic'. He was also very relieved as it would have been a blow to my independence – I would have had to have had a special fridge to keep the drugs fresh and spend an hour each day attached to a tube. Travelling would be impossible – can you imagine going through customs with a fridge?

~

I took an hour off, walked to M&S to see if they had a good yellow T-shirt (they hadn't), then on to the Royal Academy, where Norman was discussing a show of antiquity with an Oxford professor. I had the book on Pliny under my arm so I was delighted to meet him, then, light of foot, I bumped my way along to Waddington's and was given a Barry Flanagan catalogue. I walked home via the National Gallery and saw the quite ravishing little *Nativity at Night* by Geertgen tot Sint Jans.

~

Back at Bart's at seven.

Ken came and we worked on *Wittgenstein*, we are halfway through the script and had a difficult hour trying to imagine the way forward.

I received a whole wodge of Xeroxes from Manchester – the comments book from the show, some bad, some good, but all quite passionate.

After over two weeks coming in each day morning and evening I'm very tired, longing to be detached from the needles and drips.

HB appeared at three and started all the systems: hoover and washing machine; computer and printer; iron and microwave.

When HB comes back he takes several hours to settle. A Hinney Beast is a creature of habit and has to go round its territory re-establishing itself. When a Hinney Beast has done this it slowly calms down and its growly nature subsides, after that it is very happy until it makes the next move, say to Dungeness, when the whole process repeats itself. I can imagine HB sitting in one room for days on end, this would make him most happy.

~

The Serbs set fire to the great library in Sarajevo that housed the Bosnian archive – people risked their lives to save manuscripts. Neo-Nazis in Rostock set a refugee hostel alight – there is gloom here. The Somali war is so hard tonight that an entire nation is starving. The world is so small now it is as if the backyard is on fire and the millennium I will not see stands like a triumphal arch commemorating mankind's hollow victories – the winners will be the losers and we, who live in this selfish society, will face the greatest loss of all.

Thursday 27

I've come back to St Mary's to have my eyes looked into by the eye specialist, Mr Migdal. The place is the same but there are new staff, I don't recognise anyone here. How relieved I am not to have had an operation this morning. I must try and cheer HB up, he's had a hell of a fortnight. It's much easier for me to cope. I know the parameters of my health. He has to take care of the unexpected and is a slave to his conscience where I am concerned. It's a difficult tightrope for both of us, I must not take anything for granted.

~

The little grey man over from me is fretting as he had to get to Sussex; 'I can't read. I'm going blind.' A little later he picks up a newspaper, struggles with it for a moment and then throws it back on the table.

My eyedrops, which sting, have stopped me reading and so I'm writing this in a haze of belladonna.

The little grey man's face has fallen into tragedy. He looks like Jean Cocteau without the poet's refined arrogance. The room is full of men squinting in the dark in different states of illness, some barely able to walk, distress and anger on every face and a terrible resignation. The death of the strong is the worst as they have to be knocked from their pedestals to the ground.

Jean Cocteau takes off his glasses, he looks about with an indescribable meanness. He has black slip-on shoes, blue socks, grey trousers, a Fairisle sweater and a herringbone jacket. The posters that plaster the walls above him have endless question marks, HIV? AIDS? AIDS? HIV? Are you affected by HIV or AIDS? AIDS? ARC? HIV?

This is a hard wait, I want to get out of here, forget.

The shattering bright light of the eye specialist's camera – he says the retina has healed well. The photographs blind me with white, the after-image dissolves in a second to the colour of the blue sky, as the photographs progress the colours change to pink and the light changes to orange. The process is a torture, but the result stable eyesight, worth a hard twelve pills a day. It must be my association with HB, lover of computers and king of the keyboard, that brought my luck on the computer which chose my name for this drug trial.

As I left St Mary's I smiled at Jean Cocteau. He gave a sweet smile back.

~

HB and I walked to the National Gallery. HB very meditative, he spent a long time looking out of the window as I searched through books on Pliny, Wittgenstein and Bacon – my reading is mammoth for colour. Dillon's is much easier to find books in than any other London bookshop, my eyes were so fuzzy from the eyedrops that I had to ask the assistant to read the index of the *Natural History* to find out which volume I wanted.

Then I went on a search for yellow and found a T-shirt reduced to £5 in Covent Garden, huge relief.

Friday 28

I take the DHPG six times a day, two pills at a time with food.

HB said recognising one of the boys he knew from the gym – once a body-builder, now skeletal – wandering about in the HIV clinic would stay with him for life.

~

HB has put so much grease on his hair it looks like an oil slick, he says if he swam in the sea guillemots and seals would die in it.

~

At lunchtime Norman said that Francis Bacon had left all his money to his boyfriend John, whom he had picked up, and not José, who had picked him up. He bought me a Craigie Aitchison tie from the Royal Academy. Norman said he found the scrabble for property in East Germany distasteful and would not, even if it were offered, take back anything.

He thrilled about his daughter, at seventeen months she's counting and has a muddle of two languages.

~

I had missed my appointment with Ken, who was understandably cross. We mapped out the rest of our script and then walked through Soho where I bought a silvery Chinese instrument for *Wittgenstein*, then through Covent Garden to the lavish new Tesco.

~

HB went out with Peaches who greets him with 'You are so cool' with a gleam in his enemy eyes. HB flirts and jokes, and looks happier – the washing machine has been dying and this preoccupies him, he watches i's noisy death throes anxiously. Peaches is worried that his sexuality is out of control; priapic, he can manage ten orgasms a day. I say I think that he should feel lucky that it is possible, it seems rather puritan not to celebrate if you have the capacity. In my case the DHPG seems to topple tumescence for good.

~

I put on my yellow pyjamas to start yellow.

Sarah and Alison came by for a second. I recited a little of the book and told them the latest scandal: Prince Edward is not gay at all.

Saturday 29
David Lewis drove me to Dungeness.

A large pile of letters from *The Garden* showing last Monday, all very affirmative except for one abusive one, spurred by the *Independent* and sent via OutRage!. It said I made sado-masochist films of self-hatred. If I do hate myself I've never noticed it. The more letters I get from these old-fashioned 'gays' the more I'm glad of the queer.

Sarah said that she had sat down near two young men, business types, at Valerie's in Soho. They were venomously tearing into two pretty boys sitting across the restaurant. She said she could bear it no longer and said: 'Can't you take your homophobia elsewhere?' They were furious and told her they were gay. After they left the two boys invited her over. Little incidents like this point out to us that sexual preference does not make us a community, if we were there would be far more of us on the demos and we could change things. It's not us who hold things back, we are doing things – books, poetry, radio, TV – it is the assimilationists who are the enemy.

The letters brought some other surprises: one told me that Stephen Ward, of the Profumo case, had been expelled from my old school after a pillow fight – the boy he was fighting with had a brain haemorrhage and was found dead the next morning. It went on to say that Dirk Bogarde's life-long companion had also been there, and was a charming and well-mannered boy.

A letter from John Sainsbury to say he will be here on Saturday next to discuss the Wilde statue. I do hope he goes for something abstract, I don't think it's worth adding another portly Victorian to the London streets.

I worked through the evening and cleared the replies to forty or more letters.

Norman said that Hugh Casson was one of those Englishmen who always replied to his mail. I'm much the same.

When Vera Russell had written a third time telling the president of the Academy that Norman was unacceptable as the secretary – 'You know, Hugh, we have known each other so long' – Casson called Norman in to his office and said: 'I have another of *these* letters, why don't you draft a reply.'

Sunday 30
I had a terrible nightmare in the small hours and got up at dawn. A gale raged through the night and the clatter of things blowing about kept me

awake. I'm alone today writing this at seven. There is a break in the clouds though the wind is spinning my little garden silly.

~

It's eight, the wind is still howling round the house but there is blue in the sky and a chink of sunlight in the rushing clouds, and my migraine, which has made me rather sick, is subsiding like the storm.

~

Alan came with friends and made an enormous pasta lunch. We walked along the deserted beach and collected holey stones and driftwood; Alan left and soon after Sandy and Alfie arrived. We had lunch at Demetrio's restaurant, then discovered a huge metal circle on the beach, which Alfie rolled back, like Sisyphus, all the way to the front garden. We had a strong cup of Assam and watched the last of the sunset from the new room. Sandy had found a book from the time of making *Caravaggio* in her bookcase and brought it back. This must be one of the very rare occasions in my life when anyone has returned a borrowed book.

The garden continued to take a battering. I tidied up the cold frame and planted the tub at the back with cowslip, allium, snowdrop and rosemary.

Monday 31 – Bank Holiday
The rain falls sparkling on each leaf and scarlet hip, the mushrooms push up.

~

This is an old English Bank Holiday, stay inside, faces pressed to the window. Thomas the black cat slinks through the sage bushes sparkling wet, he shakes himself. A bright little bird carries on looking for grubs in the elder, quite unconcerned. A roll of thunder and lightning over the sea. I wonder how Derek's guests are coping in the army tent. I phone him; 'Nothing much is happening, what shall I write in my diary?'

His advice: 'Invent something spicy.'

I find my faulty eye worries me just in the morning, less as the day passes. John Adams's setting of Walt Whitman's 'Wound Dresser' melancholy; tap of the rain or a curious bee on the window; the gale has blown itself out and away.

I have Erasmus's *In Praise of Folly* and work on yellow, the rain falls; a grand calm.

SEPTEMBER

Tuesday 1

Stayed in all day. By ten in the evening the colour manuscript had doubled to over ninety pages. We had two small breaks. I rebuilt the garden sculptures and Gingerbits cleared the last of the wood from the building, it all looks quite smart.

~

On the way back from the Light Railway Café we found several of the corkscrew tank defences and a rusted bicycle seat that became a dragon to defend our work against the evil weather – the gales are back, the garden is tucked up for the winter, the first bulbs planted where the shrill wind can do no damage.

Wednesday 2

HB calls to say the phone had rung late into the night with people enquiring after my health. He described them as 'the telephone tree glitterati'; he said most of them gave me two weeks.

~

When Peter Logan rang me I knew something was amiss – he told me Karl had committed suicide two days ago in NYC. It came as no surprise, I imagined Karl had done this long ago.

~

I met Karl one evening at Mario Dubsky's home in Archway. Karl was sitting on the kitchen table wearing a Moroccan jellaba – immensely handsome with chestnut hair, grey eyes and the smile of an angel, one of those mysterious smiles you see in archaic sculpture. He looked like the young Mars in Botticelli's painting. He had arrived that afternoon, so I offered to show him the sights of London – we took off into the night and arrived, very late, at his hotel in Lancaster Gate. It looked rather grim so I invited him to come back to Liverpool Road. He spent his first night in London in bed with me.

Karl was nervous and bright, he had came to train as an architect at the

AA. He soon gave this up and transferred to the Slade. His paintings were not a great success, the best were rather stiff and formal watercolours brought back from trips to Morocco. This did not matter, as Karl had a small fortune from his family who were the Kelloggs. This fortune was always expected to increase when his grandmother in Phoenix died.

He was entranced by England and the English, and his small fortune gave him entry into the more Bohemian circles of the aristocracy. He also became friendly, though never intimate, with all the young artists.

His life followed the wildest path of the seventies in a flat above the Shaftesbury Theatre near the British Museum. Decorated with Arabian junk carpets and hangings, and bits and pieces from Morocco and India, his bedroom papered with clipped pictures of football heroes and naked boys from *Physique* magazines, his bed was always unmade, with a tide-line of come and KY on the walls.

Karl was a back-room boy, who chalked up his conquests on a blackboard as if he were playing darts. He had the first and biggest collection of pornographic magazines and seemed happy only when getting fucked, until that was all he was doing – the theatre, concerts and friends were abandoned for the bars, where he would disappear into the dark in a black leather jacket.

In 1970 I went on a holiday with him to Venice. A priest abandoned his prayers in St Mark's and invited him to San Senolo – the lunatic asylum – for lunch, putting him into his bed while he prayed for the madmen in the church below.

Auden could have written *The Rake's Progress* for him – they did, in fact, meet on several occasions.

The madhouse in Venice was a premonition of things to come – he had a series of nervous breakdowns. I once had the unpleasant task of committing him in London. I loved him dearly, but his instability frightened me – he would regress to a furious five-year-old, overturn tables, throw books and vases round the room, and threaten to throw himself through the window. He became nervous, his sentences an incessant psychotic babble that ended with a hollow laugh. He would have lunch at four in the morning, go to bed at midday, then wake up an hour later. Perhaps Karl's psychosis was brought on by his passion for acid with its jewel-like illusions. Through all this I remained in love with him, but increased the distance, he was always threatening to descend.

When I saw him in New York two years ago he seemed more distracted than ever – he had discovered he had the virus. This didn't worry him as he collected used condoms in the bars and parks and ate them – he confided this to me with a feeling of desperation. The mechanics of sex left him an exile to his own emotions. Karl's craving for love was boundless, he spent every moment of his life either imbibing culture to bolster his insecurities or cruising.

He met a mousy little Greek architect who drew him away from his friends and paraded his beauty on show-off holidays. Karl lived in increasingly desperate poverty – he languished forgotten and penniless in Hoboken. Not only was this flat desolate, but by this time he had lost nearly all his friends as his behaviour became increasingly erratic.

Peter said he had written recently to say he had run out of resources to cope with his madness. His last dash was stopped by an Immigration Officer at Heathrow whom he embraced as he gasped 'Thank God! England'. He was eventually turned back.

Karl's architect stole him from us and now wanted Karl's paintings – sharp, acid gouaches, which he could have easily paid for while Karl was alive.

Now Karl will be forgotten, all the promise, excitement and beauty vanished, the thousands of lovers will also not remember the boy from Buffalo with the smile of an angel. His ashes are trapped in an urn in Brompton Oratory with a collection of others waiting to be thrown into a lake in Kathmandu. After an overdose and an early death he remained the eternal traveller.

~

Back to Phoenix House where Sarah and HB were embracing, 'We're allowed, we're going to have children.' Sarah had all sorts of unmentionable information, then we walked round Covent Garden, looked at my musical instrument – a chromium lyre – for the film. Bought trousers and ended up in the Stock Pot having liver and bacon. Sarah unhappy that she wasn't going to get 'crucified' at the cathedral demonstration as she is going to be on holiday. I had brought her the crown of thorns with its ruby drops of blood from Dungeness. It's very fashionable-looking – perhaps she should wear it back home on the bus.

~

HB packs to go to Newcastle. In bed very early. The drugs make me drowsy and cause my terribly irritated skin that never leaves me alone. I find myself rolling up my trousers and scratching my legs. This morning I put on my trousers inside out and had to change them in the taxi to Ashford.

Thursday 3

Ken and I had a great meeting at Bandung. Tariq Ali is the enthusiast whom you dream of as a producer: he has flair and enough wickedness, he's a fine politician when it comes to organising things; lots of good gossip and a good eye for the best. The Spinoza film is very well put together. I think, like myself, he realises that nothing will ever change here.

~

A long discussion about Wilde initiates a film project – set in Paris at the end of his life in a room, a café, on a bridge.

Saturday 5

David picked me up at Phoenix House at 7.30 and we were down to Dungeness just after nine. We cleaned the house, put up the poles in the garden brought down in the storm and then worked on the book of film stills for Japan.

At 11.30 John Sainsbury rolled up in a new BMW sports car and seemed very happy and very relaxed, he had been opening a new Sainsbury's at Ashford and brought a huge smoked salmon, which we ate for lunch.

A long discussion about the Wilde memorial. John is very for it though he thinks a plaque on the opera house would be the best. He's not against a committee – I suggested Richard as chairman and a long list of names. We can't ask the current political establishment as Wilde would have loathed them and the project would be jinxed, so could we look to a more affirmative establishment? Vanessa Redgrave, Terry Eagleton, Lindy Dufferin, Simon Watney, Marina Warner, Jeremy Isaacs, Norman Rosenthal, Jacques Lang, perhaps Mary Robinson could unveil it – at least that would keep David Mellor off the platform.

I can see it will be a rocky process whatever we do, as so much hangs on Wilde politically as well as artistically. Everyone I've mentioned the idea to is enthusiastic.

John walked to the sea and left for Preston. David left to see friends in Canterbury. I wrote nearly forty cards in reply to the post generated by the showing of *The Garden*. Bed by nine.

Sunday 6

David here again for work, he rang Gen P. Orridge last night – his case is in the hands of Amnesty International, the hounding of him and his family from this country is a disgrace, as was the programme that started all of this in which I appeared. Channel Four excused themselves by saying 'my image was too small to recognise'. In spite of this everyone did recognise me and the tabloids were here the next evening. Gen was in Nepal and Thailand, and then left England as the police gutted his house in Brighton and confiscated a lifetime's work. The police told David that ███ ████████████ █████████ ███ █ ███-██ ████ █ ████ ███ ███ ██ ██████ ██ █████ ██ ███ ██████ ██ ███ ████ ███ █████████ ████ ███ █████████ ███ ███

Monday 7

A very successful meeting at Channel Four when it was decided to carry *Narrow Rooms* forward.

HB inducted on to his gym course. He says everyone on it has a secret cash-in-hand job: the £100 they receive in dole and housing benefit doesn't stretch far enough, they all live in terror of being discovered but have no alternative.

Tuesday 8

Worked at Bandung all morning with Ken on Loony Ludwig; we are making bright decisions. At one we walked down Kentish Town Road and on to Habitat to look at furniture. Then on to David in his plush editing suite to work on *Blue*, which is coming on fine. Quite exhausted. Home at seven.

HB bouncy. We walked to Tesco's and came out at sunset, all the street lights on against a deep-blue sky. It's become very cold and a T-shirt – yellow today – and my old Cornish smock do not keep me warm.

Wednesday 9

HB is scratching my head as I write. I have a horrid headache that is slowly going. HB is cross about the alarm that kept him awake all night at the Marquee Club across the road.

~

Arrive at Bertaux's at 8.45. Michelle preparing the upper room – a mass of cakes and everyone most happy. *The Maids* was a great success.

Ken and I spent two hours in Bertaux's sorting out *Wittgenstein*, then we met up with the two Annies – costume and sets – and visited the neat studio at Waterloo.

~

Check-up at Bart's. I have a storm of black floaters from the retina, which is flaking. I've noticed that if I wear glasses they cut out the edge of my vision field and make me feel quite normal. I had my blood pressure monitored for the headaches, this seems quite normal. My boils are being left to themselves. It was another very productive day.

~

Rang Lynn Seymour, who said she would be delighted to play Lydia Lopokova. She said Fred Ashton used to dread going down to the Keyneses' home as there was no drink. Lydia Lopokova was taken to the library each week by Alan. He said she used to garden nude, only wearing a hat; said in the middle of the three-day week: 'Pity I can't telephone Maynard, as he'd sort this out.'

~

HB bumped into his friend Anton, who had returned from two years in South Africa to find fourteen people in his address book had died. HB hadn't realised Anton had left London and had assumed he had died also – at first he thought he was seeing a ghost.

HB is worried that all his friends are dying. He thinks that he will be the only one left and lonely. He says if he was put on a life support machine and comatose he did not want to be turned off *ever*. Meanwhile I scratch myself to sleep.

Thursday 10

The eye clinic is almost empty except for a cross-looking leather boy who is noisily chewing gum. A very beautiful young man is wheeled in in a black dressing gown. He looks like a Buddhist monk as he has lost all his hair. He does not take any notice of his surroundings but looks up at the ceiling with a beatific smile. My stinging eye drops are in and the ward is turning to a blur.

He asks for coffee. 'How many sugars?'

'Two please.' He's hungry, the nurse offers him a biscuit.

The young monk is taken through by a large bearded man with a kind smile wearing a white shirt and grey trousers. He walks very slowly. The black dressing gown is, in fact, a winter coat. I can see them both through the glass door. The monk's drip dangles from his arm. His friend moves a chair and puts his feet up, his voice has almost disappeared. I can't quite hear what he says though he is still after biscuits.

~

I'm to have extra photos taken so I can work on a CMV painting.

~

To Richard's via Rassell's for alliums to plant in the garden. A TV interview about queer art, then back to David's edit suite to work on *Blue*. The little black floaters swirl around and make me giddy. I feel I am on a tightrope that I could so easily drop off. Everything rushed with *Wittgenstein*, the colour book, *Blue*, *Narrow Rooms*, the Japanese book and me slowing down. I told James last night that if he wants me involved in *Blue* he must put his skates on. He didn't seem to be too worried.

~

I have an image of me, very sick, eating dried biscuits, slowly and very deliberately. My eyes are so blurred I bring the writing to a halt.

~

The book of the drug trial is a blue book, it hasn't been filled in yet. Phone calls to Bart's so I fall into the system, blood tests, blinding photos – there are white threads in my left eye, my right is healing well. I have been blessed with a life that avoided structures, now all that's changed. I couldn't have imagined falling to queues and questionnaires in this place.

A girl in the corner says: 'My microwave is coming through from Crusaid, but they want it back the moment you peg it.'

Her friend gives her support. She says: 'He thinks I'm all right if I look it but I feel terrible. Eight years of this, somehow it might have been easier without all this.'

There is a Spanish family with an interpreter, I've let them jump the queue. The girl is 'going out to make a hundred quid, I need the dosh to buy clothes'. HIV a way of 'existing'.

'I have a grant of £650, what will that buy?' asks the other.

Saturday 12

Dungeness. The sisters of Perpetual Indulgence all here for the anniversary of my sainting, with a congregation of sixty. We built the altar with a large teddy bear, a first birthday cake and a bubble bath duck. Simon Sebastian looking tremendous with a silver nose piercing, which looks like an upturned Dali moustache. I was given a very beautiful sculpture made from a Portuguese sardine tin – of an articulated figure like Ned Kelly. The sun shone and it was a good deal warmer than last year. My good deeds were read out and my gorgeous nose praised – it was all very affecting. I know I'm not to take this too seriously but my feelings were rather emotional. What miracles have taken place? I think the best is that we are all still here. After the service we all walked to the sea where the most intrepid paddled in the waves. The Sisters talk of manifesting and making new saints. Mother Ethel from Down Under tells them to get a move on, they can't decide. They all left for a nuncheon at Alan's.

~

A clear navy sky with ghostly white clouds rolling towards the sea, the moon turned the Ness a luminous grey so that at four it was almost daylight. I woke up thinking the dawn was breaking.

Sunday 13

The garden is planted for winter, the cuttings have all taken although the rabbits are tucking in. My gorse circle has been dried by the winds of the last month, none of the cuttings seem to have taken, so I replaced them. The Californian poppies have flowered for a second time, as have the marigolds, which come and go throughout the seasons. I took honey from the hive and put the combs into boxes, very sticky business that I would have preferred to do some weeks ago, but the weather has been so windy.

I have to be here at least two days a week at this time of year to keep Prospect going; weeding, planting the alliums, the bees and distractions like yesterday keep me very busy.

~

I painted two pictures based on the CMV, they look like the messy photos of my retina.

~

Derek Ball disappeared to some club in Margate last night and hasn't reappeared this morning.

~

Sundays seem a bit hit and miss here, as erratic as the autumn weather. The emptiness of Dungeness has reasserted itself, no nuns changing in the loos of the Britannia Inn, no worried-looking tourists. I walked along the beach gathering sticks for my pyramid protectors, one lone swimmer.

Monday 14

I wonder if my tunnel vision will reflect in the films. Conversation at Bertaux's about funding films. Here we are with a budget of £200,000 and the BFI expect a feature-length film – seven minutes of film a day on a ten-day shoot. Is this exploitation or is it a gift? We have no sets and one lighting set-up.

Peter Greenaway gets a fortune to make Dante. I think Dante would imprison him in a further circle of hell for the courtesy.

~

A terrible exhausted depression descended on me. Sandy was late for the costume meeting and I collided, very hard, with the bathroom door. HB found some ice and made an ice pack, and I nursed a very sore head and virtually fell asleep during our meeting.

Holding on is psychologically difficult and sometimes counterproductive. Ken said his grandmother rang everyone up and said 'Come over.' They all went round. She said 'Goodbye' and snuffed it. I would say on the balance I'm OK, except for the inevitable depressions.

I must guard against being too demanding, HB is more than an angel, he cooked me lovely supper and I couldn't eat it, he sadly cleared it away. Since he started eating his favourite marzipan he has been in a good mood. Marzipan is HB's tranquilliser.

Tuesday 15
I'm feeling much happier today.

~

Meeting with Channel Four and BFI production, Ludwig is pulled back and forth. Ben Gibson talked for half an hour and I quite honestly didn't understand what he wanted – he talked in filmspeak: genre, Godard, Lacan. This is like ploughing through Marxspeak – the sort of opaque intellectualism that tries to define something new and doesn't quite grasp what it might be; it leads to linguistic murkiness.

~

Ten minutes later, Jan said that after he saw *If* he was thrilled at the use of black-and-white/colour footage, which drove the critics mad with theory. Much later he met the cameraman who said they had run out of money and colour film stock. I don't believe any film-maker made a film that was any good from anything other than practical considerations. Ben mentioned *Man to Man*: 'Good lighting and camera but spoilt by fussiness.'
  I said: 'Tilda's make-up reduced her to a convention – *Spitting Image*.'
  Left work at six, happier as Jan said he would find us some Schoenberg piano pieces and play them on the soundtrack.

Wednesday 16
I arrived at Basilisk at 9.30 for my appointment and there was no one in the office, slack and sloppy. James arrived in a very good mood a minute later, I am becoming a monster. James said he couldn't understand what was going on at the BFI either, everything is left to the last minute. Ben's thought that we should delay filming is typical – and would be the worst-case scenario – fucking a schedule, losing actors and technicians. Where do these mismanagements come from? It's odd how producers are always in a state and film-makers calm.

~

The interest rates are going to put us all out of work – it's all East Germany's fault. Manfred said it would have been better to keep the wall, how uncharitable! All they got was a fireworks display and a Pink Floyd concert – no wonder the swastika's flying again, Adolf and the Nazis put on a better show. Laissez-faire capitalism will destroy us, we don't need the ideology, but we do need a five-year plan.

~

HB and I walked down to St James's Park and fed the ducks. 'Don't worry,' says HB, 'I'll look after you.' We watch the starlings wheel around in the twilight. HB asks, 'Is this what floaters look like?' HB is looking sexier as time passes.

Thursday 17
This morning there are photos in the newspaper of Hitler's body, buried and dug up several times by Stalin who liked to gloat over the corpse.

Friday 18
Autumnal day, fine blue mist floating through the trees as the rain pattered down.

~

Dr Crowley rang to say the CMV study with DHPG looked as if the best solution was the drip. I decided to continue with the pills.

~

I met a lad on the street, he threw his hands in the air. 'Living with AIDS, more accurately dying from it.'

~

The Romanov bones are being DNA analysed in Cheltenham.

~

Ken and I are casting – all you really want to know is if you are going to get on with these people. Ken described Sarah Radclyffe and Richard as 'Eighties people'.
   'What's that?'
   'Well, they have to fill empty spaces, horror vacuii is the medical term, bigger and bigger until they pop like balloons.'
   Delicious tea in the eau-de-nil café with Karl Johnson, who described his childhood in sparkling language.

Saturday 19
HB says I'm the blue cheese mouse. He sniffs out my 'second-hand cheese' from the market stall in Berwick Street that sells past-its-sell-by-date cheeses and throws it all down the rubbish chute.

Sunday 20

Howard came at nine with HB who was going to get a cold – he could tell this because his tattoos were standing on end. We drove in ever brighter sunlight to Prospect, bathed in one of those last warm days before the weather turns. Swallows flying low across the garden, red admiral and painted lady butterflies on the verbena, cascades of bright-red nasturtiums and Californian poppy.

Back to London at midnight.

Monday 21

A really jolly morning getting narrative from costume. Everyone very happy, my only command is to keep it that way, no long faces while we're filming.

Some very wicked photos taken by Howard, of HB snipping off his manhood with a pair of shears, fell out of my diary on to the floor during the meeting.

Nothing new happens. 'What should I write about HB?'

'You know there are things forgotten that would be worth remembering.'

~

Ken asks questions:

What was the best sex I ever had?

I don't think location made much difference, probably in bed rather than up a tree, it was probably powerful sodomy.

What do I think of living with someone?

It's a co-option into their life, I can't think of not living with someone. I'm certain I'm as happy as anyone. I've spent years alone.

Is it difficult?

Not really, though I put walls around my life to do it. I don't go rushing about cruising and I certainly don't bring strange boys home – there are three of us already: him, me and the HIV. I worry about letting HB down by snuffing it.

Where would I live if I wasn't here?

Not possible to contemplate. Berlin destroyed by unification, Rome too exclusive, Paris no room for minds like mine – Peter Greenaway territory, home of the worst since the war, no queers in Paris except in the bars.

~

Had a brown sauce lunch. Sandy is coming with colours. We are so far ahead with the pre-production that we are sitting twiddling our thumbs. Sandy turned back to get the fabrics.

Tuesday 22

Very dark morning with thundery grey clouds and the metal beer barrels thundering down the ramp into the pub next to Bertaux's. Even the croissants were heavy. Anna, who has been here for forty years, calculated the number of coffees she has made and we both swallowed our pills.

Walked home in a spattering of rain. It was so dark I was barely able to see out of my fuzzy eye to write. The students are back at St Martin's, the windows cleaned and blazing with light. Next to no news in the papers this morning, just everyone giving everyone else conflicting advice. Little interest in the obituaries either, though it looked as if some young man had died of an overdose rather than AIDS. I read through the lines on these write-ups; though the papers have become a little more open lately, the obituaries are an exclusive club.

~

Sandy asked me how many women were in the wards. There is usually one; they are still mostly drug users working in the sex industry – my observation from overheard conversations.

Everyone complaining about the lack of light, December in September.

The lad at Cornellison's said his joints ached and that meant a deluge.

Ken rang up with a cold. I shop for more books. No one has *On Certainty*, neither Better Books, Foyle's nor Waterstone's – I've wasted an hour in the rain – Compendium? No. I wonder if the shops understand my impatience. Standing in Foyle's you feel as if you were in *Huis Clos* – it's a Sartrean hell on earth.

Hopeless bookshops. Desperate, I bury my quest and turn to Yves Klein.

~

Static and hopelessly airless today.

~

Carried on my book search, fruitless. Gave up and looked at fluffers instead, then caught a taxi to Bandung, wearing my bright-red hat that makes people laugh.

~

Piers had put my paintings on show at Richard's and he's sold another. I've no money at the moment and there's a fortune locked up in Richard's financial instability.

~

HB fretting over the dying washing machine, stands at the kitchen door ears pricked for a spark as it turns this way and that way and no way whatsoever, dribbling on the floor. He won't let me intervene – Northern Pride. He sits writing but won't let me see a single page, as he says I'll thieve the ideas. HB reads everything I write and says this or that is a quote. I don't know how lives and diaries cannot be entwined or run parallel with the crossings.

~

Long conversation at Bandung about Ludwig and my idea of introducing a Martian space -dweller.

~

Tilda and Ruby Rich came for lunch in the pale-green café run by the Greek man in a muddle. Conversation about the replacement of the Soviet Party Secretaries by the Orthodox Priesthood. Tilda said at Easter there was a banner in Red Square across from Lenin's tomb proclaiming: 'Christ has Risen.'

Tracked down an *On Certainty* in Blackwell's in Oxford. The rain pours down, my eye weeps as the taxi home slows to a snail's pace. Part of the world is blotted out, the CMV spreads like ink in the eye.

~

HB calls me an infidelitous pig for looking at the fluffers – he is in the kitchen repairing the washing machine. Read *Culture and Value*.

~

HB says my sleepless nights are caused by my frequent afternoon naps. He sits typing. 'Fur Beast, you're not going to sleep, are you?'

'No.'

Wednesday 23

It rained so hard in the night that London was flooded. HB collected my new photo albums from Paperchase, I read the *Independent*. A young man had dropped dead on a grouse moor. His obituary writer described him as 'cruising the bars of Manchester', I remember him screwing in the back rooms of Heaven.

Did cruising start in the fifties? It's such a post-war term, did Epstein cruise his wife in the Soho cafés pre 1914? I've never been adept at cruising, particularly the streets, out of misplaced propriety. It takes Ken to chat with a stranger on Tottenham Court Road and end up with his pants round his ankles in a park. My infidelitous nature means I pass at least ten lads a day whom I would be glad to fuck. It always seemed to me that the easiest boys were the brightest. What was the point of complaining no one fancied you if you fancied no one in return?

I thought that the words 'cruising the bars of Manchester' gave a new dimension to the obituary. David Mellor: 'He was fond of actresses', or Fergie: 'The Duchess had a passion for skinny dipping.'

~

I found a small book of humour circa 1804 in the bookshop – it wouldn't raise a smile today. I took my Martian harp by taxi to Bandung and the day began. I can't help feeling, as we cruise through Kentish Town, that London is much improved, though much duller than it was when we lived here thirty years ago. I was travelling on this bus route in 1964 to the Slade. Little remains of the view, though the bus stop just beyond the entrance to the VCL is still at the same spot. I can be certain Dillon's bookshop has displaced the café. Outside, a boy splashed with white paint in his hair and under his nose like a Chaplin moustache, all the boys along the street look as if they have been to the gym, muscly streets, how did we dare wear 501s? The young are so conventional now, not a surprise in sight – tight-arsed boys aping a fictional fifties.

The embalmer's is still there on the corner of Prince of Wales Road. Death is the last commodity to bankrupt, embalming hope eternal, no one rots easily; full of preservatives from processed food, we all go to the grave semi-embalmed by Sainsbury's.

> *If someone is merely ahead of time it will catch up with him one day – our greatest stupidities may be very wise – I could imagine someone thinking the names Fortnum and Mason fitted each other.*
>
> (Wittgenstein)

Everyone is having copyright problems; copyrighting a philosophy – surely that is impossible. Ludwig's theories should prove the picture, his theories are not connected or reproduced in this text.

Martian. Ken faxed the Martian text and I rewrote it.

~

A thin winter sun. My head aches at the frontier of vision, my stomach churns, turns, a dull thud in the eye, my neck irritated by a rash I have had since I first fell ill.

Am I happy? Yes. Continuously entertained by HB and his sad long face as the washing machine dies in the darkened kitchen.

~

Tony here at lunch. I signed the colour contracts and talked over the will.

Thursday 24

The day got off to a muddle when HB, who is a perfectionist, couldn't find Howard's outrageous photos that I had put in 'a safe place' after they fell out during a meeting two days ago. I puzzled all day about where I put them and my mind remained a blank. I am more and more unhappy with my amnesias, which put me into a panic.

~

At Bertaux's my corner had been squatted by a couple of noisy youngsters, outside the rain fell in a wetting mist. I went to the bank – shrinking – and then with a sinking heart to St Mary's for eye tests and blinding photos. The grey day reflects my unhappiness and the fouled sheets I left poor HB to launder this morning.

~

The stinging drops are in, the reading chart which has a flaw – as if you read with your good eye first you can remember the letters, to whose benefit? My illusions. The nurse asks me if I mind being called by my first name, this seems a little mystifying, but apparently someone complained.

There is a new poster amongst the HIV: *Murder. Did you see him on Tuesday the 2nd of June?*

I'm still feeling as if the bottom of my stomach has fallen out.

'33974,' the doctor calls. I run out of words as the line blurs on the page.

~

Unhappy. Wait. Walled up in this living tomb. There is another new poster: *AIDS death rate halved by new drug*.

Distant overheard conversations about T-cells, this appointment, that appointment with destiny. The two lethargic goldfish barely swim as the water dries in their tank. Are they forgotten? Thank God it's a grey day as the sunlight shuts my eyes and my dilated pupils fuzz till teatime.

I've noticed a huge poster: *Speak Out, Male Rape*. Under another: *The way we live now*. My neighbour says his eyes are deteriorating very quickly, he has very painful arthritis. Eleven o'clock and still waiting for the dragging minutes to pass. I'm very tired, a heap of old clothes collapsed in the chair. Is this depression the gift of the drugs? I feel less and less like fighting, giving up, giving in. Writing blind now. It's so slow here I'll never get to Rassell's or Richard's studio. Yawning void.

~

Rassell's for bulbs. Lunch with Richard at the Italian. Richard hopeful about the painting.

~

At Bart's for two. I find the sweet, cheerful man from this morning's clinic is having a blood transfusion, we have a conversation of the spirits; he says to fall into depression makes you your own enemy. The dull thud at the back of my eyes, no vistas or long-term views. I worry about this chemical depression, others suffer from it; there is a happy drug, one more pill; I refuse it. My eyebrows crawl with irritation.

~

The books have arrived in the ward – all the Penguin Classics.
  Blood, needles, more blood.
  The slow pharmacy is even slower today, I sit waiting an hour for 73 to turn into 74, get your pills before your diagnosis.
  It's a long, long wait.

Friday 25

I had the most terrible migraine last night and ended up taking six painkillers to get rid of it. This morning I'm very wobbly and my eyes fix so I can no longer read the paper.
  HB as sweet this morning as Tate and Lyle, but sad that his friend Garry cried himself to sleep over him.
  HB jokes if he doesn't get a triple distinction he'll kill anyone who does. HB is very happy this morning, good to old jugsy eyes.

~

There is a sort of panic lurking. I rang the doctor. He says migraine does leave you unable to read. A thin, damp drizzle is falling, the car lights still have haloes from my eye drops. I write in the taxi in jerks and stabs as we rattle along, the roads are as bumpy as New York avenues, they were never neglected like this when I was young. As the private houses and shops were spruced up the public utilities were run down – what they call infrastructure, abandoned pavements, roads so uneven that the blind must be in fear of falling to Australia. Maybe it's the traffic volume.
  Mr Mellor was sacrificed for John Major last night, well done tabloids! Pick 'em off one by one.

~

We are dealing with copyright – the *Tractatus* allowed; what about *On Certainty*? A video has arrived with Bertie and Maynard. Both have that slow, clipped speech of Edwardians, very measured and the words pronounced in twos. Keynes's suits will definitely be mauve. Tariq is amused by Bertie's silver hair and bushy black eyebrows.

Ducking requests from photographers, use Howard. I want to be screened from reality like the Queen on the stamps.

~

Alan drove me down to Dungeness. He said that Europe, on which we had all pinned hopes for legislation, had turned out to be a dodo, in all its years of existence had only touched reform of the injustice we suffer on two occasions. We could expect the Tories to go in for more fag-bashing. The police presence at the cathedral demonstration had included special anti-terrorist men and Alan was certain they had changed their identification numbers – they were on the lookout for blood.

Alan had no regrets for Mr Mellor and praised John Smith. The Labour Party this time seems to have chosen its most competent MP for the shadow, Mr Smith is a good talker.

Saturday 26
Swallows swoop low around the house, my black floaters swim low across the landscape.

John Adams' 'The Wound Dresser' makes me feel quite weepy. There are moments in this unequal battle against the HIV when one is overcome, then someone arrives to rescue you.

This morning Cary, my American airman friend, wrote from his airbase. He and his friend Bruce are off to Ireland, he's at the delightful age of coincidence. I wrote last week about Wittgenstein, whom he could not find in the base library but he had bought a second-hand book on Klimt and stumbled across the portrait of Margaret in the white dress.

Three young gardeners stopped by – they were from Holland and had made for Prospect on the way to Great Dixter. They spent over an hour here and were amused by the formal garden in front of the house and the informal one at the back.

The garden has never looked better, there are enough flowers splashed here and there, all is neat and tidy so the circles show well, the rain has kept everything green and healthy, the hosepipe ban, which could do in the plants that have not established themselves, had no effect, everything has seeded: valerian, poppies, cornflower, teazle, mallow, even the large thistles though the slugs eat them as fast as they grow.

I played 'The Wound Dresser' again, no tears this time. There are more swallows than floaters circling the house.

Sunday 27

At dawn I saw the first robins streaking through the plants outside the kitchen window and up on to the posts; they don't stop still for a moment.

The clouds have taken the sunshine with them and, although it is warm, a slight breeze is up. There is seaweed along the shore and the smell of salt air. The old boat that I make the full stop of my walk has gone, someone has taken it.

At ten the robins are still with me, they seem to have decided to stay. I work at the front of the garden and walk along the beach collecting stones. Three unpleasant men who have come to angle shout at me: 'You're the one who makes porno films.'

I cross the shingle and confront them. 'I'm making a film of a philosopher.' This was met with incomprehension, as I think this man who wouldn't let me go with his questions had barely enough words to string them together. All of them were middle-aged and ugly; it's a pity there are no sharks in the Channel. Disentangled myself and came back to my gardening. This is the only unpleasantness I have encountered in six years here.

~

Migraine. I planted up the sempervivums that HB 'rescued' from McDonald's where they were dying, waterless in semi-dark. McDonald's does a good job in torturing plants.

~

The sun went in and I spent the next two hours working on the new paintings. The black foil works, OMINOUS, FATAL, CMV, the paintings give rise to much wider thoughts than the diary – could I paint pornographic pictures so offensive no one will put them on their walls? I'll try later, the challenge of the dimwit on the beach.

Monday 28

For the third day the sun came up calm and perfect. A most beautiful day. T-shirt weather.

My robins still in the garden. I worked hard from dawn to sweep and clean the house before Christopher arrives in his cheerful chug-chug taxi. My eyes seem worse in the morning. I tolerate them for five or six hours and by midday I'm used to them. It's much harder to find a pen or a book, anything misplaced. I wonder if the migraines are caused by the dizziness or the storm of floaters. I didn't want this diary to become just a catalogue of ills though they have nudged themselves nearer to the centre of the stage.

Christopher has given up his idea of emigrating to Italy and talked about moving here. We had lunch at the Light Railway Café, then picked wild mushrooms. A discussion on *Narrow Rooms*, then home via Great Dixter.

HB bruised all over from taekwon-do.

Tuesday 29

Nabil will play the Martian, this is a relief as to find a child to replace Jody will be difficult. Jody is growing up and making value judgements about his work – my invention of the Martian character to give him a part failed miserably.

~

Mr Lamontable apologised to the Bundesbank. Germany cancelled the celebration of the V2, which probably killed more people in the making – 20,000 slave labourers – than it did falling from the sky.

~

The number 134 bounces towards Bandung along the grey London streets. There is talk on the radio of a huge underground city in Moscow where the Party were to retire for thirty years after the H bomb dropped.

Wednesday 30

I woke this morning very clear-headed, almost well again, clambered on the number 134, northward bound. The film is cast, crewed and designed. The cameraman, James Welland, is great, calming.

~

It's strange how you can hear your father's voice speaking through you as you get older. Tariq said he had the same experience. I find myself talking like Lance.

OCTOBER

Thursday 1

The legal and police professions are crowned with dishonour today – Eric Bentley is to be pardoned, the death rot creeps through the dying hulk.

I have a friend who joined the Freemasons, he was caught speeding. The lodge assured him the policeman would not appear at the court case – dismissed in Kent. Eric Bentley was not so lucky. Anyone who plans to commit a murder should become a Freemason first. HB says the police have no reputation after a whole succession of miscarriages of justice, class resentment and the British disinterest in any form of service. The boys in blue probably fought in the playground with their neighbours, now they can arrest them and if they wish, frame them. They only behave if they are told to do so.

The *Independent* rang me to warn me that the tabloids – this time the *Express* – were reviving the lamentable and untruthful *Dispatches* programme on Gen P. Orridge. The police, according to my informant, were thinking of prosecuting Genesis and Paula for their body piercings and tattoos. Really! What is this world coming to? The programme might have successfully investigated child abuse, but instead encouraged a malicious tabloid trial of Gen, who has had to leave the country to protect his daughters. The police have impounded his papers and work, and Gen has lost house and home. I spoke to both Jon Savage and David Lewis. We are quite powerless in all this as no one has the resources or the time to sue, though I believe Amnesty might take on his case. I can't think of a more responsible father than Gen, his children are the happiest. The authors of this programme should be brought to book. For a moment I appeared as a Psychik TV spokesperson in this drivel, a telephone call to C4 brought the response: 'You were so small and there for only a moment.' Long enough for the *Mirror* to register it and send two journalists down to Dungeness late on a winter's evening.

~

Met Carol Myers in the Algerian Coffee store. *Edward II* won the film prize at Dinard.

Bought Boston ground for filter, papers, and took a taxi up to Bandung.

229

Another quiet, sunlit morning.

October 1, in shirt-sleeves. When the sun shines it makes me dizzy, aggravates this blind eye. Some part of me dares this blindness to progress, it says I've seen enough.

~

I left HB happy on the way to work. My cheap trousers had dyed the wash, my yellow T-shirt has gone green.

His college gang is causing mayhem: 'You be the red group, you be the blue group, you be the green group and we'll be the . . . alpha group.' The dykes and fluffers have banded together, they tell off the tutors when they say anything remotely sexist or anti-gay, then shout 'You stupid poof', 'dizzy dyke', 'fat queen' at each other, then turn back to the tutors and say 'It's the new queer politics' as way of explanation. This terrorises the confused straights, one of whom confided that she'd 'dipped her toe in the waters of lesbianism'. They grabbed her and said: 'You're coming for a swim.'

~

We write a synopsis of *Narrow Rooms*, all murder mayhem, which we fax to Christine in New York.

Ken and I walked to a photographic shop and looked at a new camera – I'm set to have one to look for stills and locations; then we looked at a rainbow of silk shirts on a stall by the station. I came home with an armful of Wittgenstein books and my musical instrument.

Ken talked of my dislike of the theatre. He wound me up, as the Theed Street studio is next to the National: 'Should we eat with your friends?'

'What friends?' The grubby little culture of the theatre, a queue for privilege outside a pawnbroker's shop. The gay press congratulating it on a betrayal, the gay press: Tory bodies and Labour heads. *Testa di sinistra stomacho di destra*. I feel so alienated by this society I could rejoice in setting a touch-paper alight and watch the whole lot flame.

Friday 2

Early breakfast at Bar Italia.

Ken and I walked to the studios for our rehearsal. Ken: 'I hope I'm in the diaries, write something complimentary.'

Why do I feel so alienated? I made my own space outside the institutions. Am I glad I did it? Yes. What I found in these institutions were dead-beat heterosexual toadies and a whole lot of queens who gave their tacit approval. As a young man I hardly met anyone whom I could admire, except those who refused to make a mark in that world and who are no longer known. Everything was a compromise in a society which was riddled with death-watch.

Something to remember about the hetero toads is because they breed they never take risks – they're protecting the future. Did I ever want kids? No, it didn't pass my mind once.

~

At 3.30 Christopher came in the old taxi and took me to Dungeness. He feels *Narrow Rooms* should be partly set in studios, the rest filmed outside. We drove across the marsh to look at locations, but he was rather unimpressed. Christopher said Ken Russell once used Bournemouth for LA, it always looked like Bournemouth – if you pull the horizon in and work as pinched as I do you can create an illusion. It's the hedgerows in the fields that give the game away here.

~

Dungeness is as quiet as a mouse now. I'm here quite alone. HB is in Newcastle.

Saturday 3

It rained very hard during the night; dawn came with little light, grey and suddenly cold. Dungeness quiet and deserted except for the whine of a plane somewhere above the clouds and the cries of seagulls at the sea's edge. A migraine hovered over my left eye but after a bath and breakfast of toast and sweet grapefruit it retreated. I tied up the pyramids which protect the gorse from the rabbits. Why should rabbits take such a liking to my spikey cuttings? There is little out now, just nasturtiums and Californian poppies, the blue-green sea cabbages are beginning to shed leaves and the scarlet hips on the roses have turned a deeper red.

~

Along the beach I find more metal chains to fix the sempervivums on the roof. It is very desolate: a pile of railway sleepers marks the passage of a boat into the water, but the boat is nowhere to be seen in the grey mists that hug the water.

~

Richard phones. He is now in such crisis, both personal and financial, and so obsessed with his cash flow that he is finding organising an evening to talk about the Wilde memorial almost too difficult. Seventeen letters could be posted in one hour, but after several weeks he is still muttering about contacting Jeremy Isaacs at the Opera House.

Art dealing is the paradise of snails. Richard is besieged by good advice, but seems certain to sink like the *Titanic* with the orchestra playing – the Auction in *The Rake's Progress*. He lives in the past, there bankruptcy is seen as a personal failure. If I were him I would reap my profits from my losses but keep everything turning over. Now it is too late, even the big boys are selling their Beuys to keep their walls hung. Richard is destined to turn turtle in his immense and beautiful home in Edwarde's Square.

The result of all this ambition is to leave his helpers helpless while he rages at the financial index and transfers his anger to them; it's a form of torture. Richard has immense and almost boyish charm, he is truly stylish, but John Major has put the torpedo in. In this world everyone talks of recovery while sustaining the loss, the cash flow is nippy like the early frost, it turns bright people desperate.

Richard's situation is paralleled in Paul, who pathetically rings doorbells as he and his friend Mario – now without work, or hope of it – struggle to pay their landlord with their friends' ill-gotten gains. I put a stop to the last £1000, as I myself no longer have it. Every penny goes into propping up Richard, and Paul, like all of us, is living beyond his means.

~

Richard is hanging on to the picture frame for dear life and I'm hanging on to life for dear life. I would rather be alive than dead, I'm too curious about the here and now.

~

Recession, like famine, never happened to us – the abundance of food at Tesco, everything and more than anyone could want. What happens when the shelves run bare and the melodic chime of the cash registers ceases? HB says I shop only for luxury items, he gets as many calories at half the price. The tired lady forces the food past the electronic eye like stuffing a foie gras goose, beep beep beep.

~

Diamond drops of water sparkle in the breeze that sways the acid-green nasturtium leaves. Will a gust blow the diamonds away? Gurgle of water in the gutters. The postman arrives with too many letters. Simon Turner rings to say he can't visit tomorrow as he has left his driving licence in France. He's off to Ghent for the *Blue* concert next Sunday, which I'll miss yet again. My angelic harp will not be played, though I expect to see it as part of Nabil's intergalactic wheelchair.

~

OCTOBER

Last week I found a card from the cultural attaché in Stockholm stuffed into the crevice in one of my wooden dolmens. As I stood this morning in front of the door a large seagull picked it up and flew off with it firmly in its beak.

~

The rain still pours down. Out on the beach one of the old wood and corrugated sheds has been demolished. There is a pile of new material for the garden: chains, floats and large iron hooks. This is the third hut that has disappeared from my view in a few years.

~

The rain fell. Ken rang. Unsuccessful cruising last night – the boy he liked said: 'Hands off, you're not my type.'

'Who is who in types?' he asks. 'Do you think Anthony is my type? Is Tilda John Byrne's type? Or HB yours?'

'They all have an age difference, two young men brought up competition.'

~

The day passed in dull grey and the rain kept on. I almost decided to travel back to London for company, no sign of anyone here.

I have a sinking detachment from everything going on, a feeling brought, I suppose, by the uncertainty of my situation. Where before I could ignore this, now it is impossible. I lurch through the day listless, even Ken's observation that *Narrow Rooms* would be a great film leaves me little excitement – so many winter days before a possible shoot. Could I get through long days which start in the dark?

My food today fails to taste, unease, passing blood in my pee. Yesterday afternoon I fell asleep, the copy of *Narrow Rooms* fell to the floor. I walk through the house tripping over imagined impediments.

~

The whole country is in the lurch, absolutely lost in the monetary storm. Everything is falling apart: the roads, industries, health, education, foreign policy and the blessed £. I have felt that the appeals to recovery are hollow, the slide is permanent. Frightened bankers try to drag the unwilling electorate into the monetary union, all *they* see is Brussels interfering with their potato crisps or ruining cheese. The fate of the invisible money which flies around the world at the press of the button seems as remote as the virus. How can one muster enthusiasm for erms and exchange rates? Capital fails to deliver, if the £ goes down the shares go up with the prices and the queues of unemployed, 1,000 more of them each day. Everywhere there is failure of nerve, failure of intellect – look at the ghastly Legoland of post-modernism thrown up without a care for social value. What happened to the serious Utopianism of modernity, Vries, Corbusier? Even the Hayward Gallery is better than this.

~

The evenings are closing in, the rain still pours.

Sunday 4

A wild easterly blew up in the night. I woke at the wolf's hour with a searing migraine over my left eye as I tossed and turned. Piled up pillows, even that making little comfort. Got up and swallowed Panadol with cold dark water in the bathroom. Nothing shifted the pain so I sat through the night in my new room and dozed. Baths and cups of tea in the dawn pushed it back.

~

The windows of the house are frosted with salt and the gale has whipped up the sea. There is no one on the beach and the fishing boats are firmly on the shingle bank, though there is a glimmer of sunlight behind the misty sky.

~

I worry lest I should be unwell – the film starts tomorrow. HB worries lest I ignore the symptoms. Surely this is not a return of the Toxo brain infection; should I take this seriously? I remember telling my friend Jake Winters not to worry about his headaches. Nine months later he was dead from an inoperable brain tumour.

~

Horrific shots on TV of junkies outside the opera house in Frankfurt, like the cardboard city that is built around the National Theatre: the junkies, fools' gold, excess profit, criminality, tourniquets and blood spattering the hair, a queue like a soup kitchen returning bloody needles, HIV.

~

A large container ship passes like a shadow in the mists in front of my window. The gale has blown all my sadness away with the cobwebs around the eves. Now the sun comes and later Alan to drive me back to London.

~

The Sunday papers are full of little lost Britain in the land of the ECU. Perhaps this country was always lost but being lost and losing it are not the same. I'm certain this must be one of the pleasanter parts of the world to live, but will this always be the case? Economics, which were always tailored to their own advantage, quite shamelessly by the Tories, have now turned and bitten good and proper. While the rest of the world was building a future we were buying and selling it on a property-led boom – Mrs Thatcher's illusion. The boom was a runaway inflation and as houses doubled and tripled in value their owners colluded, believing they were richer. Now they're out on the streets, boom turned to bust, and the mortgage companies are knocking on the door.

There's an article that equates Barnsley's good fortune with the number of £700 designer jackets being sold. These are probably designed in Italy, made in India and sold here. I wonder what people in Barnsley do when they are not buying expensive clothes.

Monday 5

HB came home late last night, leaving his young friend Garry crying. While we slept, a jet slammed into a tower block in Amsterdam. The jet was almost empty, but 200 people were fried in their sleep. I've often wondered when this would happen, as the jets cross high above the city.

~

At Bar Italia by 7.30, leaving HB rather happy in the bath. I kissed him goodbye.

'Is that all I get?' he asked. 'There is competition for my love.'

~

I grabbed my chromium lyre and caught a taxi to the studio, a cold sunny day was dawning as we crossed Waterloo Bridge.

The Wittgenstein Shoot at Theed Street Studios

To turn philosophy into cinema for £200,000 in a twelve-day shoot, philosophy being antithetical to film – where language exists in a supporting role – is a tall order.

Wittgenstein believed in the green valleys of silliness rather than the heights of intellect. My first decision was to take him at his word and invent an extraterrestrial: Mr Green. The period in which Ludwig lived was obsessed with Martians; I was brought up with a daily diet of them in every comic, they were always green – little green men.

My task was to make a philosophical film, not a film about philosophy, and for this the lack of budget came in handy. Terry Eagleton's script was a vital foundation and remained so throughout the filming. It was set naturalistically in Cambridge in the thirties and was, in its conception, totally conservative. The location would, I felt, be impossible, it would all look like a hand-me-down from a Merchant Ivory. This would betray my cinema of less-is-more into the cinema of convention. To redefine film, like language, needs a leap – in this case into the black drapes, which defy the narrative without junking it.

~

I saw a television documentary the day before we started working on the script, which followed the same line of thought; in fact, it was structurally very near to our screenplay, but totally lacking in humour or any visual imagination, with endless shots of fjords. When, through lack of funds and much against my own wishes, we introduced black drapes into *Caravaggio* they worked wonderfully, as the cardinals wore scarlet. In the Tate Gallery is a startling Miro with primary shapes and colours on a black ground. Black has its own elegance, creates an indefinite space – but to work, colour has to be introduced.

I arranged the costumes so that Wittgenstein resembled a little grey man who had wandered from a social-realist film into a flamboyant England: Keynes was dressed in a scale of lavenders and mauves, Russell in red academic's gown, Ottoline and Hermine across the spectrum. It quickly became obvious that the costume houses would not be able to help, so we made the costumes and I took a decision that, as far as possible, they would not change – Tilda has the same hat and dress throughout the film: more money saved; the budget again becomes the aesthetic.

Having pared away the costumes the props were next on the list and were ruthlessly eliminated. There's only one moment of set-dressing – a pitcher plant graces the first shoot of Ottoline lying on the purple and yellow bed. It took Howard and me the better half of a morning to get a saracena expert with bright-ginger hair in a house in Mill Hill to part with it. Each plant had sentimental attachments, this one, twenty-five years old, cost £25 and was dug up the moment I was losing any hope that we would acquire it.

Colour, sets, props all under way, I realised we could not afford a soundtrack – I invited my friend Jan Latham-Koenig to play Paul, Ludwig's brother, who had Ravel compose the concerto for one hand. I abandoned the multi-layered approach to sound Simon created with me in *Caravaggio* and *Edward II*.

We worked through the end of summer in Bandung, before transferring to the studio in Theed Street, just round the corner from Waterloo Station. It was easy to walk there. Up at six each morning, I wait for Aurelia at Bar Italia to switch on the video and fruit machine, and open the door for my breakfast cappuccino, fresh orange juice and cheese roll.

I wear my blue overalls, a heavy black coat from the fifties and scarlet Chinese cap. I became obsessed with clothes and colour working on my colour book, wearing a series of co-ordinated T-shirts from M&S. I realised, apart from socks, pants and shoes, I had hardly bought any clothes for twenty years. John Byrne wearing his elegant grey tweed suits and Tilda in Yohji Yamamoto made me look like a scruff.

~

Theed Street studios is a shoe box for pop promos. All the old team are here: Morag, on make-up, transformed HB into a teenage dream matinée idol and herself one afternoon into Frida Kahlo; Sandy on costume; Annie sets; James Welland on camera.

Walking through the empty streets on the cold and sunny mornings I knew I would be greeted with smiles at eight when we set up the shots for the day. The quota quickie – masters in the day, close-ups at night. By the second week we were running very late on our seven o'clock deadline. On two or three days we passed nine, finally stuck at ten and, on the last day, midnight.

My state is one of exhaustion fuelled by a will to get to the end. On two days I thought I wouldn't have the energy to get to finish, I had to negotiate my visits to the clinic and get runners to collect pills.

~

Was *Wittgenstein* a gift or an outrageous exploitation which I allowed to happen? Should I have stopped the TV slot becoming a film? When we wrapped at midnight I was surrounded by tired eyes. Were they happy?

Saturday 17
In a delirium after completing the two-week shoot. Crossing Covent Garden, I stare in the empty shops, cross the piazza, wondering if I will stumble into an IRA bomb – the Sussex is boarded up, in front of it a table of floral tributes. The bombs go off nightly, one alongside St Giles church, in my short-cut alley – the flat rattled with shock in the blast. HB was first on the scene before the police cleared him off. Returning home, I had an altercation with the most impolite policeman, one of a group standing about doing nothing but aggressing anyone who asked them a question.

~

Met Steve Farrer in the Presto at eight. It was cold and pouring with rain. We talked of the BFI and its dependence on goodwill to get its films made. It would be possible to see *Wittgenstein* as an exploitation of goodwill – they have put me against the wall, raised the stakes without paying for them. Budge says the provisions for post production are inadequate, everything would have progressed in an orderly way for a fifty-minute TV programme, but a seventy-two-minute film in 35mm is a different ball game. The BFI must make this up – we've achieved a miracle for them; they must acknowledge this by finishing the film with adequate funds.

Sunday 18

A restless night alone – HB is in Newcastle, so I did not have him as a doorstop to my tossing and turning.

Awake before seven and out to Bar Italia with a *Sunday Independent*, a front-page editorial: TIME RUNS OUT FOR MR MAJOR. If Mr Major is a goner, as the *Sun* declared yesterday, no one could be happier than I. All honest Britons will march next Sunday to support the miners. The British ruling classes, riddled with death-watch, have declared this old home unsafe and prepare to desert the ship – sailing away on their liquid assets. Outside the sun shines on the empty street gripped by the first chill of the coming winter.

~

Howard arrives at ten, having spent the night prancing up and down in one of Maynard Keynes's lavender suits. He says the betrayal by the Nottingham miners in 1984 was unforgivable, they single-handedly destroyed the unions.

We are sailing through the sunlit city, its streets empty of life.

~

HB rings me to congratulate me on finishing the shoot. I think the BFI has got this film at the expense of my friends who have worked for nothing: Howard got £500 for two days' work and was there for the whole shoot; John made all of the dresses for the promise of a painting; Sandy gave away her fee to pay for the costumes; my own £10,000 for transforming Terry Eagleton's very conventional script into cinema and providing them with an eighty-minute film in twelve days for £200,000 – my experience and talent are, as usual, at the bottom of the cash flow. The lad who went the furthest with the least: one-take Derek. What would we have gained with an extra week? I expect little in spirit, but this could have been the most elegant quota quickie that British Cinema produced.

I am very happy I have made a sophisticated comedy that more accurately reflects my state of mind than all the previous films.

~

We are now stopped at Blackheath service station, having collected Ali, who is jammed in the back between the old black globe and the pitcher plant.

Howard says that Ali has a future as a petrol pump attendant, Ali says she'd have a better career as whiplash Sue, dressed in skin-tight leather.

Ali's great-grandfather was a communist, he was given a communist funeral with no mention of God.

Layla [Alexander Garrett], who played the Russian professor in *Wittgenstein*, was happy to have left the Soviet Union. John Byrne and Tilda wanted to emigrate there.

Howard's grandfather Jack was in a mining accident at twenty-one and lost the use of his legs after being buried alive for three days. The company gave him two weeks' wages as compensation. He lived a very unhappy life, violent and resentful.

I mention lunch and Howard says: 'I can't believe I ate a rabbit pie.' Howard had sworn as a child to his dead bunny, Benjamin, never to eat a rabbit and had kept the promise. Last Sunday, as we ate a pub lunch, Howard said: 'My chicken and wild mushroom pie is delicious.'

I said: 'My rabbit and port one isn't so good and it's full of mushrooms.' And the awful truth dawned.

~

The coldest October day anyone remembers. Howard and Ali transplanted the lavatera, which had sprung up and made the back door inaccessible. We replaced it with the wine-red rugosa that has struggled in the front garden, then rearranged the back room, so it is ready for writing next week.

Monday 19

I spent the morning shopping for clothes, something I haven't done in years: I found some cast-offs in a second-hand clothes shop – a particularly beautiful work shirt and an old Harris tweed jacket. In the market, an old pair of motorcycle goggles – a first prop for *Narrow Rooms*.

Spent some time with Zelda Cheattle in her gallery, where she is exhibiting some photos by Angus McBean. A cold, grey day. Took the number 134 to Kentish Town late in the afternoon for a screening.

Changed seats on the bus – an aggravating lad munching his way north, noisy eater, with loud disco headphones.

~

The £ plummets, Mr Major besieged on all sides, the miners plan a march, what we have dreamed of for over a decade is about to happen. It's a pity we can't string this Mafia up – that's what I would like to see, public execution for the betrayal of decency. All the old people look sad and miserable, glumly travelling north in the mined streets. There was not a smile on the number 134. A surly driver – it was never like this when I first came here thirty years ago, the conductor welcoming the old on board, chatting with them, asking them how they were. This sadness is Mrs Thatcher's legacy: ugly, uncaring, short-sighted, with a clever and arrogant stupidity. She should be drowned in England's tears.

At Bandung I saw the little film, elegant and rather funny, there are no dud performances, everyone rose to the occasion.

~

Later, on my way back from Hampstead I picked up a taxi driver who was determined to get asked back for sex. I was very circumspect.

'Have you been on the Heath?'

'Yes.'

'What's it like tonight?'

'Oh, OK.'

He then told me about a friend, a sexual tourist, in Thailand – the boys are kept in cages there, and Moscow – more open than here. I'm certain the conversation was a code for his own behaviour. 'What sort of videos do you watch?'

'Oh, this and that.'

I left him in Denmark Street, still angling for an invitation home.

Tuesday 20

Went to Mr Eddie, the Berwick Street tailor, to have HB's trousers copied secretly so I can have a pair myself, then on in the pouring rain to Richard's to paint. Richard is still in crisis, under the illusion things will improve. That makes him a minority of one; there is no crock of gold at the end of the recession.

Piers and I painted *Mania* and *Blind Date*.

My eyes are giving me more to worry about. I can't read a paper any longer, though the headache has disappeared this afternoon.

Wednesday 21

The sun came out. My right eye is a mess, like a strobe light cast on a flock of black starlings; my headache continues. Why should I care about anything with death and dissolution staring me in the face?

The second of the two programmes I gave one of my days to – this one on Michelangelo – was screened last night without a look-in. I told Lorraine I would do nothing more for the media unless I received master copies of my interviews and the rights to exploit them in any way I saw fit.

The *Independent* telephoned – they want me to write a piece on Robert Mapplethorpe.

Eleven o'clock – I buy an Angus McBean photograph from Zelda Cheattle and then take a taxi to Richard's through cold and sunny London.

I find myself upset this morning, everything I do to calm my frayed nerves useless, like an idea turning over and over in the night. The dark eye makes me dizzy, panics me on street corners. I fall over myself, trip on the cracked paving stones. I am gloomy, irritable and very unhappy with this struggle. All the friends I valued are dead or dying, a time falls into history, the adventure and euphoria gone. I write as we circle the Victoria monument, aching with the fatigue of living. I wish I could die along with HB's washing machine.

~

At Richard's started *Blind Maniac*. Richard tired, unshaven, had an osteopath round to fix his back. Completed my piece for the *Independent* on Robert – it brought back some canny memories overshadowed by his gift of two ivory and diamond skulls that I mounted on a ring. By teatime I've finished two paintings – *Mania*, and *Blind Date* – and have started a third, *Blind Maniac*. Richard says he enjoys me working here, it distracts him from his problems. The paintings are an assault on the perimeters of my life; like a wicked schoolboy, I dream of blasphemy. My life is like porridge without salt.

~

Came home to find HB sitting in the dark watching TV. His washing machine had expired, dried out and come back to life.

Thursday 22

Four weeks since I was last on my round of the doctors. I dread St Mary's – the flashbulbs in my eyes are more shocking than the operations and illnesses, my whole self winds itself into a steely coil.

My old friend Gawain walks in with a pink cyclamen for his doctor. He says after Ken died he gave up his business and bought a small flat in Paris, where he paints and makes pottery. Gawain and Ken disappeared from my life years ago. They lived in NYC until Ken died. It was difficult to talk across a hospital waiting room and when I returned from the eye drops he had gone into a consulting room.

~

Ken was the younger of the two lovers in *Sebastiane*, I'm glad that his youthful vigour is preserved on film.

He was a wild boy, the strigils in the bathhouse scene his contribution to the film. I shot Super-8 of him in Anthony's flat one June afternoon in 1975, he looked great reflected in the floor-to-ceiling smoky mirror walls of the derelict space, stark-naked except for a pair of cowboy boots, demonstrating the strigil with a bottle of olive oil from the kitchen before he pulled me into bed with him. There's a moment in *Sebastiane* when he surfaces from the water, smiling in slow motion.

Ken made love to the world. Once it would have been a terrible shock to have been told he had died, now barely a glimmer passed across my face in the waiting room. Ken was obsessed by men with large cocks. It was boys like him who did so much to melt the icy waste of propriety in the 1970s. He died for our happiness, a dream lover from an easier time.

I think of Ken as a hero of our times, it took considerable courage to do the love scene in *Sebastiane* – even more to do it with a hard-on. Ken was not a porn star, but a serious photographer. Gawain's brief encounter with me left me sad and also strangely elated for the rest of the day.

Friday 23

I'm running a slight temperature this morning, possibly the violent and uncomfortable boil, as big as an egg, that has flared up in the last few days.

Piers and I drove to Dungeness through a terrible traffic jam. We were already delayed as the hire firm wouldn't give him a car – Richard has not been able to pay him and funds have dried up. Richard owes money to everyone, but seems to have walled himself up with his art treasures, like the sleeping princess.

Saturday 24

I switched on every heater in Prospect and slept well in spite of my painful boils, which have given me a temperature.

I had the most magnificent dream: I had come to India, and found myself in a great and crumbling city – all purple and tawny sandstone, with magnificent awnings protecting the buildings from the sunlight, which cast long shadows like summer's early morning light. The city was crowded, though I found myself alone on the street in the company of a young man who was my guide. The atmosphere was so vivid that I awoke believing I had been there.

~

At eight the bathroom was warm as toast but as I made breakfast I realised that the water was cold in the tank. Back in the bathroom the floor was awash – I had not noticed the hot tap was left running.

Sunday 25

A wild storm blew in during the night, rattling the corrugated roof, buffeting the house in fits and starts, a high sea running down the channel with a huge tanker sending up plumes of white spray like a rock.

I'm warm in the new room, but with a slight headache and a temperature brought on by my infection.

~

Giles came, but I was not in the mood for visitors. I made excuses and replanted two of the roses that have struggled so unsuccessfully with drought and salt these past years. I'm glad I'm awake and it's light – at night I'm prey to fears and can never sleep with a gale blowing after the hurricane that huffed and puffed like the big bad wolf at the door.

The broom is burnt black with the salt, as are the marigolds, even the red hips are falling from the dog rose, the sea kale are dying back, but the artichoke looks set to defy the winter. My next-door neighbour thinks he has sold his house for £60,000 – I can't really believe this. He talks of his wife as his 'ex', driven to distraction and alcoholism by the lonely winds that blow across the Ness.

I live in a twilight here from day to day, neither earth nor heaven, the pain circles month after month breaking you down.

HB says he would give anything to give me a day free from this and says if we could swap bodies, and I promised to look after his, he would let me borrow it, but the reality of a sunny day might drive me insane and enduring this would kill him.

~

The gale is so noisy that I can barely think. I put Frescobaldi's *Primo Libro* on, its spidery clarity fights the bass roar of the gale across the Ness. I look for a sign of life across at Ness Cottage. Are Brian and Sheila up yet? There are days when I can imagine that if I disappeared no one would be aware of my absence – this is one.

I venture out, but I'm driven back by the rain. The sun suddenly appears, thin and silvery from behind the squally clouds.

Monday 26
The wind has died away and the sun is up bright and early; the dust cart grinds past and then silence returns, so complete I can hear myself.

It is several weeks now since I was here for more than a few hours. The days here pass quick as lightning: there's washing, cooking, writing, paintings and the garden. Getting up in the morning, shaving and breakfast take me nearly an hour. Everything is slightly slower as my sight hinders me – reading, writing and concentrating is very difficult; picking up a book, looking for a reference, much harder. Where did I put those specs? I'm hovering round *Blue*. I know I must rewrite it, but how?

~

Walked along the beach in a blue-grey sunset with wild orange and pink flashes of sun, the clouds reflecting the light in layers of opalescent splendour.

From my writing table I survey half this magnificent landscape with the lights on the reactor brighter by the minute as the sun fades. A bright yellow-green light has opened in the clouds above the transformer and the avenue of delicate pylons, a lonely crow flies towards the dying light, a black shadow.

Tuesday 27
The rain has set in, driven by a cold wind so persistent I cannot leave the house. Even the birds have taken shelter.

Wednesday 28
Nearly a week of my own company has left me longing to get back to London. My infections seem to be healing and though the nights are as restless as ever, sleep does come. I'm proud of my handwriting which still looks good even though impatience and my blurred sight conspire to ruin it.

The sun has returned and the sea turned a deep violet. I have never seen it this colour.

Thursday 29
Impossibly long journey to Ashford with the aggravating taxi lady.

Waited for ever for a bus to Camden, gave up. I hate being blinded – I know I won't come to terms with this, I'm as unhappy as all the desperate people crowding the pavements. My diary slips into the dark, the taxi driver has put on some dreadful music from the fifties, ghastly sentimental tunes.

Friday 30
Aurelia pulls another cappuccino and the gang of Italian men talk at each other foghorn loud. I stare at my crumbling face in the mirror.

The autumn chills me and the taxi takes me fast to Edwarde's Aquare, where I paint the morning away – *Now We're All Being Screwed by the Cabinet*, *Sex Bomb* and *Blind Date*. The paintings have become more unpleasant – all the bottled-up horror flying across the canvas.

~

In the evening walked to Robin's and James's exhibition in Lamb's Conduit Street with short-haired fluffers, so many that HB's friend Garry felt uncomfortable. The glamorous breakfast TV Tory Ivan – the financial adviser, Simon Watney and Emmanuel Cooper, all of us much older than the rest of the fluffers crawling around the art works. Then on to the Metro to see Della Grace's new photos. Ended up sitting cross-legged in the Thai Paradise with Richard, Mary Rose and Alison Wilding, who had come from the Tate.

Saturday 31

David and I drove to Dungeness on the calmest autumn day with woods golden yellow. The bees were out in force and the back room almost too hot for work.

So many visitors: Maddy, who was a *Blue* enthusiast, and Derek with two very young men, dancers whom he had met in dubious circumstances.

We spent an hour watching the saracena catching a really droppy bluebottle, which flopped down the tube to oblivion.

Derek made us a great supper, but I fell asleep between the rocket and the spaghetti. He drove me back as he could see I was whacked. I felt all the breath of life drawn away under the lighthouse in the reactor's glare.

NOVEMBER

Sunday 1

All Hallows. The dead circle the cottage in a high grey wind. I walk along the shore, the maroons go off and the lifeboat topples into the surf; all those lost at sea in the iron-grey waves. A calm has swept in. I'm not feeling so out of sorts this morning, only my sightless eye, absent in the morning, stares across the waves, but there is nothing there – no galleon with its masts down, no passenger liner turning turtle.

Monday 2

HB's birthday, the photo of him and Gary Stretch arrived from Donny in LA. Very wet and windy, the streets marbled with fallen leaves. HB took the first draft script of *Narrow Rooms* in to the film company.

At 3.30 we showed a rough cut of *Wittgenstein* in Andy's in D'Arblay Street.

Tariq, Ben, Terry, Ken and all the Bandung production. From the moment Terry walked in, late, following his agent, I knew we could be in for a rough ride, but hoped that this bright little film would dispel all misgivings. For an hour or two after the film finished a row blew round the room. I soon became 'Mr Jarman'. The film was 'full of errors', this word from an English professor made me see red. This altercation should have taken place months ago, indeed I wish it had – I knew the moment Eagleton and I left Tariq's generous table that we were chalk and cheese, the taxi journey home had passed in such a forbidding silence. That when I was told to 'get on with it' as Terry was 'Wittgensteined out', it was a bit of a relief. Terry's criticism of Tariq – 'You would never have dared treat Howard Brenton this way' – is such a far cry from the world in which I live and work: literary dinosaurs locked in combat. We make the films sparkle by working together – everyone throwing ideas and thoughts into the crucible, perhaps being queer taught us to bury ego. I can't see how I could collaborate when my letters – 'If there is anything you dislike about this script please let me know' – were unanswered.

Tariq behaved impeccably throughout, though I could see his old friendship with Eagleton was under considerable strain. He tried to explain the pressures of low-budget films to no avail. As Terry's agent chipped in –

'For her the script *was* the script' – I flew to my feet and told them they were all behaving out of line. How could I have negotiated this minefield?

To me, making films was an attempt to make work a joy. There are those who are life-giving who know you cannot live by rules, who know that 'error' is the weapon of the jailers of truth.

There are no words in a movie camera and too many at Oxford, where the right way of doing things is fanatically protected by business.

Terry's script was the foundation, without it the film would never have been made. I tried to explain this, but I was a rip-off merchant, a cinematic rag-and-bone-man, picking up the crumbs from the high table, academics as kings. This sort of man has had too much attention paid to him, we take the knocks and they take the credit in legally binding documents. In all my life I have never met such uncouth and surly bad manners. Don't believe that the toads on the left are any better than the toads on the right. In the two hours not one pleasant, or even slightly encouraging thing was said.

The only comment about the film came from Sarah, who said if she had not been sitting next to the grandees she would have cried.

~

The paintings lurched further into the void – we painted and slashed *Help*, and then attacked *Now We Are All Being Screwed by the Cabinet*. I dip my hands in the paint and then claw the canvas as if I am trying to break out of the limits of my painted language. The canvas is a cage in which I perform – 'Old Monkey' as HB calls me, poor Old Monkey. Old Monkey collected some smashing trousers from Mr Eddie in Berwick Street. I paid with cash. He said no one does that any longer. I said it gives me the feeling I have robbed a bank.

We are all on our uppers. I live in the moment. The past is filled with shadows and, like Johnny Rotten, my nightmare shouts: *No Future*. I live in despair, though I don't believe I should give in to it. The undone years, the hopelessness, thank God I won't be butchered for an idea, or the lack of it.

Wednesday 4

I'm wearing my rust-coloured trousers. The sun's out and I'm on my way to Bandung on the bus. James and I had a most successful meeting at Bertaux's, *Blueprint*, *Forget-me-Not*, *Speedwell Eyes* or plain *Blue*? Money is coming through, Nigel Terry, John Quentin, Diamanda Galas and Brian Eno are all discussed.

~

I'm fizzing with fury over the Eagleton row. James says the scriptwriter for *Peeping Tom* is still giving lectures about the way Michael Powell mistranslated his work. James was totally dismissive, he called them 'scribblers'. I have always been the first to protect the integrity of my collaborators but they in turn had to believe they were making films, and in making films everyone has to make sacrifices, some less, some more. Film is a language in collision with the word.

Friday 6

HB says I'm outrageous. I'm flat on my back at Bart's with a roaring temperature and bacterial pneumonia, and contemplating popping out on Monday to run through the film with Jan to determine the piano for the soundtrack. Living with an artist must be difficult, for their attention is divided – you share them with their work.

~

There are the usual charming nurses here. Bart's is quiet, orderly and efficient, it is the work of criminals to shut this hospital down – one of the reasons given is that there are too many beds in London. Bart's is packed, it took several hours to find a spare bed in casualty as Andrewe's Ward is full. How we are, and how we are reported.

~

The paintings get nearer to my mental state, the diary tells me what is going on. My paintings are social realism – they show the collision between the unreality of the popular press and the state of mind of someone with AIDS.

~

David, the nurse who calls himself 'the trolley dolly', wheels in the breakfast saying: 'Wines, spirits, cigarettes, perfumes, duty free.' I like the humour here, which counteracts any depression.

~

At breakfast HB arrives on his way to his fitness class. He looks more glamorous than ever. We could do with some of that here. He is my lifeline in this crisis, as day by day the aches and pains drive in.

I've noticed that the diary is sinking under the weight of illness like The Raft of the Medusa; in fact, The Raft would make a great AIDS film. It could be like a fifties TV documentary, or Huis Clos all at sea – the raft is *such* an image. I'll ask HB to bring some paper.

~

The quiet, blind physiotherapist came through the ward – a symbol of courage for all of us. Doris, the lady in the bed next door, fell over when her hip 'came out'; luckily she had a friend round at the time. She said she was screaming like mad, her friend thought she'd had a heart attack.

I'm wearing a 'Save Bart's' badge. The people who wish to tear this hospital down are just property developers, the sort that ran rampant through the eighties. All the good and honest England is betrayed, a land that is heritised into a theme park where time is frozen in empty houses and outside all is falling into ruin. The gloomy fascistic classical revival says it all: ugly cheesecake arches and pediments. I'm all for that style in Bath or Cheltenham, but in the land of the living?

~

Tariq telephoned. 'Oh, it's my revolutionary friend.' This intrigued the nurses, they came over and asked me who he was. Doris is wheeled out and a tearful girl is wheeled in, her voice a sad whimper. I sympathise with Doris: 'I know what real pain is like, it's awful, it takes over every thought and action till you do not exist, it's like the loudest noise you can imagine.'

I'm sweating it out, the sweet nurse called Shelley says goodbye, she says she's going home a little early for good behaviour.

The white flashes in my eye. A bed is wheeled in with a 'get well' balloon. There is a television in the ward, but no one has switched it on – a miracle. Television is a form of torture in hospitals; I succumbed to it alone in my room at St Mary's. I much prefer the bustle of the ward.

Saturday 7

The lights are up, it's seven. I've had a very sleepless night in which other people's misery leapt out of beds and circled in the dark. It's difficult not to feel swamped by the groans and whispers. Jim, the Glaswegian next door – he replaced Doris – is not quite as menacing as the alcoholic who lurched out at me in a meths haze on the doorstep a month ago; subdued by illness and withdrawal symptoms there are the remains of a human. Fragile and very insubstantial, he caught his death sleeping rough, soaked through.

The sad girl with the head injury asks for this and that, and the nurses can't deliver – it started when she had to wait for a doctor to prescribe some painkillers so they seemed set against curing her pain, this relationship has carried on. The nurses say: 'Well if you do that, you will probably go back to square one.' She is the unhappiest person in the ward. In many ways I'm happier in hospital – I can escape from myself – you see the whole world without stirring abroad.

My new drugs are Fluconocillin and Kephtaphadin. I sweated a bit in the night, always uncomfortable as you wake wet and cold, and at four in the morning – the time the demons lurk – one is never on sure ground.

I've been talking to Jim. At first I was rather nervous, but he's obviously not going to have visitors and, next to him, I have an embarrassment of riches. He welcomes my question: 'I hope you're feeling better this morning, Jim?!' with a broad smile and tells me his chest symptoms. I feel the ice is broken. I've always found talking to strangers very difficult, perhaps that's the legacy of being a bullied child, you draw your horns in. Maybe it's the key to creeping out of my protective shell.

I dreamt of HB doing his taekwon-do breaths. Sarah, who came to visit, said he was very sexy doing taekwon-do; we are going with her and Alison to see Dreyer's *Joan of Arc* – my favourite film which lay in the back of my mind making *Edward II* and *Wittgenstein*.

A very jolly teatime. Tania came with lots of Bertaux goodies and Ken too. He brought me a saucy magazine with lots of nude fluffers, over-muscled and small in other quarters – as if they had been dipped in icy water to meet the present limits in taste.

The *Independent* would not print the word 'arse' in my Robert Mapplethorpe piece – they changed it to 'anus', on the grounds that it was a family paper. I'm an *Independent* reader, but I find all appeals to family values quite valueless. Pose the question 'what is a family' and then ask yourself where the values come from. Did your family sit down and discuss its values? Mine certainly didn't, the rules and regulations were imposed from outside and reclaimed by the regulators.

Robert's high jinks have made him a gremlin to haunt propriety. I can't see how a photograph of him giving someone a blow-job is obscene – as the V&A obviously thinks. Who's protecting whom and from what? Then, we were not much good at enjoying ourselves. Now a culture of denial, frozen in false and deluded ideas of sexuality. I've always liked people having sex in saunas, I wish they'd do it in the street.

~

Feel inadequate, I fell out of love with Ms. Headbang. She fell over after three bottles of champagne and I don't know how many Bucks Fizzes. She is horribly selfish, commandeers the telephone and when someone rings in does not answer it, so the man next to her, who is very ill, slips trying to catch the call. That she has lost the hearing in one ear should teach her a lesson, it's certainly only temporary. I can understand the hard-pressed nurses' impatience.

~

David Hurst rang from Italy to say he had heard I was dying, 'Don't worry,' I said, 'I've been doing that for years, I'll tell you when I manage it.' The Italian bluntness in these matters is quite refreshing. I'm certain if I were Roman they would be filming this and projecting it in some stadium with a lurid chat show host and some scantily clad nymphets taking bets on a wheel of fortune.

~

Ms. Headbang has just been wheeled out.

Horrible, noisy, screaming children allowed to wander everywhere, making a nuisance of themselves without a thought. Noisy families talking at each other. An argument in the newspapers about whether Old Mother Windsor should pay taxes. The royal family seem hell-bent on self-destruction; what a relief there will be when they have gone – the corpse we all sleep with.

Jim says he wants to stay here – avoid his friends. He can hear the hearse revving for him.

Sunday 8

Doris left us; and Gladys – in her housecoat of little pink roses – almost before she knew where she was; and Florence as well – who was grumpy – and her friend who sat by her bedside as forcefully as an Egyptian crocodile god, with her heavy maroon hat and talk of the difficulty in crossing the road. Widows of Hackney, all the old names passing through. Will their names be forgotten in time?

I love old women, in other circumstances I would have married an older woman. They seem to have such funds of humour and knowledge compared with the elderly men; these, born in one war and lived through another, are the generation of my parents. Full of practical wisdom rather than media values.

I wonder whether our generation will have these quiet resources and stoicism?

~

There is no night here, as the casualty ward is busy late. Last night a drama was played out on the other side of the ward, illuminated through the frosted-glass partitions like shadow puppets. At two a.m. the shouting of a young deaf-mute boy rose to a squeal and the nurse found him dying in his vomit. For the next three hours doctors and nurses in increasing numbers fought to save his life. Coughing and groaning, the beep beep of the cardiac arrest machine, the roar of oxygen and the inability to communicate without shouting.

'Michael, Michael, Michael. Spit it out. That's good, Michael.'

Then observations about the state of him. It was disturbing, frightening.

The groans and his inability to speak added to the terrible feeling of impotence in the face of death. I had to remain an onlooker, there was nothing I could do.

We all lay in the twilight thinking: will this happen to me? It probably will.

The nurse this morning said: 'He's in intensive. I hope we saved him.' He didn't seem too certain.

~

HB and Peaches here performing their sisters act, they exchange camp compliments: 'You are *so* cool.'

'You're beautiful.'

They went to see *The Last of the Mohicans*, didn't like it, said it kept you at arm's length, and the make-up and costumes were atrocious, everyone looked like they lived in a launderette. The worst was the battles – crowds of yuppies not knowing what they were doing. Colin's report on Kenneth Branagh's new film was even worse – mind-blowingly trivial. I won't see either. Which of my peers has added a jot of vision rather than gold in the bank?

~

I've become much more friendly with my next-door neighbour Jim. He is determined to get off drink and is waiting for a visit from his social worker tomorrow.

He had a terrible experience: he had a lung op. in one of the other wards, as Andrewe's Ward was full up. He was 'barrier nursed' – no one would wash him, the cleaners refused to clean the ward and all but two nurses handled him at arm's length. They couldn't get rid of him quickly enough, but he was still there ten days later as they didn't want to move him. This surprised me – I thought these reactions were a thing of the past.

Andrewe's Ward is wonderful, all hands stretched out to help, but God help you if it is full. On my last visit I was reluctant to be discharged in case I had a relapse and ended up elsewhere.

~

We settle down, and then all hell breaks loose in an endless family row with a weeping Joy and her husband: 'I can't take any more!' – she tries to pull out her IV drip.

She has epilepsy, her husband doesn't seem too bad, a bit fraught.

'I'm not ill now.'

'But you could be, Joy, you'll be all right.'

'I want to go home.'

She is terrified of the hospital. He's much more practical than you might think.

Joy, who should be called Misery, is now getting angry. We have all endured the family row for two hours. A nurse finally cracks and intervenes. Joy seems to be severely disturbed, she doesn't listen to anyone, her husband gets up to go home. 'He's leaving me, he's deserting me!'

Another hour has passed, Misery is still screaming and shouting, the whole ward is up in arms.

'What she needs is restraint,' says Jim – they did this on Andrewe's to a man running around naked.

'He's leaving me. I want to go home' – sobbing. They've called her husband. 'Home. Home.' She's very incoherent, the nurses are extraordinarily caring, but she is unable to take their kindness to heart. I know they will not let her go, she is incapable of walking across the floor without two of them helping her. Suddenly there is silence, then she's swearing: 'Fucking bastards. Fucking bastards. You're fucking bastards. I wanna go 'ome, I wanna go 'ome. I'm a prisoner 'ere.' Louder and louder.

Another half-hour and she is still crying. The atmosphere is threatening. After twenty-four hours of psychological pressure my feelings about hospital have changed a little, it is extraordinary that we should be marooned down here in all this chaos for days on end. It's the endlessness – bang goes another night in recrimination, argument and tears. Finally they let her go home. How many hours had we endured?

The nurse said, 'Goodbye Joy, nice meeting you.'

~

Jim was the most compassionate, shrugged his shoulders. He's desperate to get out of here into a hostel to avoid going back on to the drink; he's fitter and brighter every day. I do hope the turn of fate that brought him here can be undone.

Monday 9

A green temazepam bomber buzzed me into five hours' sleep – a record – so this morning I feel rested and by 8.30 I'm sitting in bed, dressed, waiting to go to the screening which Dr Peter gave me permission to attend last night.

I feel perfectly rested, asked HB if he would organise a desk at Phoenix House and a seat. This would stop me falling asleep – as soon as I lie on the futon, whatever the time, it rolls in. 'Of course,' he says, he will get me one today.

There is an article in the paper RUDOLF NUREYEV BOWS OUT. It's so sad. I so remember his leap to freedom all those years ago and meeting him, holding his costume, stark-naked in his dressing room, saying: 'Well?' Me scarlet, speechless.

~

253

At 9.30 I left for *Wittgenstein*; Colin, James Welland, Jan, the gang, Tariq, it went down very well. I said to Colin: 'You see, Terry is Bertie and I'm Ludwig.' Colin roared with laughter.

Tariq asked him at the end if the film was Wittgenstinian. 'Very,' replied Colin.

~

Back here, another X-ray, then all the quiet broken by a poor old lady repeating the misery of yesterday: 'I want to go home, I don't want to die here.' Over and over. Sometimes a whimper, sometimes a shout. The doctor promised me more sleeping tablets, I'm going to need them. She said the Andrewe's Ward, with eight beds, had been full from the start, they had five patients in other wards at the moment. There is a twenty-bed unit on the way, but it won't be ready till next October. They had a crisis meeting about this and the hospital has assigned them two beds in another ward.

~

Jim comes down and sits on the bed, says he's been sent upstairs to a terribly noisy open ward, he wishes he'd been left down here, he's a catalogue of woe. He says that in overstretched St Mary's a doctor arrived with an insulin injection, thank God he was clear and bright: 'I'm not a diabetic.'

'Yes, you are.'

'Well show it me on my notes.'

The doctor found 'check for induced diabetes' – his medication could have lead to that, in tiredness his notes had been misread.

~

I'm still here, just.

~

HB arrives, then Alan and Gingerbits – with a hairstyle and new gold spectacles. Gingerbits says Alan flew up the motorway in a muddy showerbath from the huge lorries, which he slipstreamed all the way. English boys are obsessed with their hair, they spend hours teasing it into shape, stroking the results in bathroom mirrors.

I fall asleep, happy to have made my little comedy.

Tuesday 10

Dreaming of my film *Sebastiane* on my green bomber last night. It has been so misinterpreted, gay icon, or appropriation of straight icon? It's Sebastian who is slaughtered as a result of his rejection of a plural sexuality. He prays to a solar conquering god Apollo, Mithras, Christ, who demands his 'whole' attention. They steal his love and turn it into a weapon of denial. Sex cut across the reading in all the viewers' eyes: they saw a naked, handsome man, they did not see him as a spirit. No character in my films is more than a spirit, Ariel, they are not flesh and blood by any imagination.

~

I'm continually reinventing my own past, it is not static.

~

I was on the attack, gaining confidence with gay liberation year by year, making friends, out cruising, fucking boys in bushes, in gay bars, saunas, picking them off the streets, taking them home, talking, talking, when, where, why, how shall we do this?

I looked at boys' eyes and their arses on the street, I didn't miss one boy who passed. What was there on the screen that mirrored the ecstasy I found in bed? Nothing. *Victim*, forget it; *Sunday Bloody Sunday*, boring South Ken and I didn't want older men unless their company was a delight; *Un Chant d'Amour*, unheard of – buried years before by propriety; Pier Paolo, kindred spirit, but after straight boys with their jeans down allowing him, like a slave, to service them – dull fun.

I wanted to ride the arses of the willing and able through waking nights with the moonlight sparkling in abandoned eyes. It thrilled me to initiate a boy, stroking his legs and gradually and gently entering. When you heard him say 'Harder, harder!' you had won, not only for yourself, but against the heterarchy – who were busy building walls to contain half-formed desires, their lives of poverty symbolised by the purity of wedding gowns and the parents and grandparents peeking between the sheets. Mine were not invited.

At the opening of *Sebastiane* I asked my father, 'I bet forces life was never like that?' He replied that the film was quite accurate, forces life was mirrored there.

~

My sex life is that of an old man now, though I did attempt to revive it last night by my own hand, but it was not unconnected with that past. I conjured up Ken, the boy who laughs in the cleansing waters of *Sebastiane*, who covered himself with oil, produced capsules of old-fashioned poppers in glass phials wrapped in cotton wool, and had me fuck him on Anthony's enormous and ruined bed in the bright sunlight, lithe and glistening with sweat, with his come all over the sheets and walls. What a journey from the day I pushed my cock into Ron's arse ten years earlier when neither of us knew where we were going and the feeble strokes were stymied by guilt.

Fucking Ken, with his antique bronze strigil on the bedside table, we rode back into an antiquity of fable, not an Eden but a Paradois Paradise – we were Alexander and Hadrian and every boy since then, power, conquest, surrender, my paradise was whole, balanced as the rhythm of the pendulum, back forth, pleasure pain, but none of the guilt. Not the biblical Eden where the queer was but a chip off the straight like poor Eve made from Adam's hand-me-downs – who, in Christendom, will always be pushed around.

By twenty-five I knew it was brighter to be queer and alive, and not straight and dead to life. I always wrote of getting fucked in my books in order to break down the repressive world in which I grew up, where the queens wittered on: 'He's butch, she's bitch.' It might be a description of an act, but hardly a state of mind. I found myself deeply criticised in one of the first pieces written on my work as a passive and therefore negative force in film-making. The observation is short-sighted. All the passivity in Wilde and Genet has had a greater role in changing perception, the active colludes with the straight, reinvents it.

~

Oh, bugger the hospital. I'm stuck on the payphone, raging again. The boring cultural commissar Ben at the BFI faffing around, wasting time with ideas that are already obsolete, all of them wanting to become artists without knowing the meaning of it. They are driven by a collection of prejudices and perceptions, mostly gleaned from books.

~

Long talk with Jim about the royal family. I said let the newspapers act as terrorists – it's the only way we'll get rid of them, every affair published, photographed. Any of the nurses here could beat Lady Di in the caring. What's so special about her caring? It's just power dressing, actually quite sickening.

Let them shiver, they are the false pretence, unmasked, they're exploding with their own ugliness in showers of arrogance and diamonds. Give the crown jewels to Boris Yeltsin, let him fire them into outer space. Turn the Palace into an hotel, Windsor Castle into a conference centre, violate history, put the royal tombs on sale at Sotheby's – they'd look good in a Japanese department store. Disperse the royal collections, sell the carpets from under their feet.

~

Tomorrow the Synod will vote on the ordination of women priests – it is a delightful outcome that the Church should tear itself apart. I hope it is as destructive as possible to that prison of dreams and desire. Let the trumpets blast the walls of the churches till they fall into picturesque ruin.

~

I must be feeling better.

~

Big boys are pathetic in the face of pain. The canula has him shouting out, how did he break his leg? Playing football. He is visited by a series of dull-faced centre-forwards and girls with long, crinkly pasta hairstyles.

~

Three o'clock and all is quiet. Jim has been taken to a hostel in Commercial Road. He was so nervous he forgot to say goodbye. I was half asleep. The blind physiotherapist came and said I sounded more out of breath. Is this why I'm sleeping?

~

I keep thinking of Dungeness, the unopened mail, my plants.

I feel something lurking round the corner. I said to the doctor: 'I know what we are all thinking but not saying. It's this: "I don't want to die in casualty." ' I want a quiet room in which I can make decisions if I'm well enough. I asked: 'Do you prioritise patients?'

She said, 'Yes.' I don't want to move from here, I've got to know everyone and I can cope with the occasional mayhem.

Wednesday 11
Tania, Andrew, Sarah and James all here, a very nice day. A quite cute fluffer has come in and a tramp who looks like a fakir. I'm allowed to go home but I must stay in bed. I'll have my Hinney Beast cuddling up tonight. I am very weak, breathless – my lungs crackle and pop, but have not snapped. They have fourteen AIDS patients: eight in the Andrewe's Ward, the others scattered and three at home with no beds at all though they have organised doctors and nurses for them.

~

I'm waiting for HB, most gorgeous of all fluffers, to sweep me back to Phoenix House.

Friday 13
I came home yesterday very much the invalid, breathless and exhausted by the week in the casualty ward and my pneumonia. I slept all day and by the evening had a slight temperature, which I sweated off during the night. The

Augmentin – antibiotic – has turned my stomach to water. HB says I should be in diapers; he's right. This morning in the darkness his bare foot found my soiled underpants on the floor: 'Eugh!'

'Don't move them, it's an artwork, poopants, in a limited edition.' For some reason this caused a burst of croaky laughter.

~

Colin rang, he said he had sorted out the Eagleton situation and thought the *Blue* script great and *Wittgenstein* as ground-breaking as Ken's *Debussy*. He offered to get money for the *Blue* script. I suggested he took on *The Raft*, as Brian Eno had contacted us and offered money, or music, for the project.

The second of the great architectural historians who taught me – John Summerson – has died. Unlike Pevsner, I remember little of him, except a distant urbanity of a pre-war generation. If good manners could be made concrete, Sir John was that. It was my fortune to be taught by two of the greatest architectural historians of the century and not just taught but tutored – we were such a small group. As a student I was unaware of the calibre of the teaching – at twenty I had no structures or comparisons.

~

HB is a Spartan. 'It takes a lean dog for a long race.' He picked up a copy of *Boyz* to take to the lads in Newcastle, where it is unavailable. 'I don't know why I'm doing this, it enshrines everything I hate' – all the dumb convention of identifying oneself with a group. HB hates the bars, the haircuts, all the consumerism of that culture, he is an austere HB.

~

David visits. A friend of his, who is a leading light in ACT-UP Paris, has fallen in love with an English girl. He has a reputation of being staunchly gay and he's worried that his new-found heterosexuality will destroy his reputation – she has spent the last few days changing herself into a 'man', so they can live together without fear of scandal. They've been out a couple of times with her dressed in the toughest leather. This is a most interesting reversal of 'the love that dare not speak its name'.

David walked me very slowly to the bank and back here at eleven.

Doorbell rang, 'Oh, David, see who it is.'

'Fortnum and Mason.'

'Oh, go on, it's somebody playing a joke.' Ludwig's observation on Fortnum and Mason had kept everyone in laughter on the film. But it was! An enormous hamper sent from Tariq.

~

Neil Tennant rang, he's in the middle of a new album.

Piers arrived with one of Richard's beautiful hall chairs, so I sit on a throne. My great friend and film supporter Dagmar Benke, who made all my work of the eighties possible, had not been able to ferry *Blue* past her editorial board. I told her it would be great for her blind viewers, as indeed it would.

I'm much perkier this afternoon.

Saturday 14
Last night my mind raced so I slept not a wink.

Driving to Dungeness with Howard we got to the hellebore nursery very early and found it closed. Howard wants a purple hellebore. I want a black and green one for HB. I left two notes in the flat: 'woodbeast corner' and 'metalbeast corner'.

All the leaves are blown down in Kent, the brightest colour is now in the holly berries. Coming across the hills and valleys shrouded in smoky mist we discovered an antique shop in a village, with a most charming elderly man. It was like the antique shops of my past – all of a muddle, nothing arranged, nothing polished, in all the Victorian bric-a-brac everything was simple, furniture, old photos, farm implements all as he had found it.

He showed Howard and myself around the shop and then upstairs. 'This used to be the doss house,' he said. 'I was born here.' I admired an extraordinary Victorian photo of thirteen people in their ill-fitting best. He said: 'Oh, you can have that. No, no, I wouldn't take anything for it.' We chatted for at least forty minutes.

I bought a very fine William IV elm chair for £120. We named the day the day of gifts, and drove back through the rain with an old table and campaign chair. I remarked: 'That shop is in the 1950s, we just visited the past.'

'Granny, what did you do in the sixties?'

'Dyed my hair and wore a kaftan, beads and bangles, grew marijuana, danced naked at festivals, rioted at the Embassy, took up transcendental meditation, experimented with groups of both sexes, slouched on cushions in the arts lab watching Andy's *Chelsea Girls*.'

'Mummy, what did you do in the 1980s?'

'Bought a house in deep suburbia, bought some clothes in Covent Garden, bought a Porsche and mobile phone. We didn't have the time for music. We watched the ads to inform our lifestyle, gave up smoking, took up drinking, cheered when Maggie sent the troops in and framed the unliked Arthur Scargill, cheered her through the Falklands, swilled the North Sea oil in trinkets.'

In the seventies my studio in derelict Bankside cost £2 a week. We had studio shows and the most extraordinary crowds – no one thought twice when Lord Goodman came, I suppose we thought it the norm then. The Sainsburys, John Betjeman, Conran and Rothschild, Frederick Ashton. I'm not certain this happens nowadays. That Establishment was witty and much more open.

Invited to dinner by Lincoln Kristen in NYC, by Merce Cunningham to watch his classes at Westberth, or by Philip Johnson to the glass-house for a day and shown his picture collection – 'Make yourself at home' – I usually didn't follow up the invitations with the exception of the Sainsburys who showed me immense kindness. John could walk through any door and showed me a hidden London. I was all ears and eyes, and he watched my face with delight.

I treated all this as no different from going out for the night, I wasn't impressed. The world turned. *Le soleil* somehow set. I didn't regret a moment of that past but embarked, like Jason of the Argonauts, until they grew smaller and smaller on the quay of the past and then disappeared into history.

The eighties assaulted mind and body, the media connived to change something common into something 'controversial' – as good intentions didn't sell tickets. My God, it was queer to be queer – 'Oh, he's a type' – you could see it in their eyes. There were no smiles in the eighties, just 'right' ways of doing things, all the lanes and alleys of England were made straight. They fretted about me as it was difficult to buy off a film-maker – too expensive – and the road to exile in Hollywood was barred by an artistic immigration policy, there were no queers there. I struggled here with the cinema of empty pockets.

~

Here is a tale that transcends new-fangled prejudice and old-fangled political analysis.

My grandmother Moselle had a maid called Peachy, silvery frail, her hair in a bun, a gentle old-fashioned dress sprinkled with pale-blue flowers on a sea of pink. Peachy dusted the Indian ornaments – the Taj Mahals and wise old monkeys, the little jade pig with precious-stone eyes – while I played with Gran and her amber beads, which picked up little snips of paper as we glued together the Christmas chains. Peachy had butterfingers and ornaments were smashed and restored with glue so they looked like a set of exotic toffees. The third wise monkey lost his head, the little jade pig its left eye, the Taj Mahal was cracked and splintered – Peachy's duster was a ball and chain, and she and Gran quarrelled and laughed and spread the pink tablecloth for tea, and rested from work and quarrelled again. 'Oh Dekky, oh Dekky, you're Granny's love. Wash between your toes or they'll all fall off.'

Gran's Harry died at fifty and Peachy's Bert hardly older, and madam and maid befriended each other; in service was kindness.

Peachy knew her Dekky as 'Sugar' and Dekky knew Peachy as 'Peachy', and Moselle called 'Girlie' called 'Gran' called 'May' fretted and flustered as Peachy dusted, smashing the finials from the Parthenon clock, that ticked off time in the darkened hallway, until that fateful day in the fifties when the pressure cooker exploded, blowing the gas from the old iron cooker, and nearly extinguished the argument for ever.

Many years later I was summoned to Northwood by my mother, Miss Betty, who was dying of cancer. 'Peachy is coming to tea, Derek darling, she is longing to see how her Dekky looks now.'

A frail old lady, clutching a gift for Dekky, her gardening-mad darling – a grape-vine to plant on the southern wall. 'Dekky, my darling, you look so tall. You know I am ninety and still going strong and Ron's coming to tea.'

Peachy sat on Miss Betty's chair, Betty made the most excellent tea. 'Oh, your cakes are always so tasty. Darling it's lovely to see you, your smile is the same.'

We sat at the feet of Peachy who sat in the sunlight, silvery thin. The doorbell rang and her middle son Ron walked in – Ron had travelled from Australia, a handsome man, a millionaire.

'Miss Betty, Miss Betty, how wonderful to see you.'

'Come in and sit on Grandad's chair.'

And Miss Betty, now dying, worried about. And the years rolled back and she was still a girl, and Peachy sat in Girlie's chair till the sun set on her silver hair and the two of them wept as they parted.

~

Is time the something of nothing?

Sunday 15

I sat on my new campaign chair and the canvas split.

At 12.30 Nico [Nicholas Ward-Jackson] took Ken [Butler] and myself and his girlfriend Squirrel to a smashing restaurant and fed me oysters. I adore oysters, I can't count the times I've had them.

He asked me how I had met HB. In October 1986 I attended a film festival in Newcastle, then called the Tyneside Lesbian and Gay Film Festival. The festival was run by Peter Packer and was a vital focus, and though it's still lesbian and gay, it isn't called that any longer after Section 28 – a censoring of life and language by the criminal element in Parliament.

I was on a panel that included Artie Bressan and Wieland Speck, and while I answered the questions I couldn't keep my eyes off a young man in an immaculate suit with a very sharp haircut and bright, intelligent eyes. He sat in the front row, lounged casually in his chair. The chat came to an end and both Artie and Wieland remarked: 'Did you see that young man?'

When we went to the bar we saw him drinking with some friends. Wieland was crazy to meet him and so was I, so I said: 'I'll go and ask him to show us to a club or pub.' I walked over and said: 'Hello, I've come from the others to ask you if you could take us to a bar.'

His first words were: 'I never go to such places.'

But the answer was friendly and so I said: 'Could you just show us the way?'

'All right,' he said, and he and his friends showed us the way to a bar called Rockshots.

I thought I might see him the next day at the twelve-o'clock talk before I went back to London; to my disappointment he was not there.

Two months passed and I had to ring Peter with something to do with the festival. Before I put the phone down I said: 'There was a young man in the audience who will not leave my mind.'

'I know who you mean, Derek. I'll give you his phone number, but he's *trouble*.'

I looked at this number all over Christmas, I couldn't think how I could dial it. He might slam the phone down. Whatever would he think? I was not in the habit of phoning strange men. Suddenly I had an idea – I'd phone him at six p.m. on New Year's Eve before he set off to celebrate and wish him a Happy New Year.

I think the phone went very quiet after I did this, but he carried on talking. I asked him if he had ever visited London, he said he'd never been. 'Well, I'll leave my phone number and address with you. If you want to visit give me a call.'

He said: 'It's hardly possible. I'm living in Middlesbrough researching sonar for the MOD.'

I complemented him on his immaculate suit, rather foolishly, and rang off.

At the end of January he phoned: would it be possible to come for a weekend? The days flew. I was in a turmoil, I had discovered my HIV status on 22 December – maybe that's what had spurred off the phone call. I waited at King's Cross and he stepped out of the train, more handsome than I remembered. We spent the evening walking around Trafalgar Square, Piccadilly Circus and had supper at Rabin's Nosh Bar in Windmill Street, which, to my relief, he liked. Back home I said: 'Well, I'll make up a bed for you, but I have something I have to tell you, I'm HIV+.'

He said: 'That doesn't worry me, I'm not here for sex.'

Another month passed. He came back and then returned again in two weeks. I stood in King's Cross with my heart pounding. He said: 'My contracts are up and I'm thinking of taking a job at RSRE in Great Malvern.'

I was taken aback and said: 'Why don't you come and live here. I only live in one room, but I'm certain we could manage.' He said he'd think about it.

A month later he rang: 'I'm not taking the job, I'm coming to London.'

That's how I met HB.

~

Nico said: 'That's incredibly romantic, don't you think, Squirrel? Have you ever written that down in that diary of yours?'

'No,' I said. 'He's a very private person, who's coped with the invasion of his privacy that comes with living with me.'

'Oh, but you should do, Thumper, you should! It's much better than any of the Isherwood stories.'

~

Well, that's my version. HB has his. He remarks: 'You never write the good things down.'

~

Nico drove me back to Phoenix House: 'I've made you overtired with talk.'

'No, Nico, I've got to get on with life, I have so many projects that I've turned myself into an invalid of the mind as well as the body. Doing nothing would be a waste of precious time.'

'How are you coping?'

'Well. If you believe in nothing there's nothing to lose.'

~

I exist in the spaces between these words.

Saturday 21

St Bart's. My doctor said he thought I was a little better, my breathing regular compared with last week. I'll be here for at least ten days, but it is a welcoming place and the nurses could not be more kind and fill in the gaps of our incapacity. I'm fearful of losing my memory. I don't dare to visit Andrew Heard in the room next door – I'd probably give him PCP or the opposite could happen. He won't take AZT, which would cure his condition, so he will live the rest of his life in amnesia.

Sunday 22

The problem with illness and HIV is that one infection follows another like a goods train. I've developed the violent gingivitis that revels in antibiotics, so more pills.

Dr Mark comes in and examines my mouth, says I seem brighter. Howard rings. He and Karl are taking HB's cupboard salvaged from Manchester to Dungeness and picking up books.

Monday 23

Last night I asked Dr Mark for a 'green bomber' sleeping pill and had a good night's sleep. Most nights my mind races and I stay awake.

~

I'm in much better spirits this morning. My day starts at six with a first drip – Gancyclovir for the eyes – then an injection. I have a bath and shave before I'm wired up to the next drip – Trimethaprin, for the PCP; it takes over two hours.

I've arranged the room so I can write colour; I finished the medieval chapter and started on Leonardo.

Blood taken, lunch served, oxygen cylinder bubbling away – I'm a tangle of wires and tubes. There's a gap and then everything repeats itself in the evening until 12.30. I had a new tap put into me to administer the drugs intravenously and I forgot to take my pills – at least twenty of them.

~

Howard and Karl visit. Howard brought the paper whites that I planted at Dungeness and they fill the room with scent. I've also been given a beautiful little cyclamen, which has only a few more days to live.

With the radio, my phone and my writing materials I'm quite busy – in fact, the hospital room makes me concentrate, as death and mortality stalk the corridors, held at bay by the laughter of the nurses. I'll be out by Saturday or Sunday.

We discussed making Bart's *the* AIDS hospital, like the Lazar house of leprosy. St Bartholomew's church could be our resting place, a memorial to this terrible wasting disease. I wouldn't wish this on my enemies; by comparison the trenches seem clean-cut, final. The disease is a mental concentration camp, which barely a handful of those unaffected could begin to understand.

I see the hospital as an escape to sanity – everyone here has knowledge of the problems and is willing to help, full of smiles.

I feel comfortable here, just as I did years ago walking for the first time into a room full of queer men, at ease.

Karl and I planned the garden of railway sleepers which I'm going to push ahead before Christmas; after that *Wittgenstein* is finished and we'll paint the film *Blue*; I just cannot think of a name for the colour book, *Rainbow's End*? No, that won't do, *Iridescent*? *Pearl*? *Shrieking Colour*? It will come.

My doctor came in and said he will put me on a higher dose to dam up

264

the CMV. I'm talking with the energy of Dad after his stroke, breathless. There is one triumph in all this – I've done in the molluscum on my face.

~

I completed the chapter on Leonardo, my temperature remains normal. The paper-white narcissi from Dungeness fill the room with a heavenly scent. More pills and a mouthwash for thrush, you see the pharmacy trolley wheeling down the corridor and the pills dropping like confetti. I so much want to be in Dungeness, but I am happy here as everything that assaults has a chance of being stopped.

Tuesday 24
I came off the steroids, my temperature soared. A bad day, it grew worse.

Wednesday 25
A bit better today, though my temperature climbed. I waited an hour for an X-ray and worked on alchemy. James here talking *Blue*. David has a finished script, we noted the music and cleared up mistakes.

My breathing has improved. I'm not hooked up to the oxygen hissing all day and night. Old tortoise comes out of his shell.

~

Poor HB had to sit shivering on a corner till midnight, as Phoenix House was cut off by a bomb in Stephen Street – James said by a disgruntled employee of the BFI.

~

My nurse Mun, who is Japanese, brought me a beautiful book on colour, with exquisite illustrations.

I sit here in my Japanese work overall, indigo-blue. Mun read the characters: 'plum tree valley'. Blue is the colour of Japan. I noticed this before anything, flying over the blue-tiled roofs of Tokyo. There is no word for blue in Japanese.

Thursday 26
Tania and Michelle came in with cakes for the nurses, the doctors are doing their rounds.

It's been a busy day as my drip failed again and it was not until eleven that it got going. I've weaned myself off oxygen, though my fingernails look a little purple.

Drips: six hours a day Trimethaprin, two hours a day on Gancyclovir. I'm hooked up and immobile for eight hours. I become impatient, the mobile phone is a blessing, as is HB's little wireless. The music on Radio 3 is good, if a little old-fashioned – a fifteenth-century lament by Lamb for two friends who died from plague.

~

Told HB to keep to the main roads where the car bombs are less likely to explode, there is a danger zone behind the Phoenix Theatre, as MI6 have their headquarters across the street. Two bombs injured people in Manchester today.

~

I lie here in the snaky drips, 'pilled out' you might say, with a heavenly scented pot of paper-white narcissi that I grew in Dungeness.

~

Andrew Heard is here with complete memory loss, he hardly recognises a thing. Gilbert and George have come in every evening to talk to him, kindness itself. They're old friends – one certainly needs friends like them at this time.

HB very shocked. He said the body snatchers had come for Andrew, only recognisable by his tattoos. We are all travelling on the last train to oblivion.

Friday 27
This room is a monastic cell, the windows are frosted glass, the sun does not fall through the permanent blinds drawn across them. I am illuminating my book on colour, which I think I will call *Bliss* – I don't want to end in sadness, rather, if I was able, singing.

~

I lay awake last night and dreamt fitfully of Frederick Ashton – chain-smoking, gentle, while the dancers whirled around him, the still centre of a spinning top. 'Never say a thing in twenty minutes if ten will do.'

Fred was precise and a great ballroom dancer; on the night I heard Elizabeth Welch sing for the first time 'You're Too Young to Remember', he took off on to the dance floor with the Duchess of Argyll, her iron-grey hairstyle clamped on to a witchy face, she came a cropper, to everyone's consternation, on the slippery floor.

'Oh, Derek, when you're old like I am no one phones you to ask you out, they think you are too busy.' I phoned quite often. Fred would come to parties at the warehouse where we played charades – I was Edward, he Wallis Simpson, he kept all of us in fits.

'Come on, Margot, it's time for lunch' and then whispered in my ear: 'Derek, if you have any problems with the dancers, I'll sort them out, but Rudi, you'll have to deal with him yourself.'

Bill Bundy, who lit *Jazz Calendar*, took a dislike to me; nothing I suggested could work. Then Fred's voice came out of the dark: 'Stop behaving like Maria Callas, Bill, this is only a little ballet.'

I last saw him at Sadler's Wells at a show by Lindsay Kemp. That night a man in the seat behind persistently jabbed his shoes in my back. I turned round and complained, and he did it even more. I turned round and said: 'If you do that once more I'm going to spit in your face.' He did, I did, and he and his party crumpled in disbelief. One more reason why I don't go to the theatre any longer – he did me a good turn. Meanwhile Sir Fred was spinning, conserving his energy.

~

My drip clogged up and my temperature climbed. By the time a new vein was located I was coughing, losing breath and on oxygen again – I'm absolutely dependent on the Trimethaprin.

~

The paper whites keeled over in the night. I've made a sort of Japanese bandage for them with white paper, they look very elegant.

The food here is good though I hover on the edge of hunger – plaice today, excellent milk puddings: semolina, rice, sago, childhood memories. Will they make junket?

The days pass marked by the eight hours I'm tied to the drips and Radio 3, which is playing watery Bach recordings, sweet and inconsequential, nothing much to get my ears around.

It occurred to me this afternoon that the medium with which we discovered the world is glass – transparency.

Saturday 28

A good night. I woke up bathed in sweat, but my temperature had dropped to normal, the awful breathlessness of the PCP had gone, I feel I've turned the corner, as at moments, stuck on the drip, I feel I'll never get out of here.

~

James came round. The BFI on *Imagining October*: 'It's so dated.' You could say that about *Battleship Potemkin*. Long discussion about film and finance, and which short should go out with *Wittgenstein*. This is a delicate subject in which I am going to have the final say.

It's very quiet in here today.

~

Michelle and Tania sent a large box of cakes for the nurses and brioche for me. Food poured in: Garry, Peaches and HB brought me a delicious blackcurrant tart.

~

Howard came with his camera and took photos of me in bed, which passed the afternoon. Howard is having a terrible time finding somewhere to live, but he's happy with the lurid purple shirt I gave him. He said it was perfect for a visit to *Vogue*, who have decided to publish his *Wittgenstein* photographs. With that and the book – which will have fifty photos – the decision to get Howard to record the film has paid off.

It's eleven and I'm off the drip and ready to go to bed.

Sunday 29

A violent rash that burns and itches has flared across my face. I've been given a cortisone cream that stings. At 3.30 Marvin is coming to record the hospital sounds for *Blue*. I finish writing iridescence though my hands shake with palsy. Other patients in varying states of skeletal decay wander the corridors. Poor Andrew is still forgetting everything; he has no sense of direction and a memory as long as a sentence. What a blessing to have writing and reading to fill in the time.

~

HB brought in an anthology of seventeenth-century poetry, I particularly love Donne and Marvell, Donne's '*Busie old foole unruly sunne, Why dost thou thus through windowes and through curtaines call on us?*' makes up for this shadowy room where the sun never falls and light is provided by six fluorescent tubes glaring behind glass panels in the ceiling.

~

It's twelve and I am still in my yellow pyjamas. I fall asleep. Richard comes, he is more exhausted than I am, said his trip to Sotheby's brought home the depth of the recession. He hopes to get my paintings exhibited in a New York gallery. Says he has to make a large deal – a surrealist painting he wants to sell to the Japanese – as the whole dizzy spiral into bankruptcy will start again in January.

Paintings are the tulips of our time and the petals have blown. I feel much sadness over Richard's plight. It's a good thing to fight the shadows but to lose yourself in the dark? He has started me painting again. I'm always welcome to come and go, and leave a dreadful mess for Piers to clean up. Piers mixes the paints and we talk ourselves through the new paintings: 'I don't think this one goes as far, or is as good as that one.' We started with brushes, took up the kitchen knife and then rubber gloves, dipping them in the pigment, clawing the paint on the canvas, fireworks of colour and tortured scribbling, they look like my inner state, something film can never express, ideas there are endlessly swallowed by budgets which preclude a wild unhinged approach. Passionate pigment.

~

HB here at seven. He took the old washing machine out on the Charing Cross Road, put it in a phone box and went back for his camera. By the time he got back downstairs the washing machine had vanished.

We read Andrew Marvell and then he went home, taking a huge bundle of washing with him – a challenge for his new machine.

Monday 30
Up at six, on the drip. Wrote until released from the DHPG and Trimethaprin. My equilibrium has returned, I feel level-headed.

~

I'm up and dressed in my blue boiler suit. Walked to the shop to buy the *Independent*, a new pen and some chocolate peanuts. Lunch – macaroni cheese and cauliflower, and frogs' spawn milk pudding.

~

Michael Palin recommends *Modern Nature* as his book of the year, says I'm tetchy. He's right – I couldn't have been otherwise.

~

The young Glaswegian nurse who took my blood this morning said she was so pleased to work in the AIDS ward. Casualty was sometimes a nightmare – trying to get blood from a meths drinker, frightening; the geriatric ward the most unpleasant, none of the old people would let her anywhere near them, they swore at her, one punched her. I could see she longed to return home.

~

I'm off the drips tomorrow, on to the oral DHPG and something to attack the PCP. You should see my face, like a purple baboon's arse in a snowstorm.

~

HB is in Bosch heaven. All the coloureds are swirling about in a halo of soap, almost silent, bright lights – red and green – flash. It arrived at midday, Peaches waited for it. HB came home in his lunch break, plumbed it in and programmed it with the whites.

269

~

Della Grace visited, brought *Quim* magazine that the sex police at Gay's the Word banned along with her book *Love Bites*. She showed me pictures of her girlfriend, brought me a photo. I think her work is courageous and as open as she is. The sex police are the vinegar dregs of the right-on, they set up structures with all the oppressive rhetoric of Catholic commands. What would happen if *they* had the power? Enforce a world-wide ban on these images, the Jesse Helms of Marchmont Street. If only we had a bookshop like the Prinz Eisenhardt in Berlin – where you can buy what you like without feeling pressured. I'm always welcomed there, sit down for a cup of tea. At Gay's the Word that stony British silence and the dislike of any form of personal success – a betrayal of the grey collective. Della said they were quite happy to stock a book of hairy men with hard-ons, but not her wild and entrancing photographs. Before she left I said: 'Don't worry, your star is in the ascendant.' She said next year will be her year, as it is the year of the cock.

DECEMBER

Tuesday 1

Slept well and ate a good breakfast. The doctor came and said that hardly anyone went totally blind with toxoplasmosis. This put my mind at rest, as I feared it would gallop in from the night like drawing black velvet curtains.

Wheeled through the hospital for an X-ray. If that's OK, after eye tests at Mary's I will be out on Thursday. God what a lot to keep in the air. I'm the juggler, with two films, a book and a script all under way.

David has been looking through the scripts in the archive – a great surprise as *Jubilee* had some really macabre dialogue which never got into the film, the four-week shoot erased dialogue in favour of image. The book has napkins scribbled with ideas, letters from Toyah [Wilcox] and the original plastic surgery notes from Adam Ant. It is full of mad drawings of camera angles, invented for the mind rather than reality. Perhaps I drew them in as we filmed. *Akhenaten* has quite wonderful watercolours by Christopher in a large book with the king's name on the cover hammered in brass.

Wednesday 2

A woman crying in the night, my green bomber put me to sleep. I woke at four and wrote an introduction for the *Wittgenstein* book, then I fell asleep and woke again at nine.

My temperature is playing up and I am still terribly breathless. I told my doctor I felt on a razor's edge. He said they would not release me until they had done the ward round tomorrow – there might be one or two things brewing and I could come up in a rash, so no Dungeness this weekend. And the sound dub? Let's keep our fingers crossed. I'm happy to stay, I'm not certain I could look after myself – HB is right in the middle of his course, although he says he will give it up for me, sweetheart.

~

Stravinsky's *Persephone* on the radio – I must get the CD. There is a Stravinsky season, all his music has an unmistakable fingerprint.

Fell asleep and sweated it out, 98° by 4.30. My breathing is easier, but my energy is so low. I ate my lunch. Tomorrow I go to see Clive Migdal at St Mary's about my eyes, then back here for the five-o'clock doctors' round.

Thursday 3

Oh, dear, another day begins and there is so much to do. I think it best to do one little thing a day and carry on.

Up at seven, shaved, bathed and took a taxi to St Mary's. It was almost an hallucination driving through darkened streets across the city. The driver got me there quite quickly in spite of the rush hour. I arrived before the clinic had started, but the doors downstairs opened, climbing the stairs did not wind me as I thought it would. I sat alone for quite a while before others started to arrive. I am able to get about, but very weak. Perhaps I've grown too fond of my little room in Andrewe's Ward for my own good.

~

Slight night sweats, but if nothing brews up by this afternoon I will be allowed to go home. Living becomes a long shot – at moments, with all these drugs and drips, you imagine you are knocked for six, will never sit up or walk out except in a body bag. At least I have HB to look after me, some people are alone.

~

Some new posters: *Survivor's Clinic Times, Psychology Clinic Times*. The eye drops are in, vision blurs, the *annus horribilis* continues, problems everywhere for everyone. A strange purple man with long hair in a band talking to himself and walking fast hither and thither with loud boots, he is building a tower of plastic mugs. I wait and wait. The wheelchairs arrive. It takes all morning whatever time you get here. I think the CMV has started up in my right eye, I feel the black closing in. Maybe this is because there is so much talk about eye conditions – which are becoming more common as people live longer.

Michael Corder here, visiting a friend. I didn't notice him as my jugsy eye blotted him out, there is a retreat into sickness.

~

A terrible indecision about leaving Bart's. The last thing I want is to be re-admitted within the week. I have sweats, but my temperature is below 97°. Nothing showed up on the bronchoscopy so the doctors are a little puzzled, the PCP treatment worked. Tony said these illnesses start each other off, they hunt in packs. I went to Mary's where my eyes were checked out and OK.

272

Very late, HB and I tossing coins – the best of three said leave. I decided to stay here another night and see if I slept without a sleeping pill.

Friday 4
Woke at one, did some writing and then fell asleep till eight.

~

HB says I'm as thin as a rake and plans to fatten me up; my long hair is awry. I will go home.

~

Staggered back to Phoenix with Howard, unbelievably weak. Sandy came with a warm winter jellaba from Morocco and looked through Howard's photographs. Then a very cuddly HB came home. We had lunch, risotto at the Presto, I came back and lay on the bed.

~

HB munches at a plate of HB fare.
   'What's that, HB?'
   'Cheese.'
   'It doesn't look like cheese.'
   'Wensleydale. Would you like some?'
   'No.'
   While his back is turned I steal a piece. It's marzipan – he's eaten a whole pound of it.

Saturday 5
The night punctuated by wailing sirens as the police rushed this way and that after the IRA.
   Very weak and palsied, my hand shakes so the tea slops off the cup. HB says I've shrunk. I'm on the fourth hole on my belt, usually it's three. I am eating – which is a surprise as I imagined that the pills would have put paid to that. I'm light as a feather, the slightest gust could blow me away. Wobbly Saturday.
   The Lesbian and Gay Centre is to close due to 'mismanagement'. It was pretty out of focus so perhaps will not be much missed. Somehow serious thought is always absent from these institutions – there was a space for paintings, lectures, meeting rooms, they could even have had a small cinema, but the bar was the focus.

~

HB's improvements: a new radiator, a washing machine and a new proggy mat from Newcastle, it is big and all shades of green.

~

HB and I had lunch at the Presto, HB ate a huge plate of Christmas pudding and custard – he's got a little bit of marzipan which he's hidden in the cupboard. He has very long hair, which looks silky and gorgeous. He doesn't like it, though I think it's rather handsome.

Sunday 6

I slept very well, I haven't felt this rested in years. Weak at the knees, dozy. HB up at nine, later and later, the first thing he does is sort out my pills.

Late last night I finished my phosphorescent ghost poem as my temperature hit 99°, but today it's down to 97°. At moments I feel I might recover from this assault though I hardly dare believe it. Part of the lethargy has been caused by lying flat on my back for nearly four weeks, muscles unused evaporate. I must have lost a stone or more though I haven't weighed myself.

~

HB came to Bertaux's, met Mathilde the dyer and Tania's artist friend, Michael Clarke, who is to take a photograph next week. Tania made me a huge glass of fresh orange, coffee and croissant.

I wrote a piece on the blue grotto for *Blue*.

~

HB and I sit at our desks like school swots. I write with my gold and violet pen, HB clatters across the keyboard, he is going to get a distinction. He says he is doing it to show the straights – whom he, and his queer classmates, attack at every opportunity, undermining their self-confidence. HB is on the warpath.

~

Alison and Sarah came and drove us to the Barbican, where we saw Dreyer's *Joan of Arc* with an orchestra, simple and very effective, a kaleidoscope of close-ups from every conceivable angle.

Monday 7

There's an article in the newspaper – apparently you can get buried in your own back garden, there is no law against this, though the Department of the Environment might complain.

Tuesday 8

I'm much stronger today and well rested. I slept well for the third night running. HB is on the final run for his exams.

~

We worked hard on the sound. When I came back home my temperature had risen over the 99° mark. HB threatened me with the doctor – quite honestly, I'm such a ruin at the moment, I hardly know *where* I am. I stagger along the street, my feet wandering this way and that, out of control. Crossing the road with my blind eye makes me weave and stagger, I go very slowly. My physical self is out of control. I don't think anyone understands how disorienting this is, they see you standing there looking relatively well and think that you are your old self, the self they know, and that you can answer them with all your wits about you. My hand shakes, my legs pack up under me. I am a little stronger.

Wednesday 9

In the sound studio we are putting the sound on the Martian – Quark, Charm and Strangeness. Gingerbits's typing still not done! I don't think the colour book will get completed at this rate. I told him this morning: 'It's a race now!'

Thursday 10

We finished the sound, and proof-reading the book of *Wittgenstein*. I came home. HB, Karl and Peter here. They'd spent the day tidying the studio at Richard's.

Friday 11

Up at seven, a cold rainy day. HB growls that I'm making too much noise talking to myself getting my pills organised – he gets out of bed at six and doesn't even speak until nine. He hates my new leather gloves, says they are strangler's gloves. I touched him on the back of his neck and he jumped out of his skin.

Aurelia made me a cappuccino at the Bar Italia, which at 7.30 is an Italian bar before the rest of Soho arrives. I picked up my letters and read them in a taxi on the way to Bart's. I'm sitting waiting for a chest X-ray, the first in the queue. Dr Mark said I looked much better. I feel much stronger. I'm still sleeping more soundly than I can remember; last night I slept till dawn without a break.

~

Corrected the *Akhenaten* script and the first three colour chapters, *The*

Colours of Colour? The *Akhenaten* script is baroque, written in poetic-operatic, Egypt and incest. It could be made very simply, against sand floors and whitewashed walls, and though there is a small fortune described in golden statues, they are not necessary. The *Wittgenstein* approach would work wonders – Fortuny dresses would look great on both men and women.

Saturday 19

Howard, Ali, Karl and myself drove to Dungeness along our scenic route – via Hellebore Heaven in Hawkhurst, where Howard bought a purple-black seedling from Elizabeth Strangman.

We had breakfast in the greasy spoon, the tea was so bad that Ali had to buy a KitKat to get rid of the foul aftertaste. It rained and rained. We arrived at Prospect at one – where Peter was waiting, almost about to give us up for lost. Fifty railway sleepers had been dumped at the side of the road and were wet and very heavy. We decided to build the garden at the back, beyond the beehive. Karl and Peter managed to move nine of them before the dark closed in.

Ali cooked a huge meal for all of us which we ate at five, though it was so dark it seemed like midnight. Howard and Ali took off back to London.

Early to bed.

Sunday 20

It poured with rain all day, making it almost impossible to work in the garden. There were a hundred and one jobs to do, as I've hardly been here since September – except the odd Sunday trip with Howard. All the fires are going and Brian has insulated the roof so the house is very warm.

The garden is strangely out of sync as the rain and warmth has driven the flowers to sixes and sevens. There is a dark-purple wallflower in bloom and marigolds – which are wind-battered by the easterly that is blowing in burning salt from the breakers. The acanthus and artichokes are huge and looking luxuriant in the midwinter dark. I noticed the wallflowers have seeded themselves in every nook and cranny, there are poppies and cornflowers, nasturtiums and drifts of Californian poppies. The large thistles that flowered last July have self-sown with teasels, valerian, mallows and daisies – the wild flowers are all looking well set.

In the lakes along the road to Lydd the islands have disappeared into the flood, the water is higher than I have ever seen it.

Late in the afternoon we drove to Appledore where I bought a magnifying glass and a palette knife. We met friends of Peter's in the garden centre, one of them the young man who wrote me a letter asking if I had a spare copy of John Boswell's *Christianity, Social Tolerance & Homosexuality* – as wherever he went said I had bought all the copies.

Home via New Romney, where the church has been restored and cleaned, a dazzling white in the indigo sky.

It is dark now. Peter takes off for Deal to equip his new home, El Ray – a converted railway carriage out by the nuclear power station. BNFL sent us a rather optimistic calendar with pictures of ruined abbeys and idyllic landscapes with the actions we are to take in case of a disaster printed on the back.

Monday 21

Cold but not raining today. I cleaned the floors and made breakfast. It is almost more work having people stay here than to be alone, somehow you have to make space.

Howard drove me to Deal – still a beautiful seaside town, the houses fronting the sea are kept spic and span, and the concrete pier has a drab charm, the cafés are unchanged since the fifties, chrome and illuminated mirror mosaic columns. Howard and I parked in the car park facing the sea. I felt we should have brought a sandwich pack and thermos.

We got stuck into a very good second-hand bookshop. Howard fell for the girl behind the desk with hair black as a raven. We bought Boswell and the *Pearl*, and a book of days, then Peter took us to a second-hand clothes shop where I splashed out on more Harris tweed, which warmed me up.

The hills from Dover to Deal shrouded in mist, Howard and I decided that the drive west was more scenic, though the chalk downs have their own lost and bleak beauty at this time. 'Welsh,' said Howard, not much cheer for Peter who is recovering from a stint of Welsh animosity near Bangor.

'What do you expect?' asked Alan. 'These Celtic languages have no urban tradition; they are rural and fascistic, pre-thought – eighth century.'

The Welsh sheep sprouted canines and bit poor Peter. He fled back to Kent, said Bangor might as well have been Bosnia and he a Muslim – he is still smiling after his agrarian ordeal.

'What,' I enquired 'do the Welsh eat? Is it perhaps the radioactivity in the rain that fell from Chernobyl?' Peter says he found it quite impossible to cross the language barrier – he might as well have outfaced the great wall of China as befriended the sons of Glendower. He started to learn Welsh, as the farmers he lived with spoke no English; they warmed to this but not to him.

~

Karl put up a new washing line. I put up the Christmas tree – a branch of fire-blackened gorse with some very old and tarnished decorations. We built the vegetable garden by the washing line and, as the sun faded at four on this the shortest day of the year, we ate a huge high tea with a roast and a very good bottle of red wine.

Christmas Day

The day is quiet and grey, a mist hangs over the land, cold and silent, not a breath of wind. Peter is in Deal, Alan says he will be here at midday to take me to the Sisters' Margate nuncheon. I've spent the morning writing and correcting the colour book.

HB is shut in Phoenix House with his M&S oven-ready dinner. Why do we spend our Christmases apart? Perhaps it confirms the need to reject family at this time. I know if anyone asks me to spend Christmas with them my heart fails. Peter asks why *should* we get together on this day? The tears of repetition – is Pegs weeping into the turkey at my sister's? The requests to attend become even more desperate as the world grows old.

A large black crow flaps listlessly over the garden on its way to the sea's edge, not a breath of wind, utter hush. I bring in the coal for the fires – it is such a luxury to be alone here, ploughing through Horace for a quote to ring the new garden.

> *Why do we aim so high, when time must foil our*
> *Brave archery? Why hanker after countries*
> *Heated by foreign suns? What exile ever*
> *Fled his own mind?*

Blessed silence. These are the first hours that I have been alone for weeks: the cacophony of the hospital, weeks staggering around Phoenix House, a sharp pain in the lungs and the dark pushing at my right eye, dodgems along the pavement.

~

The day passes. I wait for Alan who will be here by two – or three country time. I ring HB, but, as he promised, the phone is off the hook. Richard rings, he's off to Christmas lunch. He says he has champagne for me and will drive here tomorrow.

~

The ubiquitous Derek Ball will not be here for Christmas – he has flown to Mexico for a tequila vacation in Acapulco. The festive season here as dry as a bone.

Rescued by dear Alan and the Order of Perpetual Indulgence who took me all the way to Margate, where Turan sat us all down to lunch with phallic crackers, his dishy Dutch boyfriend André – who knows how to wear those baggy khaki trousers so you miss nothing – and the OPI in festive habits with bright beads and a touch of Berwick Street.

Turan's house overlooks the Margate bay – a breathtaking view. As the light faded we played pass the parcel and old 78s of Doris Day and Carmen Miranda.

At eight Alan drove me all the way back here via Canterbury – it is such a physical and spiritual wreck of a memory it is best seen at a distance, you can just suspend belief as you see it from Straight Street. The pilgrims of our time end up in the car park, or avoiding the concrete litter bins in the pedestrian precinct. No badges of St Thomas in the high street Ratner's, no hair shirts in Laura Ashley, the only artist who could celebrate this trash – Jeff Koons with his wife 'La Chipolata'.

Boxing Day

In the middle of the night the cold water tank in the attic overflowed and I woke up surrounded by drips, fortunately none on the bed. Turning the taps on solved the problem. A cold wind got up in the night so I am well shuttered in, wearing Sandy's very warm Moroccan jellaba, which turns the heads of the Boxing Day tourists on their way to the lighthouse.

~

My doctor Mark, telling me he was leaving to do research, said: 'I have good news for you, you have survived your doctor!' Everything has gone so quiet in the last four months I feel as if I have survived myself and most of my friends. Do I make a list here just to remind myself? Peter, Terry, Howard, David, Tom, Karl, Ken, Patrik, Billy, Robert, Tommy, Paul – most of them in their twenties and thirties – all had a bright future snatched from them. As I record their names I wonder where, or on what words, my pen will stop. It should be 'Amen'.

~

The wind has died, the December grey has pulled back so the power station seems but a stone's throw across the shingle. I hope to do some gardening, transplant a rose or two, but it is too cold and I am being 'sensible'. I won't paint, I'll write.

I walked briefly to the sea, blown about by the gale that has blown up. I have spent the entire day alone – except for two long phone calls from HB, who seems quite happy dodging the bomb scares on Charing Cross Road.

The wind howls through the night and the drip from the water tank starts again at five.

Sunday 27

The sun is almost through the bank of clouds, which move like a wall across the grey sea. The wind has been in the east for over a week but this keeps the pither stoves white-hot. I'm surprised how deserted the Ness is this December, only the two intrepid Jehovah's Witnesses have called. They didn't wish me a happy Christmas and looked taken aback at my jellaba – which all the saintly witnesses wear in the terrible watercolours in the visual deserts of the *Watchtower* and the ineptly named *Awake*. I stood in the freezing cold, looking like a prophet; they did not drop to their knees. This lot are so blind, they could spend an afternoon with God attempting to sell him his own story. As I shut the door I took heart in the stories of my desert garden, which will be here long after Jehovah and his Witnesses have vanished.

> *Alas my dayes be now done*
> *I wot I must dye soone*
> *For damned I must be*
> *My legges rotten and my armes*
> *And now I see of Feendes swarmes*
> *from hell coming for me.*

I painted, *Fatal*, and CMV – the colours acid, muddy, unpleasant, annoyed. The sun came out so I tried to find the strength to work in the garden. This is difficult as I am just able to manage the scuttles for the stoves. Walked along the beach but was driven back with only a handful of sticks. Nicky rings to say he is setting off from London, Julian isn't going to make it, neither is Richard.

~

The sun is still shining, the power station is dissolved in the late afternoon mist – opaline, iridescent.

~

Nicky and Robin came, cooked me an excellent lunch of spicy sausage pasta, and then as the dark closed in we drove across the marsh to Appledore. Nicky lost a glove and some mince tarts. At 6.30 they left for London.

Monday 28

Dawn came apricot blush, brushed in as if in watercolour across the sea. There is not a cloud in the sky this morning.

I was woken by the CD, which switched itself on mysteriously at seven and played Sibelius loudly. I got up and turned it off, disturbing a flock of greenfinches clambering up and down the rose bush outside the kitchen window.

I hauled my wobbly ten and a half stone (I've lost a stone and a half) into the garden and rearranged the iris bed. This should have been done last

Today dawned blissful, not a breath of wind, warm and the sun out, a great silence. Sunday 12 May 1991

I worked in the garden, split a clump of thrift and the purple iris, planted out mullein, sweethearts and soldier's tears. Wednesday 3 July 1991

BELOW LEFT: *Should I be plain ordinary Joe Saint, or something a little more* glittering? *The canonisation of Saint Derek of Dungeness of the Order of Celluloid Knights.* Sunday 22 September 1991

BELOW: *Dreamy weekend. Peter and HB put up the poem.* Monday 17 May 1993

HB has put so much grease on his hair it looks like an oil slick, he says if he swam in the sea guillemots and seals would die in it. Friday 28 August 1992

It's become very cold and a T-shirt, and my old Cornish smock do not keep me warm. Tuesday 8 September 1992

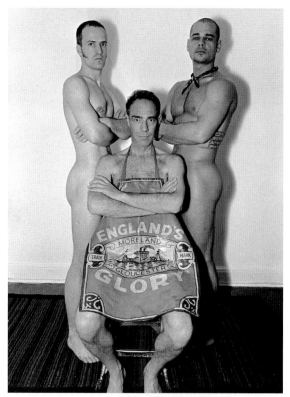

With Jordan's apron from Jubilee 'England's Glory', and a scattering of sequins we took off. Saturday 13 February 1994

Gay Law Reform Now. A very orderly non-violent and good humoured march. Derek Jarman, Sarah Graham, Jimmy Sommerville, Peter Tatchell, et al. Thursday 6 February 1992

HB has rock-hard hedgehog hair that would break a comb. Sunday 16 August 1992

Surely a world first for civic gay pride. Friday 15 May 1992

ABOVE: *HB looks for salvage furniture for Prospect.* Monday 22 June 1992

BELOW: *Gingerbits clearing the last of the wood from the building.
'It was the size of a loofah!'* Tuesday 1 September 1992

The lads, HB calls them 'the Dungenettes'. Jarman, HB, Howard Sooley, Peter Fillingham, David Peshek. Sunday 16 June 1991

An impromptu gay bar had sprung up, full of old queens like myself and little bevvies of hair-cut boys with shaved necks, looking like seals. Jarman, Ian Whitworth, Alan Beck, Malcolm Sutherland, Gingerbits. Saturday 4 July 1992

Aren't we all secret nellies with tough-as-fuck exteriors? HB with Peaches Minnelli. Friday 22 May 1992

We talked about Radical Drag but it was just Dressing Up. Thursday 12 March 1992

They are writing about us in Pravda. Jarman and HB attend the 17th Moscow International Film Festival. Thursday 18 July 1991

BELOW: The prisoners of Chateau Marmont. Jarman and HB attend the LA opening of Edward II. Saturday 22 March 1992

All the young queer film-makers there for a panel which was obsessed with violating the political correctness of seventies gay lib. LEFT TO RIGHT: *Stephen Cummings, Todd Haynes, Simon Hunt, Ruby Rich, Derek Jarman, Isaac Julien, Tom Kalin, Sadie Benning and Lisa Kennedy.* Monday 27 January 1992

My aim was to be a pioneer in aeronautics, but my experiments ended in teenage failure and I gave up. Karl Johnson as Ludwig Wittgenstein. Thursday 8 October 1992

…my revolutionary friend. Tariq Ali on the set of Wittgenstein. Friday 9 October 1992

Wearing my bright red hat that makes people laugh. Sunday 5 June 1993

Filming Alexis Bisticas' The Clearing. Sunday 5 June 1993

The vegetable garden is up: peas, purple rocket and spinach. Monday 17 May 1993

For me there is little rest, the fires are tended, the floors washed, the beach combed, breakfast cooked and this diary written. Friday 29 January 1993

Quite a trip for old wobble, who was at one moment thinking of abandoning the whole journey. Venice, paddling in the Adriatic. Sunday 13 June 1993

HB has very long hair which looks silky and gorgeous, he doesn't like it, though I think it's rather handsome. Saturday 6 December 1992

New York food is overproduced, your pudding comes with your main course, venison in cherries, veal in apricots. Saturday 2 October 1993

Spring runs along the balcony touching HB's pots. Sunday 24 January 1993

A wonderful time, ate ourselves into putting on weight and in the excitement my ataxia was forgotten. Monday 14 June 1993

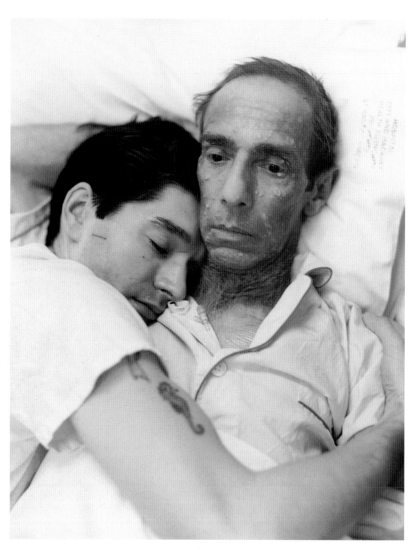

HB true love. 14 February 1994

summer, it can't be the best time to do it, but it is satisfying as it looks much neater. I've muddled the pale-blue and tawny-yellow plants which, even if they do not flower, have such fine leaves to decorate the garden. I'm lucky with the irises as they usually come into bloom after the last of the spring easterlies have done their damage.

~

Alan came with his friend Bambi. We drove to Appledore and stopped off in New Romney, where Bill's grocery was open, bought pasta and back here Alan made an enormous meal, while Bambi listened to George Crumb.

Tuesday 29

A hard frost, the ground like iron, I had to give up my gardening though the sun is shining as if it were the Alps. I'll have to be careful, as the pills I am taking make me light-intolerant.

~

Invasion by midday. Gaye arrived, rather fast, from Oxford, two and a half hours, then Peter and Karl. The wheelbarrow had collapsed, so Gaye took me to the garden centre and we bought a very good new one and some hellebores. The sun shone all day and the Ness became busy with fishermen

The sun set just after four behind the power station, the sky glowed crimson for half an hour. Gaye drove me back to London where I met up with David and took him to the Ragam. Talk of *The Raft of the Medusa*.

The flat had been left spic and span by HB, whose telephone message I missed.

I was in bed by 9.30.

Wednesday 30

Spent the morning being checked by Dr Mark. My X-rays and chest are improved, though he is worried by a spot on my lung. Could it be TB? There is yet another course of experiments. It is my last meeting with him, he is going skiing and then writing his research paper, most sorry to see him for the last time.

The pharmacy took over an hour sorting the pills so I left, it really is too long, an unbelievable nuisance and costly too – as I'll have to come back by taxi – the better part of £7 to collect them.

I bought a new George Crumb CD and came back to Phoenix House.

Gingerbits arrived at 12.30 with the colour book typed, *Chromatic Chameleon*? We went to lunch with John Maybury, then 'shopping' – window-shopping past the very expensive boutiques in Covent Garden – the place was packed. Gingerbits very excited by a fluffer who followed him round.

~

I caught the 5.30 from Charing Cross – a most uncomfortable experience – hemmed in by a couple loaded up with bargains, eating chips and hamburgers, and slurping huge icebound Cokes, sneezing and snuffling along with the rest. Slowly southwards past Pluckley, Headcorn and Marden, to Ashford. The train is a horrible reminder of the horrible lives of my fellow citizens, I feel as sympathetic as cyanide; in fact, I wish my presence killed. As we shuffled past the darkened stations I could feel misanthropy hanging like the black death in the airless carriage. I gulped at the air whenever a door was briefly opened. I don't think my 'fellow' travellers shared one brain cell amongst them, resigned and crumpled faces like discarded Christmas wrapping, mouths downturned, vacant eyes, Thatcher's rat-faced mortgagees, deservedly bankrupt – hopefully to the grave: some soggy cemetery in the South-East.

~

Karl had kept the fires burning, so Prospect was warm and cosy when I opened the door at eight. Was I glad to get home? Yes, I think so. Anything would be more comfortable than the train journey and the fires keep the cold – which it is, very cold – at a distance.

Thursday 31

This morning the Ness is frosted white, the earth shimmering white in the watery sun. I wrapped up well and 'explored' the garden. Karl has finished the new flower bed, which looks grand. The huge piles of earth at the kerbside have shrunk and today are providing a feast for the flock of greenfinches which have reappeared. I dug in manure for the hellebores though everything is so frozen I decided not to plant them. Cleared around the back of the house – the plants seem to be doing better than ever in the cold, dry and windless days. I have marigold, borage and rosemary in flower this New Year's Eve, and bulbs shooting up in every nook and cranny.

Dunged the second of the lateral flower beds in the afternoon sun. Cooked potatoes and fish – still ten and a half stone today, I need to put on weight.

1993

JANUARY

New Year's Day

Up at seven on a freezing, frost-bound morning, the nuclear power station floating above the mists, which hug the ground. The cold has flattened the broad-leaved plants; they lie collapsed like dishcloths in the silvery frosted rime. The frost as blue-grey as the santolina.

Nigel Terry telephones – says he can't stand London any longer and is contemplating moving back to Cornwall. Thirty years of the city growing more inhospitable and its inhabitants ever uglier have finally persuaded him, he says he feels unsafe in the streets.

Alasdair rings in despair from his estate at the end of the Blackwall Tunnel: 'I've grown to hate the East End, anything to leave this place.' He lives under siege from gangs of subhuman children on whom psychiatrists and social workers in their dozens make no mark. 'Yesterday I was attacked and punched in the face, trying to help the shopkeeper defend himself against a gang. He has to deal with everything, including shotguns.'

These were my two phone calls to welcome in this New Year, probably my last, as my strength ebbs. It doesn't bring hope or happiness.

Jon Savage and Neil Tennant arrived, then Alan and Howard.

Howard and I recounted our lunchtime journey to the George in Lydd – which always has an element of witless travellers falling into a trap in Dracula's castle. The congregation at the bar swivelled round to take us in, the proprietors had to confer with each other to decide if we could have 'lunch', this was so *very* English. Can you imagine this anywhere else in Europe? Begging for a meal on New Year's Day?

Alan says the reason for the stony silence of the Kentish is that they are descended from criminals who escaped at Gravesend docks on their way to Australia, they, and their descendants, have been lying low ever since.

~

Howard said he felt optimistic for 1993. HB called, sweetheart.

Saturday 2

All the drains at Prospect are blocked or overflowing, it is freezing cold, but very sunny. Peter has departed for Deal with his gang of market girls.

Howard lets out a scream from the kitchen – he has spread his toast with redcurrant jam which has turned into earwig pâté.

Po Chü-i *Winter Night*

My house is poor; those that I love have left me.
My body is sick; I cannot join the feast.
There is not a living soul before my eyes
As I lie alone locked in my cottage room.
My broken lamp burns with a feeble flame;
My tattered curtains are crooked and do not meet.

As I grow older, gradually I sleep less;
I wake at night and sit up straight in bed.

Howard drove me back to London in the early evening. It was bitterly cold and I felt sad putting the lights out and draining the tank at Prospect. I've worked there for nearly two weeks and the garden is in order for another month or two, the manure spread and the hellebores planted.

Phoenix House is strangely deserted. I long to see HB, it seems ages since I left for Kent and he took off for Newcastle – God alone knows how he will react to returning to London, he always sounds quite different when he phones from the North.

Sunday 3
The day passed correcting the scripts that David is typing up for Random Century. A second pass at *Akhenaten* – which could be made into a film, something I would doubt of *Sebastiane* or *Jubilee*, which were.

A bitter chill embraces the London streets. I had a bite to eat in the Stock Pot but felt cold and rather nauseous all day. My face has returned to the shirt of Nessus mode. I bash my head on the pillow and decide to survive – for another year. Jon Savage said my survival reproached the harpies. I feel my inexhaustible thirst for new projects is drying up, to put pen to paper becomes harder by the day and less of an adventure.

Monday 4
HB returned from Newcastle last night looking fit, furry and rested, complained of his life of drudgery tied to the washing machine and settled into the old routine – the balcony is hung with whites in almost Mediterranean manner though how they will dry in this cold God alone knows.

We walked to the market – where there was nothing – and back past the bookshops, briefly into Anne Creed and Shipley's, and then back here to make the phone calls that will catch up with a wasted December. I don't know which is the more disruptive, Christmas or illness, both have taken up so much time.

I received a letter from Overlook, the New York publishers of *AYOR*. They want me in New York City in February, the BFI want me to go to Berlin and Howard and I have a yearning for Cairo and the pyramids – of course none of them will happen.

Tuesday 5

I had a very disturbed night as my stomach collapsed – sweet HB, got up, cleaned me up, remade the bed and left for the gym at six.

Met Simon and David at Bar Italia after nine and then up to Camden for a recording session with Quentin. I nearly didn't make it here this morning as my stomach is so shot up, but I pulled myself together and now I'm feeling much better.

Howard came round and took photos of HB, who had constructed an enormous DA haircut, which sat on him like a *Coronation Street* confection.

Wednesday 6

Charing Cross Road was quiet – three incendiary bombs had closed the roads, so we did not wake up till nine. The oil tanker that blew around the Shetlands broke up during the night, spewing 80,000 tons of oil along the coast.

Simon collected the Chinese glockenspiel and we had coffee at the Bar Italia, which was empty, but very noisy – Aurelia pulling her cappuccini, and the odd macho Sicilian lad with the beetle-black hair and vociferous arm movements who sat doing nothing.

~

In the evening HB and I gave an interview 'How We Met' for the *Independent*. HB bouncing up and down telling 'the truth' – his side of how we met and of his life as a kitchen drudge. HB cleans and polishes so constantly, if he wasn't a drudge for me he'd be a drudge for himself. He says because he lives in the most public AIDS household in England it 'wouldn't do' if someone came round and the toilet wasn't '. . . *hygienic*'.

~

The rain poured down, it's warmer.

~

Rudolf Nureyev died from an AIDS-related infection, the television news pussyfooted around the subject, said he had died from a 'wasting illness'. Norman and I talked of Karl's suicide – Norman thought his madness was induced from advanced syphilis; also Norman's Italian friend who drove himself over a cliff in September because of debts of £100,000 – he had attempted suicide twice before this success.

Thursday 7

St Mary's all morning with eye tests, drops and camera flashes – there is a slight query over my left eye, we will be able to double-check it in two weeks.

~

Back up to the sound studio by midday for the last recording session, this one with Nigel.

~

Oddly qualified obituary notices for Rudi – it's obvious nobody particularly liked him, though they admired his dancing. He was described as antisocial, enigmatic, a mystery, vain, even a 'Peter Pan', though I remember him as wrinkly. Rudi was bored by the sort of society that a ballet boy of his time was subjected to; his impatience with the coffee table leap that he had made into the swinging sixties did not captivate him.

Boys, and lots of them, were his sole interest; as far as I could see dance was just a means to this end. He was really only happy in the back room – I saw much more of him cruising the King's Road at four in the morning than anywhere else. He was determined that you would fall for him, actually insisted that you did. It wasn't that he wanted to sleep with everyone – there wasn't enough time for that – but he wanted to be certain that if he clicked his fingers he could.

Inadvertently and naïvely, I turned him down – I didn't recognise the offer, though he was stark naked the first time I met him. I felt he was a bit of a prat. The Royal Ballet would forgive him all his indiscretions as he was their box office.

Rudi, unlike poor Nijinsky, was in control, I can't imagine him any other way. Nijinsky, who didn't know who he was, became the spectre of the rose. Rudi was always Rudi, being Romeo or some other sawdust princeling, zapping around the stage to unsightly applause from a thousand theatre queens who tumbled into bed with him in their minds and in their hundreds.

Rudi was a Don Juan, his insatiable lust for cock was never satisfied – a sad little man from Siberia, with more than enough charm and no charm at all.

Saturday 9

Howard and I drove to Prospect. We stopped at the garden centre – an enquiry about hellebores brought an uncomprehending reply: 'What are they, indoors or outdoors?'

Howard clarified: 'Christmas roses.'

'Oh, they all went.' I don't think they ever had them. I notice that garden centres are increasingly desolate, there are sacks and sacks of compost, peat, piles of badly decorated pots, mounds of stones, palings, flagstones, a thousand fertilisers but *no plants* – I expect these need too much attention and tend to die.

~

A foul, closed-in day with the rain blowing in horizontally across the Ness. Along the shore a thousand white seagulls faced the gale, behind them white seahorses flying across the wintry sea. It was too wet and windy to see much. Cold rain flying in the eyes like the stings that punctuated Tarene's protecting veil.

~

The January green of the garden is bright in the rain, it comes up like an old picture new varnished. I am quite in love with my huge artichoke whose fronds have defied the worst that December could do. The garden almost looks its best at this time of year as the plants mind their Ps and Qs, and don't blur at the edges, sharp in the shingle.

We walk along the seashore. Howard takes some photographs and gets *Witters Gitters* into *Vanity Fair*. People arrive and I duck. The wind is really roaring around the house.

~

Some hapless people had their garden 'done over' on one of those improving garden programmes, the results always look like Sainsbury's forecourts – the flowers arranged in a patchwork amid concrete sets and edgings. The sunbathing suburban had her garden proudly recorded by the June cameras, as on a day as inhospitable as this the fuchsias would look silly dancing in the freezing cold.

Sunday 10

Up in the night, the overflow dripping – I weighed myself, I'm up to eleven stone.

The rain pours down and chases us back inside, moments after planting the *Hellebore foetidus*. After that, even to imagine leaving the house is an impossibility, though as the wind is now in the west it is warm.

We left Prospect at four in freezing rain and drove to Appledore, then on back to London.

Monday 11

Hundred-mile-an-hour gales batter the Shetlands, snow is drifting across the north.

My blind eye hedges me in, and my skin burns. I don't complain, just confide it to the diary.

Rang Gingerbits in Canterbury and gave him a blasting. It's over ten days since I gave him the corrections on the first part of the colour book, he has no sense of time passing. I need to work and the manuscript isn't even typed up – two hours' work as my life and ability to concentrate slip away. I don't think I'll ever finish the book; I have a feeling it will be a jumble, which someone else will hash together.

~

More on Rudolf in the papers and a request to do 'HIV and the Arts' for *Newsweek*. I'm not at all certain that anything other than a sense of continuity across the generations – the chance of a young dancer to see the 'great dancer' sitting on his sofa at the edge of the stage – has been lost. Rudolf had leapt his last long before the HIV had carried him away. I feel the same about Freddie Mercury – is one less Queen album any loss? The answer has to be no.

How many more journeys did Bruce Chatwin have to make? How many more photographs did Mapplethorpe have to snap? Hadn't all of their work been completed? It's friends like David, a twenty-four-year-old at the Slade, who are the loss.

No ninety minutes of cinema could deal with the eight years HIV takes to get its host. Hollywood can only sentimentalise it, it would all take place in some well-heeled West-coast beach hut – the reality would drive the audience out of the cinema. We don't lack images – just good ones. Could you imagine an AIDS ballet brought to you by Rudolf, or the HIV album from Queen. Thank God they didn't.

I see it as an aesthetic tragedy, the rubbish flogged to raise a few bob, the motel aesthetic of the hospice, the deadly little paintings hung haphazardly on hospital walls to cheer us up. I can understand Larry Kramer's impatience, but if everyone started to write or play this tragedy, even more images of banality would be washing around our minds.

Even documentaries cannot tell you of the constant, all-consuming nagging, of the aches and pains. How many times I've stopped to touch my inflamed face even while writing this page. There's nothing grand about it, no opera here, just the daily grind in a minor key.

~

Paul called by and told me he was HIV positive. I'm afraid I was just practical – asked if he had a good doctor and said: 'Well, I always thought you were. I would be surprised to meet someone who wasn't.' He did look slightly taken aback. The wells of sympathy have long run dry.

~

I spent the evening with Gerard McArthur who was lamenting the coverage that Branagh's little 'film' has achieved. '*Peter's Friends*,' said Colin McCabe, 'is the worst film I've seen in years.' But there it is at the Engels' Lumière, promoted by the one distributor who prided himself he was involved in film. They turned down *Edward II* and didn't even come to the *Wittgenstein* screening. There is more at stake here than my vanity, there can be no cinema without exhibition.

Despite Howard's sterling involvement to have articles in all the major glossies, all that is on offer is two weeks at the ICA, the Minema, or the little screen on Baker Street. Two weeks at the ICA is accepted, we have no choice. Our publicity budget is just large enough to print a poster, but not large enough to publish it. I spent the afternoon with Liz Reddish discussing tactics. How do you promote a film with nothing?

Gerard said I was the only critic of the Branaghwagon: 'Everyone thinks like you, but you are the only one to express it.' Why give that cultural ineptitude space? His *Hamlet* is a dull, suburban nervous breakdown. Culture never had a chance, no one ever had any value other than the quick buck. A vital intervention – say Brooke's *A Midsummer Night's Dream* – never affected anything, the banal paid no attention and the flat-footed plodded on. As for *Witters Gitters*, it's going to be a success though no one will pay much attention. I won't make the BFI's fortune, so perhaps I will be given a week to make my next film, everyone will work for nothing and *enjoy it*. There's no point in renewing my union subscription. I've been forced, years ago, to ignore all their rules.

At least I will always have an audience – unless the genetic engineers have their way.

Tuesday 12

Andrew Heard in the obituaries this morning at the age of thirty-four. During my last stay at St Bart's he would wander into my room and look perplexed before being led back to the television, where he sat, like a rag doll most of the day. Gilbert and George came in nearly every evening and sat with him. He knew they were there, they were old friends, but once they had gone he had forgotten them, out of sight and out of mind. I didn't think there was any hope for him, he refused to take AZT – which might have just alleviated the symptoms, but it wouldn't have saved him, whatever was creeping through his mind had lodged permanently. I've thought of Andrew most days. I was going to find out what had happened, but didn't dare. AIDS to the left of me, AIDS to the right, into the valley of death.

Andrew stares out of the newspaper, one last entry before bowing out for ever. Unlike Rudi, Robert, Bruce and the others, Andrew is a loss to the arts as he had only run the first lap. I'm glad that he has died so quickly, just eight weeks opening the wrong doors.

~

Howard came at ten with Ali and we drove off to Woodbridge through the Dartford Tunnel. We decided to have something to eat in Colchester, but the town had been ring-roaded out of existence, the corporate lettering on its shops gave the place the uncomfortable feeling of a large supermarket rather than a country town and the buildings that hug its edges are in the neo-rural style of the eighties – DIYs of design, acres of tiled roof aping barns, an Italian hill village, six water mills and the lazy Lutyens classicism, all broken pediments. We left quickly, almost colliding with a learner driver on one of the many ill-designed roundabouts.

At Beth Chatto's nursery we bankrupted ourselves on hellebores, black auriculas and a silvery sage, said hello to Beth and then drove to Brian Eno's house in Woodbridge to pay our respects to Simon and Marcus – who is engineering the music for *Blue*. We had tea and left in the gloom.

I bought Rilke at a second-hand bookshop and then came back to London.

Picked up HB and all descended on the D'Aquise, where Lynn was celebrating her birthday – Ron Peck, Keith Milow, Anne Berthoud, Nigel Greenwood, our very loud party singing 'Happy Birthday', just the sort of group you dread to encounter in a restaurant.

Nigel said Mapplethorpe was snapped up by a group of fringe aristocrats and spent his time being entertained in their ruined acres. Keith complimentary on Robert's subject matter – this was no risk as he was bankrolled by Sam, he couldn't put a foot wrong, and if he had fallen it would have been into a basket of currency.

Keith told us that the Battenbergs had had their paintings re-framed at the taxpayers' expense before exhibiting them in the Sainsbury Wing and then charged the same taxpayers to see them.

The dinner ended with the tale of Maria Callas's ashes being scattered in the Aegean, blown into the face of the dignitary, blinding and choking him on live TV.

Wednesday 13

To Metrocolour where the 35mm blow-up of *Wittgenstein* was shown, it all looks good to me, Simon Field persuaded to give us three weeks at the ICA. It poured with rain and blew umbrellas inside out.

~

Lilies that fester smell far worse than weeds. Rudi was buried in his evening dress with his medals and favourite beret. A wonderful picture of a mourner clutching a photo on the cover of the *Independent* under the heading: AT NUREYEV'S GRAVESIDE THE BEAUTIFUL GROW OLD.

~

In the evening Lynn and Digby walked with me to Heaven for the Bart's benefit. Tania and Michelle performed *The Maids*, which is still very disturbing. Thirty years ago when we performed it at King's we expected the Lord Chamberlain's shock troops to arrest us. I can't see why *The Maids* should have been found so offensive, except for its assault on privilege – which must have put the frighteners on the Establishment accustomed to maids, footmen and flunkies.

Thursday 14

Afternoon, photographed at Richard's with Keith. Richard was invaded and coping manfully, as wan and pale and distracted as he can be.

~

Keith said that after the fire at Windsor this very glum man said: 'When it was up it was 'ers, now it's down it seems to be ours.' Which pretty well sums up England.

Friday 15

My stomach collapsed this morning for a second time. The whole of my dinner with Richard shat out as I opened the door – indescribable mess. I cried, more in fury than anything else, as HB cleaned it up. Last time my trousers, socks, shoes, everything ruined, this time I was luckier – it took half an hour to put things right.

I'm in the wars – in the middle of the night I knocked over the metal chair, which I did not see out of my jugsy eye, waking HB with a startled cry. I felt foolish. This is my second accident this week – at Lynn's birthday in D'Aquise I collided with a plate brought by one of the waitresses who was serving it over my shoulder, the impact nearly made me pass out. Ice was brought to stop the bump on my temple. I don't know if I am walking faster, but the looming pedestrians have become more of a menace and the white flashes in my eyes more insistent.

Lunch at Poon's. Keith very funny relating a Dame Edna scene in which she performs under Munch's *Scream*: 'I must introduce you to a fascinating Scandinavian artist, Scream, this is his masterpiece: *The Munch*.'

Saturday 16

Splendid meal at eight in Richard's candlelit studio, Tariq appeared in a cotton wool white wig with a mask. Richard had placed two large paintings behind the banquet.

Peter worrying about his Welsh maiden. I told him to forget her. Who wants to be married to scenery? People who hail from these postcard childhoods, and won't let you forget it, seem so retarded, often the more ghastly these places are the more they are defended. People who come from 'somewhere' enter life old-fashioned and rather regressive. The cool thing is to come from nowhere and then the future can flourish.

At ten we waited for our double-decker bus to take us to the Metro – it didn't arrive, we got there by taxi. Fortunately HB had some cash in his pocket.

I forgot that I had asked James to screen *The Queen Is Dead*, so the audience was quite thrown when it started, I told them not to worry as it was only three songs and, as this was a cast and crew screening, they could chat through it.

The cinema was crowded but not full. Jill [Balcon], John Quentin, Karl, Peaches and HB all there; Tilda was 'ill'. *Wittgenstein* looks pretty good with an audience.

My criticism of being married to scenery comes right over into the film, which is set nowhere. It demonstrates that the historicising attitude to biopic is totally irrelevant, questioning all of that in one black drape. It all goes to show that Vienna is just a grand piano. Places are no longer of much interest to the sophisticated, after all they are all the same: you buy your Thai meal in Soho and your steak and chips in Bangkok.

Sunday 17

Dungeness. There are a few surprises. While Peter digs holes for the hellebores we find the first snowdrops peeping through the pinks, which have covered large areas of the front beds, more bright marigolds and a few purple crocus in bloom. In spite of the wind and cold there are a few buds breaking on the elder, and the poppies and cornflowers have doubled in size since Christmas.

The first splatter of rain sparkles on the windows, I was going to clean them, but a wave of lethargy kept me wandering around the garden. There is a gale blowing, though it is not cold – gales disturb my equilibrium.

I've put some plants out and placed the Appledore crucifix under the Florentine trumpet. The garden looks a January delight; in spite of the gales everything is ready to contend with the summer, which besets the flowers more than the cold and dark.

~

HB rang me, pleased with *Wittgenstein* as he has received many complimentary reviews, though he is unsure about the make-up, says it makes him look like a drag queen. I didn't dare tell him that when he gives up worrying about the make-up he will acquire a more relaxed attitude to acting. He's excited by the piece he engineered in the Sunday paper; I think he has probably been as blunt as only an HB can. I'm waiting for Peter to drive by and deliver it, but I expect that will be late as he brought *another* new girlfriend to El Ray last night.

Derek is back at 'Bohemia' after his Mexican Christmas. Simon, Marvin and David came down at midday and we ran through *Blue*. Peter and his friend Isobel beachcombed, bringing back a tray for sempervivums and a shovel-shaped anchor fluke.

Budge rang to say all the colours were awry in *Wittgenstein*. We would have solved this problem if we had been given 35mm. The blow-up seems less competent than the old ones for *Sebastiane* and *Jubilee*.

Settled down to read 'How We Met' in the *Independent*. Very well written though one mistake made me laugh: 'young subaltern' became 'young sultan'. I got to bed early.

Monday 18

So sunny and warm today I went out without a coat and weeded the front square of a thousand Californian poppies. Bee-flying weather, I wonder if they will appear at midday, there are still no clouds so there is a chance. By midday I sat in my room with the door open and still felt too warm. My garden sparkles in the winter sunlight. I transferred thistles and then walked round and round, and then to the beach. There is much new driftwood brought in by the storms.

The sun hasn't tickled the bees out of the hive, it's two already so maybe they'll stay at home. Several crocus blossomed in the sunlight, purple, yellow, and yellow with a brown stripe. Peter came back from Rye at five and put a large joint in the oven, which we ate at seven. I spent the evening reading Norman's Géricault book.

Tuesday 19

This morning the sun is burning down and the rubbish that has been around the house next door is being burnt – for months now it has blown about in gales – everything will be cleaner.

Ken rang to say how much he enjoyed *Wittgenstein* and that I looked restored in health. I have put on more weight – I'm back to eleven and a half stone, in spite of my continuously upset stomach.

I polished the front room and its floor with some liquid wax Peter brought from Rye, Prospect has the smell of a stately home now.

David rang to tell me that *Blue* would be completed on 3 March; Lo has not been contacted by Michael White about *Outcry*, they're all a bit pushy – I had the usual letters saying the money was in place. I must not alter one of my plans in anticipation. In these last moments I must keep as much time as I wish to watch the snowdrops grow and be with HB.

~

Down in Dungeness I do not bump into people or objects, London is a minefield for the partially sighted. We walked along the beach and found seagulls trapped in a fisherman's nets, Peter waded out to release them. A peacock butterfly flew across the garden.

Wednesday 20

I have had three charming letters for *Wittgenstein* and the party that Tariq gave, all from the over-sixties. Letter-writing has died for the younger generation, strangled by the telephone wires, strangely, they do not ring. I suppose to write 'I loved the film' is easier than to say it.

~

I'm making the psychologically difficult transition to a new doctor. On the phone this morning to St Bart's, where I will join a candlelit procession this afternoon. I can pick up my medicines while I'm there. My face is red raw, people think I have been abroad, that this is sunburn – it's chapping from the cold salt wind at Dungeness.

~

The black oil slick recedes but clings to *The Raft of the Medusa*; my pills will be ready by four. Struggled with dates for Berlin, *Wittgenstein*, America and the garden. Colin rang to say the *Wittgenstein* book looked great, though he thought the Eagleton script too conventional – that's why I altered it.

Ken is having dinner with Maria St Juste this evening – he calls her Maria St Witch. I become less inclined to sacrifice myself on the altar of Tennessee Williams. Would I not be happier in the garden? I'm going to clear the decks of all this work and settle down.

~

Excellent lunch at Poon's with Tony going through all the written projects. Tony wants to write a biography, which I think could be fun; we are to do some interviews.

~

We marched from Bart's to St Paul's for Evensong. I had bumped into Connie [Giannaris] by my front door and he came with me. The candles blew out, though some people had brought lanterns. A tall boy, short-haired, in leathers, walked with us. I offered to light his candle and got talking. As the service began he said: 'We have something in common, we are both Miss Worlds.' Now how could such a lad be a Miss World? He looked great as plain Burnel. We left the cathedral before the Credo. I crowned myself on a chair, picking up my umbrella, and forgot my scarf.

After St Paul's we sat in the Presto, had a zabaglione and spaghetti. We didn't leave until eleven. Burnel went on cruising at a club called Crews. Connie told us stories from Greece; he had broken a leg on an escapade.

Thursday 21
St Mary's, John and Jean Cocteau in the waiting room. John has been admitted to Andrewe's Ward, it's knocked some of the sparkle out of him. He's had problems with prescriptions, says he can hardly stand by the evening, overwhelmed by exhaustion.

~

A translucent girl dying in the waiting room of the Wharfside clinic. Last August she had a needle in her neck. She sits crumpled and awry in a wheelchair, with her eyes focused on oblivion, her head bowed, with a shock of hair standing on end. You can almost see through her, she is as transparent as a shrimp, luminous with decay.

The eye specialist unhappy: a young patient had stopped taking her drugs and had gone blind – if he had known he could have saved her sight. My CMV seems still to be static, no advance. The flashes in the eyes, 'Look up, look down, look left.' Oh, how weary I am.

~

HB walked with me to the British Museum on a rather fruitless search for a grey scarf. The BM is wrapped for restoration like a Christo.

~

The phone rang and rang, HB put on a message saying the answerphone no longer took messages.

Friday 22

My face has gone a flaming, irritating purple. I stagger to Bar Italia. People stare out of the corner of their eyes, no one quite looks at me, the spoon falls off the coffee cup. I don't notice Antonio pick it up. Yellow roses scatter their petals, a large bunch sent for the publication of *AYOR* today. By the door the pale-green hellebore flowers and seeds itself. I feel my grip on life ever more tenuous, my movements are ever more erratic. Maybe I'll be run down crossing the road, putting an end to my burning skin – HB says it looks less red today.

I finish the corrections for *Blue* and *Little England*.

~

HB returned at lunchtime saying he'd had a good exam.

Jimmy Somerville rang, we talked of HIV in the press – the huge gap between descriptions of prevention and the realities. There are no descriptions of the difficulties of living day-to-day with it. Flaccid old age, a vodka too many and who could cover this limpness with rubber at a moment of excitement – another scenario.

The Battenbergers' sensational Camillagate tape is published in full, with a picture of the fruit cake prince. Where will the press probe next?

HB is leaping around the flat stark-naked!

Saturday 23

Breakfast with Tania at Bertaux's. *The Maids* is going well. I tried to enthuse

Tania with the idea of performing *Voix Humaine* or Camillagate behind the counter at four. She asked after HB. I said we couldn't expect him to go to the performance, he fell asleep at Berkoff's *East* and also *The Vortex*; to go to the theatre for him is a sweet snooze. Tania said his description in 'How We Met' of his return from the hospital without me made her very sad.

~

Ian Shipley lent me £100. I bumped into Christopher, we went to the photo gallery and I gave him one of the Angus McBeans; then we walked in the rain to Berwick Street where I bought ten pounds of Seville marmalade oranges.

Christopher talked about the weather and Lee's journey to New York to help Terence Davies research into the police. Olivia – Terence's producer – described him as 'So delicate'. Christopher says he's very tough and tells filthy jokes. ██████ ███████ ██████ ██ ████████ ██ ████ ████████ ████ ██████████ ███ ██ ███ ███ ███ ██████ ██▓▓▓████ ████ ██████ ██████, ██ ██████████ ██████████ ████ █████. Does pink champagne dye you? Ken Russell looked like a big round tomato with cotton wool white whiskers the last time I saw him. Christopher left at 1.30. I looked out the window and saw him walking down Charing Cross Road until lost in a sea of umbrellas.

I've drunk too much coffee, my mind turns in circles. I sit here itching, reading the chapter on the portraits of the insane in the Géricault book, flitting like a butterfly into the Hart Crane poems. It's only 2.30 and the grey winter day is drawing in, darkness licking the window-panes.

I walked through Covent Garden, bought a scarf in a sale, popped into the oriental carpet shop where the boys were drinking G and Ts. Picked up the *Radio Times* – an article on *Edward II*; this is good as it uses the film to talk about HIV.

~

I spent the evening with Danny Maggott and his friend Brian at the LA, which was quite packed. I found a chair in a corner upstairs and talked to many people. At three a young Australian gave me a lift home in a taxi. He was going to Bar Italia for a coffee; he assured me it was open. Burnel, at the bar, said he had spent the afternoon dancing naked with an Italian and a feather boa.

Sunday 24

This morning, tired, I retreated from Bertaux's where everyone was talking too loud. Tania threatened to shut them up. Bar Italia was like a church service compared.

Spring runs along the balcony touching HB's pots, the black celandine and green hellebore are in flower, the hellebore is surrounded by seedlings that have germinated in the last few days. There are two purple-black flowers lurking in the viridian-green mouseplant, a scatter of yellow jasmine and two snowdrops under the honeysuckle. Everywhere I look the first unmistakable signs of the return of spring and I walk through all this vigorous growth as fragile as autumn thistledown.

~

Edward II strangely shrunk on the TV, the announcer warned that it had explicit scenes of male homosexuality. I wonder when these warnings will no longer be necessary. Will the sexual naïveté of the British ever be replaced by maturity? Or will straight people fail to grow up and remain in the childlike stage of eternal development they have made their own? I have a worrying stitch in my stomach that comes and goes – maybe it is Aurelia's strong coffee, but I've come to take my pains seriously; they advance like shadows up the waist until they blot out the light.

Monday 25
David L. and David P. driving to Dungeness; David P. says the TV audience has to be warned as I'm 'the spawn of Satan'.

~

AIDS the movie, living with AIDS, Dining on Death, Harlequin Punch cracking skulls, children among the corpses, ring a ring of roses, public execution.

We worked very hard mapping out the first scenes of Géricault, packed in at ten.

Tuesday 26
The jasmine flowered in the night.

Bright sun and a touch of a breeze shimmering leaves, a keen frost thawing through the drainpipe into the water butt, drip drip. There are clumps of snowdrops out, the longer they have been planted the more settled in their beauty, those of last autumn look a little straggly. Snowdrops are the most difficult bulbs to plant successfully and since the Turks were banned from digging them up from the wild they are very expensive, so the bulbs are left on the shelf, dry out and fail.

After lunch the rain set in so cold and windy we stayed walled up, working on the *Medusa*. At eight we drove to the supermarket.

It's three years today since I witnessed the nuclear power station blow its top – HB rang to say the diary entry was reproduced in the *Independent*.

Wednesday 27

A sullen rain fell all morning, the sabre-rattling westerly died away, in the stillness the raindrops hung like diamonds in the dog rose. It is very warm. I repair the circle that has been turned over by some shadowy beast for the second night in a row. David drove me to the nursery in Appledore where I bought thyme and a *Yucca pinnata*, past their sell-by date hyacinths and vegetable seeds. Then back here to work on the *Medusa*.

James prevailed on David to leave for London. I was unhappy to see him go, but gave in fairly gracefully – I don't want him to be the wishbone in a tug of war. As it is, we have done very good work on the Géricault script and tomorrow, weather permitting, I'll work in the garden.

~

Mr Clinton is fighting to change the ruling on gays in the military, all the media reporting is malign, suggesting that the services will be besieged with fags trying to join up, forgetting that there are thousands in there already.

~

My dying eye shuts out so much it helps the January light fail quickly.

Thursday 28

The mystery continues, the stones are strewn across the shingle.

~

HB arrives in a mist, it closes in and muffles the sound of the waves, even the lorries drive past in a whisper. I plant the white hyacinths under the elder – I'm hiding all the bulbs under the shrubs and roses where they are safe from the trampling feet of visitors. HB wheels the heavy barrows of compost about the garden until driven inside as the drizzle turns to rain.

When the weather draws in the beach becomes even more secret, there is rarely anyone here, just a couple of men far out in the mist digging lug; the drip of the rain in the water butts with the notes of faulty plumbing; the passing lorries trailed by the mist thrown up from the road, their headlights on at midday; the foghorn that warns the ships sounding its melancholy note.

Puddles spread across the drive, the crow and the seagull sit on the telegraph poles, too wet to quarrel.

~

The lights failed, but came back, the army started firing at each other on the Lydd range, rattling the windows.

~

David P. staggers across the shingle and collapses. I ring his father to take him home to Hawkhurst. My problem in Dungeness is that everyone who comes here collapses with mental fatigue or illness. How many times has this happened? Far too many. I end up with more worries and work than if I was here alone.

David's father came at seven.

Friday 29

My garden is unhurried this morning, it is ten and it's still asleep: not one of the sparkling raindrops falls from the rose, the crocus are lightly furled against the damp, the sun hovers in the clouds but gives up and pulls them like a pillow across her face.

Stay at home. Only the snowdrop bell rocks gently to and fro as a breeze springs up. An immobile morning, becalmed, the sea withdrawn across the sands, the luggers dig in slow motion, the nuclear power station in a freeze-frame. I hold my breath, my eye flashing like a camera shutter. The sun makes another attempt to pull itself from the shadows and view the world, it tips itself across the green in the garden and promenades across the shingle.

~

For me there is little rest, the fires are tended, the floors washed, the beach combed, breakfast cooked and this diary written. Am I a sightseer, or do I live here? A hobo in a ruined coat trudging in circles, like the sun, stay at home.

~

The kind antique dealers from Rye have arrived and are clearing the attic, six years and it's packed to the rafters with bits and pieces, pots and pans, floats, chairs, a wheelbarrow, the delivery bike and the old chest.

~

Lorraine telephones: there are more photographers on the way from Japan – they sent me a long letter and won't take no for an answer; they reply by fax with appeals to the Buddha.

Saturday 30

I'm holding my breath, like the weather, for the first daffodil. The mists have gone with the milkman, and the sun puzzles in the clouds and laboriously pushes them aside, hesitates, and then floods the Ness with light and the day starts sneezing and coughing.

I pull myself from the shadows with the frantic activity of a snail. The snowdrops ring in the morning, naked maidens. Blue courts the sea, flirts in the sky and pulls me into the garden with my trowel. As I worked the postman came with letters and an envelope of reviews of books and paintings sent from my publishers. The reviewers don't like the angry assault of the paintings and *AYOR*, they would prefer the rustic melancholia of *Modern Nature*. I must be the spoilt child, huffy and ill-humoured, but this illness leaves little space for resignation. If you are fighting back you have to pick a quarrel. One day the paintings will be seen as more than tantrums and will seem to be wet with my tears. I can't quite grasp the pandemic as my eyes cloud over. Am I the blind hell-hound barking at the door?

It is strange that our lives should have been so excised that *AYOR* should only be seen as autobiography – much of it is charting a path through a continual assault that continues even in the news today. What possible threat could there be in allowing us to declare ourselves in the army? Who are the young men so tender they can be killed in action but not exposed to an open queer? A situation that the major-generals see as more of a threat than a thousand Bosnians.

~

The weary sun gave up on January and betrayed the daffodil. HB and I walked over to the power station and found some of the iron pigs' tails that make the best sculptures. He dragged them back and we set them up.

Sunday 31

My fifty-first birthday, I record this with surprise. Who ever thought I would be here to record this in Trinity? Cambridge so cold and deserted, grey as the brick of its grand nineteenth-century houses, the misty quad at Trinity quite deserted. We looked up at Wittgenstein's windows.

We screened the film at the Cambridge Arts to an audience of students and the remaining Wittgenstinians.

Mrs Bevan, in whose house he died, turned to Jan and asked: 'Are you a member of the craft council?' He looked bemused. 'You soon will be.'

We had an excellent lunch: roast beef, Yorkshire pudding, crème brûlée.

Can't I remember a fucking thing?

Dadie Rylands said that he met Thomas Hardy – who was born in 1840 – the two of them spanned 150 years. He met Wittgenstein in 1929 and walked round the quad at Trinity with him for an afternoon. Wittgenstein had been impressed by his production of *Lear* and stopped him with congratulations.

Dadie missed Wittgenstein's bright-blue eyes, he thought Karl burned in his performance; said that the one thing you remembered of Ottoline was her voice, which rose and fell like a donkey braying; HB very accurate as Johnny; Michael brilliant as Bertie. He added that Keynes was more static than we had made him.

Mrs Bevan thought Karl caught Wittgenstein perfectly in all the scenes in bed, though he had been a little more forceful (Germanic) in his bearing.

We were all becoming less inhibited, then lunch was over and we were on our way back to London. I would have loved to have spent more time with Dadie in less formal circumstances.

~

As we drove back, Colin asked me of my attitude to religion. We talked of the anger in the paintings that everyone finds so uncomfortable, it's there in the *Medusa*.

FEBRUARY

Monday 1

No sign of HB in the night. I forgot he told me he was not returning till this evening, so my sleep was restless, full of haunted imaginings about what could have happened to him. I am absolutely dependent upon his living here. He will joke I just want my clothes pressed, but at three a.m. I decided that I could not live without him.

In the morning one of his lovely cards arrived with hugs and kisses – he always sends me one whenever he leaves Phoenix House, even when we go somewhere together he manages to post one without me seeing it, so I find it in the heap of letters on the floor when we return.

~

The Bar Italia collapsed during the night, dust and dozens of workmen, Antonio at the door redirecting traffic. I went across the road where a board said: 'Best cappuccino in London – *Time Out*'. The journalist who wrote this must have left their taste buds in the office, no one will beat Aurelia. Bar Italia will reopen.

~

Met John Anthony who takes photographs of nude fluffers for magazines. He gave me a photo of the sauna in Budapest full of naked boys. He has a new studio in Old Compton Street, which was raided last week by the boys in blue. [Editor's note: No pornographic material was found]

~

Marvin [Black] and Simon [Fisher Turner] at Bertaux's. We went up to Jan's, he played the Satie for *Blue*. We had a full house, with Gaston from the Florence opera.

~

Colin bemoaned the fate of cinema, he said it was increasingly difficult to fund anything: the TV companies had retired from the fray, C4 and the BBC seemed to have been submerged by the imperatives of monetarism, the sixties were the last golden decade.

Americans consider the most conservative aspects of British life an Adventure, so the Royal National approach is a safe risk. This was confirmed again today by an apoplectic newsletter from Louisiana denouncing *Edward II* – accusing me of deliberately making a film for homophobes, of naïveté. Even the tongue-in-cheek 'improved by' was taken quite literally as was 'take an old play and violate it'.

There never was any structure to put cinema like mine on an even course with other foreign films. My audience in the States arrived fifteen years too late and only after Gus Van Sant had been so supportive and had his successes.

I'm writing this as I prepare to go to the BBC to record a *Face to Face* with Jeremy Isaacs – who has always been a staunch supporter of my films. I am nervous as I expect this is the last time I will appear on TV and I want to convey some of the fun of my life and less of the gloom and doom. The balance I have achieved in *Wittgenstein* much more clearly reflects my situation than *Edward II* or, for that case, *Caravaggio* – if torture crept into my life it was with the HIV and nowhere else. Everything was resolved when that stone was cast into the near tranquillity I had found – after that it was a roller-coaster with death and dissolution. I do hope I don't appear as washed out as I feel; thank God for the make-up lady between me and the lens.

~

Good interview with Jeremy. It was difficult at moments. I find myself hesitating on the questions of sex on the Heath. How anonymous is anonymous? A hornet's nest of taboo sex, HIV, casual partners, this is one you can't win.

~

Ken's Ackerley play *Prisoners of War* very well done in the New End: a gang of military fluffers in a Swiss sanatorium, lusting after each other with a lack of language, though Ackerley's words are sharp and remind me of RAF Abingdon.

Maria St Juste there. She said Jimmy Dean was a bore, always phoning to find out what Marlon Brando was up to. Maria got her chauffeur to drive HB and me back to Phoenix – HB embarrassed to get out of the stretched white limousine in case someone he knew saw him.

Tuesday 2

Spent the morning signing hundreds of books – there won't be one without a signature. HB goes to work. He has to wear a pink and purple uniform – like a packet of prawn cocktail crisps, designed to be so ugly that no one would steal it. I nearly knocked him out in my blindness this morning.

~

In the evening to Nicky de Jongh's talk, on homosexuality and the theatre, in the Gustave Tuck Theatre at University College. A strangely ancient audience – the first question: 'Do all homosexuals have such unhappy lives?' I went mad. Nicky enjoyed my interjections, the audience loved it too.

~

Dinner at the Presto. Young Sean O'Connor on crutches, but looking rested and well, chasing after a bearded fluffer in the restaurant – a bit skinny for my taste. Glad to get back to HB who was attacking the VAT return at midnight.

I fell asleep, forgetting my pills.

Wednesday 3

I signed more books for the publishers and then returned home in a freezing mist with a flaming face. If only my irritated skin would just return to normal for an afternoon – it is so distracting to be the leftovers at a lunch with a cohort of mosquitoes and the odd wasp. What is more annoying is that people stop you and, pointing to the irritation, ask, 'Oh where did you get that tan? Where have you been?'

'Oh, St Bart's.' They think this is an island in the West Indies. As this has set in it has rather destroyed concentration, it's like trying to remain calm as you are suffocated on the rim of a volcano. If I'm not bumping into things I'm certainly bumping into myself – the CMV blots out even more of the weak winter day, so I am living in a twilight, perhaps I should say *my* twilight.

Thursday 4

Sarah, Alison, Peaches and HB take me to see *Dracula* – a truly unmemorable night out. A group of shop assistants and window dummies from Next in a perpetual twilight. So bad that I revised my opinion of Francis Coppola, surely anyone who had talent would make a better stab at this – after all, it is not virgin territory. HB said it was derivative of *The Last of England* – Diamanda Galas shrieked over a red sky with black racing clouds.

Atrocious performances by Gary Oldman, Keanu Reeves and Anthony Hopkins – particularly silly. Tension 'sustained' by a thumping, illiterate soundtrack, Annie Lennox sang a song over the credits. Bring back Murnau.

This is why I never go to the cinema. The last film Coppola made was terrible as well, but this topped it. If I had been given the budget for the Kensington gore alone I could have made a feature film but, of course, it's my fault for getting involved in such a silly medium; you only had to take one step to Hollywood and you could never turn back.

Dracula is the perfect role model for the state of the cinema, there is no critical tradition, so who in the audience in Leicester Square had seen the Murnau, Hammer, or anything for that matter? The pea-brained critics deserve to be shot for giving it good reviews – don't say it too loud: they're all paid off, they have their brains in the till.

Friday 5

To Dungeness down the catkin lanes to Hellebore Heaven where we bought an iridescent purple and creamy new plant from Elizabeth Strangman.

A temperature of minus four has not stopped the garden; the daffodils under the dog rose are out and the rose is breaking into leaf.

Howard particularly fascinated by the appearance of an aconite, which has survived from some other year. Howard dug in manure in the new bed and planted thyme from Appledore, and primrose and pulmonaria from Hawkhurst.

Five o'clock, a very cold and misty day closes. Howard, far in the distance, walks back from the seashore in the empty landscape.

At seven, in the dark, Howard left for London.

Saturday 6

This morning grey and cold, the dead light of February. My daffodils flare into life to illuminate the spring.

~

Today is the day to look for improvements. My dizzy self makes my inspirations lacklustre in the gloomy light. I have to be ruthless, especially on this teeth-chattering day when the crocuses wrap themselves up and even the snowdrops tremble.

A large group of seagulls, stone-cold as my pebble garden, form a circle that echoes the henges of the front garden, every now and then they take off like the floaters in my eye.

~

In spite of the cold the bees appeared, rather unsteadily, and shortly after HB from London. He went for a long and lonely walk towards the power station and returned as the rain set in with a burden of curly irons for the garden.

I worked on my politically incorrect *Medusa*, inventing a character, Soubriette – a black slave girl in a grass skirt by Versace.

~

Larry Kramer on TV renouncing sex, sadly, but perhaps sensibly, purposeful politics fuelled by denial. He seemed focused, had even sorted out a graveyard for himself, something we talked about. The graveyards here are so grim one hardly has a choice and to be surrounded in death by mouldy crosses, simpering angels, trite phrases like 'dearly beloved' too hard to bear even stone-cold. Perhaps, as I suggested to Jeremy Isaacs, I should pack my bags and disappear without a trace.

Sunday 7

A damp, silent morning and rather warm, the garden looks at its best, the blue-green spears of the allium, the rich green wallflowers budding, a powdering of blue on the rosemary. HB dragging the last barrowloads of manure across the shingle leaving maiden tracks in the stream of time, chased inside by the drizzle.

~

HB said some lad who called by some time ago was also tickled to death by the virus. The scratching is now continuous. I'm not certain if the top of my head, my shoulder blades, or my legs are the worst, they certainly are in irritable competition and it puts me out of focus. I'm struggling with my ebbing life and decomposing bodily function.

~

Howard arrives, says it rained all the way from London. The sun came out in Dungeness and the bees swarmed out of the hive in a bad mood, stopping him from digging the vegetable redoubt.

~

Mid-afternoon we drove to Appledore where we bought a hoe and a utility shovel, then on to the garden centre where we found herbs for 89p. Peter came for tea and we thought up names to embroider on a hat for HB – *tantrum Geordie meteoric*.

I went to bed early, driven between the sheets by itching.

Monday 8

Up at dawn, dismal drizzle. Seagulls noisily outfacing each other, deserted shingle, the dustman's cart the only sign of life and a group of fishermen in yellow oilies. I wrote my letters, or rather postcards. I never know if this post is in solidarity or if some desperation lurks behind it.

~

The anaemic morning curls in the mists, even the fishermen are washed out of the view. Purple and white crocuses appear like arrows from nowhere, penny whistles for the spring, the floral band strikes up, a tintinnabulation of snowdrops. Howard inspected the Ness, mused over the broom, which comes and goes like a tuning fork. We contemplate tree peonies amongst the valerian, then do a freezing photo session as an easterly has sprung up.

Tuesday 9

Supper at Maria St Juste's with Ken, HB, Michael White, Robert Fox and Paul Scofield. Maria in the role of carrying the torch for Tennessee, Paul here to meet me – he loved *Edward II* and wants me to direct the film of *Outcry* with him and Vanessa Redgrave.

Borscht and steak en croute – HB food.

Maria recounting tales of fighting it out with Edith Evans: John Gielgud remarks from the stalls that if Maria leaves the stage to get a glass of water Edith will be upstaged, Edith said: 'I'll take that risk.'

Tennessee crossed and recrossed the dinner table in a funk; I had the picture of a little white mouse shivering in a caged corner. Maria said he begged Kazan to let him touch Marilyn Monroe's breasts on a night out when they all ended up in bed together. Kazan said: 'No, she's mine.'

Maria likes animal furs – her house is a museum of cushions and throws made from the endangered and extinct. She said to her daughter: 'So wicked to Mummy! How cruel of you to go all the way to China and not bring Mummy back a snow leopard.'

The dinner ended with some well-intentioned simping, particularly over the idea of casting Marlon Brando, which Ken described as a perfectly dreadful idea – he thought it would sink the project.

Wednesday 10

Jackie, the pharmacist, analysed my pills and thinks the Fansidar might be the culprit that burns my face. I think that the inflammation from the tip of my toes to the top of my head is less violent today, the redness has gone and with it the obsessive itching that has left me so vulnerable.

~

We worked like crazy today: a screening of Greg Araki's *The Living End*; then I wrote a review of it for the *Guardian*; lunch with David Aukin to talk over the dragging feet at Channel Four – I know they don't want to make *Narrow Rooms* but can't quite come to tell me; a radio interview and back here for supper with Richard at the Presto.

Thursday 11

A screening of *Blue*, everything went well. Connie loved the film – it does give you space for the imagination by locking you into the blue. It's possible to imagine faces and places without the incidentals of location and casting.

~

I came home in a haze of indecision. I think the next piece should be *Medusa*. I lay on the bed and scratched for an hour.

~

HB squirting an aerosol. He says: 'I'm making the summer come faster with CFCs.'

Lynn is on the phone from NYC, we are dreaming up names for hats – HB is a *Somnambulist*, Peter a *Recidivist*, Howard an *Obscurantist* and I'm a *Controversialist*.

Friday 12

Women's Hour. My sweet friend Sarah Graham the casualty of homophobia in the tabloids – the *Mail* and the *Sun*.

She had discussed the idea of serialising a lesbian novel on the *Hour*, the programme was interested, Sarah contacted Silver Moon and – this was a mistake, one she admits – Ben Summerskill at the *Pink Paper*, to find out which novel might fit the bill. Ben overreacted with a shock horror *Woman's Hour* story, picked up by the *Sun* with comments from a dickhead Tory MP and the *Mail* with a picture of a *Woman's Hour* presenter with the caption 'Vile'. *Woman's Hour* denied the story without even contacting Sarah, issued a press release admitting it might be a mistake of hers and withdrew her work placement after she leaves college in June. Sarah is distraught and philosophic in turns.

This shows the pathetic compliance with reaction at *Woman's Hour* and the myth that we live in an open society.

I'm going to write a letter to *Woman's Hour* pointing out their lack of morality in this matter, these little defeats are as important as the major ones and more insidious. Can you imagine that discussing literature could lead to this hiatus? *Woman's Hour* is more shocking than the *Sun* or the *Mail* – where we expect this irrationality.

~

Discussion about Larry Kramer, who upset people with the remark 'They're all dead', concerning the myth of the seventies' wild sexuality. There was no more or less sex in that decade than any preceding it, it was just more visible. His remark is untrue: many, but not all, of us are dead. A complete mis-reading of that time and a self-hating denial. It all seemed so calculating as he took us round the graveyard. He admitted that he had not found love in his life.

I'm a supporter of his intervention, but not of his observations on our sexuality. In the middle is the muddle of sex equated with love – too much sex never made anyone short-sighted, but love was another matter. I never felt I was using my anonymous lovers or that I was used by them, we always parted happy. The Judeo-Christian fuck-up annihilated in the orgasm.

~

David and I are driving in the mist to Dungeness, losing our way and planning a scarlet film in a choking hellfire: smashing glass, madness, a horror film with HIV as a conscious beast rustling around, hysteric laughter, Beelzebub, legions, PCP is summoned, HELL ON EARTH, red generated from sulphur, demonology.

~

The crambes are sprouting purple and the *Crambe cordifolia* is two inches high, the buds on the roses are breaking and the first daffodils are well out. At three we leave for London.

~

I do not mind missing my spring flowers, they will bloom and I will imagine them.

Saturday 13

Had a rather restless night without HB, this morning I had a Valentine from him. Left a beautiful blue watering can for him on his desk. My itching recedes, though it has not disappeared – the Fansidar was the culprit. I can live with it now as it is not burning.

~

Apprehensive about Peter Tatchell's Valentine carnival, but even if there are a dozen of us that should be a beginning. Should I dress up or be sensible and go with my warm black coat? In the end Sarah threw one of the gold surcoats from *Edward II* over a jellaba. I put the other on and topped it off with Jordan's apron from *Jubilee* 'England's Glory', and in a scattering of sequins we took off for Bertaux's on the way to Soho Square.

The clientele at Bertaux's goggle-eyed us, something as a child of the fancy dress of the sixties I was used to. Then up to Soho Square where within an hour we were joined by 2,000 others with pink balloons, a samba band, the Sisters, and a float for gods and goddesses – of which there were many. After a brief opening speech we took off for Old Compton Street to rename and reclaim it Queer Street. The float jogged and swayed down the street, the girls from Mildred's café gave up their waiting and poured on to the pavement, people leant out from windows and waved, and pink balloons sailed above the rooftops in a St Valentine sky – a burst of blue and sunshine after days of grey.

Peter leant out of a window and unveiled the new name high above Compton's, everyone cheered and I declared the new name and the street open. The whole event had the feel of an early Pride march, it reclaimed a political edge to the street demonstration and made me feel happy and, judging by the faces, most others felt the same.

Sunday 14

Before I fell asleep I noticed my left eye had blurred, leaving a hole in the TV image. I tried to fall asleep without worrying that Berlin or the trip to NYC might be off. This morning it all seems to have stabilised, just an infection brought on by the cold, not another dose of toxo.

~

Sunday morning cold and grey, another February day.

~

I worked hard and tidied up my desk, which has become a tip.

~

HB rings to wish me a happy Valentine and that he has left a present of some ice cream for me in the fridge.

Monday 15

HB back last night in a fussell rustle like a poltergeist cleaning up the dust and glitter of the Valentine's carnival. Most of the shops did good business and are very complimentary, except Camisa, the Italian grocer, who had a fit.

~

At 11.30 I went for a check-up to Bart's and ended up with a drip in my arm, chatting to Howard – the two of us were booked on the six o'clock flight to Berlin. I had jogged myself out of my introspection to make the flight and here I am, back at Phoenix House talking about euthanasia with HB, disoriented and with closed eyes, side-stepping CMV. How much longer will I hold out in this twilight zone pursued by a procession of infections?

Tuesday 16

The sun came out and I crept along the traffic-jammed streets to St Mary's, glimpses of daffodils in parks and squares, Sussex Gardens clouds of pink almond blossom. For a moment I decided to fight back, push the exhausted depression that has clung like the February mist.

HB gorgeous today. I left him watching Michael Jackson and Oprah Winfrey – Jacko has a childlike manner that is quite mesmeric, making this banal interview fascinating, neither child nor man, of no gender, he resembles an actor from the kabuki, an eternal geisha with a deathly smile. Elizabeth Taylor appeared briefly with a bouquet of platitudes, then disappeared.

~

I fell asleep at four yesterday, dozed through the evening. I think I should cancel the trip to NYC – I don't have the energy to make it less than a trial.

~

Dr Philip looks in my eyes, maybe the lesion is active. I sit scratching, a dustbowl of irritation. I can see the sun outside, although the windows open on to blank walls and fire escapes.

He saw a lesion in my left eye. I rang to cancel the journey to the States on Saturday, then caught a cab to Richard's where we had lunch – he has lost Piers who helped me paint my show.

On to Bart's to be stuck on the drip of Gancyclovir. It seemed to take an age – I was released at 3.30. Back and forth, back and forth. I fell into an itchy gloom. How much longer can I hold out? I feel I am looking at life through the plate glass of a shop window.

Gloom on the news about Bart's. I don't know where we will all be put. Everyone who has been put in the Colston Ward is unhappy. They've taken eighteen beds there as the AIDS ward is full; we were to have a new facility that won't open in my lifetime. Get ready to die in a corridor in casualty. The uncertainty gets harder as you lose control.

Wednesday 17

Back amongst the gas bottles and fridges at Bart's, 10.30 in the morning, all looks the same in spite of the Health Minister's threat to close us. Nurse Gary says: 'You should see what I've got for you.' I'm going to try to drip myself so I can go to Prospect Cottage for the weekend. I cast my envious eyes across HB's plants on the balcony, he warns me off as I leave.

I can no longer see straight, dizzy, with one eye missing. I can hear conversations somewhere to the right. I imagine I'm in the wings of a theatre, a drama of life and death carrying on, whispered rather than shouted.

Thursday 18

HB and I at Bart's. He learned how to connect the drip of Gancyclovir, about thirty procedures including mixing the drug.

In the afternoon we watched *Blue*, this cheered me up.

Friday 19

I feel a little less exhausted today, HB has got the drip to a fine art. Who would have thought this was how we'd end up?

Ken came to lunch. I performed *Medusa* for him; he said my audition was so good I'd got the part.

Saturday 20

I'm in the car with HB and Howard. HB sees a shar pei in High Holborn and gets excited. HB got three distinctions in the post this morning and calls himself 'Dr Killpatient'. We arrive at Bart's for HB to pick up saline for my drip, chased around by traffic wardens outside the hospital, even though there is not another car in sight.

Howard's queen of the night hellebore was stolen from his front garden – just shows you what they're like in Clapham.

We get trapped in a traffic jam at the Isle of Dogs. HB asks: 'Can you see where we are, Fur Beast?'

'No.'

'Well, that was a nice trip to Dungeness. Did you enjoy it?'

~

Dungeness. Peter brought hats: Howard's *Obscurantist* and HB's *Somnambulist*. Peter dunged the new beds while Howard Phostrogened the roses; HB slept with the television on. I opened a pile of letters and pottered. We bought plants at Hellebore Heaven, an origanum from Crete and two cistus, which will be planted tomorrow. Everything has started to grow, the crambes are pushing up their purple shoots, the snowdrops are nearly over.

Sunday 21

HB humming in the bath, sleep-in Sunday. I was up at sunrise with the barrow and utility shovel mulching the front beds in a sharp little gale that set in with my DHPG dreams at four a.m.

The white crocuses from my sainting are out, but blown flat. HB sets up my drip and counts the syringes, takes a painting down and hangs the drip on the nail in the front room. He finally closes the net curtains as he is stark-naked.

Brian comes and passes the hour with stories of paintings.

HB collects barrowloads of manure, we plant the cistus. It got greyer and colder as the day passed.

Several young photographers stop by to shoot the garden.
At 2.30 we had a minute of snow. My good left eye has fuzzed out.
I wrote my letters.

~

Derek Ball brought us back late in the afternoon and HB hooked me to the troublesome drip. The dreammares took over: I sailed off to India yet again, this time on a friendly elephant.

Monday 22
Michelle nearly faints in Maison Bertaux as her Austrian partner comes in in a fur hat and coat made of lots of little minks, which slither out of his sleeve – he calls them Montgomery and Alexander, they predate fake fur.

~

I took an age to get to Bart's where I had a new canula put in. I wasn't home before midday.

~

Tariq rang to say *Wittgenstein* had received a bear in Berlin.

~

Two o'clock and no sign of HB who took off at six for his work. I wonder more each day if I should give up film-making and rest up.

Tuesday 23
Shrove Tuesday. HB is to make pancakes tonight. My canula packed up last night so I'm in hospital again. I had more strange dreams – walking up a vertical wall with a yogi like a fly. I had a very itchy meal with Richard at the Presto. I was so irritated I had to go home but I slept well enough to enter my dreamscape.

Dr John Sweeney says I can have a Port-a-cath – a permanent line that can be used almost immediately – on Thursday, which should put paid to all these needles.

Nigel Terry very funny about Tilda. Tilda is being reproduced as an *Orlando* doll – I think the term is 'merchandised' – and is most unhappy about it. Tilda, who is not an innocent, fights for herself and becomes the most difficult of the least difficult, fighting the ambitions of the system. In the latest stupidity she is described as 'my muse', why not 'he's her slave'? Whatever she is she's the grit in my oyster that produces the pearl of peerless price. I can't believe I'll like *Orlando* – though it's made with friends. Something tells me the visual side will be botched, *Sight and Sound* references to Greenaway.

Wednesday 24
Constantine here for breakfast, said he couldn't bear the low self-esteem of the British – forty per cent wanted to emigrate, another thirty per cent couldn't find a good word for the place. Politicians jumping on the Liverpool child murder bandwagon, making all the wrong suggestions, vitriol and desperation, none turn the spotlight on themselves, it's always someone else or some time else to blame.

Liz Reddish called by with some jolly *Wittgenstein* posters all brightly coloured like a circus programme, the more it looks that way the better.

HB and I settled down with *Narrow Rooms*.

David Lewis came for a Greek lunch, the conversation took up where Connie had left off. I sense a failure in a generation that did not set its sights high. David Hockney who left the world with a passport to the art world – a world of sophisticated acceptance. *A Bigger Splash* shows how straightened our lives have become.

I cancel more interviews.

Thursday 25
Up early and without breakfast to get my operation at Bart's for a Port-a-cath. Very irritable skin, which burns and itches, and stops me reading, even writing. Prickly as the hedgehog in *The Holy Sinner*.

Got to 'E' block by ten and sat in the waiting room with the news on the television, all bad news and freezing weather.

~

The operation took away the morning, they glued electrodes on me in case I had heart failure. The anaesthetic burned up my arm terribly, then nothing till I came round in shivering spasms and was wheeled over to Andrewe's and put to bed amongst friends. I find this room, which is shaped like a crumpled box – it has ten walls – most comforting. I'm sore from the op. but that will disappear quite quickly.

HB came at eight, arrived with tickles and yoghurts, said he had a rowdy day at the swimming pool. He said there were good reports in the *Guardian* for *Wittgenstein* and *Variety* had described him as handsome.

Friday 26

I returned to India in my dreams, a land transformed to the jewel-like order of a miniature, woods, trees, timber mills, agrarian bustle, not a speck of dust to mar the hallucination. I bought a copper bowl for twelve rupees and sat in a train marvelling at the order like a Bruegel in a rainbow.

I'm happiest now when asleep, the days seem long and deranged by lack of sight. I had hoped never to wake up from the operation, but knew I would. This morning I ache less.

Saturday 27

A slow drip. Howard arrives, he is wearing his *Obscurantist* hat. Stuck on the bed after a very itchy night, I thought I would never get to Prospect Cottage. We stopped off at Bart's for drips and drugs, and then took off on the Hastings road to the Idencroft herb nursery. I pottered around like a geriatric, bought thyme and other herbs, and had tea, the cold north wind rustling through the pines. Hellebore Heaven, then home to light the fires. We passed a man on the road with a back pack: 'Income: £1 a year, purchases: 6 boxes of matches, Result: happiness.'

Howard struggled with the drip, the tubes came alive like an octopus and sprayed the caustic drug all over the living room. At a second attempt we got it right but the drip was not functioning and stopped halfway.

The snow blew in from the white cliffs, blotting out the sun.

Sunday 28

Icy cold morning, with snow still on the ground and a whisper of a sun through the clouds. It is so cold outside, the daffodils have all wilted, even the tough artichoke is lying flat. Howard is polishing the floor with HB's lavender wax. I write my letters. It's freezing outside, a roguish cold that nips the fingers. I put my nose out of the door and quickly back in.

In the newspapers a forty-three-year-old father says 'We have pleaded for him to be sent to a secure place' about his thirteen-year-old son who lives in the ventilation ducts in the Byker estate in Newcastle and preys on the residents – the police describe him as angelic. Over the page the exploits of J. Edgar Hoover take up several pages – Eddie liked flowers and boys and files.

MARCH

Monday 1

Bart's by eight. My dressings were changed, a new needle put into my arm; dripped with Gancyclovir, I escaped to my permanent haze. At eleven to the sound dub for *Blue* at De Lane Lea. My face is aflame and my stomach went in the night so I was up endlessly. I bought a walking stick to menace the wandering pedestrians on the Charing Cross Road.

~

A telephone message to say that Mark McCormick had committed suicide.

Mark gathered stories like lichen. Born into the aristocracy of wealth – his great-uncle Silas had invented the combined harvester and his family's companies made all the agricultural machinery for the Midwest. His mother lived in a copy of Versailles surrounded by imperial Easter eggs. She was so horrified when he left his wife for a young man – described as the most handsome in the US – that she ordered him never to cross the threshold again and held a society funeral for him where she buried an empty coffin complete with headstone.

The arguments of inheritance of a billion dollars ended when Mark said 'Fuck you', walked over to Wall Street and became a commodity broker. He made so many millions that he retired when he was thirty-two.

Mark was tall, thin, nervous and incredibly intelligent, he was also generous.

His impetuosity never left him, he offered to buy *Caravaggio* outright for $1 million and threw us a lavish opening night party at the Saint; on our last meeting he offered to fund OutRage! but I realised that would be forgotten as soon as we said farewell.

Mark's huge apartment on East 62nd Street had charming doormen, but the sun never fell inside; the curtains were always drawn and dim electric lights burnt perpetually. It was a mad jumble, hardly offset by the only empty room, the bathroom – painted to look like the inside of a marquee on a St Tropez beach. Mark collected a strange mishmash of unrelated and unnecessary objects – the cupboards were filled to bursting with designer clothes, the shelves displayed thousands of porcelain and plastic pigs. His West Highland Terrier dogs, Hope, Pain and Anguish, growled at each other as Mark flicked between the ninety television channels.

On top of the television a photographic memorial to Jimmy, the beautiful boy – he had gassed himself in his car in the garage of Mark's country home.

Mark repeated his messianic truisms constantly, they flashed up like TV adverts and took wing in the middle of the most mundane conversation.

Mark would dance each Friday night away and in the morning he would climb into his car and drive into the country. The eighties were a time for opting out, none of us danced much then. I no longer had the stamina for a hangover, so Mark went alone.

And now he is dead, the same way as Jimmy, in the same car, in the same garage, in the same house.

Tuesday 2

We sit in the *Blue*. In Waco, Jesus is in a stand-off with the Feds, he's shot four of them and is badly wounded in the crossfire.

Intricate landscape of pain, all at sea, leaving one's senses.

We finished *Blue* just before midnight. The concentration was absolute. Simon Watney came to the studio just as we started. Simon Turner got charmingly and completely drunk. I think the film is magnificent – it's the first time I've been able to look one of my films in the eye. Cinema catches up with the twentieth century, this is the first feature to embrace the intellectual imperative of abstraction, it's moody, funny and distressing; it takes film to the boundary of the known world, the River Oxus.

The film is dedicated to HB and all true lovers.

Thursday 4

This morning I woke late, curled up in the warmth with HB I forgot the time. We were at the hospital by 10.30. It's been a strange few days, physically and psychologically closed in. I walked through myself and emerged the other side with my spirits revived.

~

I'm back in the waiting room, eyes dripped and fuzzed. The repetition – here I am in the waiting room again. Hell on earth is a waiting room, but today, after days of despair, my spirit has returned.

~

I weaved my way back home with my new walking stick. HB says the red film should be called *The Allotropy of Sulphur*, we would film sulphur changing from yellow, through orange and red and finally turning black.

~

A letter from Leland, Mark's amanuensis, saying he missed us, posted just before Mark's suicide.

~

I'm back in the X-ray waiting room, this time for my Port-a-cath, they want to see if it's in the right place. The soreness has nearly gone – it's a week since the operation. There is a bright young lad next to me who is on chemotherapy and has nearly all his hair. He is full of spirits and smiling, chatting to his parents.

~

My X-ray is called. I look rather funny, one half of my hairy chest shaved, half a Fur Monkey – as HB would say. Now I'm down in immunology. The doctor says I can have the metal staples out of my wound – I'm well stitched up.

I left the hospital at three, caught HB just before he went to work. I fell asleep thinking of my strange life.

At eight Nicky de Jongh rang and drove me through the streets, as star spangled as if I was on hallucinogens. Battersea Bridge with its silvery white light bulbs looked like the entrance to Paradise. At the Battersea Arts Centre we watched a strange little play, *The Divine Words*; it had flashes of genius and would have made a great film by Buñuel.

Nicky took me to Joe Allen's where I had chops. My mind drifted across the room, distracted momentarily by the handsome waiter.

Nicky, who muffles up to write his articles, shrinks behind his woolly hat, which looks like Scrooge's nightcap. The evening was a wonderful escape from sitting in front of some wildlife programme with all the furry little beasts eating each other.

Friday 5
Worked at the third draft of *Narrow Rooms* with HB.

Saturday 6
Warm but overcast. Drove with HB and Derek Ball to Prospect. We talked about burial, cremation, services, memorials. People don't usually talk about the end of life; we did, with considerable merriment.

Shopping at Sainsbury's and some herbs from the Greatstone nursery.

In the evening HB and I worked on *Narrow Rooms*.

Sunday 7
Still overcast and very warm. Up early in the garden, planting the cardoons. A young Spanish architect, who had read *Modern Nature*, appeared from

the view. He had a camera but took no photographs.

Dozens of white crocus from the sainting are out at the back of the house. There had been a strong easterly, the pulmonaria and hellebore were casualties, as was one of the elders, but the one nearest the house was protected from the wind and has not blackened.

~

Brian the builder rang to say he might have to dig a new soakaway as the kitchen drain is blocked with beeswax.

HB is cleaning the salt from the windows, giving a sharp view. The daffodils, which bent double in last week's frost, are upright.

Monday 8
Derek drove us back to London in the evening. The flat was indescribably cold, but HB warmed me up with hot water bottles and rice pudding. This morning he was off at six. I tidied up my letters.

Tuesday 9
A very busy day, which started with a check-up at Bart's – I'm off Isoniazid and on evening primrose oil, down on cortisones as my blood pressure is up. We activated the Port-a-cath with Gancyclovir. All this took three hours.

I arrived at Richard's at midday. I gave three interviews: the first for Japanese television on HIV; the second for the radio on censorship; the last for *The Late Show* on *Wittgenstein*.

Into the taxi for the first screening of *Blue* with a very merry audience, which included David Robinson. Afterwards a good spaghetti at the Presto.

Wednesday 10
A second screening of *Blue*, which included cast and crew – everyone left elated and with a great sense of relief that I have been spared to make it.

I spent the afternoon sewing the buttons back on to shirts and trousers, I managed to thread the needle on a second attempt. Flushed and hot, I read a chapter of *Voltaire's Bastards*.

Friday 12
After an hour's dripping at Bart's, David and I drove to Prospect in bright spring sunlight.

The bees were gathering pollen from the gorse, a large and solitary bumble bee twirled dizzy with joy in the orange stamens of the crocus. The *Crambe cordifolia* have put out their first leaves and the *Crambe maritima* are sprouting deep purple; the lovage by the front door is growing as fast as the clock; there are wallflowers and rosemary, and the roses are breaking bud; the lavender is on the move. I planted purple sage and blue thistle.

Sunday 14
The sunny days are over, it's back to grey and a hint of rain. The visitors have returned to London, the best surprise Connie and his friends – we all walked along the beach.

Monday 15
HB covered me with Lanacaine to try and stop the itching, I am cold, I am hot, I put my freezing hand on my burning forehead.

HB and I walked back from the eye hospital in Marylebone, following my shadow on the sunlit streets.

Tuesday 16
Spent the morning being dripped at Bart's. At three the DHPG was delivered here with a fridge.

Wednesday 17
Robert Tiffany, whom I got to know as we sat waiting for our eyes to be tested at St Mary's, is recorded in the obituary columns of the *Independent* this morning. It seems so little time ago that we chatted as we waited. I never really found out what he did, but today that's clarified – he was at the forefront of the fight against cancer at the Royal Marsden Hospital and revolutionised practice. I could tell that he was very distinguished, good-humoured, charming, with a bubbling smile. I popped into the ward to see him at Bart's once, but he was too ill, and now he has gone. How terrible all that I record has become.

~

HB rubbed me down with an emollient. Howard and I saw the elegant Robert Ryman show at the Tate.

Thursday 18
Spent the morning at the eye unit at St Mary's, then fell asleep. Many tributes to Robert Tiffany in the *Nursing Times*. My eye specialist Clive Migdal said he had died suddenly – of kidney failure.

Friday 19
The *Wittgenstein* book arrived at the BFI at midday, it is very well done. Ray Monk in the *Guardian* defending the Martian, another piece in the *TLS*, he likes the film.

HB 'cross' – I stole his Twix bar and his ginger beer, both intended for his lunch at work. He has to be there before the shops are open. He is so furry.

Saturday 20
Drifted across to the NFT opening for *Wittgenstein*, very nicely done. A gorgeous teddy bear – the prize awarded to *Wittgenstein* – arrives from Berlin. HB walked me home across Waterloo Bridge in the cold.

Sunday 21
Could not get up. Burning eyes, face. Sad.

Monday 22
Should I give up?

Tuesday 23
I'm still here.

~

Spent the morning at Bart's, temperature 102°. Blood tests, X-rays, my lungs are clear but I might have MAI – a kind of TB carried by birds.
  Several people congratulated me on the *Face to Face*.

Wednesday 24
Awake all night, scratching. My face is closed in, burning. I dream of waking up feeling well – what a miracle – there are none.
  We drove to Dungeness and returned.
  Shivering, with a high temperature.

Thursday 25
Up at 10.30.

Friday 26
Wittgenstein opened at the ICA, Ray Monk very supportive.

Saturday 27
Drove with Howard to Prospect.

Monday 29
Spent the day in bed.

Tuesday 30
Did the same.

Wednesday 31

Corrected proofs of *Sebastiane*. De-escalated *Medusa*. Cinema: made by the cunning for the dimwitted.

APRIL

Thursday 1
I don't remember anything that happened today.

Friday 2
New measurements for my shirt of Nessus in the hospital.

This is a terrible destruction of my friends.

David Dipnall	Art student
Robert Fraser	Art dealer
Billy Gibb	Designer
Terry Lear	Musician
Paul Treacy	Costume designer
Paul Bettell	Film-maker
Rudolf Nureyev	Dancer
Ian Chamberlain	Actor
Patrik Steede	Writer
Karl Bowen	Painter
Robert Mapplethorpe	Photographer
Howard Bruckner	Film-maker
Ken Hicks	Photographer
Mario Dubsky	Painter
Graham Cracker	Designer
Max Gordon	Architect

There are six or more others dying, including myself.

~

HB has pestered the doctors and I have a complete new drug regime. What is it that burns? Is it Dapsone or Fansidar? Now I am on Foscarnet, please God this works. My life is becoming a nightmare, would it just be a bad dream.

Saturday 3

Howard and HB at Prospect, they have gone to Starvecrow Lane. I sit here with the letters and Sibelius.

Easter Sunday

We are going to Ely for the day, Ken, Tariq and myself. My skin, St Anthony's fire, has changed, looks as if badly sunburnt, the tickling is reduced. I slapped on a new lotion last Tuesday, it was as if I had put my skin in developer – I was covered by flaming spots, but these seem to be fading slowly.

I have emerged from weeks of complete disorientation today – although I can't see, I can see straight.

~

Today two celebs with HIV in the papers: Kenny Everett, who seems a stupid man – witness his outburst at Tory conference to bomb Russia – and Holly Johnson, who is charming. I think their decisions will help a lot, though I'm not certain quite how.

Thursday 8

St Bart's. I came here two days ago, it's Thursday. My raging skin vicious as sunburn so it hurts even to a light touch. I'm certain it is St Anthony's fire that is lamented at the great altar at Eisenheim. The sheet of flame had pushed me into the zoo, a distressed polar bear walking backwards and forwards past the bars. As my ability to think slipped away I could do nothing but sit in the corner, it became impossible to walk in the street.

I stopped eating, lost two stone and kept a constant temperature of 101° for three weeks. To open a letter became a major task, to answer it impossible, HB did everything for me. I couldn't write the diary – something that has never happened with the other illnesses. I felt dizzy, retired for whole days to bed, I burnt, I struggled through sleepless nights to find a cool pillow, my scalp itched, my back and arms burned, a recommended lotion turned my skin to salami. I'm brown as a berry, people in the street asked: 'Where have you been on holiday?'

To one persistent questioner I said: 'Oh, just in hell.'

As the Clock Ticks

As time passes my reality turns to your myth,
The sand runs through my fingers, when, where, who,
I am the demon in Christ's pudding,
I am the bad threepenny bit surrounded by frails,

Currants and sultanas, swimming in brandy,
Why don't you toss me, heads or tails,
Kiss my arse,
I'm the will-o'-the-wisp,
Flames which circle round,
Spectral, an eternal mist,
Here is the Christmas red,
The holly-pricked fingers,
Put on your gloves, risk of infection.
I am the blood on your hands,
Who cares a penny for silver thrupence,
I am the demon of sulphur,
I smell of rotten eggs,
Teeth and eyes.

Thursday 15

I noticed my writing is more erratic, it seemed some inky spider had spun a web – my hands shook. To get in or out of a bath excruciating, took half an hour – taking the plunge. I won't make another film, I will write no more. I closed my eyes, hung my head and endured the pain; there was nothing – if being ill is painful then I can only describe this as terrible. I seriously contemplate suicide – not in my nature.

The doctors have changed my drugs several times, yesterday the dermatologist came to visit and put me on creams and lotions and pills. 'We will have to take a skin sample.'

I said: 'You can have it all.' You see I'm going mad. I said: 'If I'm really ill please let me go.' The idea of death is so sweet, all this struggle over, no more journalists ringing to ask me if I'm dead – so they can make a few last pounds, then get some other poor soul.

The hospital is such a joy, the people so charming, the nurse sat with her arm around my shoulder for half an hour. I was shivering, naked and couldn't lie down as it was too painful. Your skin is your major organ and therefore can be lethal.

Today I just hurt, the agony has subsided, my brain scan is clear. I'm eating, the shaking and wobbly walk just the state of shock. My lungs are OK. I have decided to give life another go.

~

This afternoon the sun came out. I walked with HB, who is more handsome than ever, to 'lung functions'. I'm shaking with shock, my mind erased. My skin has started to peel away in the burning fiery furnace. I can survive the destruction of the body, but the mind?

Friday 16

Calm is returning, my shocked and shaking body less palsied. Howard brought some exquisite photographs of the garden.

My beetroot skin is turning a lighter shade of pale.

Both Diane and Peter Logan, old friends, turned up. We spent a merry hour.

Today is the first day for three months that I haven't scratched incessantly.

~

You can't imagine the tedium of a film festival with its jolly brochure with you in it. The agony of jet travel, finding the guide who takes you to the 'same' hotel you stayed in somewhere else, everyone you meet you've met before. 'Have you seen this?', 'Have you seen that?' I lie – secretly I've seen nothing. If you see nothing you might get half an hour's walk in the sun.

In the hotel the food is always the same, the groaning breakfast banquet of tropical fruits. The rest of it is interviews – each journalist from each country wants an 'exclusive' to ask you the same boring old question about a film you made some time ago and were attempting to forget so life could go ahead. See you next year.

I remember the trip to Paris to open *Caravaggio*.

I took off on the train to Heathrow and got muddled in all the terminals, no one seemed to know which one. I climbed back on the train and collapsed in Phoenix House in a rage. The frantic organisers of the reception in Paris, who were at Charles de Gaulle airport to meet me, telephoned. 'I got lost in the airport. I won't be able to come until Heathrow is designed for people to travel.'

They were incredulous. What a relief.

Saturday 17

Had my skin biopsy taken on my lower back, felt next to nothing. Nurse Shaun started a genocide action on the molluscum on my face with liquid nitrogen, red-spotted fuming attack – like an old steam train that can't pull out of the station. Enough farts to blow a hole in the ozone layer.

~

The television brings a poisonous diet from Srebrnica. I start a book on gardens, read Marcus Aurelius – then get bored; we should have read it at school. It's a book for instructing the young. I'm now about to open Martial's *Epigrams*.

Life is returning to some sort of reality; the terrible burning skin has gone now, it is just irritated, the white bits are beating the scarlet, like a lobster in reverse. I'm eating again, sleeping, I can open and read a letter and I have started to enjoy visitors.

~

My plan to visit Colmar is hatching, an hour in front of the Eisenheim altar. The sensory deprivation, the terrible effort to hold myself together so every thought was trapped in my burning body is gone, four of the seven veils are off.

~

Andrew Logan came at two, just as I finished a very good lunch: chop, purple cabbage and semolina pudding. We talked of old friends in Miami and ashrams in India. He said I've lost weight. I'm putting it on. Everyone else is trying to lose it like Divine – if I walked in here as fat as Divine they would all applaud. Andrew was wearing fuchsia, he's quite the most stylish of my friends, in a queue for the cinema, on the streets, anywhere – he lights the place up. He isn't flamboyant or showy, in fact, it would be difficult to think of him as anything but quiet and charming – Andrew's fuchsia is somehow tempered with restraint, he doesn't look like a suburban garden in August, more like an Indian prince with his courtesy and fine features. Though these are hard times, everything about him is smiling.

~

I must not allow myself to be trapped by Dungeness, there are other horizons and probably little time.

~

HB shocked us by picking up a daffodil and plunging it into the liquid nitrogen for burning my molluscum. It came out smoking. He flicked it with his finger and it shattered into a thousand pieces.

~

Peaches came in with a big smile. He had been picked up by a Spanish lad who 'fucked the arse off him' for six hours. He's coming back for more tonight – three sessions rather than one. It's four years since anyone did that to me. His tale excited all of us; sex, thank heavens, can still be enjoyed. 'He had a great big juicy cock with plenty of precome, did not have an orgasm, he did not want it to stop.' When he reads this I hope he jerks off.

> *When you say quick I'm going to come*
> *Hedylus I go limp and numb*
> *But ask me to hold back my fire*

330

And the brake accelerates desire
Dear boy, if you're in such a hurry
Tell me to slow up, not hurry

Martial

We walked to the sixties exhibition at the Barbican; the total muddle of gloomy pedestrian walks, miles of them, high in the air, deserted, windy and confusing, didn't help to put me in a good mood. HB refused to go in, said the admission price was extortionate; in the end he gave in. His long black hair makes him look rather wild.

The exhibition was a survey of painting, mostly pop and op with a few worthies like the Boyle family. It was like looking through an old magazine.

When I looked at the pictures I could only see the people who painted them: Paul Huxley, with the face of an angel, a smile, quiet reserve, but warming; Richard Hamilton's razor-bright intellect. There were some fine paintings: Ron Kitaj, who doesn't date – the painter whose show bowled me over in 1962. David Hockney's sly Cain and Mabel paintings; John Latham's burnt books – my God I wish I had one of those, it would have been very easy to ask for one then.

Most of the show innocent and natural, political simpletons, but at least political – Pauline Boty's work was interesting for its feminist observation, very new then. It's a pity she died so young as she might have painted a good picture.

Before lights out D. came in and we spun a few fisherman's tales of large ones he and his arse have seen. I still find sex fascinating though I'm quite beyond it; the drugs have done in the orgasm. In many ways this is a relief; I can get on writing and reading, and sleeping early, though the years spent cruising were never a waste of time: I had all my best ideas at four in the morning in some back room, being blown by some cute fluffer.

I slept quite well without a green bomber.

Sunday 18

I'm up early, it's six. The nurses are stirring in the background with today's pills and potions.

I'm beginning to look the desired shade of white favoured by Edwardian beauties. I'm rather gaunt, too much weight shed in the struggle. I haven't felt happier in months, to emerge from solitary confinement, which was overwhelming me with numbness, it almost seems like a former life.

~

Visited Phoenix, back in the land of the living after my holiday in sensory deprivation. Sunny, with a breeze, a perfect spring day. I'm thrilled to be out.

331

Sarah called by, looking well and full of life. She was wearing a 'Dyke' T-shirt and pranced about in HB's leather jacket, dead butch, she's going to borrow it to go to Sadie Masies. It's nice to see someone so happy. Peaches popped up after another night with Spanish Fly: 'Last time was for you, this time is for *me*.' He's not attractive, an army boy with a broken nose who just wants to fuck.

We walked around Covent Garden, HB in a smashing suit by John Richmond – black with rainbow bands like medals at the pocket. Peaches bought a book by Pierre and Gilles, which makes Boy George and Mark Almond look attractive! I wonder what they could do for me.

~

A bit of a fluster, the *Sun* tracked me down, expecting my imminent demise. I couldn't care a fuck what they write. QUEER FILM DIRECTOR IN HOSPITAL HIV ORGY. I rang Tony and I said I'm going to ring them up. If we don't confront them we'll never change anything. It was great. I called the reporter darling: 'Oh, darling, I'm perfectly all right. Would you like lunch tomorrow?' I made myself as charming as I could. He was off the phone in a trice. These intrusions are all right for me, but dreadful for HB.

~

Peter Logan came by, he was full of Andrew stories – apparently he is not always as happy as I have drawn him, but the glass house is a joy. Peter says it's boiling hot, you hear a rumble and all the windows close automatically. Michael says its own temperature is nothing to do with us. He crawls about on all fours collecting buckets of camellia petals so they don't block the drains.

~

A good way to meet Francis Bacon, if you had the misfortune to meet him, is in Daniel Farson's book: witty, serious and full of anecdote, it brings the past alive.

Monday 19

I managed to broach the subject of funerals. This is always difficult as no one wants to do it; there is a deep superstition that to do so brings one on. More often than not they are dreadful sort of gimcrack affairs, they don't have any life. I should hold a service in a circus merry-go-round.

~

Two weeks ago, at Dungeness, HB disappeared, I thought mysteriously, on the bike for hours. I said: 'You know, I think I should be buried in London,

Highgate or Earls Court, it would be easier.'

He said: 'I spent Sunday finding out about the graveyard at Old Romney with its spectacular yew. I'm not cycling sixteen miles for you to change your mind.' So that is where I am going to end up and, if life permits, he'll join me.

~

It's six and quiet. The *Sun* was followed by the *Standard* who were slightly apologetic. I could feel they were just gathering news – so strange to be rung up and asked if you are dying when you could well be.

~

At Bart's, chatted to a very attractive young man whose lover has been here for three months. He comes in at lunch each day and sits in the little TV lounge. The sign on the door says 'Visitors – no more than quarter of an hour'.

Nearly all the people here are frail, hair as white as snow, sallow, hollow complexions, an ill assortment of dressing gowns and tubes, which look like the furthest steps in some post-punk jewellery competition.

Today even the irritation on my head is subsiding, but slowly so as not to give me too much hope. This itching has been going on for two years, though only chronic since Christmas. It's an extraordinary thing, was so imperceptible at first that I did not notice.

Dr Peter came in at eleven and said I could be discharged, just pop in for the next ten days. What a relief! They need the bed and I'm better than I have been for a year. The nutritionist lady got me so hungry that I walked over to the café in Smithfield for bacon and eggs – I could easily live at Bart's, they are so wonderful here. Living on the fringe of medicine.

~

Michelle charming at Bertaux's, she had made me special cakes. *Wittgenstein* doing rather well, they've printed some more of Ray Monk's book, which is pleasing – he was so generous about the film.

I walked about, but with the London crowds coming at you it's a disorienting and rather frightening experience, half the speed, then they grind me to a halt. I can see a little more, but they look at my scarred face as if I was a zombie. I wonder if they realise how cruel they are, not a thought for anyone. I'm certain I was like that once, but I have had a good lesson – I console myself that I am a better person than I was a decade ago; room for improvement yet, but I've taken the first steps.

Tuesday 20

The girl at the flower stall gave me an inky blue anemone. I'm stopped everywhere by young people, charming, slightly embarrassed. It's worth talking to them as the glow they give counters the lergies.

~

I've started talking to myself. I walk around the room saying: 'Derek, you're such a fool, you've had the pen in your pocket all the time.'

HB says: 'They'll lock you up.' But actually it's the opposite, I've found a voice again, even if I have a couple of weeks feeling like this I am with the blessed.

~

Spent an hour at Bart's, then went for a walk – a most beautiful spring day, almost too hot for the streets. I'm still buying books to remind me of what I would read if it were possible. It's a habit I can't lose, the pleasure of browsing, the strange encounter.

~

The Overlook press are to print American editions of *Modern Nature* and *Dancing Ledge*, I've never seen one of my books second-hand, it would be fun to buy, especially if someone had written in the margins or turned a page down.

~

HB very growler about my cough, I can't do anything about it – Dr Peter says: 'No More Drugs.' HB came in washed out from his lifeguarding. He fell asleep at four and rose at 5.45. He said he'd been a danger to the swimmers all day – dozing off in the muggy warmth on the poolside.

This illness is much worse for those who care – after all, I'll be out of it soon. The idea of death is rather entrancing, getting there not that much fun, particularly for a physical toughy like myself. Life now is a little like eating the leftovers from a feast, profundities are transparent as a glass negative – half seen, half believed, in the tripping twilight where I reside.

I'm writing this with a gold Waterman, my great extravagance, in violet ink! Dead camp, or should I say soft butch? In any case I'm still all right, forty-eight hours of bliss.

Wednesday 21

I did not sleep last night, maybe forty winks. When the blackbird sang I became a young lad, lying awake next to the boy of his dreams. HB dozed and I looked at him in the twilight, not too close as if I stare at him in the night he wakes with a start. This morning I have that delightful lethargy that comes from lack of sleep.

~

The Waco Christ at the end of the Branch Davidian line has achieved telly immortality, he burnt himself to death with his followers, suffer little children to come unto me. This aiding and abetting God's purpose cheered me up, it was getting boring watching the compound. TV newscasters wrung their hands in horror. I hope the idea catches on amongst the born again – a spiritual cleansing, fan the flames over the fanatics.

~

I bought a book on the yew, if I'm to have a vegetable immortality at Old Romney I should get acquainted with my host.

Thursday 22
I met Howard at Bertaux's at nine, he was wearing his pale washed purples and pinks. He will grow old with the elegance of Virginia Woolf, but with none of her neuroses. We walked to the publisher Thames and Hudson, where Thomas, who smiles gently, commissioned a book of photos and writings of Dungeness, these have to be completed by September. It was a very happy hour.

I took off to Dickie's and ate an enormous lunch in the trattoria – an excellent salad scattered with bacon, had a sudden passion for Campari with soda and downed two. A strange Italian-Armenian opposite who drank olive oil like whisky – he was also wearing pink, but you have to know how to carry this off, he looked rather aggressive.

My new Edwardian beauty look, pale as a rose, is slightly marred by the 'cigarette burns' that have turned almost black with the molluscum burnout. People notice a spot and forget the rest. I wobbled back to Dickie's with my trippy eyes. Howard pushed the studio into order, there are two large canvases of my eye from the CMV probes. I said: 'Let's make £10,000 before tea.'

Dickie laughed. 'That's the way to think, Derek, you must be better.' So I weighed in and completed both canvases by five, wheezing and dizzy. I asked Dickie to come up, as, quite honestly, I cannot see this work. *August Date*, *Pizza Pie*, it pulled the bolt from the inaction of these months. They are more violent. We are going to do *Windsor Castle* and *The Wacos*.

~

Later, at Dickie's celebration for Alison Wilding's new show, HB growled a little and then smiled as the food – a stew – was HB fare. Ken looked sober and happy behind his glasses, and talked of Ruskin's house and dove cottage and the drizzle.

Edwarde's Square in its usual spring luxury, the wisteria is breaking bud. I had a wonderful day, productive, good food, good conversation. Phillida Barlow recounted a Wittgenstein anecdote: her father was researching into trauma in Newcastle where Wittgenstein was a porter at the infirmary; they befriended each other and the philosopher was constantly at her home. Her elder brother had a book, *The Little Boy and His House*, one of those imperial picture books – the boy had an ice house in Greenland, a paper house in Japan, a straw house in Africa and a brick one in England. Wittgenstein pored through it forty times and then said: 'You'll learn more of my philosophy in this book than my own.'

Back at eleven.

HB, a sweetheart, held my hand.

Friday 23

As I sat in the cool and quiet of the morning, the almost imperceptible slap of a letter on the slate in the hall – a letter from John Berger that made me sing. I should not, of course, quote private letters, but self-obsessed old ruin that I am . . . He had just seen *Edward II*: 'It is a work that comes out of the night of experience and it burns and gives light.'

~

We passed a girl who looked like a potato, she was wearing a grey T-shirt with 'evolution' written on it.

~

Phil Rabin's Nosh bar stung HB and myself £19.50 for a plate of salt beef, soup and a drink. I nearly fell into my noodle soup; HB produced his wallet. We came here on our first date, half the price then; once you could get this lot for ten shillings.

~

Lunch with my sister and her daughter Kate, who is planning to go to India. Gaye was looking tired and rather pale, she said she was rung by her uncle Edward after my *Face to Face*: 'I never knew my mother was a Polish Jew!'

I walked over to Mayfair to see if anyone could mend my silver pen, which I dropped in Bart's, it dates from the twenties. 'Impossible' I was told in Burlington Arcade.

Then I went to Marshall Street Baths to see HB at work, he looked surprised and pleased.

Later at Phoenix, HB mended the pen in his meticulous manner, he sat by the window repairing for an hour.

Saturday 24

Howard met me at Bar Italia at 7.30 and we drove to Dungeness, stopping at Hellebore Heaven – where he went crazy buying orchids – then to Rye, where I bought hand-thrown flower pots – they are all quite different.

Brian had painted the house a shiny black with tar varnish, he is to restore Prospect Cottage – I'm having new windows and a diamond door, with leaded 'Love is life that lasts for ever'.

Prospect ablaze with wallflowers, although it was raining and my nose was running with cold I could just smell them. The garden has leapt away, there are tulips, the first cornflower, enormous flower heads on the artichokes, scarlet anemones and the last grape hyacinths. There are buds on the valerian and the borage is out.

I cooked an excellent picnic lunch, new potatoes, ham and salad, with a very good white wine. We worked quietly and methodically putting plants in, then Howard took photographs – there is no aggression in Howard Sooley's camera, this is what makes his work so elegant. The overcast light is very good for colour.

All the roses we transplanted are doing very well, particularly the rugosa, the hellebores look happy, two new yuccas went in, we moved the teuchrium; the *Crambe cordifolia* are in bud, the elders a bright pale-green and the cabbages are well on the way.

It was a day of moving and pottering.

Howard left at eight. I watched a Jeff Stryker video and was in bed before 9.30.

Sunday 25

Grey, cool morning, the ochre shingle and sea that is swallowed in the mist. I'm having difficulty eating, everything tastes terrible. I was sick in the night but slept like a log, up just before six. I'm very weak as I had no supper last night.

I love this grey weather – the sunlight attacks me. With my gold pen, the little diary, Mr Wobble. I've made myself a bowl of porridge and eaten an orange. The garden welcomes the day. An exquisite tulip, red and yellow and frilly, has popped up in the wallflowers, which are spectacular this year.

I walked down to the sea, my stomach rumbling like the machine-gun fire on Lydd range. A wide expanse of sand, deserted except for two men catching shrimp and another digging for lug. It's wonderful, a day alone, looking after myself quite successfully.

337

Thursday 29

Four a.m., St Bart's. Yesterday was a bit like a mosaic that someone has kicked, my Port-a-cath is coming out tomorrow at one.

HB arrived. I've neglected this new infection and he was quite rightly the spiky one – though he made me quite growly fixing the parameters of my strength and me pushing at them. Simon Watney told him he was a gem, which made me think which one? Probably an emerald for his eyes. We took off for the bank, bought pants in M&S and fruit in the market. Michelle sold me a cake for the nurses for the ridiculous price of £5 and threw in an apple pie.

Back on the ward my temperature soared back to 102°. Karl came, he has the art of silent strength, the gift of saints. Of all my many visitors during this long illness he knows the art, maybe I should say mystery. He brought the gold pen from Dungeness.

> The poppies in the Flanders
> A scarlet army
> Greet the dawn
> Time blows the scarlet petals
> Across the blood-soaked fields
> Boys charmed to flowers
> A story Greek Ovid wrote

Five o'clock has fallen into silence, the antibiotic seems to have started in on my cough.

~

Wrote a letter to the *Independent*.

Sir,

I have been here now for two weeks, first in the casualty ward and now in Colston, which cares mainly for the dying. My 'own' ward, Andrewe's, is full; and the construction of the new purpose-built Aids ward has been postponed.

Over the road is Rambling Rose, who was sedated out of kindness after two days' clucking like a chicken and screaming abuse. I escape to the 18th century courtyard and read in the pavilion to the sound of the fountain, before returning to the hospital church of Saint Bartholomew, which itself is cool and filled with the peace of time.

Time is running out for this great national institution. 'I am not in the heritage business,' says Virginia Bottomley. Aren't we all in the heritage business? Without our past our future cannot be reflected, the past is the mirror. Every profession has a history and the medical profession's starts here.

This is the world's oldest hospital, founded in the 11th century by the monk Rahere. He fell ill with a quartan fever on a pilgrimage to Rome and was commanded by Saint Bartholomew in a dream to build a hospital. When he returned to England, he was given the gift of this land in 'Smoothfield' by the King. Henry VIII confirmed Bart's as a hospital, the old buildings were gradually replaced and new ones built. The architectural history can be traced from that time.

Bart's is not one of the new Habitat hospitals; its rooms are high and cool, but the voracious cashflow snake is out to strangle it. All criticism seems to pass Virginia Bottomley's curtained mind. Where an ideology has taken over, I see no doubt, and, since through doubt comes insight, a certain blindness. But of course this government is not in the heritage business. What business is it in?

All of you will one day be in hospital, you will be lucky if like Ray who lies opposite, that you are near one. Ray was surprised by the recent criminal bomb blast and was brought here, his face a mass of splintered glass. Today he is a hero with his photo on the front page of the tabloids. 'Thank God this place was here,' he says, as, I expect, do the city businessmen suffering corporate heart attacks.

There are some changes that are necessary, others not; there are decisions that we deeply regret later. To shut Bart's would be a crime against the past and against the metropolis which needs its great institutions and would be impoverished without them. I am certain that there is no reader of this paper who would not be an 'activist' if they found their home under threat. Bart's is my second home and my life here is cherished.

Rambling Rose has been calmed by the miracle workers. 'Can I have someone put my feet up? Where are you, John? Are you there? Thank you.' She's drifted into silence.

I lay back thinking of things, of my tombstone, of the present I've left the past. The hospital nights are a blessing of concentration. I'm as fragile as a flower, but as happy as a lark.

The old man, very ill over the way, is informed by the Sister that his brother is dying on the ward above; they're rushing him up. I'm going to lie awake, I'll be first in and last out.

Friday 30
Op. The next twelve hours faded in and out. Howard and HB sat with me, and I think Simon was here though it is impossible to recall. I lie still to avoid

the terrible stabbing pain on my left side. I'm a little sore this morning, as I have a Hickman line in my neck, but am overwhelmed by peace, the gift of that dream drug.

~

It's six, I'm bathed, but not shaved, I've got to work that out – need more light than we have in the bathroom here. The Port-a-cath, the source of all the poisons, is gone. Delicious smell of bacon and eggs drifting down the street from Smithfield market. I went in and had some. I stopped off in the little hospital church, quite empty, and looked through *Hymns, Ancient and Modern*.

MAY

Tuesday 11

I lost my hospital diary in a taxi this morning, something I've always dreaded. We will see if 'Reward if found' means anything. I had gone to buy materials for the re-upholstering of the chairs in Dungeness, the colours were hopeless in John Lewis.

~

I bought a solid gold Movado 1940s watch in Smithfield. I gave the shopkeeper cash so I got a very good deal. I'd never heard of Movado – Esperanto for 'keep going'. The shopkeeper said the watch was very rare and I'd made the best buy he had to offer.

~

There is some bug drifting around the ward for which we will be tested tonight. HB and Howard had to squirt some cream up their noses in case they had caught it while visiting.

~

Rambling Rose is screaming. I was moved to Colston Ward from casualty two weeks ago, Colston is an open ward of twenty-four souls – mostly geriatric heart and stroke cases, with an overspill of three or four HIV patients, mostly young and distressed.

The man who keeled over next to me in casualty lies at the end of the room, speechless. The old man across the way had heart failure at five in the morning, chaos, bleeps, 'Stand back!' as they electrocuted him into existence. A little later he takes leave of us for good. 'Why did you go to all that palaver?'

The nurse says: 'We have to, families want "everything done".'

'Families are cruel, I'm glad I don't have one any longer.'

~

The days are long, start at six with drips and injections to boost my white cell count – now nine.

Later three drips for the pneumonia, which is evaporating along with my cough and breathlessness – my voice grows steadier each day. Breakfast at eight, newspaper – the *Independent*, which to my surprise put my letter on the front page last week, generating over one hundred letters and get well cards. Visitors come and go: Karl is the best – he has the gift of silence – Howard; HB, who is veering between being lovely and furious – I couldn't find any loo paper in the flat and used his flannel, which I neatly folded instead of throwing it away or putting it in the wash. He came home in a hurry and wiped his soapy face with it – it was, he said, the worst thing that had ever happened to him.

~

After reading the newspaper I walk over to Andrewe's Ward for a fortified drink and a bath, keeping my hand in the air to avoid wetting my 'butterfly'; Eumovate – for my eczema and scratching, everything except for my ankle top is nearly cured – another fortified drink, a banana and television.

~

Rose wakes, screams: 'Go away! Go away! Fuck off! Fuck off! George, George, George.' She becomes so tired she clucks like a chicken, sedated by the nurses' kindness, she is slipping away.

It's very hot, I've left my jacket behind and sit in the French blues that Karl brought me from France.

The ward is full of moans and groans: 'Nurse, nurse, nurse.' Charles, who is slipping away, talks like a repeater, wets his bed and is ashamed of it. Mark, with his beautiful Indian wife of thirty years, asthmatic: 'I'm ready to go,' large, avuncular. An Islington pastry cook wiped out by the Wonderloaf, he came here first in 1926 for a septic toe, he gets home – to my surprise, and I'm still here.

~

Dear Howard comes and we escape to an excellent production of *The Cunning Little Vixens* at the Opera House, well acted, sung and designed, slightly faulted by the lighting, too bright and repetitive at dramatic moments, easily carried by the music.

~

Debbie Reynolds wants the part of Mrs Vaisey in *Narrow Rooms*: Sissy Spacek will read the script if we make an offer; Robin is here with the beginnings of the design; Christine meets Steve in Cannes for Japanese money; C4 is on board, phew! Christine gave Aukin a blasting as he has had the script rewritten three times and hadn't read it when he went to see her in NYC. HB is very happy, so is Johnny Phillips – they are to undergo voice coaching.

~

Twelve o'clock, more drips, the white cell injection, pills. Hospital food. I've lost a stone, ten rather than eleven, nauseous at mealtimes, though a Chinese meal today kick-started everything.

~

Lunch, more fish, more rice pudding, it comes and goes like the drip. The afternoon settles in, visitors, most of them quite incapable, invade: 'Isn't he looking . . .?' 'You're looking better.' This to the vegetable at the end of the row, when they eventually realise he's not going to answer they talk about him over his head. Rambling Rose takes off: 'Cluck cluck', screams 'Go away' and then drops off.

~

Howard and I dropped off in Northwood cemetery, but couldn't find my grandparents' tomb. Went to Merryfield where the white rose is in bud and the wisteria I planted very large with a delicious scent. We took cuttings of Mum's lily of the valley.

~

East Anglia is deserted, Howard says the big fields are unwelcoming, he prefers Kentish clutter. Kent's verges have orchids, there are none here. Very few houses, ugly, painted pink, no clapboard, fine large oaks and grand horse chestnuts twice as large as anything in the marsh, large gnarled stands of tall Scots pine.

Harriet Frazer, in her Priory, turned out to be a treat. Charlie, her son, had all my reviews and had made a Super-8, *Killer Thingies from Mars*, at the age of fourteen.

The house Edwardian, with a clutter of fine paintings by Craigie Aitchison and a neurasthenic portrait of Harriet's father who she said was queer – the portrait was by Oliver Messel and very well done. Harriet most amused by my inscription for the family tomb. I had noticed how boring the cemetery was, no information on anyone, they could all have been Mr and Mrs Smith.

Harry Lytten Puttock grew sweet peas in Bexhill, worked in tea and timber, Calcutta, died before his time; his wife Moselle Reuben 'Girlie' May, brought up in Paris, bankrupted Harry with dresses from Chanel, lived with her mementoes in a peach and grey flat; Elizabeth Evelyn Puttock, ever-smiling Betty, mother of Derek and Gaye, exquisite dressmaker who looked like a film-star and hated Northwood; Air Commodore Michael Lancelot Elworthy Jarman, the man who loved New Zealand, bomber pilot, kleptomaniac, DFC. 'It's a pity our children did not inherit our good looks.' Lance worked his passage, 28 with 200 gold sovereigns in a money belt, ran the first bombing mission of the war. This tomb is placed here by their children, Derek and Gaye.

Back at Bart's rather late. Dr Lynn here to supervise X-rays; surgery for a new Port-a-cath on Thursday; sputum sample impossible.

~

The visitors go, supper arrives and the long drug evening begins. I've been on as many as six drips, now it's two as well as the Gancyclovir for my jugsy eyes. Lights out at eleven and the groaning nights begin as the geriatrics are turned by the nurses.

I rush off with my drip to the loo – my stomach has been water ever since I came here.

Quarter to nine and the night shift has arrived, the nurses are swapping notes. Rose is crying 'Oh, oh, oh, oh.'

~

On Saturday we went to Prospect fairly early, the place was a merry-go-round. We arrived refreshed after a journey up and down the lanes to Starvecrow nursery, where Howard pottered for hours. In Rye I bought a lady's watering can for the santolinas and a very well-balanced trowel. At Prospect Joanna arrived with the pea vetch, the big one from near the old lifeboat station, Nottingham catchfly, musk mallow, a host of wild plants which Howard planted.

~

Rambling Rose is really moaning now, all the strength going into 'Oh, oh, oh'. The nurse says I must wash my hair, which I'm going to do.

~

A gang of seven erected a huge baulk of timber in the back garden. Peter, Karl, HB, Luke, Howard and friends were barely able to move it, but it's up and gigantic. Derek Ball made an excellent fish stew for lunch and remarked that I was always in a hurry – true.

~

Rose ground in, 'Help me, help me, help me.' Being in the ward is an eye-opener. Last week I was aware of the endless patience of the nurses, we talked of HIV prevention. My nurse said the Italian health minister had said at a meeting that gays were getting their just deserts, hardly a helpful way of dealing with this problem.

~

The windows in Prospect will cost another fortune, but Rupert Everett has just bought *Sick* for six grand – that will cover most of it.

~

Kent is looking very beautiful at the moment, all the greens and flower-strewn hedgerows, bluebells, ransoms, purple orchid, cow-parsley and tall buttercups that used to flower in the long-departed meadows of my youth.

~

Dr Peter came and said all was going well.

Sarah here with Alison. Sarah in a bottle-green jacket and skirt reduced in a sale to £40 – a bargain – the colour looks great on her.

~

Down in Dungeness Karl is stone-picking for the cobbled path.

~

The hospital is interminable and there's always the chance that you might not leave, like Dr Simon Mansfield – 'Sexy Simon' – who was here for three months before he died a couple of weeks ago.

Robert appears each second day. We go to see *Blue* in Camden. I get out fairly frequently, my life here is like that of a dog on an extendable lead – pulled back if too adventurous. The blue turned out to be grey, Kodak trying for uniformity seems to have drained all colour from it. The worst part was the totally illegible end titles, which don't do much credit to the labs who seem to have lost their marbles. Howard said watching it was a harrowing experience. Of course, I never thought of it in that way, since it is so intimately about my life.

There is an empty bed next door to me, one of Virginia's thousands. The hospital had one bed last week but above us, owing to cuts, is the empty ward on which no work is done; as for the HIV ward, scheduled for September, nothing has been started.

~

Holly Johnson on the telephone, besieged by the tabloids. He's written a very good piece about his brave statement that he is HIV+. We ring each other regularly. I'm going to make two paintings – he has laser-printed headlines for me – the arrangement is that Karl will do much of the heavy work.

~

You should see Rahere's desolate kitchen: I'm told someone mixed all the last paint dregs in the hospital to make this particular dead grey. Colston is off-white with a grey floor. It is also pretty ramshackle, hot water never gets to its taps, you would drain a reservoir before it got warm.

~

Charles: 'Nurse, nurse, nurse.' One nurse confessed to me she liked looking after the difficult patients. 'Nurse, nurse, nurse.' He lapses back into silence.

~

My solid gold Movado ticks his minutes away.

~

Sputum, and a new bug circling the ward with a prophylactic ointment that anaesthetises the nose.

~

If Howard was an animal he would be a giraffe, when he takes a photo he leans to his right like a T that has lost its arm. He's flower-crazed, and at the moment is taking everything to his parents' home in Doncaster as he has to move – he has retained a charming Yorkshire brogue. He reminds me of Virginia Woolf, though he seems to have no dark corners. His photos are a miracle as they seem to materialise out of the day with little pushing and shoving.

~

This is my last day for some time without feeling sore. The nurses are changing the guard. What we are going to need at Bart's is a good old-fashioned occupation, so that Rahere's hospital will always be remembered.

~

Each time I escape from death's clutches I have a rush into life, this takes the form of spending more money than I have – hospital bankrupts me. This time windows, cobbles, repairs and upholstery at Dungeness, the poem, Karl, fabrics, my watch which glitters through the night.

~

A medical student came and asked me many questions – the answer to most of them was no.

~

Wrote Gaye a letter, to take 'kleptomaniac' off the tombstone – she thought Mum would disapprove. I think she's right.

~

Bath in Andrewe's Ward, no soap, Balneum, Eumovate.

~

I'm waiting for my bloods, then I'll go to Phoenix House.

~

I'm trying to remember where I have diverted from the missing diary, what happened, what didn't happen – nothing, really, just the hum of the polisher. There are no televisions on the ward, thank God. HB bought me a gorgeous ruby-red wireless for Dungeness.

~

Ghastly gaggle of schoolgirls clustering round the door of Phoenix. 'Peep peep,' I said as I tried to get past, no attempt to move. One of them said quite aggressively: 'You should put your umbrella down before you go in.'

'I am!' I shouted and then sprayed them all by flicking it.

Thursday 13

It's horribly noisy this morning – a Greek man rambles on about 'doctor engineering', my next-door neighbour shouts 'Frank Sinatra' down the phone.

Charles is pushed to the edge of silence. There is a kind new nurse who sounds as if he's stepped from *Coronation Street*; he has the gravelly voice of the lady with the blue hair.

~

Every day there are extraordinary sights, which become so commonplace I forget to record them. There is an elegant man of fifty or more with a shock of silver hair whom I have talked to on and off for the last few weeks – he has some blockage that stops him eating so I've watched him waste away. Today I walked into the bathroom, he was standing naked in the middle of the room. He snapped: 'It says Engaged.'

'I'm sorry,' I said, 'but I didn't see it.' He looked like one of those fifties Chianti bottles with dripped candlewax, his flesh hanging off him in folds. Tall, pink, thin as a rake, you'd expect the whole lot to disintegrate in the tick of my gold watch, which is marking out my own remaining time. I'm nine stone eight from eleven stone six – so hardly a picture of health.

~

At three I had my Port-a-cath implanted in the surgery department. Taken down the corridors of some Kafkaesque nightmare, beds and bright lights in every direction. The surgeon, Mr Slater, in a bubble hat – looking like he'd been to Mecca – a nice anaesthetist who used my Hickman line for the drugs, so no more needles. I woke up there an hour later and was wheeled back here on my bed. It all looks like a success and I will leave tomorrow.

~

Dreamt the rest of the day away. Nurse Alice said she had never seen me look so mellow.

Friday 14

Last orders, X-ray, blood, sputum. God, I will be pleased to leave. I'm waiting impatiently for HB. At lunchtime, after a countdown with Dr Lynn, we left. I bought vegetables and some summer seeds: nasturtium, tobacco plant, night-scented stock for the garden. Ambling home, I dropped into Muji and bought a shirt for Venice, and red roses for HB.

~

The rain is tapping the window. Thank God I've escaped the nightmare of Colston – a nightmare thronged with angels.

Saturday 15

I woke this morning feeling very sick, managed just a glass of milk; my nausea is wearing off oh, so slowly. We sat in the car driving to Dungeness, listening to dear Ned Sherrin until eventually even his endless wit paled and we continued in silence.

I've been sitting for an hour in the car park at Sainsbury's while Howard and HB are growing the mustard and cress – Sainsbury sloths no doubt prodding the produce. The rain falls in through the open electric window – a design fault, they've got the keys so I soak.

I wonder how many hours I'm going to spend in this car park with trolleys crashing into one another. The sun, thank heavens, has pushed the shower away. Does it really take so long to buy food here or is it HB deliberately squishing luxury food so it is put on the 'reduced' counter so that poor people can afford it? They've probably been arrested. All the cars around me have come and gone, I should too.

Monday 17

Dreamy weekend. Peter and HB put up the poem. We planted cistus, more artichokes, yucca, the carnations and Phostrogened everything.

The vegetable garden is up: peas, purple rocket and spinach. We planted two types of radish – a big white cabbage-shaped one and a pink globe-shaped variety.

~

Gary came and took out a super of uncut honey, and thirteen queen cells. Howard took photos. The bees formed a bridge and clustered for an angry hour by the entrance as if they had swarmed.

Brian laid concrete. I sorted out old sculptures for bronze casting, walked to the beach and combed it, brought back a series of iron rods to build a new sculpture.

HB very happy putting up the poem.

Derek made an excellent fish stew.

Reverend Peter Ford called.

Tuesday 18

I played HB's wireless this morning as I painted a landscape.

The thrift have drifted across the garden, hundreds of bobbing pink heads from one plant I brought back from the other side of the nuclear power station two years ago.

I forget my illness here.

Howard chased the browntails off the roses.

We all went for a quick meal at Demetrio's.

Wednesday 19

Along the line returning to Charing Cross, the may trees are flowering and I expected to see a rose but did not.

I forgot my watch in the bath, I may have to have it cleaned, it stopped and then started again.

~

Painted three large canvases with Piers and Karl, *Dead Sexy* was the favourite, though I like *Arse Injected Death Syndrome*. Richard made us all a smoked salmon lunch. Two exhibitions are now in the pipeline: Rome and Potsdam. There is also a possibility of New York before the end of the year.

The paint surface of the new work is bright and lively, fighting the gloomy messages. We finished at four when David P. came with his two friends whom I am to marry on 22 June in Dungeness – they are to have bridesmaids and three best women.

~

I ran out of money. HB, who always says he will 'keep' me, gave me enough to tide me over.

Thursday 20

HB has gone to Scotland and I'm alone here this morning, still weak and rather dizzy but I think otherwise in good heart. I've developed a passion for fruit pastilles, whole packets downed in a trice, otherwise food still remains a bit of a problem. It seems to nauseate and I find I can take a little before grinding to a halt.

I took the watch in not a moment too soon, it had stopped at two in the morning.

Friday 21

Today is cold and overcast, and we are expecting rain. The garden could do with it, the bugloss looks rather withered.

~

Howard thought up a good idea – to build another bed for vegetables alongside the existing bed, $11' \times 22'$, should bring carrots into the garden, beans and salad burnet.

Saturday 22

I fell asleep with the phone off the hook. HB rang the moment I put it back, he had worried and rung Richard. Poor anguished HB. I do hope he gets his quiet holiday as he looks so sad and tired, and only growls a little, which I interpret as love growls.

Sunday 23

The answering machine says: 'One fifty-one p.m.'

I've been in the hospital since nine, dripped, infused, staples out and Hickman line as well, eyes and reflexes checked – the most thorough overhaul I've ever had. The only thing I couldn't do was put one foot in front of the other – I nearly fell over.

The answering machine says: 'No new messages.'

Lunch at Poon's. I've put on three pounds since the last week – a bit of a surprise as although I'm still on fortified drinks it's difficult to eat. So far no unpleasant confrontations today, though I think I'm going to get my stick out to chase the unwary away and rattle it at those who bump into me.

Monday 24

Woke at 7.30, bath. HB cooked me breakfast. I'm still wobbly on my feet, though according to my scales I've put on four pounds so I am now just over ten stone. The new sound of Prospect is Ligeti.

Alan came with an apple pie, and Colin and Flavia with their two sons. We all walked along the beach with the wind blowing, and then went to Doreen's and bought two Dover soles and two huge crabs.

~

A red admiral has flown in, yesterday's tortoiseshell has gone.

~

Reverend Ford came to tea. He's had quite a battle to get me buried in Old Romney, they were none too happy. He showed them my God-slot television documentary, which they said confirmed that they didn't want me. He managed to sort it out, but they made three stipulations: one was that no one else was to be buried there – that is the catch because I must be joined by HB. After all that fuss we are back to square one. My feeling is to be buried in the truly awful overspill at Lydd, at least one will be certain of a welcome there. I don't think I can cope with the problems I'm going to bring even in death and I wouldn't want any of my friends to have to run the gauntlet of the churchwarden who hates the idea of an 'outsider' in the churchyard. I wouldn't want to be surrounded by such unpleasantness.

It was so strange to find this pocket of cold comfort on the marshes after seven years of good relationships, modern nature. Ah, well it was not to be – forget the old yew.

I rang a Mrs Harris at Shepway and asked her to find out the possibility of being buried in the garden.

~

Mark Booth came, we cooked Dover sole. He is very pleased with the colour book, says there is nothing he wants to alter. I've picked up some more 'colour' poems to add into the text, Dante on brown and old Ezra Pound who has a word for everything.

Wednesday 26

HB left for London. Howard arrived at four and a gale sprang up. We left for France at seven. Here we are, sitting at Dover waiting for the hovercraft. I gave Howard a turn by saying that hovercraft always capsize. I wasn't joking and suggested – to prolong the agony – he got in the icy water of the Channel wearing a life jacket.

We talked of the culinary desert of Kent, fish in batter coffins, shrivelled scampi and soggy prawn cocktails, horrible chocolate cake, defrosted lasagne, ice cream in three colours, shrink-wrapped ploughman's with rubbery 'Cheddar' that never saw the gorge, every pub the same with the same sign *Good Pub Food Here*. Whenever I see those words 'pub food' my heart sinks.

We are taking off on this windy day for a holiday that has been cancelled endlessly by illness. The hovercraft is called *Princess Margaret*, it presumably runs on gin. A hovercraft is a lumbering sort of thing, rather like a large black beetle, which you can't quite believe flies. It seems to date from another technology, like Princess Margaret. I suspect she wears rubber skirts too.

Howard drove along the long straight Norman road, up hill down dale through grey and rather poky villages straggling along the roads. There is a sort of grim practicality about them, no thrills, unpainted, dusty looking; we both thought Kent more welcoming. The French don't seem to care much about the exteriors of these houses.

At the end of the drive the little town of Vernon, near Giverny, looked great. We pottered down to Monet's garden, which was the circus you imagine. 'Meulles a l'ouver "impressionist".' There are more good food shops in this town than in the whole of London, cheese shops, butchers, patisseries to make Bertaux's blush, wines, ciders. I have never seen such plenty, any one of these shops is better stocked than its English equivalent, butter, crème fraîche, yoghurts.

Our room at the hotel looked like an Indian jungle in a most unpleasant shade of brown. Howard escaped into town which had turned from Fortnum and Mason's into a football match, thousands of noisy boys. I slept through the lot.

Thursday 27

8.15 – a beautiful sunny morning. Mr Legless sits in the car after a breakfast of milky coffee and baguettes, Howard phones his father who is sixty-one today and HB to assure him we are all right.

~

A few girls have crept back on to the streets of Fortnum and Mason's, along with washed-out fluffers with jeans and black bomber jackets and gym bags. The fluffers are all rather good-looking and all conscious of their appearance. They all still smoke – something that is fast disappearing at home.

At 8.30 we knocked on the doors of Monet's house. After a brief scramble through some papers I saw 'M. Jarman, ambassade'. We walked through the hall and spent the next hour quite alone except for twenty or so gardeners in blue jackets working amongst the thousands of flowers.

Giverny is an Edwardian garden of borders and gravel paths, huge rose pergolas run riot; it is the shaggiest garden in the world, only possible to describe in the flecks and dabs of colour in Monet's paintings. Although the white wisteria on the bridge was nearly over and the lilies not yet out, the main garden was a mass of iris, peonies and dew-laden roses, large shirley poppies and 'different' coloured cornflowers – some stripy, some almost black. Violas crept through the beds, the whole terminated by two huge beds of pelargoniums.

The garden is a delight, a kaleidoscope of colours, foliage quite important. Just the flowers, I have never seen a garden with so many flowers.

Monet's dining room was painted the same sort of yellow as my living room at Prospect, this pleased me.

Giverny is such a contrast to the desert of Dungeness: rich, watery and sheltered behind its poplars. I doubt there is a plant that wouldn't thrive here. Everyone said: '*Bonjour M. l'ambassadeur*' – who waddled along the path with his stick, bright-red hat and owlish glasses. The tourists started to arrive in horrible bright anoraks – shrieking orange green and purple, which disrupted old Monet's colour schemes. I think they should introduce a dress code. I wonder if I'm the only one to notice this.

Back to Vernon for a citron pressé, coffee and two delicious pastries.

Howard is very happy as he's found a French *Plant Finder*, which shows many nurseries around Chartres.

Howard has evaporated in a bank. Just as you give him up for lost he appears, I can detect his footfall.

Howard says he saw a Gay Search garden in a French magazine, Search and destroy. Gay Search learnt her gardening in Sainsbury's forecourts; to her credit she's a lawn destroyer.

~

Chartres turned out to be rather a forbidding place, no fun, as gloomy as the murky cathedral with its sapphire windows all overwhelming. We lit a large candle for HB, stumbled about town to find an hotel, after nearly half an hour and with relief we hit the road to Fontainebleau – even the lunch wasn't as good as the roadside café yesterday. I bought a marvellous hat in a junk shop for £6.

~

Howard is very keen on 'haughty kulchur'. We have stolen two sempervivums and bought vegetable seeds.

~

The road from Chartres to Étampes as flat as a crêpe. No hotels in Étampes except one that smelt of stale tobacco and looked as if it had never been cleaned. A really horrible fluffy white poodle, which gave us indigestion with yapping. I said to Howard: 'Let's take it into the loo and flush it away, and if its horrible brown nose appears, give it a second flush to oblivion.'

With rain pouring down we regretted the lack of a bed and breakfast.

~

At Millet le Forêt we suddenly realised that Jean Cocteau once lived here and is buried here. Millet le Forêt is quite beautiful and Cocteau's house, in its empty street, magical. The hotel was clean, quiet and very inexpensive – we bought our own baguettes for breakfast from across the square; they made us two huge cups of café au lait. The square has a most beautiful market building like a huge wooden barn with no walls. Last night it was packed with stalls selling cheap clothes and olives.

I took my usual early rest, Howard went off to the chateau to watch the swallows circling in the dusk and got attacked by a large dog.

~

10.30 and the sun is creeping from behind the clouds. I'm glad I brought my warm jacket as it's quite cold. I'm wearing it, and a warm scarf, and still feel a little chilly. I think my legs are getting a little stronger, I haven't needed my stick today and, though I'm staggering a little, I feel a little strength returning. The car window is terribly hard work, as is the first step through the door. Howard and I have established a good pattern – he goes off to take photographs and I write this journal.

~

St Blaise des Simples a beautiful little chapel decorated by Cocteau; his tomb, as simple as you can wish, is in the middle of the floor. Around the walls are huge drawings of herbs, several very beautiful small stained-glass windows, the face of Christ crucified above the altar in a triangle. There was no one about, quite silent. I picked a very beautiful pink peony and placed it on the grave, it seemed quite perfect against the rough-hewn stone.

Cocteau is a wonderful artist. Everything he touched was filled with poetry, not least this little chapel, which lifts the soul, unlike Chartres that buried it. I think on the whole I'm a person for small places.

As I left I couldn't help feeling how the French honour their artists, no silly little grass-cutting churchwardens here. Can you imagine the people of Millet putting up so much opposition to Jean being buried? Oh, the English are loathsome.

~

MAY

At eight everyone walks round Millet with a bouquet, old ladies, workmen and myself.

~

Fontainebleau turned out to be rather like a Holiday Inn, one expected cheap beds for the night. It was as ugly as Windsor but unfortunately has not been burnt down yet. We pushed on to Sens, I'm in our ruthless 'If you don't dig it, forget it' way. Having crossed the Crepeue des Etampes we are now in the Forêt sans End – we have endlessly monotonous views. Howard thought we might be in Minneapolis.

We got diverted by a 'Brocante' sign to a horrible little commuter village called Varennes-sur-Seine, with houses with stripy awnings.

Glad to get back on the road to Sens. The landscape has started to change, fields have materialised and *le forêt* is pushed back to the horizon. After Auxerre the landscape cheered up no end, we took small side roads and Howard stumbled across no less than five different orchids on a twenty-yard stretch of the verge, purple, bee and two white ones with a long tongue.

~

Vézelay turned out to be the most beautiful town, with endless views of misty valleys smelling of wood smoke. The abbey, with its Romanesque tympanum, was quiet and almost empty – you could imagine the wife of Bath on her pilgrim knees. Beckett prayed here. In the crypt were small portions of Mary Magdalene served in neat gold reliquaries.

Another candle for HB and we're on our way. The sun comes out.

~

Autun, very classical detail, the devil's tympanum, largish town. We are now on the road to Ronchamps – Notre Dame de. Big white Charolais cows in every field, the colour of linen.

~

One o'clock, cicadas. We're parked on the side of the road looking for orchids with no luck. I'm famished so I hope Howard doesn't stumble across any.

Lunch, and then on to Beaune, past a hundred *'caves de 16C'*. A cave would be the most perfect Holiday Inn for Derek Ball: *'Où est Monsieur Ball?' 'Dans un cave de 16C.* We expect he will emerge after the millennium.'

~

The landscape after Beaune became a crêpe again. Howard said the endless white lines were the most interesting part of the scenery. We got to Ronchamps at six. Every hotel was packed out with football supporters, hotel after hotel turned us away, football supporters with suitcases everywhere. I'm sitting in the car, Howard has disappeared into a new hotel, something must be happening as he's been gone for five minutes. Does this bode well?

~

We're on the road again, directed by Mrs Please to the Hotel du Soleil in Vézelay. This hotel had no one staying in it – though it had a huge dining room set with white tablecloths and a thousand untouched croissants, and a young man looking like a Bertaux's boy, who brought Thé Eléphant for breakfast.

There was no hot water, a worse situation for me than a lack of orchids, and to Howard's horror, staggering in the dark I crapped in the bidet.

~

Ronchamps – white and grey shuttered concrete like a large *chapeau*, with light wells and secret windows – was the most beautiful building we have visited. In fact. I suspect it is one of the most beautiful buildings in the world. Its use of light is something you would have to go back to the Pantheon or Torcello to find, its alabaster windows are its modernity. The side chapel with the light filtering down a matchless calm. It's as if light was swallowed up in the intervening centuries plunged into the gloomy blue of Chartres, imprisoned by the flying buttress which is always described as a 'liberation' – the iron lung of Gothic.

~

Noisy family with a man with one of those scrubby French moustaches – you could imagine all his nasty little noisy children wearing moustaches.

~

Viewing the Eisenheim altarpiece – which Howard thought looked like Walt Disney. Lunch disaster in Colmar; on we went, famished. We stopped at Hotel St Giles where the maîtresse d' said: 'Nothing hot, no Access.' She grabbed what was left of our money for a rather indifferent salad and spoke continuously to us in Swiss-German, until I said '*En Français*' – even that didn't stop her. Howard said he felt very uneasy. We pushed on through purgatory with empty pockets.

~

Our last night, the Terminus Hotel, Chaumont, another railway hotel, but this one had a grand black marble bathroom and the same enormous empty restaurant all laid out, with six waitress girls, and a maître d' all dressed to the nines. Howard said: 'This is General de Gaulle land.' He was right – Colombey-les-deux-Eglises is up the road. You cannot imagine how quiet this Monday bank holiday morning is. No cars, no people, cold and rather cloudy. The same weather that has followed us for a week. Howard has inched westwards with excuses like 'The road via Paris will be much more scenic.' In fact, there are several nurseries he wanted to visit. These all turned out to sell thirteen varieties of cider apple. It was also a clever ruse to get back to the patch of bee orchids near Vézelay, so we are about to make a two-hour trip for him to steal one that is falling out of the hedgerow waiting eagerly for a new life in Clapham.

On a long, straight road, Howard found dozens of bee orchids, took out his guilty trowel and started his grand larceny. As the days have progressed the law-abiding Howard has vanished and his 'real' alter ego – a horticultural Mr Hyde complete with cloak and dagger – has emerged. Every orchid in France trembles at his name. The Sooley, the Celtic goddess of verges and vegetation, has colonised his innermost being, a B-movie rite of summer complete with sacrificial maidens with crowns of purple orchids. He refers to the Volkswagen as 'the getaway car'.

~

French people seem to be either charming or lie, particularly the restaurant types. The woman in the restaurant here at Laon took great pleasure in taking the menu off the wall after declaring that they were only taking a party. This wouldn't matter but EVERYTHING is closed for bank holiday; you can't even get a beer. This woman was even more unpleasant than the thieving sauerkraut of yesterday. If they've decided they're not going to help they rub it in. We managed to buy a cake in a patisserie, so much for lunch. We put the foot down and got to Boulogne at six, to be told we would have to wait until the morning. We decided to belt over to Calais, where we got almost instantly on to the hovercraft, this time the *Princess Anne*.

Howard said: '*She* won't sink.'

There was quite a gale blowing. By nine we were back at Prospect Cottage. There are more potholes in a mile of Kent road than the whole of France.

JUNE

Tuesday 1
Up early, a most beautiful warm day. We planted up the new raised bed with French vegetables: *pissenlit*, black radish, salsify and other exotics. The garden is very battered by winds this May, one of the foxgloves is blown quite flat and the poppies look a little frazzled, but in spite of that it is looking more beautiful than I remember. The sage covered by hungry bumbles and the poppies fought over by my bees.

The front doorstep and cobbles are done. In the post a cheque for £1,700 – thank heavens, as I've overstretched myself with my improvements.

Wednesday 2
HB took my temperature, 101°, so I stayed in bed and ate cherries and sweets.

Thursday 3
The thousand signs in the eye clinic have been taken down, just *Social Workers' Clinic Times* and *Walk-in Psychology Clinic* are left.

~

Christopher Lloyd's article on Prospect Cottage is in *Country Life*; the photographs make it look jungly and exotic, the article precise and very informative. Of plants, he suggests sea holly – I have tried growing it, but it didn't work. Maybe I should try again.

~

I'm so weak in the legs, a washed-out rag of my former self, my strength drained away. I stagger down steps and haul myself up them. The belladonna closes in, soon I will be unable to read. Another day gone.

Friday 4
Feeling much better today, my weak legs gathered a little strength. Ate some cherries for breakfast. HB very cuddly.

Sitting here this morning, the stunning flower-strewn meadows that France still possesses crept into my mind's eye. Daisies, scabious, every

358

imaginable summer flower. There is nothing like that here any longer, just a few buttercups in the corner of a field.

Saturday 5

HB and I filmed Alexis' [Bisticas] graduation film in Hampstead. Danny Maggott was there and helped me home, via Bart's, where I was dripped. Alexis, who has been ill, seemed in a terrible emotional state, unbelievably sad. Connie said he had regressed to his childhood, with his mother and sister constantly in attendance, tears, hugs and a huge sense of relief when we could finally leave. HB played his saxophone, missed his bus and got a train to Newcastle.

It's been a sad week – Bernard Simons died quite suddenly at the age of fifty-two, from a heart attack in a Madrid hotel. Stuart Marshall, the film-maker, collapsed with heart and liver failure after flying back from the States, where he had been taken after he fell ill in some Mexican complex for alternative therapy. Stuart was one of Duncan Campbell's targets in his attack on alternative therapies. He ran Positively Healthy, whose chief achievement was to bring the problems with AZT into prominence. AZT has haunted HIV care from the moment it was first given to people in massive, and toxic, doses. From this poisoning, a thousand rows and much tragedy. I'm not against alternatives, but when the chips were down I had to take the conventional path. Stuart was brilliant, organised a whole regime for himself, but didn't see past the quacks.

~

David, my next-door neighbour, had a sore knee, his doctor has discovered cancer. He's to be scanned tomorrow.

Every view ends in illness, the whole world staggering into the grave just a little too soon. It should have begun in ten years' time, but started ten years ago and now it's all but over. I wonder if any of this will be remembered; probably not, as in the scale of human tragedy it is very light. Cholera, or other infections of the nineteenth century, are now only remembered in medical books.

~

Julian and Nick brought me down to Prospect Cottage. The garden looked more beautiful than ever with the bright-blue sage, huge fluttering white crambes, blue cornflowers and poppies everywhere – all bathed in the clove scent of the pinks that are falling all over the place. I watered the plants that looked down at heart – the new fuchsia, the acanthus and one of the roses.

Derek Ball promised us supper, but at ten we gave up and ate here, radishes and purple rocket added to the salad.

Sunday 6
Beautiful, calm and sunny morning. The garden at its best as a thousand red poppies are in bloom, jack-goes-to-bed-at-noon has sprung up from nowhere with its purple stars, which are already beginning to close. By the kitchen window the purple rugosa is in flower, along with a shell-pink rose we planted only a month ago.

~

A jolly lunch at Derek Ball's. Fish stew, white wine, eight of us all outside. The sun spilling over us out of a clear sky, France visible on the edge of the Channel.

Monday 7
Slept from eight till eight. The sun was up, my bright little garden dancing in a slight breeze, blue cornflowers and purple sage. Julian and his sweet friend Nick fast asleep, stirred by the sound of coffee-making.

Saturday 12
Heathrow. HB has gone with Howard to get me a lemon tea. I was trundled here by a wheelchair attendant, as I have acquired a new disability, ataxia, which I call 'wobble' – the HIV is attacking my nervous system so my wobble is in fact a bit of a stagger. I spent the last two days flat on my back, I can only describe this feeling as the lethargy that sometimes comes with flu.

I was very ill this morning with the worst stomach and nausea, the ataxia comes and goes, incontinence is part of it – two nights ago I pissed in the bed. The hospital has given me some huge nappies, which keep falling off. I lost one at Heathrow, the boys saw it protruding from my trousers to much merriment. HB stepped on a corner of it, one stride and I left it behind to lots of nervous laughter.

~

Boys are a bit thin on the ground in Venice, though we had a charming little sailor with many tattoos on the boat that brought us from the airport. HB has became doubly attentive so there's no need to cast my eyes anywhere else.

~

The Hotel des Bains lived up to itself. HB, Howard and Gaye swam in the grand blue pool with the swallows swooping over the water. The weather was warm but not sticky or hot and there was always the hint of air.

~

We discovered a café called Rose Café; it had the best gnocchi that HB had tasted. This put him into such a good mood he purred through the evenings.

We took a water taxi to Torcello, stopping off at Cemetiere to see Diaghilev, Stravinsky and Pound. Torcello and all cathedrals increasingly difficult to view with the darkness that my eyes gather.

~

Blue was received by the audience with an overwhelming ovation, which left us winded and tearful; I don't think Maria Callas could have had a more enthusiastic response.

Sunday 13
Richard Hamilton's painting looked handsome in the Biennale pavilion. We clattered across Hans Haacker's *Germania* and stood in front of Nam June Paik's video installation until chased out by guards for the arrival of the president. 'Which?' I asked. 'Clinton?' This didn't go down too well. If it was President Kohl he was surrounded by so many suits it was impossible to see him in the sea of backs.

~

Lunch at Montini's, then the Ca' Rezzonico, which was mostly in scaffolding, a walk via the Rialto to St Mark's – quite a trip for old wobble, who was at one moment thinking of abandoning the whole journey.

~

Howard took many photos. We've had a wonderful time, ate ourselves into putting on weight and in the excitement my ataxia was forgotten.

Tuesday 15
HB is ripping out the kitchen with many apologies. I think the apologies are aimed at himself as I don't mind what goes on in his 'office'.

Ken rang about casting. Until David Aukin's worries are settled we can't do much. We will find a group of unknowns, it's always like that: we cast with Matt Dillon and Elizabeth Taylor, and end up with Joe and Bill. I don't mind this, but it is worrying to have finance looking over your shoulder and HB has more experience working with me than most of the other 'likely' candidates.

Wednesday 16

Today I feel like a million dollars. Will I keel over tomorrow? Like last week when I just dozed off for a day or two in the heat.

A cool day, bright with sunlight that brought with it a strange quiet to the streets as if we were living in a trance. I had lunch in one of the Greek cafés in Charlotte Street, bought paint and another black diary.

HB putting the kitchen back together said HBs are noisy creatures.

Long interview with the *Telegraph*.

Thursday 17

This upset stomach is a bore – I crapped in the lift this morning. This is the fifth time I've been caught short – in the past I've tried to hang on, soiling trousers, shoes, everything. Last time I decided I would take down my pants wherever I happened to be, so the lift ended up covered in crap. HB flung his hands in the air – at the thought of some neighbour opening the lift door to find me shitting – and cleaned it up. My trousers were saved, it was a good decision. I've done it once, I'll do it again.

Tuesday 22

We came down here last Friday. It was cold so I battened down, gave the garden a miss and finished the colour book by teatime on Saturday, it was much nearer completion than I thought.

My health continues to deteriorate, the gap in the diary brought on by a sleeping sickness that had me nailed to the chair all yesterday, quite incapable of doing anything but eat cherries – which HB brings me. I have developed these fads and fetishes for food. I am putting on weight with the amount of sugar I am eating. I'm off tea, meat and the main meals except a breakfast of porridge and grapefruit. I managed a slice of toast this morning, otherwise the lethargy overwhelms me by ten.

~

Today is the day of the marriage so I must keep my eyes open and ignore the sleepy sickness.

Sven has worked hard in the garden and also polished the floors so the cottage looks smart.

~

Emma and Anna arrived for their wedding at four. Great excitement. They had woven beautiful floral crowns. We all walked to the sea, where I married them. The ceremony, which included poems and short speeches, was soon over, though we had to raise our voices as the sea was rather noisy. They exchanged golden rings, then we all ate an enormous barbecue with lashings of champagne and ended the day with fireworks. I know that Anna's and Emma's decision to get married was an important event, lesbians and gay men have no way of sanctioning their relationships.

~

I must have retired to bed at 9.30. Howard said that everybody left at about one a.m. He said it was the best wedding he had ever been to, a joyful event as one might imagine them to be.

Wednesday 23
Howard and I took off across country for the rose garden at Mottsfort in Hampshire. We got there at 4.30 after an endless drive. The gardens are a bit of a disappointment, but the roses are spectacular. Back to Phoenix after calling at King Henry's hunting lodge, where I smashed my head on a low door.

Thursday 24
Met the pop group Suede at Bertaux's to discuss a fund-raising event.
    Watched videos with James, marvellous portraits in *B2*.

Friday 25
Back at Bart's. X-rayed. I may have MAI or even a touch of TB in the lungs. I've got to have my liver biopsied for some stray enzyme, it does go on. It's eleven and I sit here waiting. What a strange end, dying amongst all this paraphernalia. Jumbo sharp safes, oxygen canisters, liquid nitrogen, Dixel, Build-up, advanced cardiac life support, buddies, Provide, Betadine, 1,000 syringes and one rubber plant.
    Charles, the nurse, has disappeared, I'm all alone. Maybe I should choose this moment to have a cardiac arrest before the new pills arrive from the pharmacy. Germs.

Saturday 26
I slept all day, hardly stirred, even for a bowl of cherries.
    Narrow Rooms is off, after cliffhanging for months. David Aukin refused HB the part of the Renderer and I hadn't the heart to replace him, though he offered for the sake of the film. I think it very strange that a project like this should be scuppered in this way. I know HB would be one of the best things in the film, Steve Clarke-Hall is going to try the BBC.
    HB made pasta for dinner, very well done. Then went to the cinema with Peaches to see a horror film.

Sunday 27

My skin has became so irritated I lie and scratch through the sunny Sunday. At 2.30 I dragged myself from the bed. If I sit upright maybe I'll be less exhausted. The ataxia defeated the planned journey to Newlyn yesterday, but left Karl and myself free to paint *Germs*.

~

A surprise at Julian's party – two straight ladies swarming all over each other on Julian's bed, the door hopelessly barricaded with chairs – ten in all, which fell at Nick's urgent push. This sort of behaviour used to be the preserve of gay bars. I had wild sex with a lad in the loos at Heaven in the *good old days*. A week later he pretended he didn't know who I was and when I persisted he swore at me. Maybe he knew who I was, but I wasn't anyone then.

Monday 28

Bright and sunny, I follow my shadow along the pavement. Sandy Broughton has died aged forty-eight; her obituary is in the paper – death, that shadowless state. The *Independent* brought this sad news. Sandy was the most delightful arts administrator, warm, open. I really don't know what to do. With my next-door neighbour David having his leg amputated, my young musician friend Spud with testicular cancer, me with the wobble.

I caught myself talking to Sandy as I walked to the shops for cheese and butter.

Tuesday 29

Christine Vachon came to breakfast, she's in London with Tom Kalin, who was in bed with a new boyfriend who Christine says is dead good-looking – Christine is having an affair with a married woman.

Julian arrived at 11.30. We took off and boiled over. It's now nearly six and we're still at Bryan's, Camden Road, Tunbridge Wells, waiting for a radiator.

JULY

Thursday 1
A blizzard of poppies. The sun's up and Nick and Julian are at work in the garden, moving soil and digging grass.

Saturday 3
I slept all day. Richard came with supper, told me not to give in to the wobble.

Sunday 4
Bart's. Waiting to be dripped. Strange dreams that grip my mind and hang on like terriers.

Narrow Rooms will never be made, the BBC has no money.

The BBC is broadcasting a dreadful service, full of silly hymns and even sillier messages from God.

It's boiling hot, the drip takes hours, and I end up watching *Kind Hearts and Coronets* on the television in the 'lounge' and I'm not back home till late. I found it almost impossible to climb into a taxi; it's all the wrong shape for the wobble. More horrible waking nightmares.

Tuesday 6
Life staggers on into a new day.

I sat for hours, waiting to be dripped, in a dingy, illuminated – fluorescents behind frosted plastic – corridor, with all the other patients at strange angles on wheelchairs. The wait was endless. I started to fall asleep. A boy was wheeled past on a bed with a beautiful face, looking as if he had been to a beautician. He was quite unconscious, the nurse stood stroking his hair.

The hospital staff rushed around with an infuriating efficiency, ricocheting from one side of the corridor to the other; apart from their frantic dartings we all remained static. I've never seen such a ruined congregation, leaning this way and that in their chairs. Eventually, thank God, as depression just about seemed to swallow me, my name was called. The doctor covered me with gel and moved what looked like a hairdryer around me.

The staff at Bart's are as confused by Mrs Bottomley's antics as any of us, quite simply, no one knows what is happening. On the way to Berwick Street the taxi driver, spurred on by the closure of Bart's, started a wild tirade against the royal family and the gate to nowhere unveiled by batty Betty for her mother at the cost of one and a half million pounds. The Queen Mother's gate is so ugly it leaves you breathless. It looks like the gates from a provincial panto, which lead to the palace of the ugly sisters. The Queen inaugurated this disgrace by pulling a cord which unveiled a large metal pair of pink bloomers.

~

At midnight I picked up a taxi in Hampstead and asked him to take me to Cambridge Circus around Primrose Hill. He said: 'Do you know how much that will cost?'

'About £9 or so. I have done this journey often enough.'

'I wish you would stop scratching, it's making me nervous.'

'I'm sorry, but I have eczema.'

'I don't want that all over my seats.'

'Do you do this to all your fares?'

'You can't be too careful who you pick up.'

'Isn't that an occupational hazard if you're driving a cab? You might have a saint or a sinner. I'm a saint.'

Julian said: 'With your head-scratching and your clothes he probably thought you were a tramp,' which gave me pause for thought.

Friday 9

The ceremony to be made an honorary fellow of the RCA.

I arrived at ten a.m. with my fellow fellows, they included Jacques Lang, Issey Miyake, Roy Lichtenstein, Alessi. I walked up to Jacques Lang, mistaking him for Alessi, and startled him by saying: 'I have one of your teapots.' He must have thought I was mad.

It was fairly spectacular – all the students graduating were all in black, white and red gowns, and we were in multicoloured robes with big velvet hats and golden tassels. There were people in gowns everywhere, including Gray Gowrie who had a gown that looked like a cheap evening dress.

The ceremony went on for hours. I was incredibly hot and slipped out of my robes to cope with the heat. All the young students tried to help me back into them, which caused rather a diversion as the state trumpeters were blowing their blasts.

As our names were called a solemn little man with a silver mace collected us and took us round to the front where we had to stand while we were eulogised with 'funny' introductions read to the audience by the public orator. We had to doff our caps to the audience who, I'm glad to say, responded with much clapping and bonhomie. The organ thundered away, the ceremony passed and it was all over.

We went to the Royal College common room across the road. I didn't feel any different, no one doffed their caps to me on the street. I expected all those art students to be wobbling around on their knees making sycophantic gestures. It didn't happen. Was it all worth it?

Monday 12
The Suede benefit took place to rave reviews from the music critics. It seemed I'd stretched out across the generations, Siouxsie sang 'Caroline Says', and Chrissie Hynde sang 'Brass in Pocket'. It wasn't too noisy though it was very hot; I suppose this is the essence of a pop concert – sweat. The Suede boys performed with panache and looked as if they'd stepped out of Dr Caligari's cabinet. Everyone seemed quite happy with the evening.

Monday 19
I'm back in Bart's in St Andrewe's with my third bout of pneumonia. Bloody hell! HB first noticed it in Rome last week; he said on Friday morning that we should go home, as I was breathless conducting an interview for an Italian union. Some time in the middle of the afternoon we clambered into a cab and as we did so I blacked out. The next thing I remember is waking up in Andrewe's Ward four hours later. Nothing of the flight or the taxi drive here remained in my mind. HB said the journey back was a mixture of farce and horror – my bowels went and I shat all over the plane. The funny thing about this – it amused him – was that some horrible yuppie types were sitting in front of us ordering champagne and being obnoxious: 'What is that terrible smell, steward?' No one would let on that it was the shitbomb I've become.

~

Rome had been a triumph. We were put into a hotel called the Forum with an amazing view which made breakfast quite spectacular. The galleries where my paintings were shown were immaculate. You couldn't imagine them being in a grander or more sympathetic environment. Two beautiful white rooms, huge, beautifully hung by Karl.

The food was as good as ever, the waiters very jolly, marvellous plates of bictola and frutta di mare; brilliant bread, the most beautiful rolls – hollow, all crust, unbelievably good – little bottles of Soave and Ferelli mineral water.

Monday 26
A week of high jinks and illness again. It's not very nice here, these

pneumonias, being stuck on oxygen. I have the worst waking dreams in which things happen, although I know they're not *really* happening. These dreams become obsessive early in the morning, seem so real. I struggle on and on and on, think that if I wake myself up completely I might be able to dispel the worst chimeras, but even awake in the mid-afternoon I feel them happening. Somehow sleep traps me in its jumble. Wouldn't it be nice if this was not happening?

Wednesday 28
I've been in the Andrewe's Ward for nearly two weeks. Tested and re-tested as Jenny and her whirring Hoover clean the corridor back and forth. Professor Pinching came to visit – he's been on holiday in Corsica. Dr Lynn went to Denmark and Nurse Marie to Majorca. Me, incredibly weak, I lie here, just able to stagger to the kitchen.

Thursday 29
So ill but out of hospital, the CMV has spread to my left eye so I'm back on 'induction'. They say they may re-attach my retina next week. It all sounds so easy except I'm the guinea-pig in the middle. I'm trying to carry on with some semblance of normality, but in a too fast slipping away.

HB drips me now twice a day, the pills cascade around, I'm lost in a sea of sickness, hardly able to stand. The district nurses come and the physiotherapist. I see all this through a haze of enveloping darkness.

~

I wish I could record something upbeat, but except for my friend Sarah and HB's constant attention what is there? Collapsed and unable to move from my chair.

Friday 30
Very restless night, woke up in a sea of sweat at four. Horrible half an hour so cold and frightful, as HB put the bed together. He realises it is beyond my control.

We started the drips and pills at eight. Somehow I never got to sleep, so I woke all muddle-headed and it was 11.30 before I was dressed.

~

Ken came for lunch, he's on a course for directors at the BBC. We must have talked about this and that but I can't remember it, mostly gossip.

~

HB and Peaches Minnelli appeared at Poon's for a plate of wind-dried sausage, then we all ended up at Bertaux's. I'm alone in Phoenix now, sitting on the large chair, recording the unrecordable.

~

HB bought a new rubber tip for my walking stick as the nurses were worried I'd slip – I take off, waving it around so the populace keep their distance, keep out of my way. Unable to breathe, weaker than a dishrag, then another tourist is bearing down on me. What a 'life'. What did any of us do to deserve all this?

HB says I'm as tough as old boots, stronger-looking than the dying boys in Andrewe's Ward.

~

How wonderful: a day without blood tests, the manometers and blood pressure. Poor frail body.

~

Six o'clock, *Forbidden Planet*, strange, sub-Shakespearean SF movie on the television. Women have a particularly bad time in universal Armageddon; they have to look perpetually sexy in strange outfits, but there's no sex – it's very cold in space.

~

The world is full of sensation, the cold summer wind in my face, the mornings become more and more complicated, though one of the joys is unpacking a ham roll bought in Camisa and eating it at Bertaux's – their croissants are too rich.

~

When *Narrow Rooms* was cancelled it took me a couple of days to realise I was a potential bankrupt; no income, debts to the landlord, ill enough to be stuck in the chair unable to even read. I have the paintings and HB pays all the bills, and now I've signed a form declaring myself terminally ill I get £70 a week benefit.

AUGUST

Tuesday 3
I wasn't bathed or dressed before eleven as the drip fell off the wall while I was asleep, HB discovered it on the floor. I then did the rounds: Bar Italia to Bertaux's, ham rolls, cheese. Michelle gave me a choux pastry from an enormous conical sugar cake they had made for Madame's daughter's second wedding. Madame told Michelle she had to wear a hat. Michelle read out part of a wedding list from Liberty, which included such improbable items as Medusa plates and fiendishly expensive coffee cups.

~

HB off to the gym. Fay Godwin left a snap of the garden at Bertaux's. I got a new pair of spectacles and read the paper for myself for the first time in weeks – it's still difficult as the fizzy holes make it hard to concentrate.

Wednesday 4
Meeting with Nigel Finch from Arena, then Howard and I drove to Dungeness, we were held up interminably by a jack-knifed lorry that blocked the road. A cold day with a roaring gale that shut me into the back room, where I listened to Gavin Bryars's interminable *Sinking of the Titanic*. Braved the elements and did a little gardening. I was very happy to return to London.

Thursday 5
The community nurse came to drip me as HB has gone to Newcastle.

Sunday 8
The nurse produced a very sweet rag doll made by one of her patients – an eighty-year-old. It reminded me of mum and her busy Singer producing dresses from the *Vogue* pattern book, white shirts and cravats, and bright Chinese brocade waistcoats. At eighteen I looked like a respectable great-uncle, M&S pullover, trousers – probably without turn-ups – shoes from Dolcis, which had one of those X-ray machines that delighted us as kids, all of us quite unaware of any danger. After all, the fifties were the atomic age.

Friday 13

To my utter surprise I bumped into Nico as I went through the outpatients. He came up to the clinic with me – he had been having a broken arm put in order. It's always a delight to spend time with him. We talked of his neighbour Max Gordon, the architect, who has died, and his brother Adrian who lived in a gilded flat in Duke Street, and died of AIDS – another flood of memories. Nico said he didn't feel sad, Adrian had enjoyed a great life.

We talked of my fortunes and his fortunes, and my painting that Nico is giving to the Tate in memory of Adrian.

I had a very complete rundown with Dr Peter and then Nico gave me a lift to the door of Phoenix House. I must see more of him, he cheers me up.

Saturday 14

I sat here working with Gingerbits on the colour book. Did we finish it?

At six Karl and Pia came, very enthusiastic about the show in Potsdam, and Nicky, who recommended I take Dexedrine – I'm so drugged up I doubt I'd even notice it.

I fell asleep fully clothed and with the lights on. When I woke at five I took my trousers off and switched out the lights.

Sunday 15

I got an American breakfast at Ed's – HB told me they had them on Sunday. It was very good: hash browns, eggs and crispy bacon. I had to bolt it to get back for the nurse. Then an orange juice with Michelle, who was up to her eyes in VAT and her Albanian waiters – the very good-looking one waving a carving knife at her. Michelle described herself as his mother. They've all decided they like the charming Serbian girl who works in the mornings. Bertaux's is much more than a tea shop – it's a continuous entertainment.

I can hardly see anything, books and newspapers are a thing of the past, no more browsing in the second-hand bookshops on Sunday afternoons, I can just about read the headlines.

Monday 16

Michelle asked: 'What were the foods you had as a child?' Junket, I've not seen that again; roast lamb, for my New Zealand father; canary sponge pudding; my mother would have a fad – walnut bread. I don't remember food playing more than a straightforward role, there were no treats except the Christmas turkey or goose and my father churning brandy butter, which we ate with the smallest portion of Christmas pudding.

~

The district nurse all of a fluster over my invalidism. The worst part is eating. I feel nauseous on the huge quantity of Gancyclovir.

It's midday and I'm waiting for HB to pop through the door, with his been-away smile.

Thursday 19

Managed to get into the bath with my beautiful watch so I'll have to send HB to Clerkenwell this afternoon to have it put in order. I'm so unlucky with it. It's just that I don't see it. This would never have happened if I still had my eyesight. Oh, dark shadows.

~

I have put on a little strength, I can stand up with less difficulty. I have got some large nappies to wear at night, though since I've been wearing the things I haven't burst in my sleep as I did two weeks ago disastrously.

~

At St Mary's a tragic sight: a mother and her two-year-old daughter screaming from the stinging eye drops, the child had CMV. Clive said they are seeing increasing numbers of children with HIV. The mother eventually quietened the child, humming to it. The encounter left me shaken. Having AIDS is like living through a holocaust.

Sunday 22

I'm in Edinburgh with Sarah, waiting for HB to come back from Princes Street with Garry. The last few days measured by the drips. Clive wants me to stay on the two-a-day dose so the bags are hung from lights and picture hooks.

~

We came up to Edinburgh on the plane, I've never seen the airport so crowded. The film festival put me in a hotel with six flights of stairs, which I couldn't possibly climb. We had to change hotels – the new one was much nicer and had one of the best restaurants I've ever eaten in. Sarah, Alison and HB had a feast of venison, salmon and cullen skink.

~

Two TV interviews, one for Germany, which went very well.

One interviewer asked me how much the illness dictated my life. At this moment almost completely, there's no life outside it, I'm locked in. My entire physical self is a ruin that hurts. Some days I want to pass away, but that is not so easy. I'm doomed to recover, very slowly and painfully.

Monday 23
This morning I feel a little more strength in my legs, which puts me in good spirits.

We are on the train: Nicky de Jongh, who saw a lot of indifferent plays; HB, who's reading one of those gilded lurid paperbacks; and self, stuck into the diaries.

The film opened last night to an enthusiastic audience and we all went back to the hotel for supper, the whole lot of us. It's wonderful to be going home on the train, flying is such a horrible experience.

~

HB complaining that no one can get their apostrophes in order any longer, he calls it 'the case of the missing apostrophe'.

~

We came home to sad news: the cinema is being closed on Thursday, so *Blue* will not run as we will never find a venue before then. HB sad, cuddled up and asked me if I was unhappy. I replied not at all, I've come to expect these sort of things. Actually I couldn't care a damn – one less screening to go to.

Tuesday 24
The day started with a disaster: my stomach went in Camisa so I staggered back dripping shit from my trouser bottoms. Sweet HB bathed me and put my clothes in the machine. You just have to put yourself into accepting it all, though it is terrible to become incontinent.

SEPTEMBER

Friday 3

I've been at Bart's for nearly two weeks. My kidneys and bone marrow are monitored under the deluge of Gancyclovir and Foscarnet. I have an injection each day to bolster my neutrophils, the infection has not cleared up yet but is on the way. Two weeks ago I had an eye operation, very sore and painful, and I have another on Thursday. I am almost blind and have certainly read my last book and newspaper.

In the day room a doctor is badgering an elderly man: 'If you don't do this you will be dead in a week.' He doesn't answer, the doctor gets impatient and then gives up, realising he isn't going to get an answer. It seems a bit blunt.

The young man across the corridor died on Wednesday. He hadn't moved or spoken for weeks, thin and emaciated like the mummy of a pharaoh or a corpse from a Danish peat bog. I think the doctors stopped his drip. The nurse said he just refused to die, it was almost unnatural.

~

As HB and I crossed Soho Square, empty in the autumn drizzle, I felt how great it is that I'm still alive; if I say it myself it's a bit of a triumph. The doctors didn't think I would survive the last pneumonia, thought that septicaemia would carry me off. It never once occurred to me that I would not leave Bart's. I couldn't care less about dying, though I hope it isn't too gruesome. I can give thanks I am not going to end up like the geriatrics on Colston Ward. Old age here is so deprived, the sense of alienation and insecurity quite terrible. I feel all my days are quite extraordinary and exceptional. I've allies and well-wishers everywhere.

~

Crossing the road, a van deliberately ran into us. HB kicked it really viciously, dented the door and had a brief shouting match with an unpleasant man who was driving it. 'Just because we're in the road isn't an excuse to kill us.'

~

I'm quite incapable of eating the hospital food so I've given up ordering it. I think it's the Foscarnet which has destroyed my appetite. During this last illness I have been kept alive by Poon's, the small Chinese restaurant in Lisle Street. The staff there smile and welcome me, ask after HB. It's inexpensive and very good, I would have thought almost the best value of any of the restaurants, and there are many within easy distance of Phoenix House.

Tuesday 7
At Wheeler's with Norman, Nico, Richard and Ken for lunch, I managed a soup and potted shrimps. The ataxia is worse – I fell over, narrowly missing a bad collision with the wall.

Thursday 9
My second eye operation was less painful than the first and it's a success, though I have hardly any usable sight, just a blur. The Western Opthalmic couldn't be more different from Bart's, tough nurses who boss you about – they wouldn't let HB ring Andrewes Ward himself because they couldn't believe he knew the direct phone number. Geriatrics are, I'm afraid, a real pain.

Wednesday 22
The Sisters of Perpetual Indulgence took a room above a pub and celebrated my second sainting anniversary with hymns and hopes. It was a great evening, everyone enjoyed themselves.

Alan was marvellous. He's good at rallying the troops and has a head-dress which gives him a certain orthodox look. Some of the sisters had blue veils. There was a lot of love in the room and it does put one in a good mood to have all this much too kind attention. Peter Whitehead was the new saint, they've chosen well. The last weeks have been overwhelming: with letters, people stopping me in the streets and singing nuns, I have received more than my fair share of love.

OCTOBER

Friday 1
Miracle of miracles! I was finally discharged yesterday and I'm sitting waiting for take-off on a Virgin jumbo via Newark to NY. The ups and downs of these weeks have left me with enough sight to get by, though it is a little like a continual twilight.

HB is carrying an enormous bag of drugs to keep me dripped; God alone knows what anyone opening the bag would think.

~

I'm quite merry today as I'm finally off the Foscarnet and already feel a little better for that. The drug robs Peter to pay Paul and wreaks havoc across the system. The doctors at Mary's and Bart's seem very happy, the eyes no longer hurt and I can read three lines down an eye chart – before the surgery I couldn't discern the letters at all.

Losing your sight cuts you off – a sort of sensory deprivation. I fell into a sort of silence. All through, HB was marvellous. Heidi taught him how to inject me with GCSF (granulocyte colony stimulating factor). Each injection costs £180 and is minute. The cost of some of the drugs is almost prohibitive. Thank God I'm not in the States as the care at Bart's is state-of-the-art. It is not possible to think of more being done to help, the nursing staff are fun, the ward hums to Jenny's polisher as she shines the floors – Jenny is a great cheerer-up when she arrives in the morning.

Good news and a great surprise – I won the Fassbinder prize, a great deal of money: £13,000. I nearly fell out of bed when I was given the cheque. It's truly put paid to financial problems. I spent £500 buying tickets to *Carousel* for the nursing staff, but that will be my only extravagance. I want to buy HB a dishwasher but he won't let me, says he wants to remain independent.

We are still waiting for take-off, here we go. I love this moment in planes: as they roll down the runway it seems impossible they will ever take off and then a miracle – you are in the air and the houses and streets become smaller and smaller. I think because of the uncertainty of the illness travelling has become a great luxury, the idea of going abroad seems sometimes remote. I never thought I would see NY again, surely the most remarkable city, and we are staying in the Chelsea.

Blue has been a great success; some of the reviews have been a bit over the edge for such a modestly conceived film; of course I'm thrilled. It's on today's front page of the *New York Times Review*. Everyone happy, not least a young man who told me it had stopped him committing suicide at a moment of great depression, something that had happened since he was the victim of a hit-and-run driver.

We are up in the sky now, high above the truly dreadful weather in London. In seven hours we'll see the Empire State and all the other beautiful NY buildings with their stunning lobbies sparkling with glass and marble.

It was such a luxury slipping into my own bed last night. I slept like a log and wonderful HB curled up looking very smashing. He spent the afternoon in a face pack like a mud man of Papua New Guinea. We do have a lot of fun.

I just downed a sizzlingly peppery tomato juice. I often wonder as I write this diary whether I should put down 'deep' insights, but perhaps the surface is more interesting and alive like the skin and really those other revelations are better left in the past as teenage memories.

The usual aeroplane films that you have never heard of are to be shown, usually something with Walter Matthau. I think I'll carry on writing the diary.

The plane is absolutely full and HB has to sit in the smoking section because James didn't pre-book seats.

Saturday 2
New York food is overproduced, observed HB, your pudding comes with your main course: venison in cherries, veal in apricots. Lunch today was inedible and the food at the festival reception poisoned me so I had a night of sickness and vomited all over freshly washed HB, who sighed, then laughed and ran himself another bath.

We retired to the diner where the food is perfect – eggs, bacon and home fries. I had this three times today. It is incredibly cheap, just a few dollars, and is well cooked.

~

A trip to the Guggenheim, light and airy and a lot of space, the exhibition was a Lichtenstein retrospective.

~

Jeff Hill gave a lunch party with Christine Vachon, Tom Kalin and Bruce Webber – who was utterly charming; he had brought his copy of *Dancing Ledge* to sign. The American edition is very handsome, larger than the

377

English edition. He asked how I met HB. When I told him our story he said it was the greatest love affair of the twentieth century.

Monday 4

HB has gone to the army surplus store. It's another beautiful and sunny day, perfect temperature for walking. We contemplated putting our shirts in the laundry, of which there are two next to the Chelsea. Except for a dearth of plugs – HB bought one for the sink, another for the bath in the local hardware store, muttering, 'It isn't even this bad in the Soviet Union.' The rooms are very large.

HB tore up one of the rickety window seats, lit a fire in the grate and snuggled up. 'Look, Fur Beast, isn't that romantic?' and set all the smoke alarms off, with piercing whistles. He ran about, quite naked, pulling the batteries out to make them quiet. No one came to see what was going on.

~

The terrible soreness in my cock seems to be on the wane. I can pee without shouting, though the pee comes out all over the place like a watering can.

~

One very interesting question asked: why *Blue* was not angrier. I said I really don't feel angry, just melancholy, so *Blue* is a true aspect of my state of mind. I don't wake up in the morning fizzing with fury. Maybe if I had to deal with the American healthcare I would be crosser, but everything that can be done for me is being done.

If this film had images it would be seen like *The Garden* or *The Last of England* – incomprehensible.

Wednesday 6

The sun stayed out in NY, bright, very dazzling. We met up with Christine and Tom, Roberto Cecuto and Stephen Frears in a grand lunch at the oyster bar. The Americans seem to like each other much more than we do, perhaps they have more work, less time on their hands. The highlight of the tour is the little diner where we fill in the other meals with endless breakfasts, eggs over easy, bacon – delicious – and home fries, the whole lot with coffee and orange juice for $3.50, something unimaginable in London, which seems wildly overpriced.

Thursday 7

Leland took us to the Cloisters, where we were met by a charming young curator who took us round. I love the Bury St Edmunds Cross dearly. We sat in the herb garden where HB pursued a mouse – mice and lizards and small creeping things really get him excited. Our relationship is a miracle, though I think he finds it difficult to struggle along so slowly.

~

Leland said he still could not believe Mark was dead, he'd had to move out as Mark had turned so violent in the last months of his life. Mark's family kept Leland in employment, but on half pay, to look after the houses. Mark left no will and a gun in a living room drawer.

Saturday 9
After a day of jet lag HB and I come to our senses, we slept very late – 11.30.

~

It was a lovely week and we came home with a possibility of making *Narrow Rooms* – as Roberto offered to make up the shortfall that we lost to Channel Four.

~

HB is off seeing Peaches, so I'm all alone. The moment he leaves I feel lonely.
 He's so rude! He called me 'Old fart sack' in front of a diner waitress; well, I know I'm almost jet-propelled. Now if I get grumpy he retorts: 'Remember what Bruce Webber said: It's the greatest love affair of the twentieth century. Aaaah.'

~

I didn't sleep all that well last night, let's hope I do tonight.

~

We walked to Ian Shipley who gave me an interesting book on art restoration. He said the second Bacon book was a bit po-faced so I left that.

~

HB stopped off at Marks and Spencer and bought me a sweater.

Sunday 10
David and James came down to Dungeness, brought some wallflowers which we planted, good value for 99p a dozen.

~

HB stayed in London to go to the gym and have a quiet day without wobbly me; walking arm-in-arm along the streets with him is quite delightful.

Monday 11

Karl painted the backgrounds of two large paintings, but we were out of red and yellow so left it at that.

We went to the Lebanese for lunch, which was a success. It's still almost impossible for me to eat; I feel hungry, take two bites and am overwhelmed by nausea, don't give in.

Tuesday 12

Spent the afternoon painting *Dipsy Do* and *Do Lalley* with Karl. Gaye arrived with Kate who had cooked a blueberry pie, then Ken arrived in an enthusiastic mood. He had seen a production of Euripides' *Ion*, which he said was a wonderful play.

In the evening HB and I went to the Greek restaurant.

Wednesday 13

Dungeness with HB. It rained and rained without stop. I sat in the back room, the rain blowing against the windows. No gardening done.

Friday 15

Painted *Bubble and Squeak* at Richard's. Mark Jordan came from Manchester and videotaped my enormous pack of Intermates being delivered. Karl helped carry them back here.

In the evening Sarah came, after editing her news programme about a porno film called *Jurassic Fuck*, which had led to litigation. She said that it took her fifteen minutes to beep out all the 'fuck's.

Saturday 16

A cold but sunny day without a cloud, which started with breakfast at Bertaux's.

Bertaux's awash with gossip: Chloë says of Peter he is 'too machoo'; Tania purrs that Peter is 'like velvet'. Peter is jealous of Tania kissing other boys – this is hopeless for him as Tania kisses *every* boy. Her flatmate Barry is a transvestite with a blond wig who brings back taxi drivers who don't care if he's a woman or not.

Derek Ball has become as rich as Croesus. He thinks nothing of buying Japanese tramps' clothes by Issey Miyake at £1,000 a throw, although these make him look like a sack of Romney Marsh potatoes. He's started to give away his cast-off garments to friends like Tania.

~

Federico Fellini, my favourite film-maker, dies, as does the young actor River Phoenix.

~

I'm finding it increasingly difficult to do anything, I couldn't walk to the bank.

~

Sat with James and David watching old Super-8s, much more material than I remember; then off to Bart's for my drip.

James and I went to a small French restaurant in Islington, spent lunch dreaming up titles for the paintings, the best was *Gaga*.

Home via Neal Street and a stroll down the Charing Cross Road.

~

I went to the theatre twice this week, *Medea* and *The Wasp Factory* – most uncomfortable experiences in which the actors shouted at each other for an hour and a half. If anything, *Medea* was the noisier. In this Diana Rigg played a mouse of a Medea with some very intellectual men wearing military coats to turn them into kings, though I thought they looked like university professors. The horror of the production were three large ladies looking like Russian Orthodox priests, who belted out the chorus with the most unpleasant singing voices that I have ever heard – I could have sworn the biggest had a beard.

The Wasp Factory had its moments, so the torture was alleviated, but I felt I would love to hear the chink of teacups. The young audience loved it.

NOVEMBER

Tuesday 2

HB led us a dance about his birthday. He made such a fuss about not getting presents that he ensured he was given them by all his friends and admirers. Then, in the middle of the day, he knocked down the wall between the bathroom and the living room, to make a bathroom cupboard so I don't hit my head on the shelves again. The noise was indescribable! I went to Richard's to escape and fell asleep on his sofa.

~

In the evening we all went to Keith's show, Brenda, Maggie, good old friends.

Wednesday 3

I'm on some appetite-inducing pills. I don't know if they are helping. Certainly, if you can't eat you become obsessed with food. I cast my eye across the menus of various restaurants with a feeling of hopelessness. The prices these days. Amalfi: £24 for a second-string Italian meal, you can eat for half that in Wheeler's. Everything is at sixes and sevens.

Michelle and Tania took me to the Ivy. I didn't eat much, a sorbet and potted shrimps.

James took me to Alastair Little's, where I managed a sorbet. The Japanese sushi is the easiest, the Tokyo Diner the most reasonable of all the restaurants; you can get a meal there for £7.

Friday 5

Nick, Julian, Tania came to Dungeness. Peter came later with fireworks. We did a little gardening, clearing the vegetable beds. Tania cooked. We waited for Derek who never showed. I tried to paint but I couldn't see. Made HB a birthday picture. I must go and get a new prescription in my spectacles as everything has gone fuzzy.

Saturday 6

It's the morning of the 6th. Tania and Peter have gone to collect the fiendishly wealthy Derek Ball – who is making £100,000 a year picking colours. Nick and Julian are gardening in the cold. George Crumb piano works in the end room . . . Quiet.

Although I accept all this it's terrible to be so ill and fragile.

Wednesday 10

We went to more theatre. Leigh Bowery as Madame Garbo the Siberian piano teacher in a brown leather outfit and a slaughter of foxes. Leigh was the brightest acting of the week. Pascal Brannan's *I am a Bee* was gentle and charming – though I couldn't for the life of me understand why he wanted to do it. Performance art has the quality of silence, which makes it more attractive than the theatre, which is *so* noisy.

Tuesday 16

The Tate threw a smashing lunch in its boardroom, my painting on the wall, lots of charming friends: Richard Hamilton, Nick Logsdail, John and Anya Sainsbury, Tilda, Neil Tennant, Robert Medley, it couldn't have been nicer. Everyone enjoyed themselves and Nick Serota made a speech. It was sad when we all had to leave, but I made a date with Nico for lunch.

~

Life is becoming increasingly difficult, even to pick up a phone. I sit all day overwhelmed by a terrible inertia. I can't see much, so, for instance, Ken's article about the paintings in *Vogue*, out yesterday, had to be read to me by Nicky. I can just make out the photos of the paintings. Professor Pinching thinks I'm probably not as ill as I think, which is encouraging. Dr Lynn said: 'We are not going to lose you that easily,' though I think my life is drawing to a close.

Saturday 20

It snowed in Dungeness.

~

A sudden unexpected letter from the Reverend Ford saying both HB and I can be buried at Old Romney. This has set my mind at rest.

Tuesday 23

We recorded the *Camp Christmas* programme with Andy Bell and a group of wild comics, the depths of our dislike for this family event was hardly disguised.

It's not easy for gay people to enjoy Christmas, the two don't mix, so the programme should lift a few eyebrows and melt the icicles.

Friday 26

My mind knocked sideways with illness. Strange fantasies and dreams – I was wondering what the world was like before the concept of antiquity, which must have altered everything. The old stone at the bottom of the street was just an old stone, no one thought twice about it. When it became a Neolithic parking post it must have changed the world for ever.

DECEMBER

Thursday 2

Off to Brussels to see the play of *Modern Nature*, it was very well done. The actor, Chris, was compulsive viewing. I think we should organise it for Edinburgh.

I like Brussels, a homely little town, perfect for an invalid. Very good food, I've started to restore my appetite. We were back before we went, it was cold and snowy.

~

More strange dreams.

Christmas Eve

Julian and Sarah are getting my drip organised, very methodical, five times longer than it takes fluffer HB.

~

Andy Bell rang and said: 'Why don't you come to Majorca?' – real mad pop star stuff. I said no, it's difficult enough here at home. What will he think of next?

~

Meanwhile life ticks to a close, thank God. I really am a little fed up, hardly able to stand. Where am I? I feel sick, though I managed an excellent breakfast that Sarah cooked.

~

More prehistoric thoughts.

~

Sarah reads out a long list of steps to women's suffrage.

~

Sat and listened to Simon's *Garden* soundtrack, which is very precise.

twice about it then it became
a real pink parking post it must have
changed the world forever"
Dec 2 off to Brussels to see the
play of dancing edge it was very marvelous
fine acting it was compulsive
viewing I think we should organise it in
Edinburgh
good to begin I like Brussels a homely
appetite we were back before we went
it was cold and snowy before we went
we've getting strange dreams Julian and Sarah
5 times longer than it takes to wake
longer than it takes Father. *
Andy Bell rang and said why

~

Peter and I are planning tartan suits.

~

I've been asked to do a book on AIDS for kids.

1994

New Year's Day
Howard and Sarah are off to London. The play is doing well in Brussels.

Birthday
Fireworks.

~

HB true love.

New Yearsday howard and
Sarah are off to London. and
play is doing well in Brussels   me

Birthday fireworks
MB true love.

A great glow of friends

Derek Ball, the bon viveur of the Ness.

Alan Beck, marvellous at rallying the troops, in a head-dress which gives him a certain orthodox look.

Ken Butler says that all men are homosexual, he can see it in their eyes.

Andrew Logan lights the place up, though these are hard times everything about him is smiling.

Visitors come and go: Karl [Lydon] is the best – he has the gift of silence.

Peaches Minnelli – A Major Broadway Legend. Peaches because his adolescent bum was once described thus, and Minnelli after Liza.

There is no aggression in Howard Sooley's camera, this is what makes his work so elegant.

Peter Fillingham, the sort of man who, if he had money, would make bad investments.

Sarah [Graham] wishes there was a cruising park for women like Hampstead Heath.

Nicky [de Jongh] is one of my friends who cares for me quietly.

Sandy [Powell] has been feted in the bars all week.

Richard Salmon has immense and almost boyish charm, he is truly stylish.

Tania and Michelle Wade. Bertaux' awash with gossip.

Acknowledgements

Special thanks to Tony Peake who freely gave his time, encouragement and advice, without him *Smiling in Slow Motion* would not have been written, or published. Turning Derek's handwritten diaries into this volume has taken many hours and would not have been possible without the help and support of many patient friends: Derek Ball; Alan Beck; Robyn Beeche, for the photograph of Andrew Logan; Hannah Black; Mark Booth; Ken Butler; John Cartwright, for the Moscow Film Festival photograph; Alison Darren, for the photograph of Sarah Graham; Brook Dillon, for the Sundance photograph; Peter Fillingham; Rebecca Fortnum, for the photograph of Peter Fillingham; Harriet Frazer; Sarah Graham; Donny Hudson, for the LA photograph; Lynn Hanke; Nicholas de Jongh; the crew of the KellyJoe; Andrew Logan; Karl Lydon; Master Frank Massar; Paul Mattsson, for the England's Glory photograph; Jane McCarten, for the photograph of Alan Beck; Peaches Minnelli; Pop-it-in-Pete and the Dungenettes; Sandy Powell; Anya Sainsbury for the beachcombing photograph; Richard Salmon; the staff of Richard Salmon Ltd; Shipley's bookshop; Donald 'Smudger' Smith; Howard Sooley; Edward Sykes, for the Gay Law Reform photograph; Peter Tatchell; Gaye Temple; Neil Tennant; June Thomas; Tania and Michelle Wade; Nicholas Ward-Jackson; Ilsa Yardley. Lifelong appreciation to the staff of St. Mary's and St. Bartholomew's hospital, London.